Drug Control in the Americas

Drug Control
in the
Americas

William O. Walker III

University of New Mexico Press

Albuquerque

Library of Congress Cataloging in Publication Data

Walker, William O., 1946–
  Drug control in the Americas.

  Bibliography: p.
  Includes index.
  1. Narcotics, Control of—America—International
cooperation. 2. Narcotics, Control of—United
States—History. 3. Narcotics, Control of—Latin
America—History. 4. Narcotics, Control of—Mexico
—History. I. Title.
HV5801.W33   363.4′5′091812   80-54571
ISBN 0-8263-0579-2   AACR2

to Hannah

Contents

List of Illustrations ix
Preface xi
Acknowledgments xv
1 Culture and Bureaucracy 1
2 The Road to Geneva 23
3 Rebuilding the Politics of Drug Control 53
4 Drug Control in the Americas, 1931–1936 75
5 The United States Discovers an "Assassin of Youth" 99
6 Control Across the Border 119
7 A Window on the Future 135
8 World War II and After: Patterns of Drug Control 153
9 "The Horror and Damnation of Poor Little Human Flies" 181
Epilogue: The Limits of Flexibility 189
Appendix: Opium Poppy Destruction in Mexico, 1944 205
Notes 211
Bibliography 255
Index 275

List of Illustrations

Photographs (following page 16)

A coca bush
A Peruvian woman planting coca
Children harvesting coca leaves in Peru
Coca leaf fields in Peru
An opium poppy field in northwest Mexico
Harry J. Anslinger, commissioner of the Federal Bureau
   of Narcotics
Destroying marijuana crops in Mexico, 1975
Destruction of Mexican opium poppies, 1944

Maps (following page 16)

Areas of Opium Cultivation in Mexico
Areas of Coca Cultivation in Colombia
Areas of Coca Cultivation in Peru
Areas of Coca Cultivation in Bolivia

(Facing page 205)

Durango, Mexico.

Table

1. Annual Reports Sent to the Opium Advisory Committee
   from the United States and Latin America, 1921−1931   page 47
2. Annual appropriations for the Federal Bureau of
   Narcotics, 1931−1950   79

He wanted to be blind.

It made it

more likely

that one day he would see.

John Fowles, The Magus

Preface

The control of drugs is primarily a twentieth-century phenomenon. Historians have only recently begun to deal with its complexities. This study is meant to expand that historical record.

Two principal reasons help explain the slow development of research on drugs. For one thing, evidence is abundant only for a select range of topics. In the case of the United States, for example, we know much about antidrug legislation and antidrug campaigns, and even something about the profile of drug users. H. Wayne Morgan's essay on drugs and American society from the Civil War to the Harrison Narcotic Act of 1914 deals admirably with these matters.[1] We know less, though, about other facets of the American drug experience. In the decade or so following passage of the Harrison law, who were most likely to use drugs and why? What was their age, gender, race? How many addicts were there? At present, answers to these and related questions are commonly accepted approximations. Without new evidence and more definitive sources, we are not likely to obtain more precise answers nor to depict with accuracy the nature of the relationship between drug users and the larger society in which they lived.

The other reason for the inattention of historians has to do more with the issue of interpretation than with the specifics of drug use and control. That is, in what historical context should usage and control be placed? Are they unique phenomena and only in the broadest sense part of a more encompassing social and political environment? Have historians, in other words, exhausted the breadth of explanations? I would argue that drug control—like other proscriptive and prescriptive reform movements in society—

must necessarily be seen *in the larger historical context of its times*. This in no way reflects negatively on the subject's intrinsic merits.

Anyone reading this study who is familiar with the historical literature will recognize at once my intellectual debts to David F. Musto and Arnold H. Taylor. Without their groundwork my task would have been much more arduous. However, although I follow the organizational paths they previously trod, my concerns are different. I am more interested in developing as thorough an understanding as possible of the context from which drug control emerged in the United States and Latin America. It is this quest for the historical roots of drug usage and controls in the Americas that informs the first part of this study, chapters 1 through 3. Only then can modern types of drug control—after 1930–31—be adequately understood, as I demonstrate in the remaining chapters.

The more I study the control of drugs, an enterprise that has consumed my scholarly interests for the better part of a decade, the more I see a need to separate myself from my own cultural biases and to minimize the chauvinism inherent in all academic disciplines in order to do a credible job. My primary interests as a historian are the development of public policy and the process of diplomatic interchange. Sometimes these interests have not served me well in making sense of my subject. But were I at the same time a historian, psychologist, sociologist, student of political economy, and anthropologist, still it would be difficult to overcome all the methodological problems posed by the subject itself.

This is not to excuse the shortcomings that must inevitably remain in this study. It merely acknowledges the need to make intellectual choices about the best approach. By providing such a lucid discussion of the concept of culture and how it can be viewed within diverse social organizations, the writings of Sidney W. Mintz and Clifford Geertz made my choices much easier. When Mintz, for instance, takes care to point out the crucial distinction between the terms *social* and *cultural*, the student of drugs pays heed.[2]

I chose to focus on drug control in Latin America, in addition to the United States, because of their geographical proximity and their historically divergent attitudes concerning drugs. In both areas there existed aggravating methodological difficulties preventing adequate comprehension of the information at hand. These obstacles had to be overcome. When I spend considerable space, to give one example, exploring the nature of cultural variations between the north and west of Mexico and the Spanish-controlled central government in the colonial era, I am laying the basis for an understanding of the existence of the relatively modern phenomenon of drug production in such states as Sonora, Sinaloa, and Chihuahua. There is, I believe, a cultural continuity that persists over time and obtains in different social situations, although in altered historical forms. This was not at all apparent in the early stages of my work. This study focuses in large measure upon drug diplomacy between the United States and Mexico, for it has been Mexico's role throughout the century both as a producer of drugs and as the principal station in the illicit international pipeline that has most concerned United States officials.

As I have indicated, one of the major problems I encountered had to do with sources. Drug-related materials in Latin American archives remain virtually inaccessible, although published documents are useful. Also, United States records prior to the mid-1930s are not as revealing as a scholar ideally desires. Helpful in minimizing these lacunae are the records of the antinarcotic agencies of the League of Nations. Taken in their entirety, the data contained in available sources, whether seen from the vantage point of Latin America, the United States, or the international arena, comprehensively portray the history of inter-American drug control.

At present we need only look at the variety of print media giving space to drugs to gain an impression of their continuing role and influence in society: *Time, Sports Illustrated, Rolling Stone,* and the *Wall Street Journal,* for example.[3] As these publications attest, we live in a time when drugs often become the mainstay of local economies, both in the United States and abroad.

I undertook this study with the hope of providing additional information and understanding about the drug experience in the Americas. The main body of the study terminates in the late 1940s because it was approximately then that the complex developments we currently associate with drugs began to appear: extensive, illicit traffic controlled by organized gangs; geographical expansion of involvement in the traffic; and the increasing use of drugs for recreational purposes. To bring that story up to date—even while restricting it to the United States and Latin America—would entail the writing of another volume or nearly doubling the size of this one. My epilogue describes antidrug activity in the hemisphere in the 1970s.

Finally, a comment about terms, usage, and a point of style. The terms *drug* and *narcotic* are employed interchangeably, as they were in most of the official documents and secondary sources I examined. Drug, of course, is a more comprehensive term than narcotic, which is more properly applied to substances like the opiates. Pharmacologically, narcotic refers to those drugs capable of producing both sleep and analgesia.[4] The drugs most frequently mentioned in this study are *marijuana (Cannabis sativa), opium (Papaver somniferum)* and its alkaloids morphine and heroin, and *cocaine,* which derives from the coca plant *(Erythroxylon coca).* My last point has to do with the use of Spanish in the text: after the initial appearance of a word or group of words that can be recognized readily, I have not italicized it.

Acknowledgments

This book was conceived and brought to life during the inappropriately named Me Decade. In many ways, it is the product of a collective-cum-cooperative enterprise.

If it may seem ponderous, even trite, to observe that in the course of writing a book one incurs personal and professional debts impossible to repay, it is also true. Numerous individuals read or discussed with me various portions of the manuscript. For their generous advice and criticism, I thank Arnold J. Bauer, Richard B. Craig, Otis L. Graham, Jr., William H. Harbaugh, Albert L. Hurtado, Richard Kornweibel, Thomas A. Krueger, David M. Pletcher, Arnold H. Taylor, Jerry L. Tobey, Joseph S. Tulchin, and Robert H. Van Meter. Deep appreciation also goes to Marvin R. Zahniser, Mark H. Rose, and Joan Hoff Wilson for their constant encouragement and friendship.

My greatest intellectual and professional obligation, one I happily assume, is to Alexander DeConde of the University of California, Santa Barbara. His continuing interest in this study, long after he approved a vastly different form as a dissertation, attests to the admirable qualities he brings to the craft of history.

Invaluable help was also provided by the staffs of the National Archives for the records of the Department of State, especially Ron Swerczek and Kathie Nicastro; the Department of the Treasury; the Manuscript Division of the Library of Congress; the Bureau of Narcotics and Dangerous Drugs Library (now the Drug Enforcement Administration Library); the Oral History Research Office, Butler Library, Columbia University; and the Pennsylvania State University Library. Thanks for assistance go as well to the New York Public Library, the National Library of Medicine, and the Pan

American Union Library; and to the interlibrary loan personnel of the University of California, Santa Barbara, California State University, Sacramento, and Iowa State University. For financial assistance, I am indebted to the University of California, Santa Barbara for funding part of my doctoral research; and to Richard Lowitt and the department of history at Iowa State University for aid in the final stages of my work.

I gratefully acknowledge the permission of the *Pacific Historical Review* to reprint material in chapter 6 which previously appeared in its pages. And I appreciate the editorial help of David V. Holtby and Joanna Cattonar of the University of New Mexico Press.

As many have learned before me, a first book entails other, special obligations: to my mother and late father for believing their children must lead their own lives; and to Bill Chiechi, Al Hurtado, and Cece Martin, historians all, who lovingly sustained me in ways I yet may emulate. The dedication is to my dearest friend for her support when support was needed most. In so giving she never forgot it was equally important to get on with her own life.

1   Culture and Bureaucracy

Drugs have played an important, if sometimes limited role in the social history of the Americas. In some cases the prominence of drugs antedated contact with Europeans. Drug use, in fact, often assumed religious or ritualistic significance—and any attempt to restrict or regulate usage followed directly from this. The *legal* control of narcotics, on the other hand, is of comparatively recent origin, beginning in the early years of the twentieth century. At that time concerted efforts on the part of authorities in Western Europe and especially the United States to eliminate opium smoking in the Orient prompted a reassessment of the societal role of narcotics and subsequently resulted in numerous efforts to extend internationally various legal forms of narcotic control.

In the United States, the domestic movement for control was the logical extension of contemporaneous local, state, and national excursions into the realm of social reform and welfare legislation. Reformers, one historian has argued, "were apprehensive over the threat of social upheaval" and moral decay in the cities.[1] Whatever the motivation behind control, the attitude toward antidrug activity in the United States was far different from that in Latin America. The chewing of coca leaves in the Andes, the consumption of pulque, the smoking of marijuana, and ingestion of hallucinogens such as peyote in Mexico, and the contraband traffic passing through Central America reflected not so much turn-of-the-century societal decay as they testified to the historical persistence of traditions that led to few demands for legal restriction. These traditions, simply put, were part of Indian and Latin American culture.

An appreciation of the concept of culture is fundamental to an understanding of the social role of drugs, which, conversely, forms part of the substance of culture. "Understanding a people's culture," Clifford Geertz writes, "exposes their normalness without reducing their particularity. . . . It renders them accessible. . . ." In describing their accessibility, "behavior must be attended to, and with some exactness, because it is through the flow of behavior—or, more precisely, socialization—that cultural forms find articulation."[2] Specifically, control mechanisms for the ordering of behavior link the innate capacities of man with his actual behavior. Indeed, Geertz argues, the control mechanisms transform the first into the second.[3]

The concept of culture therefore enhances our understanding of the social role of drugs as a particular manifestation of individual or group behavior within the larger society. Sidney W. Mintz has posited an important distinction between culture and society: the former is "a kind of resource" and the latter "a kind of arena," the difference being between "sets of historically available alternatives or forms on the one hand, and the societal circumstances or settings within which these forms may be employed on the other."[4] Accordingly, the process of cultural change, even within a rapidly transforming society, more often exhibits continuities and adaptations in behavior than the disappearance of established cultural forms. Indigenous characteristics within a changing society may seem little more than cultural anachronisms, as Herbert G. Gutman argues, but those who possess them find them "natural and effective forms of self-assertion and self-protection."[5]

How this process came to include drug-related activity among several distinct cultures in what is now known as Latin America is a subject to which we now turn.

In his evocative work, *A Cultural History of Spanish America*, Mariano Picón-Salas writes that at the moment of European contact with the Americas there ensued "an unending conflict . . . This difficulty arose from the complex and foreign ways of an imposed culture favoring privileged minorities that were relatively indifferent to the realities of their surroundings, and from the accumulation of unresolved problems originating in the Indian and hybrid masses." This clash between and within cultures accentuated and perpetuated familiar social distinctions among indigenous Americans. Scales of classification of social standing for the period of contact usually place Indians (except for the privileged few) even below slaves. The distinctions seen in caste differences throughout Latin America have over centuries remained resistant to change.[6]

Variations of rank within Indian societies, moreover, at least indirectly aided the Spanish conquest. In Mexico at the height of the Aztec empire, the nobles, or *pipiltin*, dominated the lives of the *macehualtin*, or commoners. The social distinctions were those of task and training. Montezuma II, once enthroned, deified himself and initiated a system of debt peonage for the uneducated macehualtin. This social system, through its religious and political overtones, literally drove both commoners and nobles to drink. *Octli*, or pulque, became indispensable as a means of fortifying oneself against the practice of human sacrifice, whether one was victim or executioner.[7]

Yet it was the system more than the alcoholic systenance which served the Spanish well. The integration of political sovereignty and religion in Aztec society provided a relatively smooth transition to a Spanish-dominated social order based upon similar forms. And although class differences within Indian society did not fully disappear, as seen in the role of the caciques, or former chiefs, the conquerors treated both pipiltin and macehualtin as chattel. This was especially true with the advent of the encomienda system.[8]

Peru also had a social order based upon rank among Indians at the time of the conquest. In part rank was determined by the place one held within the precious metal and coca leaf cultures of Inca society. Local communities maintained a kind of autonomy while at the same time paying tribute to the empire with exacted amounts of gold, silver, and coca. Within this system the Inca nobles symbolically asserted their dominance by conducting religious ceremonies during which sacrifices of coca were made by chief priests. For commoners, coca was more pertinent to the rigors of daily life.[9] In contrast to the experience in the Valley of Mexico, the Spanish did not attempt in the same way to utilize the political and religious forms of Inca society to assist in the conquest of Peru. In spite of the economic rewards of coca cultivation by

1550, the Spanish remained uncertain of the role coca was to play in colonial Peru, going so far on occasion as to try to eliminate its use.[10]

This action, in turn, had a profound impact upon the cultural forms of Spanish Peru. Where contact was frequent, former Inca nobles sought to maintain as much of their status as possible through assimilation and acculturation. This process, as incomplete and superficial as it was, placed the caciques over the common Indians. The caciques were the intermediaries in the tribute system between the encomienda and its Indians who worked in the mines, at Potosí for example. The cultural change attendant to this contact may have destroyed many Indian traditions, disrupted Indian society, and resulted in large-scale reduction of the indigenous population.[11] Even those Indians who had minimal direct contact with the Spanish, that is, those who lived in remote coca-growing regions, may have remained unacculturated, but not, as James Lockhart points out, unaffected by Spanish Peru.[12]

Similarly, in Mexico north of former Aztec lands, nomadic Indians, despite prolonged periods of resistance, could not remain culturally unaffected by the Spanish presence. At the culmination in 1590 of forty years of war with the tribes of the Gran Chichimeca, a period of hostility engendered by the discovery of silver in Zacatecas in 1546, the way was opened for expansion north and west of the Spanish frontier missionary system. The opening was finally secured, not by decisive military conquest, but by promises of good land, livestock, food, and clothing. Often, as in Peru, Indian caciques who were previously assimilated acted as intermediaries for the Spanish.[13]

Expansion of Spanish settlements and society gradually extended peonage throughout much of Mexico. Great landed estates on which Indians worked took shape, reducing the size and authority of former native communities. Indians had to work their own remaining lands or see them confiscated. Native villages often became cramped. As Indian culture bent under the weight of an expanding imperial one, the hacienda inexorably took its place as the fundamental social institution in Mexico.[14] On the hacienda there arose a definite social structure. As François Chevalier has noted, "Between the Spanish masters and the Indian workers, increasing numbers of mestizos and mulattoes took their assigned ranks." Those Indians who did not become part of the laboring force for the great haciendas, in effect, consigned themselves to a position of small significance on the growing Spanish frontier.[15] To be a drifter or a vagrant, or to live in a surviving community relatively free of Spanish influence, as in Peru, did not leave one untouched by Spanish society. Nevertheless, a life-style on the periphery of society helped to preserve remnants of customs and culture which Spanish expansion was steadily eroding.

Elsewhere in the north and west of Mexico, beyond the lands of the Gran Chichimeca and briefly impervious to the encroachment of the hacienda, lived other Indians—known in modern times as *Yaqui*. Residing in what are now the states of Sonora and Sinaloa, the Yaqui, whose culture was based in large part upon military strength, did not come under Spanish administrative control until the 1740s. Even then, and until 1887, the Yaquis militarily controlled their own and surrounding lands. As Spanish strength increased, Yaquis worked on the hacienda, but a level of hostility and conflict persisted over centuries until the government of Mexico actually deported some Yaquis in the early 1900s from Sonora to Oaxaca and Yucatán in order to impose fuller political subordination on them than had previously been possible.[16]

The emergence of modern Mexico did not overcome social stratification. Efforts to curtail the power of the hacienda failed; disentailment of ecclesiastical estates in the 1850s actually threatened the communal life-style of Indian villages without improving their living conditions. Intermittent economic dislocation underlined the obstacles to change not only for the Indian but also for the mestizo, who held no prominent place within the social order. Together they constituted a surplus laboring force that served further to entrap both in their inferior status. Indian and mestizo worked the land in a tragic competition—some as peons, others as tenants, sharecroppers, or seasonals. The structure of privilege was their enemy. Jan Bazant has observed that "social inequality was taken for granted by both hacendados" and their laborers.[17]

Strict social differentiation persisted in Peru over hundreds of years as well. The process of rendering tribute and servile labor originated with the *mita* system in the mid-1500s. Although its form altered over time, the social and cultural implications remained constant. (Mita itself, termed *faena*, continued after independence in 1821.) Indians, through the coca leaf culture and its revenues, played a vital role in Peruvian history, although from a position of legal and social inferiority. Contact between Indian culture and the external, more powerful political and social environment fixed this relationship of dominance and subordination directly, as occurred infrequently, or through various intermediaries. *Encomenderos* and their *estancieros*, for example, filled the latter function during the early colonial times, as in part did the caciques. It was not until the twentieth century that concerted legal efforts were made to integrate Indian culture into the larger Peruvian society.[18]

Several conclusions relevant to our primary subject of drugs can be drawn from the preceding discussion of contact, acculturation, and cultural continuity and/or resistance in Mexico and Peru. The nature of the available evidence being what it is, the conclusions must perforce remain speculative—although more directly derived in some instances than others. Specifically, a life-style of deprivation within or exclusion from the economic and social mainstream of a particular society may manifest itself as a kind of resistance or revolt by a subjugated group against the dominant legal-political culture of the society.[19] The authority of the dominant culture is not questioned so much as it is disregarded. In Peru, Indian culture in 1900 gave to coca the same esteemed place it had traditionally held. As we shall see, that a product of the Andean coca leaf, cocaine, caused problems of a social, legal, or sanitary nature in other cultures meant nothing to the Indian *coqueros*. Coca was solely a matter to them of sustenance, in part religious but largely corporal.

The connection in Mexico between various expressions of indigenous culture and narcotic-related difficulties in the external environment is less direct. What is known, however, is the historical use of substances like pulque and peyote by the lowest classes of Mexican society.[20] The Yaquis and other disaffected and dislocated peoples in the north and west of Mexico undoubtedly turned from subsistence farming to means not legally sanctioned by the ruling political class to combat their deprivation. The continued ingestion of pulque and peyote implies passive alienation, whereas the cultivation, use, and trade in drugs such as marijuana and opium demonstrate the externally directed side of alienation. That such activity might bring actual or perceived changes in economic and social status should not be seen as incidental to the mainstream of modern Mexican history.[21]

Like cultivation and usage, smuggling has at least indirect links to a long-standing cultural phenomenon in the Americas. From earliest colonial times, the mere existence of an economy tied to the mother country, whether by custom or royal *cédula,* seemed an inducement to *rescates,* or smuggling. Competitive enterprises might be discouraged or forbidden; Spain might not be able to absorb sufficient colonial goods or offer desired merchandise in return; inflation in Spain, thanks to the influx of colonial gold and silver, might reduce purchasing power in the colonies; and war in Europe might prove detrimental to trade at any time. Each of these economic uncertainties was mitigated to some extent by smuggling.[22]

Between Mexico and Peru, for instance, trade remained essentially free until 1535, but was increasingly licensed thereafter. The enforcement of cédulas establishing trade regulations became the responsibility of officials who collected licensing fees. The livelihood of these officials depended upon their fee collections or, as proved more lucrative, the acceptance of bribes to waive the fees and other regulations. Additional restrictive cédulas in the 1560s simply invited greater fraud.[23] The opening of trade between Peru and the Philippines in 1573 brought luxury goods from China to the Spanish colonies and removed precious silver to the Orient. The impact on the Spanish treasury was profound, and Philip II prohibited the trade within ten years. Much silver was lost to the crown, however: shipping points such as Acapulco helped Peru to evade the enforcement of Philip's decrees.[24]

An even more extensive culture of illicit trade emerged in the Spanish Caribbean.[25] The following analysis will necessarily concentrate upon Central America since it was there that rescates acquired special meaning. The word *rescates* refers literally to exchange or barter; a derivative meaning suggests smuggling, even ransom. What is apparent is that the word describes a pattern of economic and cultural relationships within emerging Central American society. The economic nature of rescates is clear: it is intimately linked to supply and demand for desired commodities.[26]

In the early years of settlement after the conquest of Central America, there existed an anarchic social order with few internal, unifying links. By about 1540 a less developed Caribbean zone and a more advanced Pacific zone were emerging. The conquerors were naturally oriented toward Europe, so the society promised to be transitory: men with scant desire for the rigors of long-term development would accumulate wealth and depart. As raw materials became scarce or exhausted, and the labor supply dwindled, many of those left behind trafficked in cacao to overcome their marginal existence. A social division of labor evolved wherein the Indians, at first from Soconusco and Sosonate provinces, became integral parts of the traders' schemes. Some of the profits of the trade were then exchanged in Spain for titles, *mayorazgos* (entailed property), or other advantages. Ultimately, there were two cultures in Central America, one Spanish and one Indian. The often struggling encomienda economy placed enormous pressure on the latter. By the 1570s, as Murdo MacLeod writes, there "were still some differences among Indians because of prestige, office, or religion, but in general variety had gone, and the Indian survivors of these terrible years had become the peasantry of the newly formed agrarian society."[27]

Over the next half century, rescates played a prominent role in the shaping of Central American society. Economic expansion portended more than stable social conditions. With expansion, especially through commerce in Oriental goods, came smuggling along the Pacific coast from Callao-Lima to Guatemala to Mexico. Royal officials were lax in the enforcement of the cédulas of 1604, 1609, and 1620. Legalization of restricted trade conceivably could have brought the crown additional revenue, but it was not to be. To support the practice of rescates, *repartimiento* (labor drafted on a rotating, quota basis) replaced the encomienda system. The new system brought further hardship to the poorest Indians. At the same time, Spaniards who had been unlucky with the cacao trade increasingly fled to the countryside. These *vecinos* (citizen freeholders of Spanish towns) placed added pressure on Indian land, resulting in a system of Indian debt peonage. By the 1630s a multitiered society had evolved, composed of Indians, mestizos, and Spaniards of differing means, frequently sustained by illegal trade.[28]

The second hundred years of Spanish presence in Central America did little to alter the contours of this society. The Indian population was further reduced as cultural deprivation continued in areas of close contact with the Spanish. The process of acculturation did not lose its inherent reciprocal nature, but its effect can perhaps best be seen in the competition between the poorest segments of society in depressed economic times. One partial solution to the hard times, as always, was smuggling.[29] Rescates had become a way of life throughout much of Central America, and would retain its presence and power for centuries.

The persistence into the twentieth century of rescates and social separation in parts of Central America and Mexico proved a great obstacle to those who sought to proscribe or eliminate illicit traffic in drugs. Nowhere in Latin America around 1900 would the profound impact of restrictions upon indigenous culture be more apparent than in the coca regions of the Andes. The traditions of the coqueros had survived for centuries virtually unchanged. The coca culture stood both as a paean to an ancient past and as an ironic reminder of the consequences of conflict between civilizations. The following description of the historical and cultural role of coca adumbrates well the obstacles that narcotic regulators would encounter.

Coca chewing, or *el coqueo,* thrived throughout the Andes in pre-Columbian times, and may have antedated the Inca empire by two millennia. An Aruak tribe probably discovered coca in the Río Negro area of modern Colombia and introduced it to the Indians of Bolivia and Peru. Inca leaders often limited the use of coca to nobility, old people, priests in religious ceremonies, and to *chasqui*—couriers who notified the nobility of developments in the provinces—to aid their running.[30]

As suggested, el coqueo is neither a new nor a geographically limited cultural activity in the Andes. Archeological collections of ceramic remains found in Ecuador, for instance, depict Indians with balls of coca bulging in both cheeks. The Spanish substantiated these findings at the time of the conquest in reports to their superiors. Coca cultivation was widespread in colonial Ecuador and became an important trading commodity. Yet coca chewing had nearly disappeared from Ecuador by the end of the colonial period as a result of the enforcement of several cédulas of Philip II restricting coca's use in the Royal Audiencia of Quito. (A similar cédula had much less effect in Peru.)

In the seventeenth and eighteenth centuries the Spanish in Ecuador turned away from coca cultivation and toward substitute crops such as sugar cane, bananas, sweet potatoes, and other agricultural products. This change in emphasis lessened the Indians' dependence upon coca for sustenance and earning a living. Together with the enforcement of anticoca decrees, this alteration in life-style enabled Ecuador to rid itself almost entirely of coca, leading to a more productive and diversified economy which served well the Spanish-dominated ruling elite.[31]

El coqueo has had a different history in Peru. Inca limitations on the use of coca evidently were modified in the sixteenth century. Spanish records from that time contain numerous references to el coqueo, and the dispatches of Pizarro's secretary, Vincente Valverde, the Bishop of Cuzco, describe coca use by most Indians. Cultivation of coca on the lush rain-soaked *montaña* on the eastern slopes of the Andes—as an agricultural commodity and for personal usage—greatly increased by the 1570s and 1580s. Even though some of the conquerors argued against coca's use, the prospect of substantial economic rewards motivated the viceroys to order increases in production for the domestic market. The decrees of Philip II evidently had little effect upon royal officials in Peru.

In addition to the financial lure, other reasons worked against the prohibition of coca. Several famines created the need for some substance to alleviate hunger pangs among the Indians. Moreover, there existed a demand for something that would enable laborers in the mines to work productively with a minimum of fatigue. El coqueo filled these needs since it produces a generally good feeling. By the late 1700s, almost in testimony as it were to the reciprocal nature of acculturation, Spanish troops had acquired the habit of coca chewing to sustain themselves in the field. Thus by the time coca chewing almost vanished in Ecuador, an official tolerance for the habit had taken shape in Peru where it persisted for centuries.[32]

By the twentieth century perhaps half of the Indians living in the upper reaches of the Andes were inveterate coca chewers, known as *cocaístas*. El coqueo was most prevalent in Peru and Bolivia, but existed to a lesser degree in Colombia, northern Argentina, Chile, and Ecuador and Brazil in isolated instances. Colombian and Bolivian Indians grew coca primarily for personal use, or for domestic sale and consumption. Some Peruvian coca leaves, as mentioned, found their way into the world market as the major international supply of manufactured cocaine. No South American government at the time considered measures to regulate the production and use of coca leaves.[33]

Indians were still chewing coca for reasons unchanged for centuries. The use of coca in some areas implied continued ritualistic significance from earlier eras, such as in the burial ceremony, but the overriding reason for the persistence of el coqueo was its role in mitigating the miserable living conditions in the Andes—an enduring legacy of the conquest and colonization. The passage of centuries had lessened neither the relative poverty of Indians nor the burden of endless toil, often for others, on the mountainsides. Coca chewing therefore offered the chance of an illusory escape from the harsh realities of life. El coqueo quenched one's thirst, suppressed the pangs of hunger, and enhanced the productivity of labor. In Ecuador where living conditions did not differ much from those in Colombia, Peru, and Bolivia, Indians most often turned to alcohol for relief.[34]

Attempts to control or prohibit the use of coca would fail without adequate food supplies and alternative agricultural production. Even so, proscription could not guarantee in the short term the desired, accompanying cultural transformation. Nonetheless, no single effort at international control of the coca leaf prior to 1945 directly faced this fundamental issue. Accordingly, el coqueo and the cultivation and export of coca leaves scarcely abated as the assumed benefits of coca came under increasingly close scrutiny, as will be discussed later.

The historical and cultural role of marijuana in Latin America, especially in Mexico for the period under consideration, although not as well known as that of coca, also exemplifies the resilience of indigenous cultural forms amid national and external pressures upon them. The lack of knowledge about marijuana results from the traditional reluctance of Latin American governments to demonstrate active concern about the use of drugs by their citizens. Persuasive, though circumstantial, evidence reveals the accustomed use of marijuana. For instance, as Mexican authorities began to deal seriously in the 1930s with widespread marijuana smoking, they occasionally discussed its long-term enjoyment by the lower classes of society. Also, the earliest reports in the United States regarding marijuana claimed that Mexican nationals in the Southwest and West were the largest group of users. Usage can therefore be viewed as another turn-of-the-century form of separation between the presumed national culture and indigenous culture throughout much of Latin America.[35]

In sum, the use of substances such as coca leaves and marijuana had become tacitly accepted activities in several countries.[36] As a result, drugs, inseparable from the cultural expression of countless people in Latin America, would not be readily controlled there.

It is much more difficult to determine with precision the historical role of drugs in the United States, even if special attention is given to ethnic and cultural dissimilarities within the population. Nor is it particularly revealing to talk of a subculture involving drugs prior to the passage of the 1914 Harrison Narcotic Law. The gist of what is known, however, is that usage was widespread geographically and ethnically, if not numerically extensive prior to 1914. The ensuing discussion therefore will trace in general terms the contours of usage till then, and analyze why domestic control took the form that it did. Specific historical references to usage will be made primarily to elucidate larger points.[37]

Narcotics such as opium and morphine were acknowledged as acceptable for public consumption under certain circumstances until the last quarter of the nineteenth century. In the 1770s, Dr. Benjamin Rush, who served as surgeon general of the Revolutionary Army, suggested a compound of wine and opium as an alternative to drinking rum or whiskey. Promoters of patent medicines in the 1800s brought America the medicine habit; often their tonics, such as Mrs. Winslow's Soothing Syrup, were laced with opium. Control of patent medicines occurred only with the passage of the 1906 Pure Food and Drug Act.[38] The family physician and town druggist also supplied opiates to many people. Hospitals were established where chronic users were maintained in their habits, partly because such treatment was lucrative, but also because the medical profession lacked interest in determining the deleterious effects of opium and its derivatives. Moreover, hypodermically injected morphine served well as a painkiller during the Civil War. What these disparate examples reveal is the presence of chronic opiate intoxication.[39]

Scientific evidence questioning the alleged benefits of sustained drug use was slow to appear. Opiates, cocaine, and to a lesser extent marijuana were readily available in many parts of the country. A researcher discovered the local anesthetic properties of cocaine in 1884; usage increased through its presence in snuff and nasal sprays. Fourteen years later a German pharmacological researcher synthesized diacetylmorphine, a chemical compound of industrial acid and morphine thereafter known as heroin. A similar experiment years earlier had been abandoned because of the compound's adverse effects upon laboratory animals. Yet reports around 1900 claimed heroin to be free from the addictive properties of codeine or morphine. As Dr. Charles E. Terry and Mildred Pellens wrote, "Probably no remedy was ever greeted so enthusiastically as was heroin." The Bayer chemical company of Germany used Heroin as a brand name in a mass-marketing campaign. The American Medical Association (AMA) approved heroin for general use in place of morphine to treat various painful infections.[40]

The use of narcotics continued apace until the passage of federal legislation. Statistical data regarding the extent of use and addiction are available but unreliable, since means did not exist to collect accurate information over wide and varying geographical areas. The most authoritative figures for 1915 estimate between 200,000 and 275,000 addicts in the United States. Females apparently outnumbered males by a three-to-two ratio. Many of the habitués were of middle age, from the middle and upper class, and lived in the South. After 1915, when narcotics became more difficult to obtain, this sexual-social delineation altered as poorer males numerically dominated the known addict population.[41]

To conclude the portrayal of narcotics in the United States at this juncture would be misleading. The preceding material suggests that usage occurred within a quasi-favorable environment and that authoritative opinion proffered by doctors and druggists among others overcame adverse public opinion regarding the social and medical effects of usage. Such was not the case. Narcotic use, especially of the opiates, had also been associated with vice and social decay. In their condemnation of alcohol and the saloon, advocates of prohibition inveighed against narcotics as well—so much so, it has been argued, that antinarcotic sentiments helped to define the nation's progressive reform tradition.[42] The hypodermic injection of narcotics was seen in some quarters by 1870 as a possible road to individual "dissipation." A study of opium use conducted in Michigan in 1878 found that the "influence of vicious association was relatively negligible." Whatever other assumptions researchers brought to their study, they seem always to have believed in a close relationship between vice and opium.[43]

In California, at least, such an assumption had racist overtones.

The government of San Francisco prohibited opium-smoking dens in 1875; Chinese frequented the dens far more than did other ethnic groups. Thirteen years later the federal government singled out the Chinese in a law prohibiting the importation of opium. It is doubtful that the legislation had the desired deterrent effect. [44] Racism as an element of antidrug sentiment was prevalent elsewhere, too. At the turn of the century many Southern whites viewed cocaine as a fearsome substance. Vivid images of Negro cocaine addicts destroying the white-dominated social order underlay their fears. One Georgia luminary, a Colonel J. W. Watson, held that crimes committed by "colored people can be traced directly to the cocaine habit." These fears emerged during a period of renewed racial discrimination marked by legal segregation and a spate of lynchings. Virtually no available evidence supports the presumed link between color, crime, and cocaine. In a five-year period beginning in 1909, for instance, of twenty-one hundred Negroes admtted to a Georgia asylum, only two were confirmed cocaine users. [45] However vulnerable to criticism the widely accepted link between race and narcotics may be on other grounds, it helps to demonstrate an additional aspect of the nation's antinarcotic sentiment prior to the enactment of federal control.

Taken in their entirety, the arguments against alcohol, drugs, and activities commonly associated with their use ultimately presented a compelling rationalization for legal and social reforms. Control offered a means of protecting cherished values for a primarily white and putatively mobile society; it portended order in place of chaos. And the law could be relied upon as the arbiter of dissent. [46]

Within this general framework, the motivation behind narcotic control necessarily included both humanitarian and coercive aspects. As such, it did not differ from other areas of public concern which can either be discussed under the rubric of social reform during the Progressive Era, or seen as part of the process culminating in the creation of the welfare state. To reformers, social legislation, whether prescriptive or proscriptive, marked progress against social unrest, class conflict, and moral decay. [47] The movement for social justice was frequently morally uplifting, both for the reformers and the people who were the object of their concern. Progressives believed that directed behavior, often by religious, political, and social institutions, offered the most efficacious road to reform and to a better society. Even if we acknowledge that the "new radicals," as Christopher Lasch terms the social reformers,

possessed beneficent intentions in their ministrations, reform undoubtedly had repressive and coercive features. Too often reform
campaigns reflected class or racial biases; and some activities, such
as narcotic use after the passage of the Harrison Act, became
defined increasingly as fit for coercive response. Thus, Lasch suggests that the egalitarian spirit of progressivism suborned an excep-
tional degree of intolerance toward social and cultural differences.
The Lasch argument, as the vast range of historical literature
subsequently produced attests, is too broad for specific application
in all instances. It does, however, possess relevance for a discussion
of narcotic regulation. [48]

Although the taste for liquor in the United States was momen-
tarily tempered by constitutional amendment, the consumption of
alcohol, unlike the use of drugs, remained socially acceptable to
large segments of the populace. Although drugs were widely
viewed around 1914 as a social contagion, there existed precedents
for humanitarian control of these substances. One such impetus
derived directly from the short, prior history of international antidrug activity. The origins and development of the international
movement have received adequate exposition elsewhere, and need
not be recounted except where germane to the present discussion.[49]

The movement arose in response to the usage, usually by smoking, of opium in China and the Philippines. Under the watchful
eye of Governor William Howard Taft, opium was excluded in the
Philippines for all but medical purposes. Reforms proved more
difficult in China, where perhaps one-fourth of the adult males
smoked enough opium to be classed as addicts by Western standards. At the urging of Episcopal Bishop Charles H. Brent, a humanitarian reformer from western New York, an antiopium
meeting convened at Shanghai in 1909.[50] Conferees from thirteen
nations gathered but failed to make any decisions binding upon the
participating governments. Nevertheless, the reformers had aired
the issue of international control and looked ahead to subsequent
meetings. While the conference at Shanghai was in session, its
chief coordinator, the American Dr. Hamilton Wright, who had
devoted his adult life to research on communicable diseases in the
Far East, persuaded the Department of State to seek the enactment of federal antiopium legislation. Thus it was that the Opium
Exclusion Act became law in February 1909.[51]

Wright's unceasing misgivings about the situation in China ultimately led to a series of three additional conferences at The Hague between 1911 and 1914. The agenda at the first gathering was expanded to include discussion of morphine, cocaine, and Indian hemp (marijuana) along with opium. International jealousies and rivalries closely tied to the revenue derived from drug production and manufacture effectively emasculated the efforts of the reformers. The Hague Convention of 1912, upon which the United States based its international drug diplomacy until 1931, merely urged the signatories "to use their best endeavors" to suppress illicit trade. Limitation at the source was out of the question. The powers also failed to reach agreement either on quantification of world drug needs or a workable definition of the legitimate medical and scientific uses of drugs. By the time of the Paris Peace Conference, only eighteen nations, including the United States and Great Britain, had put the 1912 convention into effect.[52]

Wright also played a prominent role in the quest for domestic control legislation. The legislative process, which David F. Musto has well described, seems important less for its particular manifestations than for its role as an aspect of the contemporary movement for social reform. An original antidrug bill was defeated when representatives of physicians and the drug trades could not agree upon an acceptable division of responsibilities under the proposed law. The problem involved diagnosis, prescription, and dispensation. In 1913 the National Drug Trade Conference and the American Medical Association, then an Eastern, urban organization whose members shared the reform spirit of the times, entered the deliberations. The two groups, Wright, and various congressmen worked out a satisfactory agreement which mandated in part that all persons, other than the customers, involved in narcotic transactions had to be registered with the government. Passage of a law by Congress was thus secured, and President Woodrow Wilson signed the Harrison Narcotic Act into law on December 17, 1914. Antidrug activity would thereafter become part of the emerging pattern of scientific management of national reform issues, one of the hallmarks of the Progressive Era.[53]

As will be presently seen, enforcement of the law did not augur well for the country's addicts. On the local and state levels in some regions of the land, however, addicts continued for a time to receive humane treatment from the medical profession. Dr. Charles E. Terry, city health officer in Jacksonville, Florida, promoted medical treatment for them. At Terry's behest Jacksonville established a maintenance clinic at which narcotics on prescription were freely available. To guard against the spread of addiction, Terry argued for city and state programs as an alternative to the dispensing physician. Similarly, the state food and drug commissioner of Tennessee, Lucius P. Brown, advocated an increased caretaker role for the state. Maintenance as medical treatment did not, of course, mean cure, but less suffering for the addict. Even the later notorious New York City narcotic clinic began operation in the hope of mitigating the ravages of a life of addiction.[54]

This method of dealing with addiction, humanitarian in conception and thoroughly in accord with certain impulses of progressive social reform, could not withstand pressure from even stronger administrative and legal impulses which in this instance comprised the more coercive aspects of progressivism. Maintenance, simply put, countenanced moral turpitude and social deviance. No fuller proof of the evils of maintenance was needed than to point to the level of addiction. But just how many addicts were there? A report by Lawrence Kolb and A. G. DuMez for the Public Health Service (PHS) placed the 1918 figure at 238,000, virtually equal to a national estimate for 1922 done in Pennsylvania—a year in which Kolb and DuMez estimated only 110,000 addicts. The city health commissioner in New York believed that there were nearly 100,000 addicts within his jurisdiction alone. A concomitant problem for health and law enforcement officials was the risk of illegal traffic in drugs; the trade made accurate estimates of the number of addicts impossible. "In recent years," explained a Special Committee of the Treasury Department in 1919, "especially since the enactment of the Harrison law, the traffic by underground channels has increased enormously."[55]

The unfavorable light in which addicts were being viewed did not necessarily preordain the nature of the federal response to addiction after the Harrison law took effect. True, that response reflected in part the attitude of a contributor to the *American Journal of Clinical Medicine* in 1918 who admitted that some upstanding citizens fell victim to the drug menace innocently enough, but characterized most addicts as "drug fiends . . . the physical, mental, and moral defectives . . . denizens of the underworld."[56] The federal response encompassed at least two other considerations as well, namely, bureaucratic or organizational disputes, and the related pattern of legal enforcement of the Harrison law.

That enforcement would ultimately turn addicts into criminals was not clear upon passage of the law. One section allowed physicians to prescribe narcotics for certifiable medical use. This suggests that a doctor could issue drugs to addicts under his care, a practice not necessarily distinguishable from maintenance. The Treasury Department, however, published additional regulations in March 1915 requiring druggists to verify whether the signatures of physicians were forged or whether the amounts of drugs prescribed seemed excessive. At the same time prosecutors for the Justice Department were arguing in court that possession of narcotics by unregistered persons should be regarded as violation of Section 8 of the law.[57]

At first the Supreme Court partially disagreed with this contention. In *United States v. Jin Fuey Moy* (1915) 241 U.S. 394, the court rejected the government's appeal for broader regulation of the practices of the medical profession. Not until 1919, in two companion decisions—*Webb et al. v. United States* (1919) 249 U.S. 96 and *United States v. Doremus* (1919) 249 U.S. 86—would the court rule that, in effect, providing narcotics for maintenance could not be considered a legitimate medical practice. Another ruling three years later, *United States v. Behrman* (1922) 258 U.S. 280, seemed to outlaw narcotic prescriptions made even in good faith.[58] That it had taken several years for the pattern of enforcement and its legal sanction to evolve is not surprising given the organizational disputes within the Treasury Department. At issue were contending attitudes on the propriety of maintenance, therapy, and custodial care, including imprisonment.

The Bureau of Internal Revenue, charged with supervision of the licensing provisions of the law, opposed maintenance and advocated strict enforcement. The Public Health Service, on the other hand, was more disposed at first to consider therapeutic or curative activities. These positions were never uniformly held within each agency, and events from 1915 to 1918–19 may have served virtually to reverse their initial positions. The Public Health Service, through A. G. DuMez of the Special Committee of the Treasury Department, disavowed the likelihood of cure and turned to punitive law enforcement. In the 1920s Dr. Lawrence Kolb of the Public Health Service would declare that an addict was a psychopath by choice. Countering this position was the difficult practical experience of Internal Revenue in accomplishing effective law enforcement. The bureau came to support a curative solution for addiction. Under its auspices, forty-four narcotic clinics were set up for the purpose of assisting gradual withdrawal, or providing maintenance for addicts if necessary. Commissioner Daniel C. Roper praised the work of the clinics in his annual report for fiscal year 1918–19, but the bureau's next report, subsequent to the Supreme Court decisions of 1919, condemned the clinics for "providing applicants with whatever drugs they required for the satisfaction of their morbid appetites" and applauded "the wisdom of the policy being pursued."[59]

The fluctuating support for strict law enforcement, judicial decisions, and the complexity involved in actually reducing narcotic use help to explain in one sense why the nation's maintenance clinics never became more than a transitory experiment which had largely ended by July 1920. The Public Health Service and the AMA's Committee on Habit-Forming Drugs both lauded the closure of the clinics.[60]

In another sense, the bureaucratic differences over narcotic law enforcement support conclusions in other studies concerned with the role of bureaucracies and institutions during the Progressive Era. Whatever its particular characteristics, the Narcotic Division of the Prohibition Unit of the Treasury Department, established in December 1919 after the passage of the Volstead Act, can be seen as representative of the organizational movement for efficient management. Strict law enforcement therefore need not be seen as distinct from social reform. In this instance, as institutionalization in a penal rather than a therapeutic or curative facility for what was essentially a medical matter (although not universally recognized as such at the time) became a major organizational objective, humanitarian social reform lost its remaining importance. At this juncture, Kolb's depiction of addicts as psychopaths becomes indistinguishable from the reality of government policy.[61] Interest-group administrative liberalism, as Theodore Lowi describes it, had replaced older, less administratively reliable ways of handling the socially unacceptable practice of narcotic consumption.[62]

To implement antinarcotic policy, the Congress provided the Narcotic Division, under the direction of Levi G. Nutt, a budget for fiscal year 1920 amounting to $515,000, almost twice that of the

prior year. Increasing violations of the Harrison law probably led
to larger budgets for its enforcement. From 1916 to 1919, the
number of known violators ranged from a low of 1,100 in 1917 to a
high of 2,400 in 1919. There were 3,900 known violators in 1920,
an average of 10,300 in 1924–26, and an average just below 9,000
for 1927–28. Of the 7,738 persons in federal prison at the end of
the fiscal year 1928, nearly one-third, or 2,529, were imprisoned
for Harrison law offenses. Daniel Roper believed that the drug
problem in the United States was out of control by 1920. Terry and
Pellens concluded that enforcement practices induced higher levels of addiction, drug peddling, and associated criminal activity. Of
America's addicts, the Special Committee observed, "From information in the hands of the Committee, it is concluded that, while
drug addicts may appear to be normal to the casual observer, they
are usually weak in character, and lacking in moral sense."[63]

In many ways, the law and the evolving organizational structure
through which it was administered had made the addict population
of the United States into a social class not unlike that of Latin
America, associated with extralegal, antisocial behavior. Official
tolerance for drugs and related activity differed greatly. Moreover,
the depiction of addicts in the United States as a coherent social
class, useful for administrative purposes, did not reflect actual
racial or socioeconomic conditions. There existed no distinct drug
culture, no unified group similar to the Andean coqueros, the
participants in rescates, or the rural poor, often Indians, who for
generations had worked the land for the benefit of others.

It was within the context of its emerging federal antinarcotic
activity that the United States encouraged Latin American participation in the larger, international campaign against narcotics. And
it is from the perspective of the aspirations of officials in Washington juxtaposed with the vastly different cultural history of Latin
America that the success or failure of the narcotic foreign policy of
the United States should be assessed.

No Latin American country attended the Hague conference of
1911–12. At that meeting it became evident that the campaign
against illicit drug traffic needed Latin American support to be
effective. This was especially true in the case of Peru, the world's

leading coca leaf exporter. The government of the Netherlands, charged with obtaining signatures to the convention by the nonrepresented states, asked the United States for assistance.[64] Hamilton Wright composed a detailed memorandum for United States representatives in Latin America which outlined the brief history of the international antinarcotic campaign and requested countries there to sign the supplementary protocol. Wright's letter pointed out that the conferees at The Hague realized the importance of Peruvian and Bolivian acceptance of the convention and concluded their business only after agreeing that "the signature of the Convention by Latin American states was essential if the Convention was to become effective."[65]

The generally favorable response from Latin America pleased State Department officials, but Peru and Bolivia withheld adherence. Bolivia objected to the linking of coca with opium in the convention and was reluctant to take any action threatening its coca industry. By the end of 1912, though, all Latin American countries except Peru indicated a willingness to sign the Hague Convention if they had not yet done so. Peru was undecided because of revenue derived from the coca trade and because of limited involvement in opium traffic, primarily within the Chinese population in Peru.[66]

In deliberations during the second conference at The Hague in July 1913, Great Britain and Germany reiterated an earlier concern that the 1912 convention would be worthless regarding cocaine unless Peru signed. Peruvian reluctance was delaying ratification by several important narcotic manufacturing states. Before the conference adjourned, Peru promised to sign the convention, but the promise was made only after urgent appeals by the United States.

The delay in depositing ratifications led to the convening of a third conference. The start was postponed from May until mid-June 1914 because officials in Washington were seeking Mexico's support at the meeting and hoped the delay might serve to lessen tension that arose between the two countries over the United States occupation of Veracruz earlier that year. With war on the horizon in Europe, the conference took place. By its final session forty-four of forty-six nations had signed or pledged to sign the Hague Convention. Eleven countries had completed ratification, including Venezuela, Guatemala, and Honduras as well as the United States.[67] Although adherence to the convention was gradual, it provided a basis for subsequent international antinarcotic activity.

Through 1920 in Peru and Bolivia, adherence to the convention did not signify its implementation. Both nations refused to jeopardize their lucrative coca leaf operations.[68] Only Mexico, of the Latin American countries crucial for control, tried in any way to restrict drug-related activity. Early in 1916 the *de facto* government prohibited opium importation. The following year President Venustiano Carranza sought to outlaw opium transactions in Baja California, but his own lack of control and the alleged complicity of the governor there in the trade (as discussed in chapter 2) nullified Carranza's efforts.[69]

These episodes presaged future difficulties that would impede antidrug activity throughout Latin America and cause concern in the United States. The overriding fear in Washington, then as later, was that illicit drugs produced in Latin America or shipped there from Europe or Asia would find their way to the United States. Compounding the matter, few Latin American states admitted the existence of a drug problem within their borders. With a rise in smuggling as a probable consequence of greater actions against drugs, concern in Washington over inadequate controls in Latin America was no doubt warranted. The legal-organizational process leading to the formation of a strict drug control program seems clear; just as apparent, conversely, is the cultural and economic background of Latin American inattention to controls in the early 1900s. The incongruity between the two would be further revealed as the United States continued to press for more effective international controls on drug traffic.

2   The Road to Geneva

Influences shaping the various responses to narcotics in the hemisphere prior to 1920 continued to hold sway. Existing problems remained unsolved, preventing the rational drug control desired by officials in the United States. Also, new dilemmas, especially concerning relations with the League of Nations, emerged to vex narcotic officials. Several Latin American nations nevertheless considered adopting stricter domestic controls, and participated in the international movement on a limited basis. The United States entered the decade hoping to exercise greater influence internationally while maintaining a strong antinarcotic commitment at home. By early 1925, however, America's goals seemed chimerical. Withdrawal of the United States from a narcotic conference in Geneva left officials in Washington estranged from the international movement. At the same time, the effectiveness of domestic policy seemed in doubt. From this nadir, new forces were at work which ultimately would bring greater efficiency to America's foreign and domestic drug policies. The transformation would help to promote concomitant, if lesser, antidrug activity in a number of Latin American countries.

The two major histories of narcotic control, although otherwise excellent, do not treat their subject from a sufficiently broad perspective.[1] Consequently, the extent of their analysis is necessarily restrictive. David F. Musto's book on domestic control focuses briefly on other contemporary developments of interest to narcotic officials and the medical profession, but does not undertake a sustained discussion of the larger issues of public policy formation and political power. Similarly, the work of Arnold H. Taylor on the international control movement, although useful for an understanding of United States relations with the League of Nations on narcotic matters, does not consider simultaneous changes within the foreign policy bureaucracy. An appreciation of the changes makes more understandable the shift in narcotic foreign policy by 1931. Through that date control cannot adequately be explained *sui generis*, but needs to be seen within a wider context integrating where possible general political and diplomatic trends with conditions peculiar to narcotics.

Herbert Hoover's belief in individualism defined the limits of American public policy in the 1920s. A protean philosophy, Hoover's individualism stressed the rectitude of voluntary, cooperative activities in service to the community. The preservation of democratic liberalism would be the primary reward of the efficient operation of public policy, whether expressed in social or economic terms. As Hoover put it, a society's "inspiration is individual initiative. Its stimulus is competition. Its greatest mentor is free speech and voluntary organization for the public good. Its expression in legislation is the common sense and common will of the majority. It is the essence of this democracy that the progress of the mass must arise from the progress of the individual."[2]

This eloquent, if roseate, statement of faith unfortunately minimized the difficulty of its realization. For Hoover, that would come essentially through associations of farmers, engineers, lawyers, and doctors among others who would provide the basis for managing the American system. Associations, Hoover believed, promised professionalism and efficiency. The role of government would be one of coordination and noncoercive guidance.[3]

But was the ideal attainable given the distribution of power within the existing political system? Hoover felt so, but his defenders and detractors both argue otherwise. Hoover viewed public policy as a means to an end. The exercise of power, as seen in the multifarious activities of his commerce department, was a tool to attack economic inequality and eliminate poverty in America.[4] Such a task, however, raised the specter of politics and public

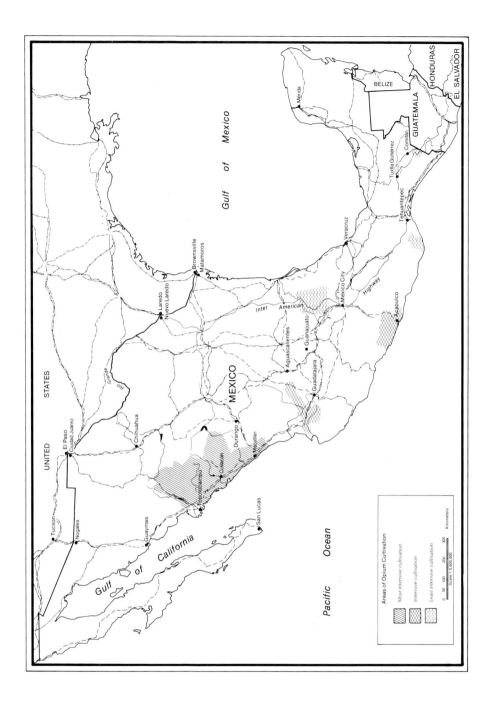

Maps of opium and coca cultivation courtesy of the Department of State, and adapted by Editype, S. Woodson.

Caribbean Sea

PANAMA

VENEZUELA

Pacific
Ocean

Puerto
Carreño

El Porvenir

Bogotá

COLOMBIA

Vichada
Rio

Guaviare
Rio

Popaván

Mocoa

Tulcán

ECUADOR

BRAZIL

PERU

Areas of Coca Cultivation

0   50   100   150   Statute Miles
0   50   100   150   Kilometers
Scale 1:4,000,000

ECUADOR

COLOMBIA

PERU

Amazon

BRAZIL

Rio Marañón

Rio Ucayali

Chachapoyas
• Mendoza

Juanjui

Cajabamba
Otuzco • • Huamachuco
Santiago de Chuco • Mollebamba
• Tayabamba

Aucayacu

Huánuco

Pacific

Ocean

Puerto Ocopa

Callao • Lima

Mantacra • • Luisiana
Machupicchu

BOLIVIA

Pan American Highway

Pan American Highway

CHILE

Areas of Coca Cultivation

0   50   100   150   Statute Miles
0   50 100 150 Kilometers
Scale 1 : 4,000,000

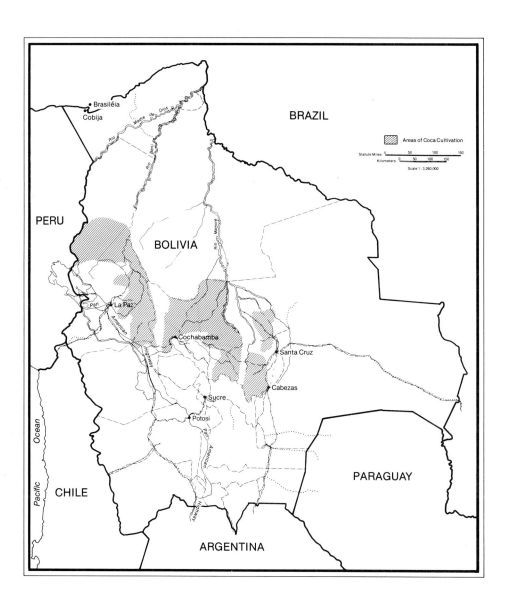

A coca bush. Courtesy Drug
Enforcement Administration
Library.

A Peruvian woman planting
coca. Courtesy Drug
Enforcement Administration
Library.

Children harvesting coca
leaves in Peru. Courtesy
Drug Enforcement
Administration Library.

Coca leaf fields in Peru. Courtesy Drug Enforcement
Administration Library.

An opium poppy field in northwest Mexico. Courtesy Drug
Enforcement Administration Library.

Harry J. Anslinger, commissioner of the
Federal Bureau of Narcotics from 1930
until 1962. Courtesy Drug Enforcement
Administration Library.

Destroying marijuana crops, Mexico, 1975. Courtesy Drug
Enforcement Administration Library.

Destruction of Mexican opium poppies near Metates, Durango, Mexico, 1944. Courtesy National Archives.

policy dominated by special interests. Interest-group pluralism need not be undemocratic, yet has the potential for being so.[5] Additionally, the efficient operation of a society based upon the ideals Hoover cherished entailed supervision. As commerce secretary and president, Hoover maintained that this supervision did not have to produce a larger, more powerful government bureaucracy. Nevertheless, it ultimately had that effect despite his desire to prevent it.[6]

Reflective, too, of the accrual of power in the executive branch largely by administrative fiat were contests between Congress and the Harding and Coolidge administrations over the course of public policy whenever public issues made that course contestable. As was his wont, Hoover tried virtually to bypass Congress, attempting, in effect, to circumscribe its impact upon public policy. The standard interpretation suggests failure or at most collaboration with Congress by the three Republican presidents. The reality is more complex, exposing deep philosophical splits within the Republican party—wounds which Hoover's social and economic activism exacerbated rather than healed.[7]

Hoover no doubt influenced his two predecessors. Even before the election of Warren G. Harding, Hoover hoped to elicit the candidate's support for his programs. He agreed to join the cabinet on the condition that Harding support executive branch reorganization, one of Hoover's pet projects. (The president also convened the 1921 Conference on Unemployment at Hoover's urging.) Likely neither Harding nor Coolidge shared the secretary's disdain for legislative solutions to national problems. Nor can we ascribe to them Hoover's faith in associational activity as a panacea for the nation's socioeconomic ills.[8] The Harding presidency did not lack leadership, however. True, for nearly one-half of his term in office Harding acted as a conciliator, apparently dominated by powerful and diverse party leaders. The president nevertheless came to enjoy his role as the nation's leader. Even before Republican losses in mid-term elections, he determined to challenge party insurgents in Congress. In so doing he emerged as the head of his party; executive power and authority were ascendant. Robert K. Murray has observed that Harding became a "practitioner of strong presidential power, deserting most of his former beliefs concerning presidential proprieties."[9]

If Hoover's influence upon Harding and Coolidge is measured by the nature of their relations with Congress, then Hoover had less of an impact upon the latter. Coolidge did not envision a major role for himself in the legislative process. His meetings with congressmen were perfunctory; and he did not do well in his early jousts with Congress. Relations with Congress produced a stalemate, at best, in the struggle for control of public policy.[10] Despite Coolidge's limitations as president, the accretion of power to the executive branch, if the commerce and state departments may be taken as cases in point, continued without serious congressional challenge.[11]

Hoover's program, never successfully realized, came closer to fulfillment in the economic than the social realm. Even so, the depression exposed the weaknesses of economic voluntarism and associationalism. The limits of his vision put Hoover on the defensive politically. Not that the early New Deal resolved Hoover's doubts about government controls and coercion; it did not. Roosevelt and his advisers managed to restore the American people's faith in their institutions, whereas Hoover's aversion to legislative activity damaged the nation's faith in representative government.[12]

The tragedy of Herbert Hoover and the serious wound the depression inflicted upon his historical reputation were far in the future, though, as he took his place in Harding's cabinet. What lay ahead in 1921 was the task of gaining acceptance of his particular brand of American individualism. Not all organized groups were persuaded of the inherent virtues of associationalism. The American Medical Association, for example, despite its increasing professionalization, rejected closer ties to the federal government, however informal. It was only in the first two decades of the century that the AMA began to grow into the national, politically potent organization that the American public later came to take for granted. To a great extent the First World War interrupted that process. Issues of importance to the organization led to a renewal of its growth immediately after the war. As we shall see, one of these was narcotic law enforcement. Compulsory health insurance loomed as the most contentious issue at the time. Despite initial vacillation on the merits of the issue, the AMA strongly opposed compulsory insurance, and the campaign for its adoption largely failed by 1920. In the following year, the Sheppard-Towner Act became law. A variant of compulsory insurance, providing for maternal and infant care, the law appeared to the AMA to be an invasion of states' rights. The association argued with varying degrees of success against its extension throughout the decade. The battle against federal health subsidies to the states, a fundamental part of the welfare legislation, was won only in the depths of the depression.[13]

As a professional association, the AMA rejected even the benign involvement of the government in an issue as ostensibly uncontroversial as child care. Hearkening to the twin causes of states' rights and opposition to state, or institutional, medicine, the organization sought to unite the profession behind its leadership. In so doing, American medicine assumed a collective, institutional form that the national association increasingly dominated.[14] In many respects, the AMA hewed closely to Hoover's associational ideal. Ironically, the more it did so the more it denied the need for an informal, complementary relationship with the government that would have emphasized the value in Hoover's larger vision of the communal, integrative state.

Contemporary developments would ultimately influence the direction of foreign narcotic policy. The most important trends involved questions of relations between the executive branch and Congress, and the professionalization, in this case, of the agencies responsible for policy making. Throughout the 1920s Congress vied with the executive branch for control over foreign policy. It is misleading to try to trace the course of that contest and describe its outcome. Neither branch of government can usefully be characterized as isolationist or internationalist; except for a few ideological purists the terms do not apply. A more profitable endeavor is to follow and analyze the ways in which executive power increased, even if not at the expense of congressional prerogatives. Often Congress and the executive branch shared power amicably. From this perspective, Senator Boies Penrose was wrong when he commented in 1921 that "Congress—especially the Senate—will blaze the way in connection with our foreign policies."[15]

Woodrow Wilson's short-term legacy of contention with the Senate has clouded subsequent views of congressional-executive relations over foreign policy. Harding's vacillation during his campaign concerning support for a league of nations did little to lessen confusion. His administration subsequently cultivated ties to the

League of Nations with care when that course suited American purposes.[16] Harding was hardly as uninformed about foreign relations as his critics have traditionally alleged.[17] Conscious of his limitations, he delegated authority, especially to Hoover and Secretary of State Charles Evans Hughes, without abdicating his responsibility as president to supervise the outcome of policy decisions. "He was the navigator who charted the course," as Kenneth J. Grieb put it.[18] The care with which Hughes, Hoover, and their subordinates tended to the daily operation of foreign policy necessarily resulted in increased executive ascendancy over policy.

Professionalization of the Foreign Service, composed of the consular service and the diplomatic corps, aided this ascendancy. Although prior to the Rogers Act of 1924, the diplomats had dominated the policy-making process, both services recognized the need for a more efficient Department of State and a more efficient policy-making process. These objectives became particularly important after the rejection of membership in the League of Nations.[19] For nearly three years the diplomats maintained their superior status. As one of them, Hugh Wilson, remarked of his associates to Wilbur J. Carr, consular chief, "They have all felt that they belonged to a pretty good club." An administrative measure in 1927 establishing a unified promotion list minimized the practical import of that sentiment. Thereafter the Foreign Service would exist as a professional organization, yet one designed to serve the larger bureaucratic needs of foreign policy.[20]

Reorganization constituted a recognition of the changed international role of the United States in the 1920s. While it is true that the nation sought to remain politically aloof from European affairs, such isolation never became absolute. In economic matters the United States was directly involved in the politics of European reconstruction.[21] Political involvement transpired on a selective basis. In narcotic foreign policy, for instance, the United States could not afford to ignore the activities of the League's Opium Advisory Committee (OAC), however bitter disagreements with the committee occasionally became. Throughout the decade, the professionalization and bureaucratization of foreign policy making, which the Rogers Act virtually mandated, helped sustain an intermittent, but vital link with Geneva. The link held until State Department and congressional officials finally deemed impractical their advisory relationship with the OAC, and revised the nature of American participation in League meetings.

Public policy in the area of drug control was not as advanced as it might have been upon the Harding administration's assumption of power. Comprehensive federal legislation was less than a decade old, and judicial sanction of enforcement practices had come only in 1919. Moreover, the Narcotic Division of the Prohibition Unit had been operating for scarcely one year. Yet a need existed in the minds of officials for public policy to tend more closely to narcotic matters. Secretary of the Treasury Andrew W. Mellon observed in 1921 that reports "made to the office of the chief of the customs division show conclusively that smuggling of narcotics in the United States is on the increase to such an extent that the customs officers are unable to suppress the traffic to any appreciable extent." Not only did beleaguered officers have to contend with narcotics smuggled from points of origination abroad, they also had to guard against the illicit reentry into the country of American manufactured narcotics legally exported. It is no wonder that several years earlier Internal Revenue Commissioner Roper had found the national drug situation to be out of control.[22] The government believed there to be slightly more than 100,000 addicts in the country, an estimate shared by Levi G. Nutt of the Narcotic Division.[23]

The problem was how to cope with both smuggling and addiction. As always, the most available tools were legal and administrative ones that scarcely differentiated between the two phenomena. The *Behrman* decision of 1922 denied as a defense in Harrison law cases an assertion of good faith on the part of the physician if a quantity of drugs prescribed seemed unusually large. Legally, the advocates of strict enforcement evidently had carried the day. The victory was won, however, only at the cost of the support for federal enforcement practices by segments of the drug trades and the medical community. In fact, the *Linder* decision of 1925 seemed to sanction their dissent from Narcotic Division procedures by modifying the strictness of earlier rulings.[24] In actuality enforcement policies remained essentially unaffected by the ruling and dictum of the Supreme Court, leaving the practical effect of the *Linder* ruling a moot question.

Changes in the administration of narcotic law suggest generally, if indirectly, the influence of Herbert Hoover upon the nature of public policy, and speak more specifically to the immediate problems faced by Nutt's Narcotic Division. In quest of more efficient supervision of the licit narcotics trade, Congress passed in 1922 the Narcotic Drugs Import and Export Act which expanded the scope of the 1909 Opium Exclusion Act by limiting importation of coca leaves as well as opium to quantities specified by the Federal Narcotics Control Board, an agency created by the 1922 law and composed of the secretaries of state, commerce, and treasury. The board was empowered to exercise strict supervision over imports and exports and to help the Customs Service guard against smuggling—a task the Treasury Department deemed virtually impossible. The AMA opposed the law, arguing that further import controls meant both inflated prices for narcotics and additional government supervision of the medical profession.[25]

Important in determining the perspective through which the government would attempt to deal with addiction and smuggling was the Public Health Service. Modernization of the PHS came in 1912 with the appointment of Dr. Rupert Blue as Surgeon General. Renowned for his work on bubonic plague in the San Francisco area, Blue took control of the service at a time when Congress authorized expansion of its practical and scientific functions. One special study concerning the health of garment workers demonstrated the need for a kind of government health insurance system for the nation's working population. In recognition of his own contributions and those of the PHS, Blue was elected president of the AMA in 1916 when the spirit of social progressivism was high.[26]

The sense of social responsibility in the PHS was reflected by its initial reaction to the Harrison law, deeming the law a measure primarily intended for the gathering of information. Such a function ostensibly did not preclude continued customary access to narcotics by addicts. As we have seen, that sentiment soon changed, entailing profound consequences for the nation's addict population. The change was both attitudinal, revealing the opprobrium attached to addiction, and practical, a function of the extent to which World War I defined the scope of PHS activity.[27] Accordingly, when Roper soured on his bureau's ability to enforce the Harrison law in quasi-police fashion and argued that a better way to handle addiction was for the PHS to conduct maintenance

operations, the Public Health Service demurred.[28] As Dr. Lawrence Kolb so bluntly suggested, curative treatment for addicts was
by definition impossible. Through its response to addiction in the
first decade of the operation of the Harrison Law, the PHS, although it had no statutory responsibility for care or supervision of
the nation's addicts, substantially contributed to the legally restrictive atmosphere within which American domestic drug policy was
formulated and implemented.

Drug control as punitive public policy in the 1920s demonstrated
more a long-term, continuing opposition to narcotics in society
than it mirrored Hoover's general aspiration to employ public
policy and private means to remedy national ills. Perhaps addiction
was an insoluble social problem best left to a legal, restrictive
response, but defining it as so almost from the inception of federal
control furthered the woes of addicts and initiated large-scale
smuggling. Management of drug laws expanded executive power,
creating a bureaucracy that quickly became more entrenched than
efficient. It also engendered strong opposition rather than support
from the AMA. Physicians did not so much disagree with the place
society assigned to addicts and their related activities, but rather
condemned the supervision of the medical profession allowed by
the legal and administrative enforcement of antidrug legislation.

In many respects, narcotic foreign policy more nearly approximated concurrent developments in the realm of foreign policy.
Relations with the League of Nations and inter-American narcotic
diplomacy offer two important examples. Despite an initial attempt
to do so, Harding and Hughes could not long afford to ignore the
League. The means utilized to maintain communication with the
League was that of sending an unofficial observer to all meetings in
which the United States had an interest. This action served to
evade the wrath and scrutiny of an anti-League Senate. The position of the observers, one historian has remarked, was "anomalous
. . . something between a guest and a spy. . . ," but no less vital for
that.[29]

With the creation of the League of Nations, supervision of the
1912 Hague Convention passed from the government of the Netherlands. At once the League Council appointed an Advisory Committee on Traffic in Opium and Other Dangerous Drugs (Opium
Advisory Committee, or OAC) and named three assessors to the
committee, including Elizabeth Washburn Wright of the United

States. Upon the death of her husband, Hamilton Wright, Mrs. Wright had taken on his life's work as her own.[30] The assessors, it should be noted, served merely as narcotic experts, not as official representatives of their governments. The OAC was to provide previously lacking administrative machinery to oversee implementation of the 1912 convention. At its first session in 1921 the committee requested the signatories to the convention to submit annual reports concerning narcotic cultivation, production, and manufacture. During the next session in April 1922, the OAC drew up draft forms for annual reports and import-export certificates. It was also asked that countries submit estimates of their narcotic consumption so an effort could be made to determine worldwide legitimate narcotic needs.[31]

Narcotic officials in the United States would not necessarily have been averse to working with the OAC. The bitter fight over the League precluded that possibility for the time being. Involvement with the OAC would have seemed to many as tacit recognition of the League. In June 1921 the Department of State therefore told the government of the Netherlands, with which it maintained communication on international narcotic matters, that it could not accept the transferral of execution of the 1912 convention to Geneva. In deciding to deal exclusively with the Dutch, the United States assumed a position unlike that of any other major power.[32] Isolation from Geneva jeopardized the leadership status the country aspired to in the antinarcotic campaign. Moreover, it made less likely the acceptance of American-influenced drug control programs by foreign nations. Most important, Washington's truculence threatened the future of all international antinarcotic activity.

Hoping to counter this situation, the Council of the League invited the United States in October 1922 to nominate a member to serve on the OAC. Edwin L. Neville, head of the State Department's Division of Far Eastern Affairs, favored participation in an unofficial capacity in order to eliminate the need for congressional consent. Harding and Hughes approved the idea.[33] At the suggestion of the Treasury Department, the assistant surgeon general, Dr. Rupert Blue, was chosen to go to Geneva. In the fall of 1919, political maneuvering had blocked Blue's reappointment as surgeon general, but he stayed with the PHS as an assistant to his successor, Dr. Hugh S. Cumming. The American government got off to a poor start with the League on international sanitary questions by effectively impeding for a time the efficient operation of the Health Section. Cumming and other officials in Washington briefly insisted on working with the Office Internationale d'Hygiene Publique in Paris, thereby perpetuating the costly existence of two international agencies with essentially identical functions.[34]

Blue first attended the OAC's fourth session held in January 1923. By sending an unofficial representative to Geneva the United States had three objectives other than acquiring a leading role in the antinarcotic movement. Primary, of course, was the goal of retarding the illicit drug trade. The United States also sought current information about the attempts of other nations to control narcotic exports. Finally, Washington hoped to initiate action against the accumulation of surplus narcotics.[35]

Blue's presence at Geneva especially pleased Mrs. Wright. She had not abandoned the lofty principles that motivated her husband. Aware of United States "zeal to force the adoption of higher moral standards" upon those countries with a history of laxity toward narcotics, she warned that "it must be remembered that a great burden of responsibility will rest upon the United States."[36] The guidelines Blue carried to Geneva, however, limited the extent of his government's cooperation. As had been its official policy for some time, the objectives of the United States continued to focus upon the restriction of narcotic production and manufacture to legitimate medical and scientific purposes.

Blue did not like what he found at Geneva. He felt that the OAC did not possess adequate machinery to enforce restrictions on the growth of opium poppies. In fact, major manufacturing countries such as Great Britain, France, Japan, and Germany opposed most restrictions.[37] Blue accordingly recommended that United States representatives to subsequent sessions of the OAC refuse to participate further unless that agency recognize and accept Washington's position. In a practical vein this meant strengthening the 1912 Hague Convention and considering a program of narcotic limitation at the source. For the next two years relations between the United States and the Opium Advisory Committee were conducted within this narrow, unproductive framework. With Blue's strict proviso as a guide, the Department of State prepared for the fifth session of the OAC to be held in May 1923.[38]

Congressman Stephen G. Porter, a Pennsylvania Republican,

chairman of the House Foreign Affairs Committee, and an outspo-
ken critic of the League's antinarcotic efforts, supported Blue's
recommendation regarding the upcoming meeting. "An effective
remedy" Porter wrote Hughes, "cannot be secured by compromise."[39] Hughes subsequently outlined five proposals the United
States would offer for discussion, including the stipulations that
nonmedical or nonscientific usage of opiates was illegitimate and
that elimination of narcotic surpluses was essential for proper control. "This government is convinced," the secretary wrote, "that no
effective cooperation can be expected unless the . . . two are
accepted."[40] The American preparations for the OAC session made
accommodation impossible. Refusal to seek compromise was
largely shared by officials in the state and treasury departments
and by important members of Congress. At the same time, nongovernmental organizations such as the Foreign Policy Association
supported the official attitude. By broadening the base of support
for their policies, narcotic authorities may have assured a lengthy
future for their particular philosophy of control at home, but in
doing so they retarded international efforts to advance antinarcotic
activity.

Porter headed the United States delegation to the fifth OAC
session. The delegation included Bishop Charles H. Brent, Dr.
Blue, and Neville. Mrs. Helen Howell Moorehead of the Foreign
Policy Association also attended the meetings. Hughes defined the
delegation's role as consultative, but authorized Porter to initiate a
discussion on limiting narcotic production.[41] The session opened
on May 24. Seven days later, proceeding as instructed, Porter told
the OAC that it could accept or reject his country's proposals as
constituted. He then left the session, refusing further debate.[42]
The Porter-Blue philosophy had reached its preordained conclusion: the United States was largely isolated from the international
movement. Porter remained combative, remarking: "If when I get
back to America anybody says 'League of Nations' to me, he ought
to say it conveniently near a hospital."[43]

Officials in Geneva, dismayed though they must have been,
recognized the importance of the United States to their efforts and
sought to renew ties with Washington. At a meeting in September,
the Fifth Committee of the Assembly decided to convene two
conferences in 1924–25. The first would be restricted to a consideration of prepared opium and the problems it caused in the Far

East, while the second would deal with the limitation of manufactured narcotics and their derivatives, and the restriction to legitimate needs of raw materials produced for export. In formulating a program of that nature, the League virtually assured United States participation in the latter conference, as we shall presently see.[44]

Latin American participation in the international movement followed an uncertain course as well in the early 1920s. Explanation of this uncertainty can be found in the nature of the directives issuing from Geneva and in the unsettled domestic conditions then prevalent. In the first place the Opium Advisory Committee had unintentionally erred in transmitting questionnaires regarding cultivation, production, and manufacture only in French and English, the two official languages of the League. Replies reached Geneva belatedly, if at all. The use of Spanish, a goodwill gesture to countries largely unconcerned about drug control, might have improved the situation. The lack of substantive data in responses further underlined the differences in attitudes. Annual reports for 1921 came only from Chile, Cuba, Guatemala, and Venezuela; Bolivia sent a partial report.[45] The import-export certificate system received even less attention. By the fifth session of the OAC only Mexico, not a member of the League, and Panama were experimenting with the system; several other countries were considering doing so. As late as August 1925 only Cuba, Guatemala, and Haiti joined Mexico and Panama in using the certificates. Peru once contemplated adoption, but decided against doing so.[46] In short, the administrative directives of the League had little impact in Latin America.

Even more important, domestic conditions worked against the adoption of controls. Mexico, for example, was burdened with border difficulties and an increase in drug use by its own populace. Border conditions in the 1920s had not changed appreciably since the end of the revolutionary decade.[47] Chihuahua, Sonora (one of the states most dramatically affected by the Revolution), and Baja California Norte continued to meet American demands for narcotics and other illicit pleasures. The situation in Baja stood as a dubious legacy of the governorship of Esteban Cantú, 1915–20.[48] While in office Cantú virtually set up an autonomous regime despite Carranza's efforts to the contrary. He cemented his hold on power, until forced out of office, by licensing gambling, prostitution, and other vices illegal across the border. Narcotics, too, were readily available. Not surprisingly, numerous Americans, including some business interests in the West, preferred Cantú's control of Baja and the enjoyments found in Tijuana to the more restrictive, anti-American leadership of Venustiano Carranza in Mexico City.[49]

As in Tijuana, so, too, in Ciudad Juárez. To some observers the notoriety achieved there was truly appalling. United States Consul John W. Dye remarked that "Juárez is the most immoral, degenerate, and utterly wicked place I have ever seen or heard of in my travels. Murder and robbery are everyday occurrences and gambling, dope selling and using, drinking to excess and sexual vices are continuous. It is a Mecca for criminals and degenerates from both sides of the border." Said an American evangelist: "I would rather shoot my son and throw his body in the river than have him spend an hour in the raging inferno of Juárez."[50] Conditions in Juárez, exacerbated by continuing economic dependency upon El Paso and by the imposition in Texas of prohibition in 1918, sparked the inflammatory comments.

The sentiments of Dye and the evangelist should not be viewed in isolation, but need to be seen in the context of the border's history since the Mexican War. In brief, a predisposition to illegal activity, including smuggling, emerged along the border soon after the war. Border areas are often regions of great opportunity. This potential took concrete form from the 1850s to the 1890s with the establishment on the Mexican side of a free zone for trade. Within the Zona Libre, whether through legal or illegal activity, standards of living were generally higher than in the interior, a result of considerable trade with the United States. Both this American orientation and discrimination in favor of the Zona ultimately aroused such strong domestic opposition that the Díaz government abolished the free zone. The resultant economic dislocation at Paso del Norte, the area encompassing Ciudad Juárez and El Paso, was particularly felt in the agricultural sector of the economy. To compensate for the socioeconomic travail of recession, Juárez turned to the tourist trade—a way of life even more dependent on the United States than existed with the Zona Libre.[51]

Tourism, of course, serves many masters; and tourism flourished during reform times in the United States, notably during the era of

prohibition. The rampant vice that Dye and others decried resulted largely from a demand being created on the United States
side of the border, the fulfillment of which had been forced to the
Mexican side by social and legal proscription. Illegal activity was
reciprocal. During the revolutionary decade, as Juárez was acquiring its dissolute reputation, Americans were carrying on an illicit
arms trade with various revolutionary factions in Mexico.[52] Although Mexican needs from the contraband trade subsided as
revolutionary violence abated, American demands—including access to narcotics—on the illegal border economy continued.

Compounding difficulties at the border for Mexico were domestic drug problems that President Alvaro Obregón and other federal
officials could not readily bring under control. In February 1923
the governor of Yucatán, Felipe Carillo Puerto, issued a decree
prohibiting trade in opiates, cocaine, and marijuana.[53] Shortly
thereafter, the Mexico City newspaper *Excélsior* called attention to
the domestic use of narcotics. Demanding corrective action against
alleged drug-induced violence by young Mexicans, the paper reported growing national concern about the spread of addiction.
Excélsior charged that perhaps 90 percent of the addicts acquired
their habit while in the nation's hospitals and sanitariums.[54] The
paper's campaign against narcotics elicited government response
when in July Obregón prohibited by decree the importation of
narcotics except for legitimate needs.[55] The high incidence of
smuggling and residual corruption of officials probably nullified the
decree at the moment of its promulgation.

The geographical and ideological configuration of forces during
the Mexican Revolution restricted Obregón's authority as president.[56] Moreover, internal conditions reduced the likelihood of
effective drug controls. That is to say, the Revolution put forth the
intoxicating promise of democracy and socioeconomic change, as
expressed in expanded political participation and agrarian reform.
While such goals necessarily raise the level of expectation and
aspirations of people in a revolutionary situation, fulfillment is a
dismayingly more gradual process. As a result, established patterns
of drug-related behavior persist even as changes occur.

Although Mexico's revolutionary tribulations have been frequently chronicled and analyzed, it seems worthwhile to recount
them briefly, as indirect, though substantial, support for the present interpretation. The Mexican Revolution did not appreciably

alter at once the life-style of many Mexicans. At length, an enlarged middle class took shape, but only as part of a larger political structure wherein persisted from times past patterns of marginality, internal colonialism, and a distinctly plural society. Access to effective political participation was therefore not easy, and many groups, especially rural ones, whether native or mestizo, remained for a long time in virtual isolation from national political activity.[57] Few previously marginal groups became organized well enough to demand effective participation or to insure that the nation responded to their political concerns.[58]

In the place of democracy, then, Mexico has experienced a modern continuation of essentially caudillo-dominated rule, even if a particular president's hold on power was brief or uncertain—as was the case until the time of Lázaro Cárdenas.[59] In effect, one ruling elite replaced another. However diminished actual democratic opportunity and practice have been, there has simultaneously existed a high degree of aspirational politics—at least until recently. Therefore it is reasonable to conclude that the Revolution redistributed and broadened the base of power, gradually enlarging the size and enhancing the power of the middle sector. To argue additionally that this process guaranteed a cohesive nationalism, as has been done,[60] seems to claim too much in view of our knowledge of those who do not share in the process.

A look at early attempts at agrarian reform further brings into question the extent of the benefits of the Revolution. As with democracy, it has been difficult to transform the promise of change into reality. It is possible, in fact, to question the putative national commitment to reform.[61] Specifically, the revolutionizing effect of the *ejido* on land reform is less than its proponents have claimed. Practical limitations of the ejido were evident even with the inclusion of Article 27 in the Querétaro Constitution of 1917.[62] The need for change was great, however. Around 1920 perhaps 70 percent of the labor force was engaged in agriculture, and an equally high percentage of the population lived in rural communities. (It is probable that 90 percent of the rural families owned no land on the eve of the Revolution.) In ten years the rural population of Sonora had increased by nearly 45 percent,[63] while Mexico's total population had declined—as had agricultural production. Significant change in the form of actual agrarian reform would not alter these conditions until after 1930.[64]

The extent of social and economic deprivation in Mexico, for which agrarian reform was intended to be a major panacea, can be depicted with some precision. There was much to be done after the Revolution; life meant little more for many Mexicans than a culture of poverty. Drawn even in the broadest strokes, gradual change is evident when differences between 1910 and 1930 are charted. Education at the primary level chipped away at the solid block of illiteracy. So, too, were slight improvements noticeable in income distribution and the general level of poverty.[65] Although statistics on unemployment, or more accurately underemployment, are meaningless in the modern sense, its pervasiveness can be appreciated when seen in the context of Mexico's traditional, persistent agricultural-village economy.[66]

If the foregoing suggests that the Mexican Revolution, however factional and regional it may have been, experienced an early Thermidorean or reactionary phase, that conclusion should not obscure the essential complexity of the revolutionary process and the richness of its ultimate achievements. The Revolution brought Mexico economic growth, industrialization, and prepared the way for modernity. There continued at the same time, nevertheless, a concentration of wealth, but with a broader social base than prior to 1910. Instead of having a leveling effect, however, subsequent economic growth and urbanization, while expanding the middle class, sustained discernible class distinctions. There emerged at length what Peter H. Smith has termed "a stable, authoritarian regime."[67] Limited political participation, social differentiation, and economic privilege for the few still characterize Mexican society long after the Revolution.

On the surface the preceding analysis does little to alter the traditional view of the rural Mexican, or *campesino*, a characterization that finds the campesino to be scarcely more than a helpless, oppressed peon.[68] At issue is not whether the Revolution succeeded in changing the status of the campesino, for it inevitably did to some degree, but rather how campesinos may have acted during the Porfiriato to gain a measure of control over their own lives—so that we may revise our understanding of their role within society.

The emerging picture suggests a life-style of mutual adjustment and accommodation, especially in terms of service and the level of wages, in contrast to one of unbridled exploitation. Not that land-

owner control suddenly became undesirable; rather, labor shortages, particularly in the center and north of Mexico, changed the
forms of control *latifundistas* endeavored to employ. Before the
Revolution the transition of the campesino out of peonage remained sadly incomplete. It was not unusual therefore to find him
out of work, dispossessed of the land he had worked for another's
advantage. In the course of modernization of the work of the
agricultural laborer to a form over which he exerted some control,
a clash of values resulted—the impact of which ironically threatened the survival of his cultural heritage. The demands of an
increasingly market-oriented economy no doubt disrupted natural
agricultural rhythms, often alienating the campesino from wage
labor even when it was available. [69]

The scarcity of work, alienation, the threat of cultural change,
and the promises of revolutionary caudillos combined to bring
peones actively to the Revolution. In the south this meant joining
with Zapata in a radical quest for land reform, consecrated, as it
were, in the Plan de Ayala. For the Zapatistas, the Revolution was
agrarian-based and political in nature, advancing a more coherent
ideological position than evident elsewhere. The northern supporters of the revolt against Victoriano Huerta, led by Carranza and
Pancho Villa, were far less unified. Villa's revolt, described by John
Womack, Jr., as "more a force of nature than of politics," com-
manded the allegiance of a diverse group of followers: dispossessed
campesinos, cowboys, railroad workers, bandits, Yaqui Indians,
and others. This congeries of social misfits and the downtrodden
gave little organized support to the nationwide uprising. An effort
to join with Zapata in opposition to Carranza and the Sonorans
failed markedly. [70]

What the Villistas brought about, however, was their own brand
of chaos in Chihuahua and parts of Sonora (for which they contended and lost)—a social anarchy whose impact was felt even after
the revolutionary decade ended. Yet the Villistas could not ordain
chaos in the north on their own. Social upheaval was generously
abetted by economic dislocation, the result jointly of internal civil
strife and international conflict. Nor were the actions of the Villistas
as directionless as has been generally assumed, despite their being
declared "outside the law." One of the principal examples of their
alleged anarchy, the raid on Columbus, New Mexico, on March 9,
1916, may actually have been a rational if erroneous response by

the Villistas to the relationship their leader believed existed between Carranza and the Wilson administration.[71] A minor aspect of that episode, but important for our purposes, and which superficially lends credence to the charges of anarchy, discloses that Villa's men probably smoked marijuana to steel themselves for the raid on Columbus.[72] Marginal men and marijuana, border troubles and drugs: whether in the context of revolution, social and economic dislocation, or simply vice, the association was clear and the message direct. Domestic and international controls had to be made more effective.

Numerous incidents occurred in the early 1920s providing authorities ample opportunity to reiterate these sentiments. At present, one example will serve to make the larger point. Citizens from Yuma, Arizona, acting in conjunction with the local Women's Christian Temperance Union, petitioned the State Department to set up a dry zone along the border with Mexico. The practical effect, the petitioners argued, would be to halt the flow of liquor and narcotics, thereby containing the "unbridled vice and debauchery" prevalent along the border.[73] Attempts at control of this and similar situations met with scant success. Drugs continued to play a discernible if veiled role in Mexican society. The Revolution had barely touched the foreign and domestic preconditions for their presence.

At the same time, the situation in Peru presented a comparatively clear picture, bound as it was to the observable culture of the Quechua and Aymara Indians. It is simpler therefore to understand the context in which drugs helped to shape the contours of Peruvian society. Primary, of course, was the presence of coca. Its use could not be eliminated, and scarcely reduced. Army officers, largely from the middle class, considered it an achievement if they succeeded in denying Indian conscripts their quid of coca. Urbanites, it seems, smoked tobacco.[74]

This type of incident reveals much of the place of the Indian in Peru during *el oncenio*, the dictatorship of Augusto B. Leguía lasting from 1919 to 1930. Leguía, who disingenuously held that "dictatorship is more popular than anarchy," imperiled the fortunes of democracy in Peru until his ouster. The fortunate coincidence of an expanding, supportive middle class and the impetus given that class during the First World War to participate more actively in national political life assisted Leguía's rise to power in 1919. The erstwhile businessman, who had failed in an earlier attempt as president (1908–12) to eliminate opposition to his personal rule, was far more successful the second time around. Armed with the support of the aristocracy, hacendados, and much of the middle sector, Leguía virtually ignored the national congress in setting Peru's political course.[75] The issuance of a supreme decree often settled otherwise contentious matters. A decree could be used as well to give the appearance of social change amid authoritarianism.

The public record is rife with statements by Leguía expressing concern over the Indian problem. Yet Leguía's actions belie his rhetoric. Indians may have comprised the majority of Peru's population, but they were inevitably exploited and, when economic or population pressures dictated, dispossessed from their lands. Leguía's first administration could not control injustices perpetrated against laboring Indians; some Andean mining centers effectively ignored the imposition of government authority.[76] The imposing realities of Andean geography offer one plausible explanation of the inhuman treatment of Indians and the government's inability to rectify the situation. A more satisfying explanation emerges when the situation is seen in connection with the economic and social context of Leguía's second administration. In brief, the president favored foreign involvement in the national economy to the point of domination. Penetration by foreign companies, many of which were United States-owned, was especially prevalent in mining, a sector of the economy with a historically notorious social policy. The inherent self-interest in the social base of support for Leguía also suggests minimal attention to oppressive conditions for Indians. More precisely, Leguía intended to modernize Peru and reward his supporters. That meant urbanization, a costly process entailing extensive federal expenditure. In light of the revenues expatriated by foreign-owned companies and the extent of urban growth, only a small percentage of Peru's expenditures and debt during el oncenio was related to the Indian question.[77]

Notwithstanding its entrepreneurial-urban orientation, el oncenio could not fully ignore the Indian problem. A study commission was set up in 1920, but its recommendations alarmed landowners and were not implemented. Much the same can be said of a similar effort three years later. Nor was there great substance to be found in the creations of two other supreme decrees. The first, in 1921, created a Bureau of Indian Affairs in the Ministry of Development; the other, in 1922, set up the Patronato de la Raza Indígena—ostensibly to protect Indians and improve their political, social, and economic lot. The former suffered from organizational problems, whereas the latter was never accorded sufficient implementing legislation.[78] The bottom line of Leguía's policy was to avoid alienating the hacendado.

The problem was not that *indigenismo* had no place in el oncenio, for the tribulations of *la conscripción vial* which began in 1920 evidence the role that Indians were to play in Leguía's modernization schemes for Peru. Service on the roads made the Indian the literal backbone of that process, but rewards were few. Human costs, measured by continued oppression and social and geographical dislocation, outweighed material advantages made available by the system of roads.[79] Rebellion by Indians against the condition in which they found themselves was sure to be repressed violently.[80] Indigenismo was acceptable therefore solely in the middle-class terms defined by Leguía. Indians would not have their problems dealt with separately, but would have them tended to only in the larger context of modernization. Consequently, Leguía's policy impeded national integration, though one may justifiably doubt whether integration was actually a goal of el oncenio. Even the recognition of surviving Indian communities after 1925 could not overcome the disparity in objectives among Leguía, his followers, and the *indigenistas*. Culturally and ethnically a wide gulf continued to separate Peru.[81]

Clearly, then, Indian policy would provide little if any assistance to antinarcotic efforts. Externally desired proscriptions on coca leaf production had no chance for realization. Coca would continue to serve, of course, the requirements of cocaine manufacturers in Peru and abroad. Evidence is sketchy, but it seems that in the 1920s Leguía attempted to control the trade in narcotics and thereby reduce domestic usage. In 1921, for instance, he gave the Bureau of Public Health absolute power to regulate narcotic imports and exports. A subsequent supreme decree in March 1923 limited imports to the customs house at Callao. In fact, Peru had made all dealings in opium a government monopoly as early as 1887. Over the years this revenue-producing measure was strengthened. Despite Peru's failure to ratify the 1912 convention, Frederick A. Sterling, an American representative in Lima, reported to the Department of State in July 1922 that the "provisions of the Hague Convention are . . . in force here and the Peruvian Government complies with all that the Convention enforces regarding opium and its derivatives."[82]

Peru could not control all drug-related problems. The *Christian Science Monitor* of August 12, 1922 revealed that Japanese interests had gained control of the coca leaf market and were probably exporting manufactured cocaine from a small port in the north. Officials in Washington discounted the report, but asked Sterling for verification. Sterling's investigation proved inconclusive. He related that coca leaves grew well in the Department of Huánuco, the area suspected of being the center of the illegal Japanese activity. He also learned that some customs officials there, often poorly paid, were receptive to bribery.[83]

From what is known of the Japanese experience in Peru at the time, it is conceivable that they were involved in narcotic activity but unlikely that they controlled the coca leaf market. By 1923 fewer than 18,000 Japanese were living in Peru. Immigration had begun in earnest at the turn of the century with the demand of sugar and cotton hacendados for a stable work force. Chief among the proponents of contract-labor migration was Augusto B. Leguía. If Japanese stayed beyond the terms of their contracts, they occasionally invested in small businesses. Japanese were not popular in Peru. Fears of Japanese domination of the nation's economy arose entirely out of proportion to their numbers and influence. During his presidential terms Leguía helped to feed the fears of colonization schemes and economic dominance. Ironically, upon his ouster from office in 1930, anti-Japanese sentiment reached a new high. Perhaps Leguía's earlier encouragement of immigration had not been forgotten.[84]

Nothing verifiable can be concluded about the Japanese and narcotics in the 1920s in Peru. Nonetheless Frederick Sterling defended Peru's antinarcotic activity, thereby demonstrating another issue over which United States representatives supported Leguía's presidency. "The Government is making an honest effort," said Sterling, "to restrict the narcotics traffic." Claiming that import controls were effective, he pointed out that a United States citizen was serving as Director of Customs—one of several major positions Americans held in Leguía's Peru.[85]

The attention given to drugs in Mexico and Peru early in the

1920s did not lead either nation to a closer relationship with the
Opium Advisory Committee. Mexico was unwilling to expose to
international scrutiny anything that might detract from the accomplishments of the Revolution. And Peru, as had been the case for a
decade, remained unlikely to place controls on the coca leaf.
Nevertheless the antidrug activity in both countries paralleled the
recommendations put forth at the three Hague conferences. Although legislative promulgation should not be mistaken for effective enforcement, Peru and Mexico were not the only countries to
have difficulty transforming intent into reality.

From Bolivia, the other major Latin American nation from which
some form of narcotic control was desired internationally, there
was no indication of any effort. Extensive domestic demand consumed almost the entire crop each year, which probably explained
the lack of regulation. Peru, not Bolivia, was believed to supply
the world's illicit cocaine manufacturers with raw material. In 1911,
for example, Bolivia exported less than 5 percent of a 5,500 ton
crop. A report some years later indicated that outsiders failed to
appreciate the significance of coca to Bolivian culture. "As is well
known," United States representative Jesse Cottrell stated, "alcohol is the bane of the Andean Indians."[86] The United States, at
least, never repeated Cottrell's error, and in future years expended
much effort imploring Bolivia to limit coca leaf production.

Officials in Washington made an unsuccessful attempt to commit
Latin America to more extensive involvement in international antidrug activity. At the fifth Pan American Conference held in Santiago, Chile, in April 1923, the United States urged the ratification
and implementation of the 1912 Hague Convention by those states
which had not yet done so. This thinly guised anti-League of
Nations measure had no impact. Peru, Mexico, and Bolivia were
not even present at the meeting. Bolivia was seeking revision of a
1904 treaty with Chile; Peru was again at odds with Chile over the
Tacna-Arica boundary dispute; and Mexico stayed away in protest
of United States nonrecognition of the Obregón government.
Other Latin American nations were not yet important to the international movement.

Latin American reluctance to follow lead of the United States
stemmed in part from uncertainty concerning the hemispheric
policy of the Harding administration. The administration had set
for itself the difficult task of decreasing political and military inter-

vention in Latin America while at the same time enhancing American economic presence. Such a transformation in United States policy would not be accepted unquestioningly, especially given the nature of American involvement in Latin America since 1898.[87]

Latin American states thus showed little interest in antidrug activity, whether under the aegis of the United States or the League. Annual reports to the OAC, for instance, continued to arrive late, if at all. In 1925 only Cuba prepared a report. (See Table 1.) Ties between Latin America and the international campaign also depended upon the importance attached to the domestic drug situation by government officials. Prior to the antiopium

TABLE 1. Annual Reports Sent to the Opium Advisory Committee from the United States and Latin America, 1921—1931

	1921	1922	1923	1924	1925	1926	1927	1928	1929	1930	1931
Argentina						x					
Bolivia	x[a]	x					x	x	x	x	x
Brazil		x[b]						x			x
Chile	x	x[b]	x				x	x	x		x
Colombia											x
Costa Rica							x	x			x
Cuba	x	x	x		x	x		x	x		x
Dom. Repub.				x[c]							
Ecuador			x[b]				x				x
El Salvador			x[d]								x
Guatemala	x[b]	x[b]									x
Haiti				x[e]					x		x
Honduras											
Mexico						x	x	x		x	x
Nicaragua						x				x	x
Panama			x[f]			x	x	x	x		x
Paraguay											
Peru							x				
Uruguay								x	x	x	x
United States	x	x	x	x	x	x	x	x	x	x	x
Venezuela	x										x

[a]Report given for cocaine only.

[b]Report given for imports only.

[c]Letter sent stating that the Dominican Republic did not manufacture narcotics.

[d]Report contained general information, but not for any specific year.

[e]Letter sent, no year given.

[f]Letter claimed that the 1921 report had been remitted.

Source: Compilation of League of Nations documents, 1921–1931.

conferences in Geneva in 1924–25, historical patterns relating to the societal role of drugs limited Latin American participation in the work of the OAC. That is, where drugs played a minimal role there was no impetus for cooperation, and where drugs were present skepticism of international controls often had a deterrent effect.

The Department of State instructed Edwin Neville to take part in the preparatory work for the Second Geneva Opium Conference. Neville offered his country's usual program, stressing the need to restrict cultivation and production of raw material to scientific and medical needs. He hoped to have the first five articles of the Hague Convention dealing with raw opium controls extended to cover coca leaves. Accordingly, in a measure directly affecting Peru and Bolivia, he proposed that individual governments should endeavor to curtail reliance upon revenue derived from drug production and trade, except for the explicit purpose of regulating commerce in drugs. Neville's proposals were more subtle and comprehensive, while less strident in tone, than prior American entreaties to the League. If adopted, the plan would logically lead to the limitation of narcotics at the source. In opposition, other participants at the preparatory sessions argued that legitimate per capita needs could not be established and also charged that production or export quotas would induce higher prices and smuggling. Prominent, too, was the feeling by some states that the proposed controls would bring about a monopoly for those countries most actively engaged in production and manufacture.[88]

The preparatory committee ultimately devised a draft program for the conference. It called for the creation of a central board to receive annual government estimates of raw opium and derivatives required for legitimate medical and scientific purposes. The board would also handle statistics covering imports, exports, consumption, and the supply of most narcotics. Additionally, the board could determine allocations for nations failing to do so or for those submitting excessive estimates. As Neville had suggested, coca leaves would be placed within the scope of Article 2 of the 1912 convention. Although the draft program contained neither the United States proposal for direct limits on raw material production, nor a British scheme for limiting manufacture, it satisfied the United States for the time being.[89]

From an inter-American perspective, success or failure of the Geneva conference depended upon which nations were in attendance and the degree to which conference decisions were implemented. It seemed unlikely that Peru would send a delegation because of the profits reaped from legitimate coca production for cocaine. During the First World War, Peruvian cocaine had been used extensively as a local anesthetic. Demand decreased after 1920, but residual needs proved fairly lucrative. The Department of State hoped for Peruvian participation at Geneva. Reiterating his government's belief in the necessity of production controls, Secretary of State Hughes declared: "Unrestricted production means uncontrollable consumption, especially when the product enters into international channels."[90] Nevertheless, exhortations by American representatives in Lima failed to bring Peru to the conference table.

Related concern over its own coca industry seemed likely to prevent Bolivian attendance. In a dispatch to Washington in 1924, Jesse Cottrell cited anticipated coca leaf production figures for the year as nearly 6,500 tons, which he felt might be low by one-third. "I have every reason to believe," he stated, "that the Foreign Office has warned the various Departments of the Government to be very circumspect in replying to any inquiries by this legation regarding coca production." The reluctance to disclose precise figures doubtless stemmed from an effort by the legation to initiate intergovernmental discussions about production restrictions. Nonetheless, Bolivia decided to attend the Geneva conference although the Foreign Office refused to promise to consider restricting coca leaf production. Nor did it promise not to increase the acreage under cultivation.[91] Accordingly, Bolivia's presence at the conference did not augur well for the adoption of improved coca controls.

Like Peru, Mexico did not go to Geneva. On its own the government initiated several measures which virtually equalled in comprehensiveness those under consideration at the conference. For instance, prohibition of marijuana cultivation was announced in June 1923. Next, Mexico made plans to assume greater responsibility for opium and heroin traffic within its borders. This action, occurring in January 1925, signaled *de facto* adoption of the 1912

Hague Convention. Then on February 7, the *New York Times* reported that President Plutarco Elías Calles had ordered judicial authorities to take stronger action against drug sellers and users. In so doing he hoped to respond to conditions that led earlier to the dry zone proposal.[92] Mexico's actions, whether effective or not, gave it a drug control system exceeded in the Western Hemisphere only by that of the United States.

Washington's participation at the Second Geneva Opium Conference symbolized the anomalous position of the League of Nations in American politics, and raised as well the issue of control over narcotic foreign policy. During deliberation over a $40,000 expense appropriation for the delegation, the Senate attached a crucial proviso strictly prohibiting the delegation from signing any convention which took a position weaker than Washington's on the legitimate use of opium and other narcotics and on the necessity of limiting raw material production. The proviso severely curtailed the ability of the American delegation to negotiate a compromise convention or even play a constructive role in the deliberations. If the delegation, led by Stephen G. Porter, looked unfavorably upon the precise stipulations of the proviso, it must also be said that it shared the general, restrictive sentiments. On this particular measure Congress and the executive branch were in accord over the nature of policy.

As such, on the second day of the conference, November 19, 1924, Porter presented Washington's narcotic control proposal: the plan required limiting narcotic production to medical and scientific needs, accepted suppression of the trade in prepared opium over a ten-year period, and supported the creation of a permanent central board to handle statistical information. The plan encountered immediate opposition and efforts to negotiate an acceptable compromise failed because of the restrictions on the American delegation. Early in February 1925, a critical Porter sought and received permission to withdraw his delegation from the conference. After its departure, Edouard Daladier of France questioned Porter's action and criticized in turn the all-or-nothing attitude of the United States.[93]

Latin American countries, too, did not have an altogether constructive influence upon the conference. For instance, Peru, although absent, could not be ignored in discussions about control of the coca leaf. In his opening address, the elected president, Herluf

Zahle of Denmark, appealed for limits on coca production there and elsewhere. The delegate from Bolivia, Arturo Pinto-Escalier, later replied, stating that his government found el coqueo to be "a perfectly innocuous activity." He claimed that the use of coca by Andean Indians presented no social danger. He noted further that Bolivia had never contributed significantly to the illicit drug traffic.

Pinto-Escalier spoke of his country's reluctance to institute controls since coca was an integral part of the national culture. Some months earlier, sounding a similar note, he had told the Opium Advisory Committee that it "would be impossible for the Bolivian Government to contemplate restricting the production of coca leaves without seriously interfering with the needs and economic life of the working population, particularly in mining districts, as coca leaves constitute for them a source of energy which cannot be replaced." The Bolivian representative therefore expressed strong opposition to a United States proposal envisioning limits on coca production.[94]

The conference concluded its work in mid-February after having adopted a convention superior in many respects to the 1912 convention. The Geneva Opium Convention of 1925 marked important conceptual and administrative progress in the world antinarcotic movement. Controls had been added to coca leaves, crude cocaine, and Indian hemp, substances which the earlier agreement failed to cover. Also, the establishment of a Permanent Central Opium Board and an updated import-export certificate system were unqualified achievements. As a result of these accomplishments, the conference improved the likelihood of future, more comprehensive international drug control.[95]

The conference could not, however, be termed a complete success. Bolivia's reservations brought into question the efficacy of controls on coca leaves. Moreover, because of Peru's absence, the persistent charges that the government there would not act to suppress illicit cocaine commerce went unanswered. A statement by Persia's minister for foreign affairs just prior to the conference underscores the difficulty there would be in getting narcotic controls adoped in South America. Moshar-ol-Molk observed:

> The Imperial Persian Government, despite its sincere desire to restrict the production and commerce of opium finds it, unfortunately, impracticable suddenly to place a prohibition on it without . . . the substitution of other products for the

production of opium, and the adoption of an appropriate decision whereby the domestic consumption of opium could be gradually stopped.[96]

The difficulty faced by the international antinarcotic reformers and bureaucrats, especially in the United States, was a global phenomenon. By 1925 it was far from certain that their solutions to the narcotic problem would ever be effective.

Just as troublesome for the international movement in the foreseeable future was the action of the United States at Geneva. The Porter-led walkout from the conference virtually severed the brittle link the OAC desired to preserve with Washington. The United States not only forfeited its remaining claims to leadership in the antinarcotic campaign, but also seriously jeopardized the movement's future. The moral zeal that Brent and Hamilton Wright had demonstrated at Shanghai and The Hague, and that Mrs. Wright was carrying on as an assessor at Geneva, fell victim to political antagonism. In place of humanitarian reform stood a temporarily unified narcotic policy hierarchy extending from the executive branch to Congress. Washington's chauvinistic isolation was counterproductive to a coordinated global fight against narcotics and may have helped delay for some time the adoption of stricter controls in Latin America. The road back to internationalism in antinarcotic activities would not be a smooth one.

3   Rebuilding the Politics
of Drug Control

For three years, until April 1928, the United States refrained from actively working with the Opium Advisory Committee. Had any State Department officials been inclined to reconsider this isolation from the League's antinarcotic activity, it is likely that Congressman Porter would have been able to prevent such a move. From his powerful position on the Foreign Affairs Committee, he controlled the authorization of appropriations necessary to send representatives to Geneva. In short, Porter virtually held a veto power over American narcotic foreign policy.[1]

During this time, Pinkney Tuck, a consul in Geneva, served as an unofficial observer at OAC meetings. Tuck lacked technical knowledge about narcotics and urged his superiors to name a more qualified observer. A change finally came at the eleventh session of the OAC when the League protested an announcement that Tuck would again observe the meeting. John Kenneth Caldwell, who had replaced Neville as chief of narcotic matters in the Division of Far Eastern Affairs, went to Geneva to assist Tuck; thus the United States resumed a policy of minimal cooperation with the League. Nonetheless, the consul's presence at OAC meetings had illustrated the extent of the rift between Washington and Geneva.[2]

After the 1925 Geneva Convention went into effect in September 1928, relations began gradually to improve. The Treasury Department, hoping for assistance to retard the flow of illicit drugs, advocated a closer relationship with the League. As a result the United States began submitting requested statistical information to the Permanent Central Opium Board (PCOB).[3] Two individuals, Mrs. Helen Howell Moorehead of the Foreign Policy Association and Joseph Chamberlain, an opium expert teaching at Columbia University, by modifying their prior support for Washington's anti-League policy, showed a desire to attain a prominent role for the United States in the work of the board. To Moorehead and Chamberlain, suppression of illicit traffic could only come with a change in United States policy.[4] Active participation in the work of the PCOB provided an opportunity for a new beginning.

Few policymakers in Washington initially shared these sentiments. The Council of the League asked the United States to take part in naming members to the board, but only Undersecretary of State J. Reuben Clark favored accepting the request. Clark wanted to use the occasion to have an American named to the board and to recoup lost prestige abroad.[5] Porter naturally objected to participation and joined Caldwell and Nelson T. Johnson of the State Department in recommending that the offer be declined. The congressman argued that to do otherwise than refuse would compromise the position the United States had clung to in its relations with the OAC. Porter asserted that the United States had not lost its leadership status in the international movement. Instead, he argued, compromise by Washington might weaken the resolve of other nations to fight illicit drugs.[6] Porter's protestations effectively blocked Clark's attempt at accommodation.

Despite Clark's failure, the United States did not revert to its prior position of isolation. Mrs. Moorehead arranged to have an American nominated to serve on the PCOB; New Zealand nominated Herbert L. May. At its session in December 1928, the Council of the League chose May and seven others as board members.[7] May's selection placed him in a delicate position. While desirous of assisting in the board's successful operation, he had to refrain from giving the impression that his presence in Geneva signaled a reassessment of his country's attitude toward the League. Though not an official representative of the United States, May provided a vital link between Geneva and Washington.

May's dexterity in his position was tested in a conversation with Assistant Secretary of State Johnson. "I told Mr. May," Johnson recalled, "that I was not at all sanguine as to the future of the Board. . . . I did not feel as constituted that it was empowered to do very much." He also cautioned May that statistical compliance with the PCOB did not foreshadow an improvement in relations with the League. For his part, May responded by admitting that the board would be working under a handicap,[8] particularly in relation to the reluctance of Iran and China—producers of raw opium—to sign the 1925 convention. North and central China, in the midst of a renewed period of warlordism, were experiencing serious famine largely as a result of increase opium poppy cultivation.[9] May might have mentioned as well that the policy of the United States handicapped the PCOB.

If the United States, subject to the caprice of Porter and certain individuals in the State Department, merely cooperated perfunctorily with the League in some areas, it engaged in outright anti-League activity in others. An important instance of this transpired just before the 1925 convention went into effect. Somewhat surprisingly, Mrs. Wright was a key participant. By taking part in the venture she may not have been trying to discredit the work of the League as Porter evidently was attempting to do. Rather, Mrs. Wright probably felt that the United States could bring sufficient pressure to bear upon the League so that Geneva and Washington would find it advantageous to resolve their differences. Attainment of this goal would restore United States prestige and enhance the international antinarcotic campaign.[10]

As early as July 1926, Mrs. Wright urged her government to take action to prevent the ratification of the Geneva Convention by other nations.[11] The Department of State did not act upon the idea until the Sixth Inter-American Conference, held at Havana in February 1928. There Washington's delegation hoped to persuade the Latin American republics to ratify the older 1912 Hague Convention if they had not yet done so. "I believe it is not yet too late," Mrs. Wright wrote Johnson, "to prevent this final step [adoption of the 1925 convention] were it made known in Havana that the Government of the United States has never withdrawn its opposition to the Geneva Convention and will never accept it in its present state."[12] Caution by the United States in Havana was in order. The meeting promised to be a volatile affair, a result of the continuing presence of United States military forces in the Caribbean. For many Latin Americans, the Coolidge administration had not sufficiently extended the policy of disengagement initiated under President Harding. Any indication of additional intervention from the north, even in the relatively noncontroversial matter of narcotics, would probably end the conference prematurely.

Even the discreet action which the United States delegation ultimately took in Havana failed to achieve the desired result of subverting the influence of the League.[13] The reason for this would seem to lie in the growing association after 1925 in Latin America of drug usage with social problems. In one respect nothing changed in Bolivia, for example. The consumption of coca leaves continued as usual. Firms with mining operations in the Andes provided morning and afternoon work recesses so Aymara Indians could replenish their supply of coca. Refusal to do so would have resulted in desertions by the workers.[14] No foreign pressure, it seemed, could dislodge the coca leaf from its customary status. Excepting the regulation of coca, the Bolivian Ministry of Foreign Affairs acknowledged that a narcotic control system similar to that of the United States would be a worthwhile addition to national law.[15] Whether this meant that Bolivia was acting to restrict illicit commerce remains unclear. In 1927, drug control officials in Washington received reports of cocaine manufacturing in Bolivia (and Peru). However genuine its commitment may have been, the Bolivian government nevertheless enacted a series of four laws from 1928 to 1931 which was intended to regulate the traffic in opium, morphine, marijuana, crude cocaine, and coca leaf exports. The ministries of public instruction and finance, and industry were charged with administering the laws.[16]

The recognition of drug usage as a social problem was more apparent in Leguía's Peru than in Bolivia. Patterns of usage changed in the 1920s until substances other than coca were found among all classes of society. Responding to this situation, a national health commission formulated plans in July 1927 to provide state treatment for addiction. Two Peruvian physicians, appearing that October before the Eighth Pan-American Sanitary Conference in Lima, admitted that the national tradition of el coqueo among Indians had blinded the government to the dangers of other drugs. Coca may have been "a gift from the gods" and "a universal panacea" for Indians but, the doctors told the conference, in Peru "narcotic addiction in its most common forms was ignored."[17] Sebastián Lorente and Baltazar Caravedo offered several suggestions as a corrective measure. Principally, they called for closer supervision of drug manufacturing nations and advocated mandatory state treatment for the rehabilitation of addicts. In addition, they proposed both increased education about addiction to combat its spread and reduced cultivation, manufacture, and sale of drugs. During the late 1920s and into the 1930s, the government of Peru failed to implement any of the doctors' proposals—probably a result of the worldwide depression and Leguía's overthrow in August 1930.[18]

Other problems with drugs increased in the face of official paralysis. The Department of State received reports of several fraudulent schemes to export illicit cocaine from Peru.[19] Also, the relatively unfettered use of opium by the Chinese population became a matter of concern. The newspaper *El Comercio*, claiming that imports of opium did nothing more than sustain the life of numerous opium dens, declared that the sale of opium through a state monopoly tacitly sanctioned the continued use of the narcotic. The paper called upon the government to ban further opium imports. Suspension of the trade in opium would have entailed a loss in national revenue at a time of serious financial difficulty; the opium monopoly consequently remained in operation for some time.[20]

Elsewhere in Latin America few countries initiated antidrug activity within their borders. In Colombia, for instance, minimal government regulation did not impede easy access to morphine and cocaine. Also, some Indians in the Chilean Andes chewed coca leaves while working in the mines there. One observer of this activity claimed that mining accidents did not befall Indians who had come under the influence of Christian missionaries, but happened only to those who purchased daily rations of coca leaves from the company store.[21] Whatever the real or imagined benefits Christianity provided the Andean Indians, these two examples suggest a more acute awareness than before of the extent and variety of drug use in parts of Latin America.

The situation at the same time in Uruguay, a country not widely recognized then as having drug problems, offers the quintessential example of this awareness. In 1928 the National Health Council complained about the spread of opiate and cocaine usage, but noted as well the government's apparent inability to handle the situation. Repeated requests for alterations in narcotic laws went unheeded.[22] Yet Uruguay had not entirely exhibited a laissez-faire approach to drug control. In 1923 the government issued a number of decrees establishing a partial state monopoly over the commerce in drugs. By placing restrictions on imports of opium and cocaine, the government intended to limit usage to legitimate medical purposes.[23] Concern, however, about drugs as a serious social problem only arose five years later. The case of Uruguay raises an important question with broad implications. If within a short period of time the nation changed from giving casual attention to drugs (the 1923 laws) to acute concern over their prevalence and misuse (the warnings of the National Health Council), how serious must the situation have been when drugs first received legislative response? As one official later put it, drug usage in 1923 had "acquired the proportions of an actual plague."[24] If this were true in Uruguay, what were actual conditions elsewhere in Latin America?

Insufficient information leaves that question largely unanswered. Such is not quite the case with Mexico, however. The government there had equated increased drug usage with social problems since the early years of the decade, as the executive decrees of 1923 and 1925 attest. Their promulgation had no discernible effect on a worsening situation. Marijuana continued to grow wild throughout the country and opium poppy cultivation flourished especially in northern states. The poppies were frequently processed into morphine and heroin. This indigenous crop, along with opiates smuggled into Mexico from abroad, served both domestic addicts and innumerable others in the United States. In a further attempt to control the situation, President Calles signed a decree late in 1927 banning the export of heroin and marijuana.[25] Two years later a revised penal code enumerated strict penalties for those persons found guilty of illegally growing or manufacturing drugs.[26]

Success in the Mexican effort depended, of course, upon effective enforcement of the decrees. As before, congruence between intent and actual procedure seemed coincidental. For instance, Henry Damm, the United States consul at Nogales, reported the growing of large quantities of opium poppies in the region, yet Damm had no indication that local authorities were trying to halt cultivation. Similar reports reached the State Department from other consular districts in northern Mexico.[27]

Revelations similar to Damm's came also from Mexicali where Consul Frank Bohr learned of the existence of a lucrative, widespread commerce in opium. Bohr managed to arrange a visit to an opium den run by Chinese nationals. There the consul found Mexicans and Chinese as well as black and white citizens of the United States. Inside the den many varieties of narcotics were available for sale and consumption on the premises; a special room was set aside for the smoking of opium. Upon Bohr's arrival the Chinese operators expressed suspicion about his presence, but Bohr's contact secured entry by buying a small amount of cocaine. The consul's report does not reveal whether he partook of the drug.[28] This incident underlines the difficulty inherent in drug law enforcement for Mexican officials.

In addition to internal narcotic problems, Mexican authorities had to cope with the ubiquitous matter of smuggling. At Juárez and Nuevo Laredo, officials rarely confiscated more than a small percentage of the quantity of drugs admittedly crossing the border. Conditions in the Matamoros-Brownsville area resulted in a consular request for a special agent to investigate the illicit traffic there.[29] The poor record of interception stemmed not only from Mexico's lack of agents and funds to patrol the border properly, but also from the absence of any cooperative antismuggling effort with the United States.[30]

Despite the difficulties they faced, upper echelon leaders in Mexico seemingly possessed antidrug sentiments similar to those held in the United States. Neither side working alone, however, could achieve the results each desired. Yet the idea of a common effort had been considered earlier and abandoned, but for reasons not strictly pertaining to drug control. The plan for cooperation evolved from the previously mentioned request in 1924 by a group of citizens in Yuma, Arizona for a dry zone along the border.[31] Recognizing the unilateral nature of the dry zone proposal, State Department officials instead issued an invitation to Mexico to join in a conference to create channels for improving information exchange on illegal drug activity. All border consuls were instructed to attend the meeting in El Paso scheduled for May 1925.[32] Against a backdrop that portended further smuggling at Ciudad Juárez and depicted Ensenada in Baja California as "an entrepôt of some [considerable] quantity of narcotics,"[33] the two sides quickly reached an agreement. Both pledged regular exchange of information on known smugglers and their activities. The pact took effect in March 1926.[34]

The treaty was not an open-ended one, so as the conclusion of the initial year of its operation approached, the United States notified Mexico of its intention to terminate the agreement. The decision resulted from an assessment by State Department officials of political and economic conditions within Mexico. Secretary of State Frank Kellogg explained the decision in a conversation with the British Ambassador Sir Esmé Howard. Painting a picture of chaos and imminent disintegration of Mexican society, the secretary described a situation in which business activity was slowing down and revenues decreasing. Kellogg feared that opposition to Calles by "radical Communists" would prevent any corrective action. "Mexico," he told Howard, "[is] evidently on the brink of financial collapse."[35]

In a postscript to the termination of the treaty, Consul Jon Dye in Juárez reacted to its lapse indifferently. He felt that the Mexican government had not seriously endeavored to enforce the accord.[36] True, the task of transforming commitment into effective action often failed, producing understandable exasperation on the part of officials who were reminded daily of the large quantity of drugs moving northward. In April 1931, when a special Mexican agent arrived in the Juárez–El Paso area to assist the consul there, William Blocker remarked that "the arrival of the narcotic agent . . . would indicate that the Mexican Government has at last decided to clean up the drug traffic on this section of the border."[37]

The vicissitudes associated with drug control activity throughout Latin America in the latter half of the 1920s prevented the United States from discrediting the work of the League of Nations at the 1928 Havana Conference. The emerging definition of drug usage as a social problem was demonstrated more, by those few governments which acted, through acceptance of the 1925 Geneva Convention than by sole adherence to the 1912 Hague agreement, as the United States desired. By the start of the meeting in Havana, Latin American nations including Brazil, Chile, Nicaragua, Uruguay, and Bolivia with reservations, had signed the Final Act of the 1925 convention; others were reportedly about to sign. These ratifications, plus those from outside the Western Hemisphere, guaranteed adoption of the convention. The action of the United States at Havana only added to its isolation from international antinarcotic activity. That is, the refusal of the United States to disavow fully the right of intervention doubtlessly limited the willingness of Latin Americans to follow the lead of the United States in other matters, including narcotics.[38]

Despite her support for the position of the State Department, Mrs. Wright knew that American policy was inherently counterproductive to effective drug control. In January 1928 during one of her frequent discussions with Nelson Johnson, she suggested that some way should be found to have the 1925 convention made more acceptable. She offered few specific proposals except the vain hope that other nations might be willing to accept an amendment to the convention so it would not be adopted in its present form. Johnson told Mrs. Wright that Porter and the Division of Far Eastern Affairs were studying the situation to determine what could be done.[39] Caldwell and other officials realized that she was right in calling for a reassessment of policy. Johnson, though, remained skeptical; he saw no feasible way to revise Washington's policy toward the League. But Mrs. Wright interposed her ideas once again. In March she urged the secretary of state to formulate a policy reasserting United States leadership in the antinarcotic movement. This meant convening a new conference.[40]

Caldwell reversed his prior isolationist stance and supported the idea. He wanted the United States to ask for a conference, possibly for 1929, and then approach it with greater flexibility than had been the case in 1924–25. Johnson was not persuaded of the idea's merit. "So far as I know," he told Caldwell, "we have no program other than that which our delegation offered at Geneva in 1925, which was rejected and would be rejected again by the powers."[41] That assessment seemed accurate, since, by its insistence on a program of limitation at the source, the United States strongly discouraged consideration of any other drug control scheme, including manufacturing restrictions. American rigidity thus obscured the cultural, financial, and political difficulties some countries had in accepting Washington's program wholesale.[42]

Renewed cooperation with the League was essential for effective drug control. If nothing else, the OAC provided an available forum in which pressure, however limited, could be brought to bear on producing and manufacturing nations. Such pressure might not have had sufficient influence if exerted through bilateral diplomatic channels. To United States officials this must have seemed especially true concerning Latin America by 1928. At the time of the conference in Havana, there did not exist a coordinated antidrug effort in the hemisphere. Whatever gains were to be made would have to originate outside the Americas. The League offered the only possibility. Accordingly, our attention must shift there for an understanding of inter-American drug control around 1930.

The League of Nations helped to resolve the dilemma for Johnson and his colleagues. In September 1929 the Tenth Assembly adopted a resolution calling for a plenary conference. The proposed meeting would be concerned primarily with reducing the manufacture of drugs to levels required solely for medical and scientific purposes. Earlier that year several OAC members had expressed concern over the reported global spread of illicit traffic. Impetus for the conference appeared after the French, previously opponents of manufacturing controls, announced a limitation program of their own. An international gathering became the next logical step. [43]

The calling of a conference occurred at a propitious time for the United States. Caldwell termed the invitation "an advantageous opportunity." Referring to the doubts Johnson held about a change in policy, he remarked: "I am not sure that progress will not be greater if manufacture and production are dealt with in separate conferences."[44] The Department of State agreed and responded favorably to the initiative of the League. Secretary of State Henry L. Stimson had Caldwell and Johnson convey the decision to Porter. As expected, the congressman voiced reservations about a role for the United States in another conference.[45] For the first time, however, Porter's objections could not withstand contrary opinion favoring cooperation with the League. Both Herbert May and Mrs. Moorehead favored participation; Moorehead advised Caldwell that the delegation to the conference should be granted the flexibility missing at earlier meetings.[46]

Buoyed by the rising level of support, Caldwell continued to press his case. He pointed out that any agreement on limitation would give practical effect to the provisions of the 1912 Hague Convention which urged that drug use be restricted to legitimate needs. Caldwell also argued that the United States had a vested interest in the restriction of manufacture because of an increasing problem with narcotics at home.[47] These arguments convinced Porter to modify his opposition enough to allow Caldwell to attend the OAC session of January and February 1930 which would consider a plan of limitation. The only proviso was that Caldwell remain an observer during the deliberations.[48]

At the OAC session Caldwell rendered assistance solely on technical matters in the preparatory work for the plenary conference. A tentative plan, drafted by a subcommittee, advocated the formation of an international cartel composed primarily of European drug manufacturers. Since the United States traditionally opposed cartels and because the plan of the OAC did not provide for controls over manufacturing as strict as the United States desired, the State Department initially decided to send only observers to the conference.[49] Yet Caldwell would accept nothing less than full participation. As such, he had to make that course the most attractive alternative for other officials.

A preliminary conference held in London from October 27 to November 30 helped greatly in that regard. The meeting had two objectives: to determine the apportionment of quotas to manufacturing nations and to devise a system for the distribution of manufactured narcotics to consumer nations. Quota allocations proved impossible to agree upon. Individual governments were therefore left free to offer their own proposals at the general conference scheduled for May 1931.[50] The indecisiveness at London likely influenced the decision of the United States to participate fully at the manufacturing limitation conference. As Stimson later informed President Hoover, nothing which transpired at London precluded an open hearing for United States proposals at Geneva.[51]

Stephen G. Porter, too, unwittingly helped to get a delegation to the conference. In the short run, his untimely death in June l930 had a salutary effect upon narcotic foreign policy.[52] From a broader perspective, the creation of the Federal Bureau of Narcotics, which came about largely as a result of Porter's hard work, provided an additional rationale for going to Geneva.

After the establishment of the Federal Narcotics Control Board (FNCB) in 1922, the departments of state, treasury, and commerce shared the responsibility for implementing national narcotic policy. The Narcotic Division of the Prohibition Unit in the Treasury Department took charge of the day-to-day work. This procedure stayed the same until March 1927 when Congress set up the Prohibition Bureau, thereby transferring from the internal revenue

chief to the deputy commissioner of prohibition the task of enforcing the Harrison Narcotic Law and its amendments.[53]

In 1929 the effectiveness of narcotic control under this method
of operation began to receive criticism from several sources, both
in and out of government. In the first place, the presence of illegal
narcotics in the country was generating concern within segments
of the medical profession. In May the head of the Eastern Medical
Society of New York, Dr. Harry Cohen, wrote Stimson expressing
his organization's concern. The society believed the officially recognized level of addiction, about 100,000, to be too small and felt
that addiction was steadily increasing. Cohen also noted that the
apprehension and incarceration of major drug peddlers did not
occur frequently enough to make the threat of a prison term an
effective deterrent to illicit activity. In fact, he argued that the
jailing of small-scale peddlers was a waste of time.[54]

Even before Cohen's letter reached the State Department, Porter was questioning the operation of domestic drug controls. He
first expressed his doubts in a meeting with various state and
treasury officials. Present at a gathering on April 11 were Johnson,
Caldwell, Porter, Assistant Secretary of the Treasury Seymour
Lowman, Prohibition Commissioner James M. Doran, and Harry
J. Anslinger—a State Department consular official temporarily on
duty with the Treasury Department as secretary of the Federal
Narcotics Control Board.

This select group met at Porter's request. Having observed the
work of the FNCB for some time, he felt that a new central
authority should exercise integrated jurisdiction over foreign and
domestic drug control activities. He judged it unsatisfactory that
the FNCB had to rely on the Treasury Department for the compiling of statistics relating to the yearly allowable amount of opium to
be imported under the Harrison law. Porter also described as
insufficient current supervision of the quantity of narcotics manufactured in the United States. Those present agreed to prepare
draft legislation designed to rectify these perceived weaknesses in
narcotic law administration.[55]

The same group convened again within one week. At that time
State Department representatives offered two bills for consideration, and the Treasury Department also presented a draft proposal.
In brief, the plans stipulated that all dealers in drugs whether
through manufacturing, selling, or shipping in interstate or foreign

commerce would need a license from a central authority in order to continue such activities. Subsequent meetings were held to formulate a common proposal.[56] At the conclusion of the meetings it became apparent that the drug control structure in the country would be revised. The administrative and enforcement system in effect had lost the support of those officials most intimately involved in control. (In January 1929 the Public Health Service had received its first statutory authorization to participate officially in the nation's drug control programs. The PHS would provide medical treatment for federally incarcerated addicts.) It remained only to be determined whether the new machinery would place greater emphasis upon administrative efficiency, as the Porter group desired, or on a suggestion of the Eastern Medical Society of New York calling for limitation of narcotics at the source. The society felt that domestic efforts alone could not produce effective controls. *"Unless the supply is controlled at the source,"* Cohen wrote Stimson, *"all internal methods of control and prosecution are useless."*[57]

Ironically, the ultimate objective of the antidrug effort in America traditionally had been limitation at the source. Yet rigid adherence to that method of control, a *sine qua non* of the nation's participation in the work of the League, had prevented Washington from exerting much influence over other countries throughout the 1920s. Dr. Cohen's letter showed that the society did not fully appreciate the dilemma facing policymakers: the United States needed to find a way to renew participation at Geneva without seeming to reject its own programs for adequate control. By considering the creation of a new central authority, officials were suggesting that they had not abandoned traditional goals, but instead were willing to try to attain them gradually.

The proposed bureau of narcotics would play an important role in this strategy. Yet as Porter endeavored to guide his bill, HR 10,561, through the House, several problems arose. First, state and treasury officials did not fully agree on the need for the bureau. Caldwell told the Ways and Means Committee in March 1930 that better organization of narcotic control at home would help the United States meet its international obligations.[58] Caldwell, it should be recalled, had just attended the 1930 session of the OAC and was adamant about securing unfettered participation in the projected Geneva conference. He meant the international antinarcotic role of the United States to be an expanding one.

In an appearance on behalf of the Treasury Department, Harry J. Anslinger showed less enthusiasm for the bureau. He declined to guess whether passage of the bill would help reduce illicit traffic. He did assert, though, that the proposed bureau would be a welcome administrative tool for narcotic officials. Reacting to this vacillation, John Nance Garner of the Ways and Means Committee observed: "I gather from what you say that the Treasury Department is not very enthusiastic for the bill . . ." In reply, the witness simply stated: "The Treasury Department supports the bill."[59]

Garner's suspicion that the Treasury Department was extending only lukewarm support to the Porter bill may have been accurate. On the day that Anslinger testified, the *Washington Herald* revealed that Secretary of the Treasury Andrew W. Mellon's own report to the committee included the following comment. "There is some doubt in my mind," he said, "as to the necessity of creating a separate bureau to accomplish what is sought in this bill."[60] Caldwell, who saw in the bill an opportunity to provide necessary coordination in the nation's foreign and domestic drug policies, feared that the committee would issue an unfavorable report.[61]

Outright opposition to the bill from the American Medical Association and the Eastern Medical Society of New York, which continued an earlier pattern opposing expanded government power, could not have allayed his fears. A member of the House of Representatives who spoke for the medical profession, Dr. William I. Sirovich of New York, introduced a substitute measure retaining the Federal Narcotics Control Board and requiring a narcotics commissioner to be a physician—such as the assistant surgeon general of the United States.[62] By March 7 Sirovich dropped his objections to the Porter bill and testified about it in generally favorable terms. His change of mind occurred after a discussion with Porter, who agreed not to seek passage of a companion bill to HR 10,561 that would have tightened licensing requirements on physicians engaged in drug-related business. In exchange, the medical associations did not oppose publicly the creation of a narcotics bureau.[63]

Just as it seemed the Porter bill would receive final approval, another obstacle appeared. Caldwell discovered that the bill would emerge from committee with an amendment providing for imports of coca leaves to the Coca-Cola Company in amounts exceeding stipulated legitimate needs. The problem was that the State Department could not legally support a bill with such a provision. Some uncertainty also existed concerning whether coca leaves could be sufficiently decocainized to meet government standards.[64] Porter counseled patience, hoping to have the amendment made acceptable in the Senate after House passage—which came on April 7.[65]

The State Department ultimately found a way to overcome its objection to the bill. The department would drop its opposition if the Senate altered the amendment so as to provide for the destruction under government supervision of the cocaine content of the coca leaves. By late April when the bill had not passed the Senate, an anxious Porter was willing to have any form of the troublesome amendment deleted from his bill. The legislation finally obtained Senate approval on June 5 with a revised section ordering the bureau of narcotics to supervise destruction of cocaine in coca leaf imports. The House of Representatives subsequently accepted this version and President Hoover signed it into law on June 14. The Porter Narcotic Act took effect on July 1, 1930, four days after Porter's death.[66]

Dissatisfaction with the structure of the narcotic control bureaucracy does not entirely explain why the bill received congressional approval. Proponents of the measure neutralized opposition to it, but the bill failed to receive more than lukewarm support from the Treasury Department, the supervisory agency for domestic control. Moreover, Caldwell's efforts to transform narcotic foreign policy probably would not have been impeded if the bill had failed. Much of the credit for passage must go to the persistent Stephen G. Porter. By devising the machinery that brought increased efficiency to the administration of the nation's drug laws, he inadvertently minimized the role of the Congress in that procedure;[67] yet his endeavors also helped to institutionalize the coordination between domestic and foreign narcotic policy—a nexus that proved to be of great value to the Federal Bureau of Narcotics in its nearly forty years of existence. In addition to Porter's efforts, another series of events undoubtedly provided the proximate cause behind the bureau's creation.

The results of a grand jury investigation into illegal drug activity in New York City early in 1930 challenged the integrity of drug law enforcement by the government. The presentment alleged "misconduct, incompetence, and dereliction" of duty against federal agents and accused some agents of "having regularly falsified their reports to Washington" concerning the number of narcotic arrests. This activity took place at the instance of Levi G. Nutt, deputy commissioner of prohibition, who apparently issued the order through a subordinate. The federal grand jury listed 354 cases wherein the agents expanded their arrest records by claiming responsibility for cases worked on solely by authorities in New York.[68]

Just as damning for the government were the strong indications which the grand jury uncovered of collusion between officials in the federal narcotic bureaucracy and alleged operators of the illicit traffic. Nutt became suspect because of the association of his son-in-law and son, both lawyers, with a known gambler, Arnold Rothstein, who was reportedly involved in narcotic activity. Nutt's son-in-law had borrowed over $6,000 from Rothstein sometime in the 1920s, and the younger Nutt obtained a favorable settlement in 1927 on an income tax assessment levied against Rothstein for the years 1919–21. The suspicions of collusion together with the fraudulent records necessitated, in the grand jury's words, "a complete reorganization from top to bottom" of the enforcement operation.[69] In sum, the grand jury's revelations, the transfer of Nutt to a position as field supervisor for the Prohibition Bureau, and the assumption of Nutt's duties by Anslinger assured passage of the Porter bill.[70]

Even before Hoover signed the bill, Caldwell was told that the State Department wanted a voice in choosing a commissioner for the Federal Bureau of Narcotics. Caldwell believed that the selection of Anslinger would afford the best opportunity for harmonious relations between the new agency and the State Department. It is representative of the forthcoming coordination among drug officials that the White House and Treasury Department quickly learned of Caldwell's evaluation.[71] Important, too, in this regard was the simultaneous request Anslinger made for information about the international aspects of drug control.[72] Such a gesture could only have assisted Caldwell in his efforts to renew United States participation in the antinarcotic work of the League of Nations.

Harry J. Anslinger officially assumed the office of narcotics commissioner in December 1930. He had compiled a twelve-year record of service in the government. Born in Altoona, Pennsylvania in 1892, Anslinger attended Pennsylvania State College for two years before going on to the Washington College of Law, where he earned an LL.B. From 1918 to 1926 he served in various consular offices for the State Department, including The Hague; Hamburg, Germany; La Guaira, Venezuela; and Nassau in the Bahamas. In 1926 the Department of State loaned his services to the Treasury Department to aid in organizing the Division of Foreign Control. Anslinger also served as a delegate to the 1926 London Conference for the Suppression of Liquor smuggling. Finally in 1929 he received a transfer from State and began serving as secretary to the Federal Narcotics Control Board.[73] Anslinger, who would remain as commissioner for more than thirty years, accepted without question the policy of strict and punitive enforcement of domestic drug laws. Under his leadership the Bureau of Narcotics subordinated humanitarian concern for the ravages of addiction to an impersonal efficiency.[74]

What the creation of the bureau portended for the nation's addict population was expressed by President Hoover in a comment on the growth of government bureaucracies. "No one with a day's experience in government," he once remarked, "fails to realize that in all bureaucracies there are three implacable spirits—self-perpetuation, expansion, and an incessant demand for more power." Given the organizational context in which drug laws were made and enforced, to have treated addicts as other than criminals would have compelled a reassessment of the objectives of drug control policy. No policymaker in the renascent bureaucracy was prepared to do that.

Outweighing all other considerations, the quest for efficiency largely restricted public debate over policy, minimized any chance of democratic decision making, and promoted an informal, arbitrary operation of government. Efficiency in public policy, of course, had its financial side as well. For Fiscal Year 1931, the national drug law enforcement budget was slightly more than $1.7 million. An additional sum of relatively the same size was appropriated for the creation of two federal narcotic farms (hospitals). Finally, the budget allotted an unspecified amount for payments to informers concerning alleged drug law violations.[75]

Had he lived, Porter might have come to regret his endeavors in creating the bureau. He had agreed with the State Department on the need for restrictive international controls on drug traffic, but he viewed addiction differently than did Anslinger. "A person who is addicted to drugs," Porter remarked several months before his death, "is sick. He or she is the victim of a disease and should be placed where treatment can be given. You can't cure a sick person by sending that person to jail."[76] That sentiment seemed to be anathema to the commissioner of narcotics in 1930, as his actions in office would soon reveal.

Flexibility rather than rigidity marked the relationship of the United States with the international drug control movement at that time. During its January 1931 session the OAC, with Caldwell's active support, enlarged the list of narcotics that might become subject to manufacturing limitations at the May conference.[77] In his instructions to the delegation Stimson told Caldwell and the other members (including Anslinger) not to oppose a convention "which would be acceptable to other governments and unacceptable to the United States . . . , provided it would seem likely to accomplish the desired restriction of manufacture." The secretary of state hoped that the United States would be able to accept any convention agreed upon.[78]

Prior to the opening of the Conference for the Limitation of the Manufacture of Narcotic Drugs, Stimson also encouraged Latin American participation at Geneva. Some hesitancy about committing themselves wholeheartedly to League-directed antinarcotic activity still existed, but over half the countries there sent representatives to the conference.[79] In attendance were Argentina, Bolivia, Brazil, Chile, Costa Rica, Cuba, the Dominican Republic, Guatemala, Mexico, Panama, Paraguay, Peru, Uruguay, and Venezuela. Physical presence in Geneva did not ensure active participation in the deliberations. Mexico, for instance, assisted in administrative procedures, but contributed little to the substantive discussions. This reluctance may seem anomalous when compared with her continuing domestic problem with drugs. Yet as Martínez de Alva explained for his government: "There [is] no problem of narcotic drugs in Mexico. Mexico produce[s] no raw material, [does] not manufacture narcotic drugs, [does] not export them and [does] not even consume them except for legitimate requirements."[80] Under Mexican law the activities mentioned were illegal unless carried out under strict government supervision. The statement of the Mexican representative, otherwise disingenuous, becomes explicable if it is remembered that Mexico, still immersed in the spirit of its revolution, was participating for the first time in a world narcotic conference and probably did not want to admit the existence of any blemishes on its antinarcotic record.

Argentina, the only other Latin American nation to play a vocal role in the conference, naively became involved in the debate over manufacturing limitations. Its representative, Fernando Perez, who had no constructive proposals to present, dismissed the argument that overproduction and excessive consumption of drugs had a direct relationship. Perez told the assembled delegates in terms reminiscent of those heard years earlier in the United States:

> The spread of drug addiction and the development of the illicit drug traffic are not the effect of over-production, but are due to the moral perversion of the drug addicts and of the unscrupulous traffickers who supply them with material for their vicious practices.

This assessment of the motives behind drug usage led Argentina to support a proposal of the Soviet Union which, if adopted, would have expanded the scope of the conference to include a discussion about whether to place limits upon raw material cultivation.[81]

In more contentious times the United States would have ardently supported a similar drug control plan. To the credit of Caldwell and his superiors, the United States delegation did not have to labor under such restrictions in 1931. Instead Caldwell and Anslinger backed a Franco-Japanese proposal based on the concept of an open and competitive market. First, each government would submit to a central office annual estimates of legitimate needs. Next, internal regulations would limit the supply of available narcotics to those requirements. Finally, the central office would have the authority to regulate narcotic traffic as a means of restricting excessive exportation.[82] If this plan had been adopted as composed, it would have ultimately resulted in limiting the production of raw narcotic material.

Because of objections, especially Germany's, to so comprehensive a plan, the scheme could not be adopted without modification. Agreement in principle was reached, however, on the need for strict supervision of the quantity of raw materials in the possession of each manufacturer. Accordingly, one provision of the 1931 convention was intended to prevent the accumulation of excessive supply. Going beyond the 1925 convention, the new one made the estimates of legitimate narcotic requirements binding on the nation submitting them. The Permanent Central Opium Board would try to curtail violations of the agreement by exercise of its supervisory and administrative duties. The PCOB also received the authority to place embargoes on countries exceeding their import and export estimates. In sum, the manufacturing limitation conference sought to bring under control by the League commerce in the chief preparations of the opium poppy and the coca leaf.[83]

The work of the conference pleased the United States government. If the convention did not exactly duplicate Washington's position, it at least embodied many of the ideas Caldwell and his associates found crucial to effective control. Caldwell therefore signed the convention and protocol of signature on July 18. He refrained from signing the final act only because the United States did not belong to the League. Other signatories included the major manufacturing countries—Germany, Great Britain, Japan, the Netherlands, and Switzerland.[84] Among the Latin American states, Bolivia, Chile, Costa Rica, Cuba, Guatemala, Mexico, Panama, Paraguay, Uruguay, Venezuela, and Argentina *ad referendum* signed the convention. Nicaragua, a nonparticipant, deposited the first ratification with the League, followed closely by the United States in April 1932. Enough nations deposited their ratifications for the convention to take effect on July 9, 1933.[85]

The presence of the United States and numerous Latin American countries at Geneva in 1931 and the convention drafted during the conference underscored the changes which had transpired since 1925 in the attitudes of the American republics toward international drug control. The United States had altered its method of administering domestic policy with the creation of the Federal Bureau of Narcotics. As of 1930 Congress possessed less authority than before to formulate policy. Henceforth legislative action would reinforce rather than define the antidrug efforts of the executive branch. By formally participating in the activities of the OAC, the Department of State reduced congressional influence over narcotic foreign policy as well. The results of the 1931 Geneva conference seemed to demonstrate both the efficacy of shared power within the executive branch and the return of the United States to leadership in the international movement. Disputes with Congress over the nature of policy could only undermine that position.

Simultaneous attempts to build, let alone rebuild, the politics of drug control in Latin America produced a closer relationship than had existed previously with the League of Nations. Several nations, particularly Bolivia, Peru, and Colombia, began gradually to perceive drug usage as a social problem. Remedial action rarely altered existing conditions, however. On the other hand, Mexico and Uruguay employed legislative and administrative means to restrict drug commerce and usage. Yet even those efforts proved largely ineffective. Financing was unavailable for proper control—if large-scale financing could have helped; official corruption became a major obstacle; and drug use as part of the cultural heritage throughout Latin America militated against comprehensive controls. Nevertheless, at the close of the Geneva conference of 1931, recognition existed in Latin America of the need for additional controls, a recognition that hemispheric diplomacy alone had not been able to produce. In the 1930s, the growth of the bureaucratic state there would contend with drug-related traditions for influence over the direction of drug policy. The United States seemed the logical choice to lead the way toward greater hemispheric drug control, whether by example or direct diplomacy. A reconstructed bureaucracy and a revised narcotic foreign policy ostensibly provided the example of sound management necessary for effective policy change.

4   Drug Control in the Americas, 1931—1936

The adoption of the 1931 Geneva Convention buoyed hopes for rapid progress in the worldwide antinarcotic campaign. Shortly after the convention went into effect in July 1933, the World Narcotic Defense Association celebrated. The association's leader, Capt. Richmond P. Hobson, a Spanish-American War veteran who had become an active campaigner for several organizations, delivered a number of speeches praising the work of the Geneva conference. In another tribute the *Literary Digest* heralded the implementation of the convention with an article entitled, "End of the Illicit Drug Traffic Now in Sight."[1]

Unfortunately, such euphoria was unwarranted. For nations steadfastly committed to the eradication of illicit drug commerce and usage, including the United States, the convention provided an additional tool to help in the fight. Nations with less systematic programs, especially those in Latin America, were encouraged to reconsider the extent of their antidrug activities. In some cases more vigorous actions would be undertaken. For their part United States officials believed that the recent integration of foreign and domestic drug policies would mitigate some of the nation's drug problems. They miscalculated the complexity of the situation.

In the early 1930s domestic addiction remained at a considerable level, a steady stream of illegal drugs, including marijuana and opium, continued to flow north from Mexico, and new problems appeared for policymakers as Central America and Colombia became important locales for smuggling opiates and cocaine from

Europe. These conditions plus a general inability to control illicit narcotic commerce by Latin American governments offered officials in Washington scant hope for success in their endeavors.

Conservative estimates provided by the Federal Bureau of Narcotics placed the number of addicts around 100,000 in 1926; six years later the official figure had increased by 20,000. This amounted to approximately one addict per one thousand people. Testifying in 1930 on his bill creating the bureau, Stephen G. Porter stated that the most reliable estimates of addiction ranged from 200,000 to 1,000,000 addicts. Porter personally felt that the accurate number approached 400,000.[2] If Porter's statistics exaggerated the real extent of addiction, the government's figures underestimated it. The point is that addiction was probably not decreasing, despite the enforcement programs being carried out under the provisions of the Harrison Narcotic Law and its amendments. On the twentieth anniversary of the law's passage, an editorial in the *St. Louis Post-Dispatch* termed it a failure which had only produced large-scale smuggling. The Federal Bureau of Narcotics denied the allegation asserting that addiction had decreased during the two decades of the law's operation.[3]

Moreover, the continuing depiction of addicts as social deviants belied the faith officials placed in their capacity to reduce addiction. In 1932 Treasury Secretary Ogden L. Mills found addicts to be "mentally defective and psychotic," easily given to the influence of other addicts. Bureau Commissioner Anslinger doubted whether addicts could ever play a useful role in society. In remarks before the Attorney General's Conference on crime held in Washington in December 1934, he commented that "we understand that none of these addicts would have become habitués had they possessed the mental stamina to resist the drug. The mere fact that they could not control their craving, and yielded time after time even when they knew from experience that they faced a jail sentence, is indisputable proof . . . that many of them will relapse to the ravages of the old habit and form underworld associates." To Anslinger, addicts were "derelicts from a sinking ship."[4]

Only occasionally in the 1930s was there heard a dissent from such views. Dr. Walter L. Treadway of the Public Health Service, reflecting perhaps his bureau's difficult historical experience with drug addiction, warned of the danger in a facile dismissal of the social and environmental causes of addiction. Treadway pointed out that addiction appeared in all social classes, although it remained more visible within the lower class. He also felt that a high level of recidivism did not so much lend support to the assertion that addiction was a function of a pathological personality as it refuted the approach which sought to control drug usage primarily by punitive means.[5] Since Treadway's views ran counter to the enforcement patterns practiced by the Bureau of Narcotics, they did not obtain a large audience within the policy-making bureaucracy.

At this time the major instance of an attempt to improve domestic controls came in the movement to adopt a uniform state narcotic law. Long before 1930 it became evident to officials that many states were defaulting to the federal government the task of enacting and enforcing adequate antidrug legislation. The Harrison law served not as a model for some state legislatures, but as an excuse not to pass complementary state laws.[6] At its annual conference in October 1932 the National Conference of Commissioners on Uniform State Laws accepted a draft proposal for a uniform state narcotic act. Under the terms of the draft, no person could trade in drugs without specific authorization. The final version of the Uniform State Narcotic Drug Act related primarily to the opiates and cocaine; marijuana was incidentally included under the general provisions of the act. The proposal also recommended the strict licensing of manufacturers and wholesalers. Hoping to create a receptive atmosphere, the Bureau of Narcotics prepared a number of articles about the need for the act. It is noteworthy that early in the government's campaign, the American Medical Association added its support for the adoption of the act. The rapid response throughout the nation pleased the bureau; by 1936 twenty-seven states had put the act into effect.[7]

The renovation of drug control policy did not proceed in a vacuum isolated from contemporary events. In fact, the economic exigencies brought on by the depression almost negated the meticulous work of the State Department and the young bureau. The problem appeared in the form of a proposed reorganization of various government agencies just as President Franklin D. Roosevelt's administration was settling into office. Among the contemplated changes was the transfer of the Federal Bureau of Narcotics from the Treasury Department to the Attorney General's office. Initiative for the change apparently came from the Bureau of the

Budget and its director, Lewis W. Douglas, who convinced the commissioner of prohibition, A. V. Dalrymple, that the interchange of agents for narcotic and prohibition law enforcement would increase the operational efficiency of the bureaus being merged.[8]

Stuart J. Fuller, a narcotic expert speaking for the State Department, offered two objections. First, any change might contravene Article XV of the 1931 Geneva Convention which required each signatory to maintain a separate, central narcotics office. Furthermore, the proposal would probably place the enforcement of narcotic laws in a situation similar to that which existed before the establishment of the Bureau of Narcotics. In a cover note on a memorandum to Undersecretary of State William Phillips on March 31, 1933, Fuller wrote, "Our Narcotics Bureau has been held up at Geneva as a *model* one." Fuller therefore concluded that to:

> abolish the Bureau of Narcotics would be regarded as a distinctly retrograde step and would discourage abroad the centralization and coordination of foreign narcotics administration which the American Government has repeatedly urged.[9]

Fuller took his case both to the Justice Department and the prohibition chief. He informed Dalrymple that the 1931 convention had been composed and signed "on the insistence of the American Government." Any alteration in the policy structure would make it appear that the United States had reneged on its antidrug commitment, causing embarrassment for the State Department.[10] Reports also reached Washington detailing concern by the Opium Advisory Committee over the proposed merger. President Roosevelt finally ended all speculation when he told Phillips that there would be no merger or abolition of the bureau, especially in view of the treaty obligations incurred in 1931.[11] The defeat of the proposed merger underscores the bureaucratic skills at work in the management of national narcotic policy by Harry J. Anslinger and his colleagues in the Department of State. After an early decrease in funding as a result of the depression, they were able to maintain appropriations for the Bureau of Narcotics at a relatively constant level throughout the depression, New Deal, and the years of the heavy fiscal demands generated by the Second World War. (See Table 2.) In financial terms at least, the stability of

TABLE 2. Annual Appropriations for the Federal Bureau of Narcotics, 1931—1950

Fiscal Year	Appropriation	Fiscal Year	Appropriation
1931	$1,712,998	1941	$1,303,280
1932	$1,708,528	1942	$1,278,475
1933	$1,525,000	1943	$1,289,060
1934	$1,400,000	1944	$1,150,000
1935	$1,244,899	1945	$1,338,467
1936	$1,249,470	1946	$1,167,400
1937	$1,275,000	1947	$1,300,000
1938	$1,267,000	1948	$1,430,000
1939	$1,267,000	1949	$1,450,000
1940	$1,306,700	1950	$1,610,000

Source: Compilation of Federal Bureau of Narcotics annual reports

funding shows that public narcotic policy had finally taken its place as a regular and institutionalized function of the federal government. With the end of the controversy over reorganization, drug policy could be looked upon almost as an entity unto itself—no longer subsumed within broader policy considerations as had been the case since 1914. By having to devote less time to obtaining support for their policy at home, drug officials were able to give more concerted attention to related problems abroad.

As had been the case for some time, the situation in Mexico and its direct relationship to drugs smuggled into the United States required much of the energy officials in Washington were expending in their effort to improve the quality of control in the Americas. A crucial obstacle to their goal arose out of the difficulties the Mexican government faced in handling its own drug situation. Usage apparently increased in the early 1930s. Marijuana smoking persisted, and heroin was found among the lower levels of society.[12] Despite claims to the contrary by the government, the decrees of the 1920s had not really alleviated a deteriorating situation.

A report in the newspaper *Excélsior* on June 12, 1931 revealed the severity and extent of the situation. In a letter to the paper, the minister of government, Carlos Riva Palacio, announced his resignation, an action resulting from his alleged complicity in a smuggling operation which was introducing illegal drugs into Mexico and then transporting them to the United States.[13] Plutarco Elías Calles, the most powerful man in Mexico and now ex-president, had the nominal president, Pascual Rubio Ortiz, accept the minister's resignation. There existed no certainty, however, that Riva Palacio was intimately connected with the smugglers. Others mentioned in connection with the operation were the president of the Federal District, the governor of San Luis Potosí, and also members of the staff of Rubio Ortiz. "The most charitable construction to put on the action of the President," declared United States Military Attaché Col. Gordon Johnson, "is that the sudden exposure of so many high officials of his Administration might be politically disastrous."[14]

In short, a government crisis seemed at hand. Mexico's financial condition, more precarious because of the depression, was worse than at any time since 1915. Credit was poor; gold and silver were in short supply. With the resignation of the head of the presidential staff, Calles's faith in the ability of Rubio Ortiz to govern effectively nearly evaporated. Fortunately for Mexico, the power and prestige of Calles held the government together. In August the crisis passed when Gen. Lázaro Cárdenas, who would become president in 1934, accepted an appointment to Riva Palacio's former position.[15]

It is not clear that the appointment of Cárdenas had a causal effect, but shortly thereafter the government undertook a reassessment of the operation of its drug control policies. Specifically, the Public Health Department sought to establish special hospitals to care for addicts: the program was obligatory and the department had to authorize an addict's discharge. Under the plan, free care would be provided for poorer addicts. Finally, physicians were to be held responsible for the condition of patients upon their release.[16] Nothing came of the proposal until Cárdenas took office as president. At the end of August 1934 the new administration published a revised sanitary code and decree of implementation. Under provisions of the code, if an addict had drugs in his possession for personal use, he would be consigned to the Public Health Department, not to the criminal courts. But if an addict supplied others with drugs, he would be subject to criminal prosecution after undergoing treatment. Most important, the Department of Public Health would constitute the ultimate authority concerning possible prosecution for criminal offenses.[17]

Implementation of the sanitary code left Mexico's drug law enforcement practices at variance with those of the United States. Policy would be set by an agency with a medical function rather than by one (the Bureau of Narcotics) emphasizing punitive law enforcement and administrative efficiency. The Public Health Department planned to treat addicts first as individuals meriting medical attention; their particular situation would determine the applicability of criminal law. Conversely, enforcement practices in the United States blurred distinctions between sale and possession solely for personal use. Whether the Mexican approach to drug control would prove any more successful than that advocated in Washington remained to be seen.

Despite the intentions of the Cárdenas administration, it was doubtful that the new regulations had a discernible impact on the drug situation in areas distant from Mexico City. In April 1935 the United Press news wire carried a story from Geneva stating that a standing committee of the League of Nations, probably the OAC, named Mexico as a nation from which large quantities of drugs were being smuggled into the United States. It also noted that Mexican officials took part in the illicit activity. The government denied the allegations, putting the blame for smuggling instead on manufacturing nations with insufficient controls over exports. Whatever the level of official corruption and complicity, the government's countercharges had a basis in reality. In Manchuria, British and Swiss interests were seeking to have the opium trade from Persia legalized: an increased trade would prove lucrative financially, particularly if the demand for narcotics could be artificially stimulated in places other than China.[18] Notwithstanding the denials, the level of smuggling from Mexico remained high.[19]

Based upon its record in the early 1930s, the government in Mexico City appeared willing to act with the United States to stop smuggling. In 1930 the two countries concluded an informal agreement for the exchange of information on drugs.[20] The following year officials sent a special agent to coordinate antidrug activity with Consul William Blocker in the Juárez–El Paso region.[21] Mexico next requested that agents of both countries be permitted unrestricted border crossings there pursuant to their duties. The State Department and Bureau of Narcotics turned down the request, although United States agents would continue to cross into Mexico with Anslinger's express approval.[22] By mid-1932 all the Mexicans had achieved was another informal arrangement for the exchange of information.[23]

While reluctant to engage in cooperative activity, the United

States took several unilateral steps to detect and prevent illegal traffic. Around 1930 private planes began smuggling drugs out of Mexico. In response, an antidrug air patrol operated from various sites in Texas starting in 1931. During the first two years of the program no drugs were seized, only liquor. Yet authorities remained convinced that smuggling by air was a prime means of getting drugs into the United States.[24]

In addition to west Texas, Baja California continued to serve as a prominent locale for smuggling. The consul at Ensenada, William Smale, suggested that the State Department pressure Mexican authorities to act by taking steps "which would reduce to a minimum the travel and expenditures of American tourists in Baja California . . ."[25] Not until Operation Intercept thirty-five years later would the United States try, in a comparable situation, to take the action Smale suggested. In place of economic pressure, a meeting was held on October 10, 1934 in Los Angeles to disseminate information on smuggling to representatives from the state, treasury, labor, and justice departments. The need for the meeting became evident after the district supervisor of the Bureau of Narcotics in San Francisco stated that he saw no reason to believe anything other than liquor was being smuggled into the United States.[26]

Such ignorance of the actual situation was unacceptable in Anslinger's Bureau of Narcotics; nor would it help matters in Baja California. In January 1935 Smale found "the matter of smuggling . . . taking more and more of the time of this office."[27] The meeting in Los Angeles provided some assistance. Communication lines between State Department representatives and Treasury agents, who had often operated in Mexico without consular knowledge, were improved. Smale and other consuls would receive any urgent information from the Customs Border Patrol Office in San Diego. In turn, they were required to report periodically to a general coordinator in Los Angeles.[28] The transfer of a clerk at the consulate, Paul Carr, to the employ of the Treasury Department provided additional help for Smale. Carr undertook most of the daily work concerning smuggling. He worked for the Treasury Department in order to avoid the necessity of presenting a formal request to the Mexican government to allow him to move freely about the Ensenada area. As noted previously, the United States had no interest in reciprocal operations of this kind. "It is inadvisable," Smale was told, "to notify the Mexican Government of the general nature of the appointee's duties."[29]

Yet as Smale well knew, the United States could do little about illicit drugs in Baja without assistance from Mexico City. Assistance was offered infrequently, however. Smale therefore could only relay information to his superiors. On one occasion in March 1936 he reported learning of extensive cultivation of opium poppies and marijuana in remote regions of Baja. The only action Smale was able to take was to have a staff member take a "vacation" in the area and report on conditions there. This and similar occurrences in other consular districts moved the United States to bring the matter of border smuggling to the attention of the OAC in Geneva. In a presentation distinguished by sensitivity for the diplomatic feelings of Mexico, and therefore symbolic of the reciprocal nature of the Good Neighbor Policy, Stuart J. Fuller declared that smuggling presented a problem on both sides of the border. In response, the Mexican delegate, Manuel Tello, promised a more comprehensive exchange of information on drugs would be forthcoming. Nonetheless, available records for 1936 do not reveal the conclusion of any agreement to augment the previous ones of 1930 and 1932.[30] It seems unlikely that the Mexicans could believe, as they had at Geneva in 1931, that there was no drug problem in Mexico.

Illicit drug activity also flourished elsewhere in Latin America in the early thirties. Most governments failed to respond even with the rudimentary measures of control prompted by smuggling across the Mexico–United States border. Instead, official inattention and incompetence, even corruption, defined the spectrum of responses to drug problems. Such a situation brought into question the extent to which Latin American governments actually had begun to view drug usage and traffic as domestic social problems in the late 1920s. It also demonstrated the difficulty of inculcating in others by whatever means the antidrug fervor of the United States. As before, the division remained in part one of culture versus bureaucracy.

Only Uruguay embarked upon a serious campaign to control drugs. In June 1931 the State Department distributed throughout Latin America a questionnaire seeking information about the situation there. Uruguay's reply showed a flurry of activity between 1929 and 1932. In May 1929 the Geneva Convention of 1925 had gone into effect. Then came the implementation of an import-export certificate system and a decree in March 1932 seeking to control further commerce in drugs. Most important, the government gave full power to the National Council of Public Health to supervise the enforcement of all narcotic regulations.[31]

In 1933 the government created the ornately titled Special Commission for the Defense Against Toxicomania and Control of the Narcotics Traffic to work with the Public Health Council. The duties of the special commission included supervising compliance with all domestic and international regulations, compiling statistics on the extent of addiction, and promoting an antidrug educational campaign throughout the country. To assist the work of the special commission Uruguay planned to spend $10,000 per year.[32]

As was true elsewhere, attention to domestic matters alone could not mitigate the narcotic situation. The Uruguayan government also had to deal with the possibility of increased drug traffic resulting from apparent Japanese efforts to establish an industrial center in the Free Zone of Colonia across the Río de la Plata from Buenos Aires. The Anti-Opium Information Bureau in Geneva, a clearinghouse for narcotics data, asked Uruguay to scrutinize closely any questionable activity in Colonia. Of particular concern to the bureau was the relative proximity of Bolivian coca fields, an available source of illicit cocaine.[33] Unlike officials in Geneva and Washington, Uruguayan authorities did not believe Colonia would become a transit point for smuggling. Dr. José Mora, a foreign office official in charge of narcotics, told United States representatives in Montevideo that Colonia had never played a prominent role in illegal traffic. Problems with illicit drugs centered around the border with Brazil. Nonetheless, Uruguay promised to supervise any unusual activity in Colonia. By the mid-thirties, it should be noted, the feared Japanese industrial center had not come into existence.[34]

At this same time Uruguay took other steps to guard against the introduction of unwanted drugs. At the Seventh Pan-American Conference at Montevideo in December 1933 the government urged those Latin American republics which had not yet ratified the 1931 Geneva Convention to do so quickly.[35] Uruguay also sought assistance from the Opium Advisory Committee. At the OAC session in May 1934, Alfredo de Castro asked the committee to make a special appeal to all Latin American governments urging the prompt submittal of their annual reports. He further requested that Geneva encourage the development of drug education campaigns by individual nations. The suggestions received substantial support, including Fuller's for the United States, and resolutions putting them into effect passed easily.[36]

Available evidence suggests that Uruguay's efforts were succeeding. Although not formally establishing a state monopoly, the government effectively assumed full authority to supervise and direct all commerce in drugs.[37] Also, the public health minister and prefect of police in Montevideo offered cash rewards to those officers who were most productive in their antinarcotic work. By early 1937 drug consumption seems to have fallen below the 1930–34 level. What illegal drugs were uncovered came primarily, as before, from Brazil and secondarily from Argentina. "Compared with cities of similar size in the United States or Europe," observed United States Minister Julius Lay, "drug addiction in Montevideo is of minor importance."[38]

Uruguay imported all its narcotics, both raw and manufactured. This fact plus careful regulation of sale and consumption did much to restrict illicit traffic there. Finally in September 1937 the government officially created a state monopoly governing the importation, exportation, and distribution of all narcotic substances. This action went beyond the more limited effort of 1923. Public health officials took charge of the monopoly. Possession of narcotics became illegal whether intended for personal use or sale to others. The law putting this program into effect outlined stiff penalties for any physician or police official who violated its provisions. Significantly, a state hospital was set up to treat addiction. Part of the funding for the institution would come from revenues derived from the monopoly.[39]

No other Latin American nation followed the example set by Uruguay. Argentina, for example, had never made a serious attempt at drug control. The government acceded to the 1925 Geneva Convention but did not actually sign the document.[40] Smuggling was uncontrolled around Buenos Aires. It was not surprising, therefore, that Argentina tended to import more drugs than allowed under the terms of the 1931 convention. In 1935, for instance, imports of morphine and cocaine exceeded the stipulated allotments.[41]

Not until three years later did Argentina enact a comprehensive drug law. In February 1938 the government placed controls on the traffic in opium, heroin, and cocaine, and began import and export supervision. In a comment on Argentina's action, the assistant secretary of the treasury, Stephen B. Gibbons, declared that the regulations were malleable enough to permit physicians to prescribe sufficient quantities of drugs to maintain addicts in their habit. In Gibbons's view, Argentina's annual estimates far surpassed the actual yearly need. A newly created Section of Narcotics Control in the government evidently did not deem it necessary to revise national drug requirements.[42]

The narcotic situation in Honduras seemed equally out of control early in the decade. In the eighteen months prior to the end of 1933 Honduras imported enough morphine, eighty-seven kilograms, to meet its medical and scientific requirements for one hundred years. The supply, far in excess of quota allotments, came mainly from France, Germany, and Switzerland, nations traditionally reluctant to adopt manufacturing limitations. In 1934 when Honduras received another twenty-two-year supply of morphine, League of Nations officials suspected wholesale forging of import certificates.[43]

Considerable amounts of the imports, including morphine and cocaine, found their way into the southern United States, particularly the New Orleans area, where local authorities managed to seize a portion of them. At least one other seizure took place in Dallas. When the smuggling continued, the United States began using Coast Guard vessels to track ships on which drug couriers were believed to be traveling. Consular officials in the Honduran ports of La Ceiba, Tela, Puerto Cortés, and Belize provided the Coast Guard with information on ship movements. The State Department viewed the reconnaissance efforts as a temporary measure which might provide a deterrent to smuggling. Such an eventuality was, of course, unlikely, given the historical role of smuggling in Central America during depressed economic times. In the 1930s as in earlier eras, smuggling became a part of the local way of life—a potentially rewarding enterprise for some individuals during the worldwide depression.[44]

Numerous Hondurans received narcotics from Europe, but one man, José María Guillen Velez, seemed to acquire larger quantities than most. (It was morphine from one of his shipments that officials in Dallas seized in 1932.) Guillen Velez, owner of a pharmacy in Puerto Cortés, accepted shipment of forty kilograms of morphine from France in 1933, an amount large enough to satisfy legitimate Honduran needs for fifty years.[45] Faced with such a serious situation, the government professed a desire to revamp its control activities. At the same time, however, Dr. Ricardo Alduvín, dean of the medical faculty at the national university in Tegucigalpa, told United States representatives that the Director of Public Health, P. H. Ordonez Díaz, had authorized Guillen's imports of opium, morphine, and cocaine. Permission was evidently granted for the years 1933 and 1934.[46]

Official corruption no doubt contributed to the ease with which drugs reached Honduras. Julius Lay reported that Honduran politicians were susceptible to bribery. The depression exaggerated the consequences of the unhappy fact that Honduras was the poorest of the Central American republics. As was true elsewhere in Latin America, especially Mexico, accepting bribes helped officials personally make the best of an economically difficult situation. Yet official corruption would mitigate in no way the impact of the depression upon Honduras. In mid-October 1932, scarcely two weeks before scheduled presidential elections, Lay found trade "nearly at a standstill."[47]

As had been the case since earlier in the century, Honduran prosperity primarily depended upon the banana industry, which was controlled by the United Fruit Company and the Standard Fruit and Steamship Company. Even had the companies not dominated the economy, the monocultural tradition would have prevented an effective response to the depression. As it was, the companies, too, were constrained in their ability to ameliorate conditions. The depression cut world banana prices, and Panama and Sigotoka disease devastated the fruit throughout the banana plantations, further damaging the nation's export-oriented economy. Although the companies contributed in numerous ways to improving the quality of life in Honduras, the wages they paid "provided little more than subsistence for workers and families" in the estimation of career diplomat Willard L. Beaulac. In 1933 wages were reduced 10 percent across the board.[48]

It was within this climate that a national election was held on October 30, 1932. The victor, Tiburcio Carías Andino, would take office on February 1, 1933. At that time, no informed person would have predicted a future of amicable relations between Washington and the new Honduran government. In 1924 the United States helped to prevent Carías from assuming the presidency. Then in 1928 the United States supported Vicente Mejía Colindres as Carías lost a relatively free election. After his electoral success in 1932, Carías immediately had to quell a revolt by dissident elements within the Liberal party. At the same time the national treasury was virtually empty.[49]

The two situations were not unrelated. While in office Mejía Colindres had kept potentially rebellious army factions in line by paying them with funds borrowed from the banana companies. (Repayment of the loans came in the form of reduced customs collections.) The vicissitudes of the depression did not afford Carías a similar option. Unable to obtain requested arms from the United States, Carías received aid from El Salvador and soon put down the revolt. The denial of the request for arms, despite Lay's recommendation to the contrary, could have only increased Carías Andino's wariness of the United States.[50]

In what cannot be interpreted as other than a diplomatic formality, Carías pledged himself to a policy of cordial relations with other governments, "especially that of the United States." The pledge included reorganization of the departments of justice and public health. What this declaration portended for drug control, or United States influence, remained to be seen.[51] Even had Honduras acceded at once to the 1931 Geneva Convention, the problem of excessive narcotic importation would have existed. In turn, smuggling would have continued unchecked.[52] When a legislative decree in March 1934 finally put the convention into effect, the practical problem of enforcement still remained—as Dr. Alduvín admitted.[53]

Essentially the problem for the United States in Honduras was that the governments of the two countries did not share the common objective of the eradication of illicit drug traffic. As a result, reciprocity—a prominent aspect of the Roosevelt administration's Latin American policy—played a lesser role in the situation than the United States would have liked. No narcotics bureaucracy existed in Honduras that would take the United States cause as its own. The tacit assumption held by Washington in hemispheric narcotic relations—that cultural and other impediments to effective drug control could be mutually overcome—simply was not relevant. There were practical limits therefore to what American diplomacy could achieve.

Several comments are in order about the Good Neighbor Policy. Its two primary tenets, military and political nonintervention by the United States in Latin America and the return of prosperity to the hemisphere, became evident within a short time after President Roosevelt took office.[54] Later in the decade, military security from potential Axis subversion became inextricably linked with the Good Neighbor Policy. Throughout, the idea of reciprocity in inter-American relations provided a basis for giving the policy its widespread appeal. In the words of Josephus Daniels, ambassador to Mexico: "The only hope of the Good Neighbor Policy lies in reciprocally applying it with justice and fair dealing between the Pan American States . . ."[55]

However skeptical of United States intentions Carías may have been, he joined in the general approval of Roosevelt's policy of nonintervention.[56] This gesture should not be construed as a thoroughgoing acceptance of the Good Neighbor Policy. As would be discovered in other countries, particularly Brazil, reciprocity could be used to domestic political advantage without being accepted wholesale. As we shall soon see, Carías realized this as he tried to rebuild the Honduran economy and cement his hold on power. In 1933 and 1934, reciprocity did not necessarily extend to implementation of a policy to curb illicit drug traffic.

Julius Lay experienced the selectivity of Honduran policy first hand. Lay felt that the prosecution of Guillen would improve the situation, but he remained pessimistic about the likelihood of any such action. An official search of Guillen's pharmacy in June 1934 uncovered no evidence linking him to the narcotics trade. "By means of forged government certificates," an exasperated Fuller declared, "Honduras has imported sufficient morphine . . . to supply her legitimate needs for a century." Compounding the frustration, it was later learned that under Honduran law the forged import certificates would not have been evidence enough to convict Guillen of a crime.[57] Lay learned, too, that Guillen served as minister of government and justice under an earlier administration and entertained hopes of becoming the president of Honduras. As such, he tried not to alienate any elements within the country, including the banana companies that might thwart his ambitions.[58] Even a League of Nations inquiry prompted by Fuller's statement did not convince the government to take action against Guillen.[59] In an ironic epilogue to the Guillen affair, which will be discussed in greater detail later, the Department of State learned that Guillen participated in at least two abortive attempts to remove Carías Andino from power in 1935 and 1936. Had the revolts succeeded, Guillen would have become acting president of Honduras.[60]

Smuggling from Honduras was not the only problem troubling American officials. Elsewhere in Central America, especially in Panama and the Canal Zone, illegal drugs were abundantly available. Costa Rica and Colombia, two countries with negligible controls, frequently served as transit points for drugs bound for Panama. United States authorities regarded Panamanian police as generally honest, but helpless to control the situation. One side effect of this condition was that a large percentage of U.S. Army personnel receiving hospital care in Panama were suspected of being addicts.[61]

If little could be done in a remedial way in Panama, continuing problems in Honduras (in addition to the difficulties posed by Guillen) made the situation there even less amenable to resolution along lines desired by the United States. Throughout his tenure as minister, Lay suspected the government of complicity in the drug traffic. It did not surprise him greatly therefore when Dr. Ricardo Alduvín, who had occasionally been helpful to Lay, resigned his post at the university. In his capacity as dean of the medical faculty, Alduvín possessed the authority to issue or withhold narcotic import certificates. On at least one occasion, Alduvín signed a certificate for a firm to import narcotics from a New Orleans company, the Meyer Brothers Drug Company, which was not authorized by the Bureau of Narcotics to export drugs to Honduras. The newspaper El Cronista revealed that throughout his service as dean, Alduvín had granted import authorizations to a select group of businessmen suspected of participating in the illicit traffic.[62]

Dr. Francisco Sánchez replaced Alduvín. He evidently wanted to change his predecessor's policy, declaring that only "pharmacies of good reputation will be allowed to petition importations of narcotic drugs through the Faculty of Medicine." Trying to assist Sánchez, Commissioner Anslinger turned down a request from the Meyer Brothers Drug Company to export morphine to Honduras. At best, Anslinger's action served a symbolic purpose. Without a strong antinarcotic commitment on the part of the Carías government, little could be done to stop the persistent smuggling. The murder of Sánchez in July 1935 testified to just how chaotic the narcotic situation had become.[63]

By that time, the Honduran government could no longer afford to ignore the problems caused by narcotics, yet it had virtually no prior antinarcotic experience to rely upon. The Minister of Foreign Affairs, Antonio Bermúdez, turned to the United States for assistance. He asked the Federal Bureau of Narcotics to send a trained investigator to Honduras. American authorities turned down the request. Shortly after the death of Sánchez, federal agents and New Orleans police had seized a shipment of heroin bound for the United States through Honduras. Distrust of the government there by officials in Washington abounded. One agent, Fuller and Anslinger knew, could not compensate for the lack of a systematic antinarcotic commitment.[64] The overture from Honduras accomplished nothing.

What concerned Carías more than drug control was the economic revitalizaton of Honduras. In 1929 Honduran exports were valued at $24.6 million, dropping to $7.4 million in 1938; imports dropped over the same period from $14.9 million to $9.5 million. Trade with the United States also plummeted, as seen in the value of banana exports: from $20.9 million in 1928–29 to $4.2 million in 1937–38. Bananas accounted for more than 80 percent of the nation's total exports; and fully three-quarters of the export trade to the United States in 1934 consisted of bananas.[65] The task for Carías was to diversify and increase the volume of exports.

Secretary of State Cordell Hull's reciprocal trade agreement program presented a partial solution to Carías. Negotiations were begun in mid-1934, and an agreement was signed on December 18, 1935. The agreement did not help to lay a basis for economic diversification, though. It may even have resulted in the reduction of customs revenues in Honduras, a liability which Julius Lay quickly foresaw. Moreover, a total reciprocity agreement might conceivably threaten banana markets in Great Britain and Germany; it assuredly would harm the import of cotton goods from Japan, a trade previously dominated by American merchants. As concluded, the agreement made few concessions to Honduran economic aspirations.[66] Despite, or perhaps because of increased dependence upon the United States, the domestic political fortunes of Carías improved. If nothing else, Honduras had obtained a guaranteed export market—not an inconsiderable achievement

in depressed economic times. However minimal, economic pre-
dictability was something the opponents of Carías could not provide.

In Peru and Bolivia, where domestic antidrug activity directly
affected the international situation, few constructive measures
were undertaken. This lack of activity proved to be particularly
disappointing to officials in Geneva and Washington. Prior to 1931
each nation had begun to consider drug use as a societal problem;
it was hoped that remedial actions might follow. Peru made a start
in the desired direction. In March 1932 a bill was introduced in
the Constituent Assembly placing restrictions on cultivation and
use of the coca leaf.[67] As before, the issue of the stability of Peru's
economy became closely linked with the question of coca restriction, as did Peruvian tradition. An official in the narcotic office of
the government told William C. Burdett, United States Consul
General at Callao-Lima, that Peru wished to comply with the
regulations of the League of Nations, especially since "the use of
coca constitutes one of the most pernicious habits of the Indian
populations." The official acknowledged that coca chewing could
not be fully halted, but felt that coca production could be controlled. In course, the international trade in cocaine would surely
decline.[68]

Upon completion of a brief trip through Peru's coca-producing
regions, Burdett reported that coca controls were unlikely. "American engineers operating some of the most important mining enterprises in the world in Peruvian highlands," Burdett noted, "have
been unable to report adverse effects from coca upon their men."
He doubted as well whether export laws could successfully restrict
illicit commerce. "There is, however, no guarantee," Burdett
stated, "of conscientious enforcement of these laws. Enforcement
is vested in the Bureau of Health, which has in recent years been
accused of more corruption than any other section of the Peruvian
government." Five different men headed the bureau between 1930
and 1932, a period when Peru was on the verge of civil strife after
the ouster of Leguía in August 1930.[69] Any hope of effective coca
control therefore seemed unrealistic. Ultimately the bill limiting
coca leaf cultivation failed to secure passage; and for the year 1932
Peru produced more than 3.5 million kilograms of coca.[70]

It was not until 1936 that the government made another attempt
to regulate the coca leaf. A planting crisis in Cuzco, a major area

for production, substantially diminished the revenue derived from coca sales. Moreover, a malaria epidemic drastically cut the supply of Indian labor. These occurrences induced officials to reconsider the role of the coca leaf in Peru.[71] No action was taken then, perhaps because of the international narcotic conference scheduled for June in Geneva. During these same years the newspaper *La Crónica* was calling for a more vigorous policy. The lack of substantive action led the Pan-American Sanitary Bureau to remark that the government of Peru did not seem disposed to waging a serious fight against drug problems.[72]

Like Peru, Bolivia failed in the early 1930s to limit coca production. Nearly two million kilos were grown in 1932, most of which were consumed domestically. International pressure to restrict production brought a response from a landowners' association in the coca-rich Yungas region.[73] Illustrating further Bolivia's rejection of proposed coca controls, President Daniel Salamanca rescinded in September 1933 a tariff on Peruvian coca in transit through Bolivia for shipment abroad. Bolivian laborers, employed in Chilean mining operations, continued to chew coca on the job. Controls on coca would not soon come to Bolivia.[74]

Except in Uruguay and to a lesser extent Mexico, the record of narcotic control in Latin America between the Geneva conferences of 1931 and 1936 was not an encouraging one to officials in the United States and at the League of Nations. Patterns of usage continued, tied as they often were to historical traditions and contemporary developments; and smuggling became a phenomenon more widespread than ever before in the hemisphere. The United States suffered most from this situation. By 1936 it was clear to officials in Washington that they could not eliminate smuggling by their own endeavors. Moreover, the perceived emerging antidrug commitment of the late 1920s in important Latin American nations proved largely illusory. The only alternative place to look for assistance was Geneva.

In trying to restrict illicit traffic, international authorities had two means available not regularized by earlier conventions. They could either attempt to control sources of supply or they could sponsor a move to increase domestic penalties for drug law violations. The OAC decided to concentrate on the second tactic. After devising a draft convention, the committee called a formal conference for June 1936. Although originally unenthusiastic about the proposal, the United States sought additional information about the scope of the conference. The Department of State hoped to broaden the agenda. "The American Government considers it important," a department communiqué stated, "that the Conference consider prevention and punishment of illicit cultivation, gathering, and production of the poppy, coca, and cannabis."[75] The League appeared to encourage Washington's plans. "Any delegation at the conference may propose any matter," declared Eric Einar Ekstrand, director of the Opium Traffic and Social Questions Section. The draft convention, Ekstrand suggested, merely offered a basis for discussion. The State Department accordingly made preparations for formal participation at the conference.[76]

Before the first session was held it became apparent that the attempt to enlarge the scope of the conference agenda would encounter opposition. Peru objected to further restrictions on coca leaves—evidently having decided not to reconsider the role of coca in society. Enrique Trujillo Bravo was instructed to reverse the position Peru had taken on the 1931 convention. He was to amend Peru's acceptance of the convention with reservations similar to those of Bolivia. He also hoped to obtain a quota for manufactured cocaine.[77] Dr. Carlos Enrique Paz Soldán, Vice-Director of the Pan-American Sanitary Bureau, suggested the change in Peru's position. In a pamphlet issued under the auspices of Peru's Sociedad Nacional Agraria, Paz Soldán wrote that exports of coca leaves and raw cocaine had fallen dramatically since the mid-twenties. As a result much of the current coca crop was being consumed domestically. If Peru were to restrict coca production, an economic crisis would occur. To placate those favoring restrictions, Paz offered several options. Peru might attempt to regulate production through the creation of a state monopoly. He suggested, too, that Peru erect its own facility to manufacture cocaine. Paz envisioned as well the establishment of a national institute to study the impact of coca on Indians, a proposal commensurate with the desires of the indigenistas. Finally, he advocated a program to educate the masses about the possible dangers of coca usage.[78]

Over half the American republics sent delegations to the conference along with Peru. These included Brazil, Chile, Cuba, Ecuador, Honduras, Mexico, Nicaragua, Panama, Uruguay, and

Venezuela. For the United States, Fuller, Anslinger, and Frank S. Ward, a legal adviser in the State Department, served as representatives.[79] The conference began with discussion of the first article of the draft convention, which enumerated offenses meriting punishment. The framers hoped that the threat of severe penalties would reduce illicit traffic. At once Fuller proposed an amendment. Although in agreement with the need to punish drug offenders, he did not think the offenses should be listed. Instead he asked other nations to "limit exclusively to medical and scientific purposes the narcotic drugs and substances to which this Convention relates." In turn, Ward explained that the absence of enumeration would make clearer the purpose of the conference. In short, the United States delegation had subtly asked for a program of cultivation restriction in order to control the usage of all drugs; suppression of the illicit trade was not enough.

In reply Portugal and Great Britain claimed that Fuller's proposal fundamentally altered the purpose of the conference and should not be considered. Fuller rejoined that any subject could be introduced as Ekstrand had stated, and noted that his delegation further wished to discuss "prevention and punishment" of illicit activities in connection with opium poppies, coca leaves, and cannabis.[80] The burden of Fuller's argument reflected his country's belief that the draft convention added little of substance to previous international agreements. Uruguay supported the United States, noting, as we have seen, that the inter-American meeting at Montevideo in 1933 passed a resolution recommending more comprehensive drug controls than those then in existence.[81]

Portugal remained adamant and sought to eliminate Fuller's proposal from additional consideration. This turn of events presented a serious problem for the United States delegation. If the amendment were not considered, Fuller and Anslinger were prepared to refrain from further participation at the conference.[82] The Department of State, mindful of the difficulties caused by such action a decade earlier, advised against any rash action by the delegation.[83]

Ultimately a committee was appointed to study Fuller's proposal and Portugal dropped its challenge to the amendment. The full conference finally settled the matter by deciding to place the "cultivation restriction" proposal into the Final Act as a recommendation rather than in the text of the convention. After this step was taken the United States delegation confined itself during the remainder of the conference to occasional observations. At one point, for example, when discussing whether to use the words "if willfully committed" in the article advocating punishment for drug law offenses, Anslinger made unmistakably clear the position of his government concerning such violations. "The work of narcotic authorities would be radically handicapped," he stated, "if, when prosecuting for illegal possession, for instance, or for illicit sale, they were obliged to prove willful commission."[84] Mere possession of proscribed substances served as presumptive evidence of law violation; it was that approach which the State Department and Federal Bureau of Narcotics wanted other nations to adopt.

The final convention did not reflect the American sentiment. Rather it resembled the preconference draft. In a cable to Washington, Fuller and Anslinger charged that countries with minimal narcotic problems controlled the formulation of the convention. Additionally, opium monopoly countries had been especially uncooperative since they feared revenues would fall if any restrictions were accepted on opium beyond those already in existence. "It has become evident," the two concluded, "that most European nations are not prepared to sign any convention which would provide for a really effective system [of control]." On June 26, twenty nations excluding the United States signed the convention. Fuller termed it "a retrograde step" for his country and found its provisions inadequate.[85] Other American republics signed the pact, including Brazil, Cuba, Ecuador, Mexico, Panama, Uruguay, and Venezuela. Honduras and Peru were not present at the final session.[86]

Years later Anslinger further explained the decision not to sign the 1936 convention. He noted that it applied only to trade in and distribution of manufactured narcotics. Such narrowly defined provisions meant that it "would afford no Constitutional basis of Federal control of the production of cannabis . . . and the opium poppy." As we shall see presently, control of marijuana was becoming a matter of increasing concern to the bureau. And even though no opium poppies were grown in the United States, the commissioner's point was clear: "Provisions of the Convention would weaken rather than strengthen the effectiveness of the efforts of the American Government to prevent and punish narcotic offenses."[87] Indeed, the convention might have proven useful to Latin American countries only marginally engaged in drug control. For the United States, however, as Anslinger and his colleagues knew, the convention added nothing of substance to its antidrug policy or patterns of law enforcement.

5 The United States Discovers an "Assassin of Youth"

In the latter half of the 1930s nothing more clearly reflected or symbolized the American style of drug control than the federal government's reaction to marijuana. Actions of the Bureau of Narcotics resulted in the passage of the Marihuana Tax Act of 1937. Harry J. Anslinger's pragmatic philosophy, joining administrative efficiency with strict enforcement of drug laws, provided formidable support for a law for which no statistically verifiable need existed. Nevertheless, the policies and procedures of the Bureau of Narcotics, which would affect the lives of addicts for years to come, were firmly entrenched by the late thirties.

The burden of the present chapter is to convey a sense of the bureaucratic and attitudinal atmosphere as it related to the formulation and execution of drug policy in the years immediately surrounding the passage of the Marihuana Tax Act. The development of unchallenged authority for the Bureau of Narcotics to define certain substances as antisocial reveals the nature of the bureaucratic atmosphere that existed. As for the attitudinal environment, it can best be seen in the adverse medicolegal perception of substances such as marijuana, whether or not governmental perception was based upon scientific, reasoned judgment.

As noted in the previous chapter, marijuana was only included in the Uniform State Narcotic Act of 1932 in a supplemental fashion. Richard J. Bonnie and Charles H. Whitebread II have shown that in order to add marijuana to the list of proscribed substances, a state would merely need to place cannabis within the definition of "narcotic drugs." By an administrative procedure, without scientific deliberation, marijuana would be seen as a narcotic by any state considering its regulation. The Federal Bureau of Narcotics evidently played a prominent role in the adoption of this method.[1]

The first instance of federal attention to marijuana may have occurred with the passage of the Pure Food and Drug Act of 1906. The act required that cannabis be labeled clearly before being sold to the public. No other federal controls were placed on marijuana until 1937. Even the efforts of Hamilton Wright failed to get marijuana included in antidrug legislation around 1910.[2] At the same time, it should be noted, Dr. Rodney True, a physiologist in charge of the Department of Agriculture's Bureau of Plant Industry, was speaking to various groups, including the Wholesale Druggists Association, about experimental work conducted by the government on cannabis. Dr. True did not mention the supposed ill effects of the drug.[3] Bureau officials would note some years later that "the hemp plant, the source of the drug hashheesh [*sic*], is one of the commonest weeds of the country; but there is little danger that it will seriously promote the drug habit." One official, Dr. W. W. Stockberger, cautioned against alarm regarding cannabis addiction. He pointed out that marijuana induced temporary elation and then sleep. And he found reports of its effects to be exaggerated.[4]

In the 1920s much of the marijuana entering the United States evidently did so through the city of New Orleans. Incidences of its usage were discovered there and in parts of Texas, Colorado, and California. Most likely itinerant Mexican laborers, employed seasonally in low-paying jobs, introduced marijuana into those areas. (To a lesser extent marijuana usage had also reached into northern, urban areas.) By 1930 sixteen states had passed antimarijuana laws, yet usage remained generally restricted to certain geographic regions and ethnic groups. Significantly, the twenties had witnessed a rapid rise in Mexican immigration. The cheap labor of the workers was welcomed, but their habits were not.[5]

With the onslaught of the depression, nonwhite minorities were subjected to increasingly critical public scrutiny. Marijuana usage accordingly evoked greater concern than was previously the case. Racial antagonism often underlay this attention. As stated in the *New Orleans Medical and Surgical Journal* in 1931:

The debasing and baneful influence of hashish and opium is not restricted to individuals but has manifested itself in nations and races as well. The dominant race and most enlightened countries are alcoholic, whilst the races and nations addicted to hemp and opium, some of which attained to heights of culture and civilization, have deteriorated both mentally and physically.[6]

Concurrent with this assessment, reports began circulating throughout the country regarding the use and effects of marijuana. Inevitably, these nonmedical reports contradicted one another. Strong testimony against cannabis came from New Orleans where exposure to the drug had been extensive. The district attorney there, Eugene Stanley, attributed to marijuana many local problems with crime. As validation for this thesis, Stanley inaccurately revived an old legend. He claimed, as would many others in the decade's antimarijuana campaign, that the Assassins, an eleventh-century Persian military and religious order, received its name because of hashish-induced violence. As Lester Grinspoon has demonstrated, marijuana's guilt by association with crime remains unsubstantiated—in fact and probably etymologically as well. But that mattered little to the crusaders against marijuana.[7]

Stanley, too, seemed to contradict himself regarding marijuana's effects. On the one hand, he claimed that it produced violent activity. Yet, he noted: "Its toxic effects are ecstasy, merriment, uncontrollable laughter, self-satisfaction, bizarre ideas lacking in continuity . . . a rapid flow of ideas of a sexual nature." The district attorney made no attempt to resolve his contradictory conclusions.[8]

At first, the Federal Bureau of Narcotics tried to minimize the impact of reports such as Stanley's. Arguing that attention to a few specific cases might generate undue anxiety, the bureau commented: "The publicity tends to magnify the extent of the evil and lends color to an inference that there is an alarming spread of improper use of the drug."[9] Two years later, in 1933, the bureau felt differently. "A disconcerting development in quite a number of states," its annual report declared, "is found in the apparently increasing use of marihuana by the younger element in the cities."[10] The change of attitude emerged as the bureau sought to have marijuana included in the uniform state drug law. Whether the perceived increase in usage was real cannot be ascertained. By

1935 when Commissioner Anslinger reported a decrease in general drug smuggling into the United States (a situation seemingly at variance with the events described in the previous chapter), he found a rise in marijuana traffic "throughout the country."[11]

Heightened public awareness of marijuana increased in 1934. The Women's Christian Temperance Union (WCTU) found evidence of its usage everywhere from schools to bridge parties. The WCTU also felt that marijuana users graduated to the opiates and cocaine.[12] The Wayne County Medical Society was assisting in a campaign to keep marijuana cigarettes from being sold to high school students. More than a hundred peddlers were reportedly operating in the Detroit area.[13] Also in 1934 the *New York Times* warned of the widespread availability of the "poisonous weed [which] maddens the senses and emaciates the body of the user."[14] In New York City squads of specially trained Works Progress Administration laborers scoured the boroughs of the Bronx, Brooklyn, and Queens trying to eliminate marijuana growing in vacant lots. In the first seven months of 1936 they collected forty tons.[15]

Despite the reported increase in the use of cannabis among all segments of society, much of the antipathy toward it remained racially motivated. The Bureau of Narcotics responded to a request for information with a statement that police officials "in cities of those states where it is most widely used estimate that fifty percent of the violent crimes committed in districts occupied by Mexicans, Spaniards, Latin-Americans, Greeks, or Negroes may be traced to this evil."[16] Also, an article in a popular magazine averred that Pancho Villa and his followers "derived their reckless courage from smoking marihuana and that most of their outrages were committed under its influence."[17] The most open and virulent anti-Mexican sentiment came from a nativist group seeking immigration restrictions. Speaking for the American Coalition, C. M. Goethe of Sacramento stated:

> Marihuana, perhaps by now the most insidious of our narcotics, is a direct by-product of unrestricted Mexican immigration . . . Mexican peddlers have been caught distributing sample marihuana cigarettes to school children. Bills for our quota against Mexico have been blocked mysteriously in every Congress since the 1924 Quota Act. Our nation has more than enough laborers.[18]

The Bureau of Narcotics may have only been interested in promoting state regulation of marijuana. By 1935, though, its own efforts plus the support which it lent others in placing anticannabis propaganda before the public stimulated a movement toward federal suppression.

No later than January 1936 Harry Anslinger was searching for a means of devising a law whose constitutionality the Supreme Court would uphold. He was reluctant to amend the Harrison Narcotic Law of 1914 for fear of impairing the enforcement practices which had evolved under it. Regulating marijuana would likely entail production controls, an activity the court might not countenance. Even if presented under the guise of a revenue-producing measure, the revenue generated would never meet the cost of adequate control. An attempt to resolve the dilemma by exercise of the treaty power, and by implementation of the "necessary and proper" clause which would legislatively support federal controls on marijuana, failed when Mexico decided not to sign a trilateral pact concerning marijuana agreed upon by the United States and Canada. Anslinger admitted that there could be no use of the taxing power, for under it and under "regulations on interstate commerce it would be almost hopeless to expect any kind of adequate control."[19] Nonetheless, the general counsel of the treasury department, Herman Oliphant, presented in the summer of 1936 the idea of a transfer tax on all dealings in marijuana. It was this device which Anslinger settled upon for federal legislation.[20]

Because of the commissioner's doubts about the constitutionality of the tax, supporters of a law sought to minimize in hearings before Congress evidence tending to weaken their case against marijuana. Potentially damaging evidence did exist, however. Although scientific investigation into the alleged effects of cannabis demonstrated an unsophisticated methodology, several studies offered provocative enough conclusions to merit the attention of the Federal Bureau of Narcotics.

The U.S. Army in January 1923 had issued a regulation prohibiting the use and possession of marijuana in the Panama Canal Zone. Two years later a group of legal, medical, and police authorities reassessed the situation. In its report the group concluded:

> There is no evidence that mariahuana [sic] as grown here is a "habit-forming" drug in the sense in which the term is applied

to alcohol, opium, cocaine, etc., or that it has any appreciably deleterious influence on the individuals using it.[21]

Subsequently the 1923 regulation was rescinded; then in December 1928 the Republic of Panama repealed its law forbidding the use and possession of marijuana. United States military officials questioned the wisdom of these two actions, arguing that usage undermined morale and led to addiction. A further study was concluded in June 1929. Again the findings minimized the dangers of marijuana, stating that "use of the drug is not widespread and that its effects upon military efficiency . . . and discipline are not great." Penalties for using marijuana were not revived until December 1930 when Maj. Gen. Preston Brown, deputy commander of the Canal Zone, forbade smoking on the grounds that it impaired efficiency.[22]

A third investigation commenced in June 1931. Its conclusions did not differ much from those of the two previous investigations. The report stated that organizational commanders, in estimating the soldierly qualifications of delinquents under their command, "have unduly emphasized the effects of mariajuana [sic], disregarding the fact that a large proportion of the delinquents are morons or psychopaths, which conditions of themselves would serve to account for delinquency."[23] This time restrictions on marijuana usage were not rescinded; and the validity of the characterization of "delinquents" as "morons or psychopaths" is not at issue here.

A report of the Public Health Service in 1929, the *Preliminary Report on Indian Hemp and Peyote,* was grounded as much in mythology (with the inclusion of the Assassins/hashish tale) as in scientific research. The surgeon general of the United States, Hugh S. Cumming, made no reference to the first two Panama Canal Zone studies. Bonnie and Whitebread have accurately concluded that the lack of interest of the Public Health Service in marijuana left the government's policy regarding the substance to be determined by the Bureau of Narcotics, a nonmedical, nonscientific, law enforcement agency. The bureau had no predilection for undertaking a thorough study to determine the effects of cannabis.[24]

In contrast to the scientific inattention of the government, the research of Dr. Walter Bromberg, senior psychiatrist at Bellevue Hospital in New York, constituted a major effort to confirm or deny the presumed ill effects of marijuana. In psychiatric examinations of more than 2,000 convicted felons, Bromberg found not a single instance of marijuana addiction. Bromberg did not deny a conceivable link between marijuana and crime, but concluded that it was more likely that alcohol would induce criminal behavior.[25] He realized, moreover, that his findings merited additional research. In a presentation delivered to the American Psychiatric Association in 1934, he identified marijuana as a "primary stimulus to the impulsive life . . ." Societal inhibitions and restraints seemed to be released, allowing individuals "to act out their drives openly."[26] Bromberg did not conclude, however, that use of marijuana led to crime, addiction, and insanity.

The Federal Bureau of Narcotics attached that particular stigma to cannabis. Recognizing that usage frequently produced pleasurable sensations, the bureau assumed that dependence resulted from its continued use. Psychological attraction or dependence was not to be distinguished from physical dependence by the bureau. All users were referred to as "addicts."[27] From this perspective, the bureau logically assumed attendant mental deterioration and regression to the point of insanity, although this view was finding medical disfavor by the time of the passage of the Marihuana Tax Act.[28] Policymakers in the federal bureaucracy had no doubt, though, that crime was a direct by-product of marijuana usage. Their own propaganda throughout the 1930s made any other conclusion impossible.

In selecting witnesses to appear before Congress to testify on the desirability of an antimarijuana law, the Treasury Department excluded representatives of the Public Health Service. During preliminary briefings before hearings began, Dr. Walter L. Treadway, one of the top officials in the Division of Mental Hygiene, offered the opinion that marijuana did not constitute a greater physical or social evil than alcohol. Treadway's views failed to receive a public hearing.[29]

The Bureau of Narcotics decided upon the strategy it would employ before Congress in a meeting on January 14, 1937. When asked if the bureau possessed a collection of marijuana horror stories it could relate, Anslinger replied affirmatively. The commissioner in turn asked a representative of the National Institute of Health, Dr. Carl Voegtlin, if marijuana usage caused insanity. Voegtlin replied that it did when used extensively for prolonged periods.[30] With its own attitude reinforced, the bureau was ready to go before Congress. "If the hideous monster Frankenstein," Anslinger was quoted as saying just prior to the hearings, "came face to face with the monster Marihuana, he would drop dead of fright."[31]

The House conducted hearings on the antimarijuana proposal from late April to early May. In his testimony Anslinger repeated the tale of the Assassins of Persia. He also distorted Bromberg's 1934 conclusions about the effects of marijuana and its relation to crime. He denied, though, that a marijuana user moved on to the so-called hard drugs such as heroin or cocaine. "No, sir," he replied to a question on that subject, "I have not heard of a case of that kind. I think it is an entirely different class. The marihuana addict does not go in that direction."[32]

Scant opposition to the marijuana tax bill appeared at either the House or subsequent Senate hearings. Only one serious critic testified, Dr. William C. Woodward, legislative counsel of the American Medical Association. In his appearance before the House Ways and Means Committee, Woodward pointed out the lack of substantive evidence before the Congress demonstrating the connection between marijuana and crime. He also noted that no representative from either the Bureau of Prisons or the Children's Bureau had testified regarding the measure. Nor was there testimony about whether young people were using marijuana and turning to crime as Anslinger and the bill's supporters alleged. And no one appeared from the Public Health Service to testify. Committee members generally ignored Woodward's objections to the bill. Instead they asked him to justify AMA opposition to certain health insurance provisions contained in the 1935 Social Security Act.[33]

Woodward evidently doubted the actual need for federal legislation to control marijuana, questioned whether the several states were turning to Washington for assistance, and found little useful in the barrage of antimarijuana propaganda. "If there is at present time any weakness in our state laws relating to Cannabis, or to marihuana," he declared, "a fair share of the blame, if not all of it, rests on the Secretary of the Treasury and his assistants who have had this duty imposed upon them for 6 and more years."[34] In short, why would the Bureau of Narcotics be able to control marijuana any better with a federal law than was already being done with existing regulations and the uniform state act? Available evidence suggests that the implicit question had no satisfactory answer; the bureau had initiated a process which would result in a federal antimarijuana law whether or not it would have any effect.

The House committee's chairman, Robert L. Doughton, felt confident that the Supreme Court would accept the transfer tax device. Under the guise of the taxing power, he explained, no law would be held invalid as a regulatory attempt if the law seemed to be a revenue-producing measure. That is, the law contained "no regulatory provisions except those reasonably related to the collection of revenue." The prohibitive character of the tax would not warrant a court's probing "behind the face of the legislation to discern motives other than the raising of revenue."[35]

Congress passed the Marihuana Tax Act on August 2; it took effect on October 1. The law imposed an occupational tax on importers, sellers, dealers, and anyone handling cannabis. The tax on a transfer was set at $1.00 per ounce for registered persons, $100.00 per ounce for those not registered with the government. Violations were punishable by a $2,000 fine, five years in prison, or both. The annual report of the Bureau of Narcotics for 1937 simply stated: "The consumption of marihuana reached such serious proportions in the United States as to call for the enactment of national-control legislation during the year."[36]

The process, of course, had been much more complex. At least five elements combined to bring about the law's passage: apparently inadequate state control of cannabis; public fear of the substance, whether real or based upon government-approved propaganda; nearly total disregard by the executive and legislative branches of scientific research on marijuana; a racist-nativist response to a generally restricted social phenomenon with no lengthy history in the United States; and the punitive-restrictive approach toward usage of drugs by law enforcement officials prevalent since before 1920 and diligently employed by Anslinger's bureau since its inception. These forces resulted in a bureaucratic atmosphere which can only be described as one in which the Bureau of Narcotics under the direction of Harry J. Anslinger possessed hegemony over the development and direction of domestic drug policy.

The conclusions in the prior section reflect an emphasis in line with the overall direction of this volume, but so far the present account of the government's antimarijuana campaign essentially parallels that of Bonnie and Whitebread. Important differences exist, however, in interpretations of what occurred after the passage of the tax act. Bonnie and Whitebread describe a four-pronged marijuana policy comprising:

    1. Control of cultivation of the plant for legitimate purposes and eradication of wild growth

    2. Pacification of marihuana sensationalism in the press

    3. Education of the federal judiciary toward strict application of the law

    4. Allocations of federal enforcement resources toward major trafficking rather than petty possession offenses.[37]

Their interpretation concerning the first and third parts of the policy seems accurate. The fourth part may be accurate to the extent that Anslinger issued such a directive, but it had little effect upon patterns of enforcement. The evidence on the second part of the policy, as Bonnie and Whitebread present it, does not support their conclusion. Antimarijuana propaganda seems rather to have continued, muted perhaps in newspapers, but no less sensational in periodicals, medical journals, law enforcement magazines, and in speeches. The attitudinal environment arising out of this persistent effort is important because of its impact on subsequent domestic drug policy matters and on the context in which narcotic foreign policy was formulated and implemented.

In months prior to the passage of the 1937 law, *American Magazine* published an article Anslinger coauthored entitled, "Marihuana: Assassin of Youth." In vivid terms the commissioner described the link between cannabis and crime. Several of the illustrative examples, such as the one in which a young man killed his entire family with an axe while supposedly intoxicated with marijuana, soon became standard and grisly fare in other tracts against marijuana.[38] "No one knows," Anslinger wrote of its effects, "when he places a marihuana cigarette to his lips, whether he will become a philosopher, a joyous reveler in a musical heaven, a mad insensate, . . . or a murderer."[39]

Presumably, Judge J. Foster Symes of Colorado understood the effects of marijuana. In the first conviction under the new statute, he commented in October 1937:

> I consider marihuana the worst of all narcotics—far worse than the use of morphine or cocaine. Under its influence men

become beasts . . . Marihuana destroys life itself. I have no sympathy with those who sell this weed. In future I will impose the heaviest penalties. The Government is going to enforce this new law to the letter.[40]

A corresponding assessment by Anslinger appeared the same month in the Minneapolis *Journal:* "Dreadful crimes have been committed and young children turned into dangerous, even murderous criminals. Maniacal and homicidal fury is a common effect, although certain races and types react differently."[41]

Writing in the February 1938 *FBI Law Enforcement Bulletin* the commissioner further asserted that marijuana was "adhering to all its old world traditions of murder, assault, rape, physical demoralization and mental breakdown." This "dangerous drug" had a close association with insanity and crime. "From the standpoint of police work," he concluded, it is more "dangerous than heroin or cocaine."[42] Had he been relating the assertion to the weed's abundant growth throughout the country the claim might have been true. It was suggested in 1938 that Civilian Conservation Corps workers undertake the destruction of marijuana fields.[43]

Various periodicals at the time adopted the commissioner's position on the deleterious effects of cannabis. With no supporting documentation, sensational articles appeared bearing the titles: "Youth Gone Loco"; "Marihuana: the Mexican Dope Plant is the Source of a Social Problem"; and "Marihuana More Dangerous than Heroin or Cocaine."[44] These stories and others expressed variants of a decade-long theme. Federal conclusions about marijuana continued to appear and found general acceptance.

Anslinger reinforced his agency's own fiction in October 1938 in a speech to the New York *Herald Tribune* Forum. He traced the brief history of marijuana in the United States. Calling for the eradication of marijuana abuse, he proclaimed a familiar litany: "It depresses, it stimulates, it turns wrong into right, it incites to violence. It distorts vision, hearing, space and time. No one can foretell the results of its use." As usual, no supporting evidence accompanied the charges.[45]

About this same time the book, *Marihuana: America's New Drug Problem*, appeared. Written by Robert P. Walton of the University of Mississippi Medical School, it offered the most extensive look yet presented on the social and medical aspects of marijuana usage. Claiming usage in the United States was reaching epidemic proportions, Walton stated that the "vice still flourishes in every country in which it has been established." Walton realized, however, that dependence upon marijuana was different from reliance upon the opiates or cocaine. Withdrawal distress, for example, seemed nowhere near as severe as with opiate addiction. He also concluded that "a formulated conception of hemp drug insanity is generally lacking."[46]

One chapter of the book, prepared by New Orleans Public Safety Commissioner Frank R. Gomilla, did rely upon antimarijuana scare tactics. Under the title, "Present Status of the Marihuana Vice in the United States," Gomilla claimed that foreigners were supplying school children with marijuana; he repeated numerous tales of brutal crimes committed under the drug's influence. Approvingly, he cited comments made in 1933 by the chief of detectives in Los Angeles, J. T. Taylor:

> In the past we have had officers of this department shot and killed by marihuana addicts and we have traced the act of murder directly to the influence of marihuana, with no other motive. We have found . . . that marihuana is probably the most dangerous of all our narcotic drugs.[47]

The appearance of misinformation continued, spreading inevitably to the medical and scientific communities. One research team from the California Institute of Technology began an article publishing its research findings by expressing its indebtedness to Anslinger and his bureau's laboratory experts.[48] A report in the *Journal of the Kansas Medical Society* found marijuana both "a cerebrospinal stimulant and a powerful aphrodisiac" used widely by adolescents. Crimes and insanity resulted from it use: "It gives a user a lust to kill, unreasonably without motive."[49]

Other efforts to indict marijuana were absurd as well as scientifically invalid. The Behavior Clinic of the Criminal Court in Pittsburgh tried to link cannabis with crime. But a court study could only couple one case of indecent exposure to its use in a two-year period. Nonetheless, the report concluded: "It is surprising that . . . there were no more than this one case of Indecent Exposure which was secondary to Marihuana Intoxication, when we consider . . . that such a response is quite typical of Marihuana usage."[50] This type of article was not an isolated occurrence in the years from 1937 to 1941.

For a final example of the widespread disdain for scientific investigation and the concomitant dispersal of tales for the credulous, it is necessary to return to the head of the Federal Bureau of Narcotics. In the Missouri Peace Officers Association magazine in 1941, Anslinger retold the story of the Assassins of Persia. Then he drew upon human fears of animal "assassins": jackals, hyenas, and mad dogs. The commissioner asked:

> Do I overstate the case when I say that a more terrible enemy to society than a mad-dog is innocently growing up in every community, perhaps, in Missouri? It is the Marihuana weed within whose leaves and flowers lurks a poison that turns man into a wild beast, destroys his mind, his will, his morals, and his soul.

He claimed, too, that marijuana "is destroying so much of the manhood of the race."

The images were indeed fearful; and Anslinger concluded with another even richer in symbolism. On the derivation of "Indian hemp," another name commonly given marijuana, he said:

> From it the hangman's rope is woven—an instrument of death which criminals simply refer to as hemp. Many a human being has been hurled into eternity, his body dangling from a noose made of this noxious weed . . . Nothing better illustrates the end of him who dallies with Marihuana. Literally he is placing his neck in a noose, and just as literally will that noose strangle him.[51]

The stentorian character of the federally inspired and often directed campaign against marijuana overpowered dissent from the official position. The opposition that existed did not have similar access to the public as the Bureau of Narcotics. A comment by the Bureau of Legal Medicine of the AMA just before the tax act took effect therefore evoked no public or governmental reaction: "No evidence has been produced to show the extent of addiction to cannabis arising out of the medicinal use of the drug."[52]

Other scientific opinion of the time seemed to support and perhaps extend this conservative assessment. Assistant Surgeon General Lawrence Kolb acknowledged that unstable individuals probably did use marijuana, but noted that average, nonpsychotic people often smoked it as well. In 1938 Kolb still seemed uncertain about the relationship between marijuana and insanity, but denied that heavy use of it produced the same physical dependence as chronic opium use. He discounted, too, the causal link with criminal activity, stating that "the prevalent opinion that anyone who smokes a marihuana cigarette and becomes intoxicated by it will have criminal impulses is in error." He further felt that false comparisons between the opiates and marijuana should not be made to strengthen the case against cannabis. Concerning the penalties imposed by the 1937 law he stated: "Punishment beyond the confinement necessary to bring about cure is harmful rather than beneficial."[53] This statement reflects a continuing belief in marijuana addiction, but it also demonstrates Kolb's growing opposition to the punitive antimarijuana policies and practices advocated by the Bureau of Narcotics.

Concurrent research by Dr. Walter Bromberg raised serious questions about the addictive properties of marijuana. He asserted that the Beam Test, the means of chemically verifying through isolation the active principle in cannabis, had no scientific validity. He thus attributed any perceived schizophrenic characteristics in heavy users to existing psychological deficiencies rather than to a direct link between usage and observable psychoses. Marijuana did not constitute, in his opinion, a strong enough substance to satisfy psychopathic personalities. Finally, he concluded that the lack of excessive withdrawal symptoms probably indicated that marijuana was not habit-forming.[54] Echoing Bromberg's findings a short while later, Roger Adams of the University of Illinois noted: "It is impossible to predict the reactions in any particular subject. An exact knowledge of the intoxication of marihuana and its deleterious effects will have to await carefully controlled clinical experiments."[55]

Bromberg had the occasion to present his findings to Anslinger at a marijuana conference held in Washington in December 1938 at the behest of the Federal Bureau of Narcotics. Various experts gathered after Dr. Herbert Wollner, consulting chemist of the Treasury Department, convinced Anslinger that a meeting should be held to discuss the current state of research into the many aspects of the marijuana problem. Agricultural, chemical, industrial, sociological, pharmacological, and economic information was exchanged. Little substantive discussion took place, and it is worth noting that after Bromberg made his presentation the commissioner quickly changed the subject. The bureau apparently rejected even the tacit suggestion that its law enforcement program might not be the best means of controlling marijuana.[56]

Only briefly for many years thereafter would serious scientific research on cannabis be able to seize the initiative from the forces of ignorance. One such instance occurred in September 1942 when the *American Journal of Psychiatry* published a paper expanding on Bromberg's earlier findings. Two physicians, Samuel Allentuck and Karl Bowman, declared that a typical marijuana user did not exist. They stated that cannabis "will not produce a psychosis *de novo* in a well-integrated, stable person. In unstable users the personality factor and the mood preceding the ingestion of marihuana will color any psychosis that might result." Marijuana accentuated personality traits, both harmful and beneficent. "Marihuana itself does not give rise to antisocial behavior," Allentuck and Bowman concluded.[57] In a comment on the paper, Lawrence Kolb acknowledged that the case against marijuana had long been overdrawn. He praised the work of Allentuck and Bowman and called for additional research on the effects of cannabis. Kolb, too, found it reassuring that, in the absence of concrete, contrary evidence, the link between marijuana and crime had been severed.[58]

The reaction of the Bureau of Narcotics was immediate and predictable. In a letter to the editor of the *Journal of the American Medical Association*, Anslinger termed it most unfortunate that Allentuck and Bowman had sought to obscure the relationship between marijuana and physical, mental, and moral degeneration. In the words of the commissioner, the two physicians "are there treading on dangerous ground."[59] To a select audience, Allentuck and Bowman damaged the credibility of the antimarijuana campaign of the federal government. The government's reaction to the Allentuck-Bowman report demonstrates the difficulty of disseminating to a large audience views contrary to official dogma on marijuana.

An editorial published in *Military Surgeon* in July 1943 offered the opinion that "smoking of cannabis is no more harmful than the smoking of tobacco." The writer termed the 1937 legislation ill-advised since it emphasized "a problem that does not exist" and "it branded as a menace and a crime a matter of trivial importance."[60]

Much more controversial at the time was the so-called La Guardia Report. In 1938 Mayor Fiorello La Guardia commissioned the New York Academy of Medicine to undertake a sociological and scientific study of marijuana use. Thirty-eight physicians, psychiatrists, sociologists, chemists, and penologists conducted the study with the aid of New York's police, prison, and hospital officials.[61] The study was completed in March 1941, but federal pressure apparently delayed its release for three years. (In their paper on marijuana intoxication, Allentuck and Bowman acknowledged the assistance of the Mayor's Commission on Marihuana.)[62]

The study traced the background of the government's policy on cannabis, reconstructing the often unsophisticated mythology linking it with criminal activity. Next the study surveyed marijuana from several perspectives: extent of use; method of retail distribution; attitudes of users toward society and cannabis; connections between marijuana and eroticism, marijuana and crime, and marijuana and youthful offenses. Usage in New York was found to be restricted generally to Harlem and part of Broadway. Users did not enjoy steady employment and had no sense of guilt about using marijuana. Finally, attempts to tie marijuana to sexual activity or crime were judged to be unwarranted. For New York, marijuana constituted neither a social nor a medical problem. "The publicity concerning the catastrophic effects of marihuana smoking in New York is unfounded," the commission concluded.[63]

Unfavorable reaction to the report quickly appeared. One observer noted that a similar study in New Orleans "gave the impression that criminals were kidding the examiner, possibly with the hope of receiving more lenient treatment."[64] The AMA's journal termed the testing methods unscientific and pointed to one case of a youth allegedly suffering from mental deterioration caused by smoking marijuana after reading about the results of the study. "Already the book has done harm," the editorial intoned. By this editorial the AMA formally, if belatedly, joined with the Bureau of Narcotics in the attack on marijuana. The La Guardia study was likened to one prepared for the Army by Eli Marcovitz and Henry J. Myers. The journal proclaimed: "Public officials will do well to disregard this unscientific, uncritical study, and continue to regard marijuana as a menace wherever it is purveyed."[65]

Karl Bowman responded to the critique of the La Guardia report by noting that the journal of the AMA omitted reference to the sociological aspect of the study in which researchers lived within the same environment as marijuana users for more than one year. He also charged that the editors failed to read beyond what they wanted to discover in the report.[66] In a rejoinder to Bowman, Anslinger offered as supportive evidence for the government's position the findings of an authority from India, Dr. R. N. Chopra, regarding the relationship between cannabis (in this case potent hashish) and crime, and insanity.[67] The comparison was decidedly inexact since hashish in India was considerably stronger than marijuana in the United States. By 1945 though, the Bureau of Narcotics had not only federal law on its side in the campaign against marijuana, but also the prestige of the American Medical Association. Any dissent from the view of the government in the immediate future would be restricted to an even smaller audience than before. Anslinger could therefore ignore with impunity such evidence and cite without compunction patently false assertions about the effects of marijuana.[68]

David F. Musto has speculated that Anslinger either may not have actually believed the horror stories his bureau spread about marijuana after 1935,[69] or that he sought to mute nongovernmental publicity against cannabis because he felt that "the problem was under control in most of the nation's communities," and any contrary suggestion might embarrass the Treasury Department.[70] It is reasonable to conclude from the public record for the decade ending in 1945, and from the evidence adduced in these pages, that Anslinger actually did believe in the confluence of marijuana, insanity, crime, and addiction. Whether the problem was under control cannot be determined with precision.[71] The character of the government's antimarijuana efforts from 1937 to 1945 suggests that Anslinger remained uncertain about the effectiveness of his agency's enforcement practices.

The commissioner clearly brooked little dissent from the bureau's marijuana policies, but his excessive attention to that subject may have impeded governmental effectiveness in handling other drug-related matters. Commencing in 1938 and continuing for several years Representative John M. Coffee of Washington proposed a congressional investigation into the overall narcotic situation in the country. The Public Health Service was to conduct the inquiry.[72] Coffee contended that the Federal Bureau of Narcotics, having failed to reduce abuse or illicit commerce in drugs to an appreciable extent, should alter its law enforcement practices. He seemed to favor clinical dispensation of drugs to addicts. The congressman's proposals never reached the hearing stage; the bureau had too many elected allies.[73] If nothing else, Anslinger had become a skilled bureaucrat.

Yet, at least one private group shared Coffee's concerns. In 1939 the newly formed World Narcotics Research Foundation doubted the accuracy of the bureau's reports on addiction for 1938. A press release from the foundation observed that the report failed to mention New York City, which had more addicts than any other community in the nation, or the state of Pennsylvania, where 29,000 addicts had been denied drivers' licenses.[74] The foundation also claimed that there existed a 75 percent rate of recidivism among former patients at the Federal Narcotics Farm in Lexington, Kentucky.[75] Finally, the foundation went so far as to suggest that ignorance or incompetence in the Bureau of Narcotics may have inadvertently aided the underworld in supplying addicts with drugs. Coffee, too, attacked the government's treatment of addicts as poorly conceived: "Victims of narcotic addiction are not permitted to receive treatment like other sufferers. The question at issue is, 'Why are they not permitted this elemental right?'" At this same time bureau officials were debating whether the confinement of addicts at Lexington should be extended from one to five years before release.[76] Regarding the work of the World Narcotic Research Foundation, Anslinger commented that "the policy of the organization is contrary to the objectives of the Federal Government in controlling the traffic in narcotics."[77]

By 1940 the objectives of the Bureau of Narcotics were clearly expressed in the bureaucratic and attitudinal atmosphere surrounding the national campaign against marijuana. The bureau's autonomy in the formulation of public narcotic policy prevented any reconsideration of the prevailing philosophy of control. Harry J. Anslinger remained the final arbiter of a punitive, legalistic approach. Within the context of emerging governmental centralization and the paternalism of the New Deal, the presence of the 1937 Marihuana Tax Act served three general purposes: it perpetuated the existence of an already well-established federal drug law enforcement bureaucracy; it extended in the guise of liberal reform a continuing, repressive form of social control whose propriety would not soon be challenged; and it supported the formulation and execution of a foreign policy consistent with the domestic drug control objectives of the Federal Bureau of Narcotics.[78] This latter purpose seemed nowhere more evident or important than in United States–Mexican narcotic diplomacy from 1936 to 1940.

6   Control Across the Border

United States–Mexican narcotic diplomacy between 1936 and 1940 offers the most demonstrable example of the impact of Washington's antidrug policies on relations with other countries. In the early 1930s the governments in Mexico City and Washington, D.C. concluded two agreements providing for the exchange of information about drug traffic across their common border. By the middle of 1936, Treasury Department agents had undertaken operations in Mexico to gather additional information about smuggling activities. Although occurring on a limited basis, these operations took place without the concurrence of the administration of President Lázaro Cárdenas.[1] The increasing strain in relations between the two countries over petroleum, commercial policy, and other matters in the late thirties gave a greater importance to common antidrug efforts than they might have otherwise enjoyed. From 1936 to 1940 United States drug diplomacy threatened to exacerbate the sensitive state of affairs existing with Mexico and accordingly brought into question the reciprocal nature of the Good Neighbor Policy of the Roosevelt administration.[2]

In November 1936 Ambassador Josephus Daniels, acting as he sometimes did to lessen tension between the two countries, questioned the secrecy surrounding the presence of the Treasury agents in Mexico. In particular Daniels objected to the appearance in the Mexico City region of Alvin F. Scharff, the assistant supervising customs agent at San Antonio, Texas. The ambassador doubted that the presence of agents in Mexico without the knowledge of the government there served any useful purpose and might offend the Mexicans.[3]

The activities of the agents may have shown that United States officials were dissatisfied with the way Mexico was carrying out the agreements of 1930 and 1932.[4] The Mexican government, though, felt differently about the accords. On October 16, the *Weekly News Sheet*, published by the publicity department in the Ministry of Foreign Affairs, lauded the joint antinarcotic efforts of the two nations, and especially noted the reduction of smuggling through the port of Mazatlán.[5] (It should be noted that Daniels failed to verify the accuracy of the report during a discussion with José Siurob, chief of the Department of Public Health.[6])

Mexico seemed desirous of improving and expanding even further its activity against narcotics. In January 1937 Luis G. Franco, chief of the Alcohol and Narcotic Service of the Public Health Department, told Daniels that he wanted to meet with United States customs agents at a border city in order to alter the earlier agreements so that Mexican agents, if need be, could cross the border into the United States.[7] Narcotic authorities in Washington rejected the proposal, just as they had turned down a similar request some years before.[8] Border crossings by agents, it seemed, would remain a one-way proposition.

Although the Mexican officials failed to secure approval from the United States for border crossings, they took other steps to increase antidrug activity. Franco and Siurob favored strengthening sections of the national penal code dealing with illegal narcotics. Such a legislative process would take many months to complete, yet the situation demanded immediate attention. "Mexico is not only an important producer of drugs," the newspaper *El Universal* observed on February 25, "but . . . also the chief distributing center for this continent." The Public Health Department quickly expanded the scope of its activities beyond simply a legislative response to drug problems. A centralized narcotics administration was planned and set up under Siurob's direction. Broadly defined, the National Auxiliary Committee's responsibilities consisted of devising ways to eliminate illegal narcotic traffic in Mexico.[9] Soon after operations began in April 1937, *El Universal* reported that the committee was considering the creation of a national narcotic monopoly.[10]

These efforts under Siurob's direction elicited a generally favorable response from United States personnel in Mexico.[11] Their view soon changed, however. In at least two instances Daniels was unable to substantiate Mexican claims of success in handling drug-related problems. The matter of smuggling at Mazatlán has already been mentioned. He also could not verify a government assertion that the incidence of addiction in Mexico had fallen dramatically since 1935. In fact, a story in *Excélsior* reported a rise in drug abuse.[12]

Available evidence suggests that Mexico's antidrug activity was having little discernible effect upon domestic conditions. *Excélsior* commented that for the campaign to be successful both the federal constitution and penal code would require amending. Changes were especially necessary in the nation's prisons, where drug usage abounded.[13] Not everyone agreed that the newly formed national committee was the proper agency to handle the situation. Ángel de la Garza Brito, who headed the rural hygiene program, felt that either the Treasury or Interior Department should be in charge. He argued that as long as the Public Health Department controlled the antidrug effort, political rivalry would supersede effective action. The accuracy of this allegation seems doubtful. During 1937 Franco had achieved a cooperative relationship among various government bureaus, and thus strengthened Mexico's antinarcotic commitment and effort.[14]

While Mexico was endeavoring to improve its drug control program, United States officials were advocating passage of the 1937 Marihuana Tax Act. The Bureau of Narcotics therefore became interested in Mexico's marijuana policy. Through Daniels, Commissioner Anslinger learned that Mexico restricted the growing of marijuana, or hemp, for rope fiber without proper authorization.[15] In fact, Article 202 of the Mexican Health Code forbade the cultivation of Indian hemp. Other provisions of the code outlawed marijuana possession, sale, use, and any form of commerce.[16] Whether the restrictions were effective cannot be determined with any more precision for Mexico than for the United States. Manuel Tello, the Mexican representative to the OAC in Geneva, claimed that marijuana smoking took place primarily among the criminal elements in his country. *Excélsior* saw no reason to minimize marijuana's suspected dangers: "Many of the crimes of blood . . . are committed under the pathological influence of marihuana . . . The number is beyond count."[17]

Whatever the extent of cannabis usage or the effectiveness of

drug control, an administrative change in February 1938 interrupted the work of the Public Health Department. Siurob resigned
as department chief to become governor of the Federal District of
Mexico City, and Franco left the Federal Narcotics Service for a
position with the Ministry of Foreign Affairs.[18] These changes
ended the first phase of United States–Mexican narcotic diplomacy
between 1936 and 1940. While Mexico's attempts to enhance its
antidrug activity had not yet produced noticeable results, a process
was under way which presaged the government's being more critical of drug abuse. Just as promising from the United States point of
view was Mexico's desire to work more closely with Washington to
halt the northward flow of illegal substances. To that end, Siurob
and Franco had met in 1937 with H. S. Creighton, supervising
customs agent at San Antonio, to discuss coordinating their countries' antidrug efforts along the border.[19] But by the time the
Mexicans had left office, no formal plans had been agreed upon.

Leonidas Andreu Almazán succeeded Siurob at the Public
Health Department, and Leopoldo Salazar Viniegra took Franco's
place at the Federal Narcotics Service. Salazar had earned a good
reputation in Mexico as a result of his work with addicts in the
national mental health hospital.[20] Shortly after taking office, he
met with customs agent Creighton. Mexico, he stated, could only
reduce the flow of illegal drugs through government controlled
distribution, with the aid of an expanded antidrug educational
campaign, and through the construction of more hospitals to treat
addiction. Salazar did not underestimate the difficulty of the task.
"It is impossible to break up the traffic in drugs," he told Creighton, "because of the corruption of the police and special agents and
also because of the wealth and political influence of some of the
traffickers."[21] During the meeting Salazar mentioned that he did
not consider it his duty to act as a policeman in supervising drug
control activity.[22] In so doing, he implicitly warned that his policy
on control would probably not parallel that of the United States to
the same extent as his predecessors'.

Despite the obstacles he envisioned impeding effective drug
control, Salazar seems to have favored the continuation of cooperation with the United States. He requested the assistance of cus-

toms agents in the destruction of opium poppy fields growing in the states of Sonora and Sinaloa. An agent from Texas observed the burning of a number of fields in April.[23]

Such cooperative activity failed to prevent doubts about Salazar's antidrug commitment from arising within the United States. Before Salazar had completed two months in office, Creighton and Thomas H. Lockett, a commercial attaché serving in Mexico City, were complaining to José Siurob about the narcotic chief's lax attitude toward drug control. The charges against Salazar were unspecified, but the reason for the criticism must have stemmed from his approach to drug law enforcement.[24] Were Salazar to minimize the punitive aspect of his antidrug activity, Mexico's program for control would become markedly different from Washington's. (During deliberations over the Marihuana Tax Act, United States officials reiterated their belief in punitive treatment for the nonmedical and nonscientific use of drugs.[25])

Before the end of 1938 Salazar began to chart a course that produced further displeasure in Washington. Proposed revisions in the federal toxicomania regulations gave the Public Health Department the authority to establish methods of treatment for addicts and to create hospitals or dispensaries for their care. Entrance into the facilities would be voluntary. Most important, the regulations included a proposal calling for the formation of a state monopoly for the sale of drugs.[26]

In reaction, R. Walton Moore, counselor of the State Department, wrote Daniels that the contemplated change in regulations, particularly the provision for drug sale by the government, "occasions no little concern to authorities in the United States." Judging from the short-lived and disappointing experience with dispensing clinics nearly two decades earlier, officials in Washington concluded that implementation of the new Mexican regulations would inevitably lead to an increase in the illicit drug trade. As Moore put it, border dispensation would "nullify the efforts being made on the American side to suppress the abuse of narcotic drugs." In sum, ambulatory treatment of addiction, by placing drugs in the hands of addicts, would create the very situation officials in Washington believed led to illicit drug traffic. Only strict supervision of commerce in drugs and confinement of addicts could eliminate the trade.[27]

The disquiet Salazar was creating in the minds of United States officials increased further with the appearance of his article, "El Mito de la Marijuana." The fourteen-year study detailed widespread marijuana smoking by Mexico's lower classes, yet Salazar had not uncovered evidence of psychoses resulting from the use of cannabis. Any deleterious effects, he argued, were psychologically induced. He also claimed that marijuana usage did not provoke criminal impulses and in fact created fewer social problems than alcohol abuse. Salazar's doubts about the harmfulness of marijuana stood in sharp contrast to the position taken by the Bureau of Narcotics during discussions of the 1937 Marihuana Tax Act.[28]

Criticisms of Salazar's findings appeared at once. A derogatory editorial was published by *El Universal* on October 22. Two days later the paper printed an article by Manuel Guevara Oropesa, head of the Mexican Association of Neurology and Psychiatry, disputing Salazar's conclusions. Next, *Excélsior* reported that many officials in the Public Health Department also disagreed with the contentions in Salazar's article. For the United States, Consul General James Stewart suggested that ridicule would provide the best means of combatting "the dangerous theories of Dr. Salazar Viniegra." And Bureau of Narcotics chief Anslinger reiterated his agency's unequivocal opposition to marijuana by referring to it as "the deadly drug."[29] When the article appeared in the December issue of *Criminalia*, the editors felt compelled to print as a counterbalance to Salazar's piece an antimarijuana study completed in 1931. The view of marijuana presented in that article approximated the position of the Bureau of Narcotics.[30]

Salazar, supported by other research on marijuana in Mexico,[31] sought to refute his critics. The proposed alterations in the federal regulations, he explained, stemmed from the generally inefficient and often selective enforcement of prior antinarcotic laws in Mexico. Salazar, it seems, did not question the propriety of antidrug activity, but differed with other officials in his own country and the United States over the best way of fighting drug problems. He described all existing international agreements on narcotics, such as the 1931 Geneva Convention, as "practically without effect." Illegal drug traffic was "surreptitiously tolerated, if not encouraged, by those same countries which have agreed to suppress it." Thus Mexico, to reduce smuggling and control the domestic drug situation, would experiment with a relatively untested measure for control, the national narcotic monopoly.

Mexico's experience convinced Salazar that the solution to drug problems did not rest with the jailing of addicts or the expenditure of large sums from the national treasury to track elusive smugglers. He felt that United States antidrug efforts, for example, suffered from this overly punitive and costly approach. Salazar wanted governments to alter their traditional perceptions of addicts and addiction. This meant revising, he declared, "the concept of the addict as a blameworthy, antisocial individual."[32]

The United States was not prepared to make such a fundamental change in its drug control philosophy. Indeed, Salazar's position ran counter to Washington's foreign and domestic drug policies as developed during the previous twenty-five years. In the view of the United States, drugs were not to be dispensed for other than express medical and scientific needs. By adhering to this deceptively simple formula every nation would insure cooperation, in Anslinger's words, with "other nations in the common effort to prevent the abuse of narcotic drugs." As the country most concerned with effective drug control, the United States had the duty, Anslinger felt, to supervise the vigilance of other countries in the fight against narcotics.[33]

Such a self-appointed task would seem to suggest success by the United States in its own struggle with drugs. Salazar held that available information offered an opposite conclusion. Arguing that the incidence of recidivism remained high, he cited statistics indicating the withdrawal of more than three-fourths of the patients from a voluntary program at the federal narcotics hospital in Lexington, Kentucky. He also estimated that the thirteen hundred addicts interned as prisoners at Lexington for drug law violations represented barely 1 percent of the addict population in the United States. The remainder, he felt, had been virtually abandoned by the government to illegal drug merchants, the result of overly punitive narcotic policies.[34] By attacking the antidrug efforts of the United States, Salazar hoped to dissipate criticism of his own proposed regulatory changes.

Not content merely with a defense of his plans at home, Salazar had Manuel Tello elaborate upon the proposals at the May 1939 meeting of the Opium Advisory Committee meeting in Geneva.

Tello, after promising the continuation of Mexico's antidrug effort, reiterated Salazar's statement that addicts would only be able to acquire drugs from official dispensaries or state-licensed physicians. The principal reactions to Tello's remarks came from dubious United States and Canadian representatives who condemned drug dispensation schemes and advocated stricter supervision by Mexico of intercourse in narcotics. For the United States, Stuart J. Fuller asked Mexico to postpone for one year promulgation of the controversial regulations. Harry Anslinger, also in attendance, minced no words reminding Tello that drug addicts "were criminals first and addicts afterwards." He doubted as well whether Mexico's proposed action would be acceptable under the 1931 Geneva Convention. Tello responded by reading a letter from Salazar defending the changes, but promised nonetheless to convey to his government Fuller's request for a delay in their promulgation.[35]

The pressure put upon Salazar by foreign and domestic critics to alter the nature of his antidrug activity so that it would conform more closely to that of the United States led to his departure from the Public Health Department in August 1939. He was replaced by Heberto Alcázar, public health director of the Federal District. Also, José Siurob returned to his former position as head of the Public Health Department, taking the place of Almazán, who while in office played a subordinate role to Salazar.[36]

Consul General Stewart applauded the change in personnel, noting that the "weakness and indifference" of Almazán had allowed Salazar "to advance his wild theories regarding narcotics and narcotic addicts." A representative of the Rockefeller Foundation in Mexico, Charles A. Bailey, told Stewart that Alcázar was "a man who will do just what he is told and will follow the policy which Dr. Siurob will outline."[37] With Salazar's departure another phase of United States–Mexican narcotic diplomacy came to a close. Domestic disputes over his policies and contention with the United States over proposed drug law enforcement changes marked Salazar's eighteen months in office. His critics never tried to assess dispassionately the plans he hoped would improve antinarcotic activity in Mexico. As a result, he spent considerable time defending himself rather than putting his ideas into operation.[38] That a national narcotic monopoly would provoke controversy in the 1930s is undeniable; but that it contravened the 1931 Geneva Convention seems less certain, despite the assertions of United States officials to the contrary. Whether a monopoly would have successfully restricted illicit drug activity in Mexico at that time remains a moot issue.

The return to office of José Siurob seemed to promise a rebirth of Mexican–United States antinarcotic endeavors. Ambassador Daniels commented that under Siurob's earlier tenure relations had been cordial, but under Almazán "the spirit of cooperation was lacking." Siurob asked for a copy of the drug control regulations of the United States Public Health Service, and intimated to Daniels that he would like to establish in Mexico a control system similar to that found in the southern United States. Frequent talks with H. S. Creighton about drug law enforcement likely influenced Siurob's thinking on narcotic control.[39]

The American impact upon Siurob's antinarcotic beliefs became more evident in November in Mexico at the annual convention of the Pacific Coast International Association of Law Enforcement Officials. In an address to the gathering, Siurob depicted drug users in terms similar to those employed by United States officials. Addicts were individuals "constitutionally or educationally una-dapted to the struggle for life; the restless not satisfied with a straight and noble mode of living, . . . the weak minds seduced by mysterious and unknown pleasures." Drug usage demonstrated "deficiencies of will power." In concluding his remarks, Siurob praised the leading role of the United States in its continuing struggle with drugs.[40] His words suggested that he was intent upon promoting closer ties between Mexico City and Washington in their antidrug activities.

Siurob's address, although showing a firm commitment against addiction, belied the nature of the policy he would seek to enforce. Drug problems in Mexico ranging from individual usage to smuggling were producing much concern among officials in the health department. In an attempt to combat the situation, new drug regulations had been promulgated on October 23 prior to the convention of law officials, but surprisingly, these statutes were virtually the same as those put forth by Salazar Viniegra.[41]

Siurob hoped that the change in policy would not elicit an adverse reaction from Washington. He felt that cooperation in antinarcotic work between the two governments remained not only desirable, but possible. He continued to apprise United States representatives of progress in the campaigns against opium and marijuana.[42] Siurob then announced that he would attend a public health directors' conference scheduled for Washington in May 1940. He also asked Commissioner Anslinger to visit Mexico to discuss the training of narcotic agents in order to deal more effectively with smuggling.[43]

The Department of State favored a trip by Anslinger since a meeting "should result in a better understanding on the part of competent Mexican authorities of the aims and policies . . . being pursued by the United States." Daniels thought that March would be a good time for Anglinger's visit since it was shortly before the start of the public health conference in Washington.[44] On February 17, 1940, however, the trip and, more important, the Mexican–United States antidrug effort Siurob desired were seriously jeopardized. The new statutes creating a national drug monopoly and providing addicts with increased access to narcotics had finally taken effect.[45]

Anslinger at once informed the State Department that he would embargo all shipments of medicinal drugs to Mexico. A 1935 amendment to the Narcotic Drugs Import and Export Act of 1922 authorized such action by the commissioner. Under the law drugs could only be exported to countries for explicit medical and scientific purposes. This stipulation did not include the ambulatory treatment for addiction which Mexico was about to undertake.[46]

State Department officials had received advance information that the regulations would become law. To have taken no position on them would have constituted tacit acknowledgment that they were acceptable. Authorities in Washington's drug policy hierarchy could not allow this unless they intended to reexamine their own restrictive and punitive methods of control. No top-level official was prepared to do that.

To explicate his government's position on the Mexican regulations, Stuart Fuller prepared a lengthy memorandum. Mexico could call drug dispensation by physicians "medical use," he stated, but the United States found such a definition inconsistent with the meaning of the term defined in various international antinarcotic agreements. For instance, Fuller believed that the Permanent Central Opium Board in Geneva would regard drug dispensation through a national monopoly as a violation of the 1931 convention. No major country except Mexico was trying to handle its drug problem with a state monopoly. "The plan envisaged by the proposed legislation," Fuller wrote, "differs completely from those followed in all countries in the world which are parties to international narcotics conventions." Even if Mexican actions were "praiseworthy," he continued, supplying addicts with narcotics "merely for the purpose of satisfying their cravings could not be regarded by the Commissioner of Narcotics as otherwise than constituting distribution for abusive use. . . ."[47]

Anslinger's embargo on medicinal drug exports therefore coincided with the State Department's view, in Fuller's words, "of settled international policy." In sum, the commissioner could not issue export permits without breaking United States law and contravening the 1931 Geneva Convention. Anslinger followed the embargo with the cancellation of his trip to meet with Siurob.[48] But because officials in Washington hoped that the Mexican government might be induced to reverse its policy, no public statements were issued detailing United States opposition or Anslinger's actions.[49]

Mexico mildly protested the embargo, but no diplomatic rift occurred. In fact, Siurob tried hard to reconcile Mexico's differences with the United States. First, he met with Creighton to discuss ways of combating a recent increase in smuggling. One means considered by the two men was allowing health department officials to act as policemen in drug-related matters.[50] Next, in conversations with Daniels and Stewart on March 14 the public health chief made a compelling offer. Mexico, he observed, was prepared to suspend those portions of the new regulations found most objectionable by the United States. Siurob promised to seek suppression of the provision allowing drug dispensation to addicts by licensed doctors. As a gesture of reconciliation, he suggested the formation of a bilateral commission to study border narcotic problems. Siurob hoped that Anslinger would demonstrate a similar desire to settle the contentious matter. Throughout his discussions with Daniels and Stewart the Mexican official reiterated his commitment to a strong antinarcotic policy. His ultimate aim, he said, was to reduce domestic addiction and to render smuggling unprofitable.[51]

Daniels found merit in Siurob's plan to alleviate the dispute. The ambassador thought that his government might show some appreciation of Mexican intentions by suspending the prohibition on medicinal exports.[52] Siurob, Daniels noted, was "greatly disturbed and would like to find a way of cooperation." The Mexican even asked, without success, for an interview with Dr. Thomas Parran, Surgeon General of the United States Public Health Service.[53] As was often the case during his tenure in Mexico City, Josephus Daniels had again surpassed officials in Washington in his efforts to maintain good relations with Mexico. Anslinger's reply to Siurob's conciliatory offer provides a case in point. The commissioner matter-of-factly told Fuller that the proper way to determine legitimate drug usage was to ascertain if the usage was "lawful under international agreements," meaning—in the view of the United States—circumscribed medical and scientific use. Fuller and Anslinger found Siurob's offer too vague to warrant a more receptive response. The Treasury Department wanted to send the commissioner's blunt statement of policy to the Mexican government, but the Division of American Republics in the State Department quashed the idea, noting that "the memorandum . . . might also give offense."[54]

Herbert Bursley of State proposed a compromise which would let Siurob rescind the regulations and still maintain his integrity at home. Bursley felt that there should be no hint of pressure from Washington on Siurob. He volunteered to tell the Mexican consul that "it might be well for Dr. Siurob to announce that he cannot carry out his program because of the worldwide shortage of narcotics caused by the European war and that therefore he is suspending or cancelling the regulations in question."[55]

By the time Siurob arrived in Washington in May for the Fourth Congress of Health Directors of Pan-American Countries, he had done what he could to improve relations over narcotics with the United States. His temporary suspension of much of the new narcotic code left Public Health Department clinics as the sole dispensing stations in Mexico.[56] On May 4 and 7, prior to the opening of the meeting of the health directors, discussions about the Mexican drug control regulations took place. Present at the sessions for Mexico were Siurob and an English-speaking assistant, Dr. José Zozaya of the Institute of Hygiene in Mexico City. Anslinger, Fuller, Bursley, Dr. Lawrence Kolb, and John W. Bulkley of the Customs Bureau Division of Investigations and Patrol represented the United States.

Siurob found himself on the defensive during the first session. Implementing the regulations, he stated, concluded a process be-

gun before he took office. He personally felt that the action might
have been premature, although he noted that the new program
had achieved some success. For instance, the first Public Health
Department clinic in Mexico City placed under government care
over 700 of the 4,000 addicts in the capital. When Anslinger asked
who provided the remainder with drugs, Siurob agreed that they
probably obtained their drugs illegally. At the close of the session
the public health chief received from Anslinger a copy of the
memorandum in which the commissioner had tersely outlined the
United States conception of legitimate narcotic usage. Privately,
officials urged Zozaya, who concurred with their drug control philosophy, to explain further Washington's position to his superior.[57]

The problem was not that Siurob remained equivocal about his
stand against drug abuse. In his address to the Pacific Coast International meeting the previous fall, he displayed a resolve similar to
that of his counterparts in the United States. Rather, like Salazar
Viniegra, Siurob felt it worthwhile to explore a national narcotic
monopoly as a means of combatting illegal drug activity in preference to the less flexible system espoused in Washington. Mexican
officials were not as convinced as United States authorities that a
state monopoly would worsen the drug situation or that it violated
international agreements.

As the second session of the talks began in Fuller's office on May
7, Siurob had evidently reevaluated his position on the new regulations. "The Mexican regulations [are] entirely wrong," he declared, indicating that the drug control policy of the United States
was a more appropriate response to the existing problem. Siurob
promised immediate suspension of the regulations still in effect,
but warned that he could not publicize the policy change. The
sensitive nature of Mexican–United States relations, arising especially out of the petroleum disputes of the late 1930s, would leave
the government, in the midst of an electoral campaign, vulnerable
to charges that the United States, as Siurob put it, was "dictating
again."

The Mexican's fear of United States pressure and the reaction it
was likely to occasion had some basis in reality. Bureau of Narcotics
chief Anslinger closed the talks by telling Siurob that only formal
suspension of the controversial regulation would permit him to
resume authorizing drug exports to Mexico. With this declaration
the narcotic policy talks ended. In seeking an accommodation over

policy differences as Siurob and Daniels wished, the ˜˜exican
government made considerable concessions while th
States did little to reciprocate. In fact, Siurob was unab¹˙
from Anslinger and his colleagues even a verbal
cooperative activity in the important region a
Ciudad Juárez.[58]

The conclusion of the Washington discussion:
the final segment of United States–Mexican d
tween 1936 and 1940. The United States had be
attempt to get Mexico to reconsider the nature
policy. Future antinarcotic collaboration was likely to
along lines set forth by officials in Washington. As Herbe.. ᴊᴀ.ᴛᴏn
of the Treasury Department told Secretary Henry Morgenthau: "I
had a very pleasant conversation with Dr. Siurob and his associate
Dr. Zozaya . . . They are completely won over to our method of
handling the narcotics problem and ask our continued help and
advice." Gaston concluded: "This is a notable victory for Harry
Anslinger."[59] Anslinger's sense of achievement must have increased
two months later on July 3 when *Diario Oficial* published a decree
suspending indefinitely the February regulations. Thereafter,
Mexican addicts would be dealt with under the more punitive
statutes of September 1931.[60]

José Siurob, who held ultimate responsibility for the care of
Mexico's addicts, may have had misgivings about the outcome of
the talks in Washington. Shortly after his return home, but before
publication of the governmental decree, he wrote Creighton and
attributed the change in policy directly to the discussions. Creighton's reply referred to "*your conclusions* with respect to the control
of illicit narcotics in Mexico."[61] On the same day that he wrote
Siurob, Creighton sent the following note to Washington and enclosed copies of the two letters:

> Realizing the position the Bureau [of Narcotics] has taken
> with Dr. Siurob, I am very happy to now have the letter of
> June 17th in which he states that he has finally come to
> recognize the inefficacy of their experiment to control narcotic
> drugs by administering same directly to the addicts. While I
> believe that Dr. Siurob has taken this position now because of
> the manner in which the situation was presented to him while
> in Washington, you will observe from the enclosed that I am

trying to convince him that he has made this change of his own volition.[62]

The publication of the decree rendered moot whatever second thoughts Siurob may have entertained about the change in policy.

Between 1936 and 1940 the United States had successfully reshaped Mexican narcotic policy. Nominally, it would conform more closely to the legalistic-punitive policy espoused and followed by the United States. The exertions of Anslinger, Fuller, and their colleagues helped force from office a dedicated public servant, Leopoldo Salazar Viniegra. Moreover, since their actions led to intervention in Mexican affairs, the reality of the professed Good Neighbor Policy of the Roosevelt administration must in this instance be brought into question. Had the drug control program of the United States been measurably more effective than it apparently was, the interference with Mexican policy might have been more understandable if no less objectionable from Mexico's point of view. Such was not the case, however.

Throughout the 1930s officials in Washington arrogated to themselves a leading position in hemispheric activity. Because of the lengthy history of paternalism toward Latin America and as a result of Mexico's proximity to the United States, this self-delegation of leadership and assumption of moral superiority led to intervention in Mexican affairs. Anslinger and others never questioned the propriety of that interference. In the context of the disputes between the two countries in the late 1930s, the politics and diplomacy of drug control could have exacerbated an already sensitive situation. That it did not do so is testimony to the antinarcotic commitment of José Siurob and his desire, along with that of Josephus Daniels, to reach an accommodation over the narcotic policy differences between their two governments.

7   A Window on the Future

The efforts of the United States that worked so well in getting Mexico to alter the nature of its drug control program would not prove similarly successful elsewhere in the hemisphere, particularly in Honduras, Bolivia, and Peru. These nations were far less receptive to diplomatic overtures from Washington. For reasons already adduced at some length, restrictive controls on drugs, whether on production, manufacture, or commerce, were not likely to be adopted and enforced in the latter part of the 1930s. The prospect of stricter controls, for which the United States held high hopes early in the decade, nearly disappeared. At best, meager efforts were made toward a now elusive goal: effective drug control. In reality, the priorities of the three nations in question (not to mention Argentina and others) lay elsewhere.

Accordingly, the United States did not overtly pressure nations in South America to bring their drug control programs into closer conformity with that espoused in Washington. To a great extent, the threat to American citizens did not seem as direct as that emanating from Mexico. It was rarely possible, for example, to trace Peruvian cocaine, let alone Bolivian, through legitimate or illicit channels until it found its way illegally into the United States. Since some of the responsibility for the spread of illicit cocaine no doubt rested with European manufacturing nations, Peru and Bolivia were even less amenable to outside pressures. In the existing situation, only rigid production controls would have helped to meliorate conditions, and they were out of the question. Only in

Central America, and especially in Honduras, did the United States show much interest in scrutinizing the course of narcotic control. Extensive smuggling from the area constituted a problem which authorities in Washington could not afford to ignore.

In January 1936, the *Boletín de la Oficina Sanitaria Panamericana* asserted that the government of Peru was inattentive to domestic drug problems. At a national narcotic hospital the needs of addicts allegedly were ignored and treatment for them was inadequate. Although the figure was probably not extensive, the government could not even estimate the number of addicts in Peru.[1] (There is no indication whether the *Boletín* considered coca chewers addicts.) There seemed to be no prospect of immediate improvement in the situation. The journal suggested it was more probable that conditions would worsen.

Travel magazine also charged that the government was not trying to lessen drug abuse, especially coca leaf chewing. It was believed that nearly three-fourths of all Peruvians chewed coca leaves on occasion. The magazine claimed, too, that most of the soldiers in the national army chewed excessive amounts of coca daily. As we have previously seen, such may not have been the case. The author wrote of the Peruvian Indians: "While many are moderate users, most are constantly stupefied with cocaine and alcohol."[2]

Desirous of limiting coca production and hoping to induce stronger antinarcotic activity by the government, *El Comercio*, a leading Lima newspaper, called for improved treatment for addicts. The paper suggested a renovation of the program at the national narcotic hospital.[3] Any change in narcotic policy would of course entail social and economic costs for Peru. As a way of minimizing the effects of a lessened dependence upon coca, *El Comercio* advocated that "the cultivation of coca be replaced by other [crops] that can give more satisfactory yields to the farm owners and which, from the sanitary point of view, do not offer dangers to our population."[4] The government evidently did nothing at the time to investigate the feasibility of substitute crops.[5]

Peru made a couple of inconsequential regulatory changes regarding coca and cocaine. Late in 1937 the director general of public health assumed full control over the internal transit of coca leaves destined for manufacture into cocaine. It should be noted that production limitations were never intended to be a part of this administrative change. In fact, the Sociedad Nacional Agraria advised against it.[6] In a related development in December 1939 the government suspended the issuing of new licenses for the manufacture of raw cocaine until pertinent regulations of the Department of Public Health, Labor, and Social Welfare could be revised.[7] This directive was issued after large quantities of raw Peruvian cocaine appeared in Europe. A potentially major step toward reevaluation of national coca policy came in 1940 with the creation of the National Institute of Andean Biology. The institute was empowered to study the effects of high altitude and rarified air on habitual coca leaf chewers.[8]

Shortly after the institute began operating, the Department of State in Washington received information suggesting that Peru intended to establish a national monopoly to supervise all commerce in drugs, especially cocaine. The United States, as we have seen, traditionally opposed narcotic monopolies. Yet officials in Washington also consistently encouraged Latin American governments to undertake more rigorous drug control measures, something a national monopoly might conceivably do. Putting aside its philosophical reservations about the monopoly, the State Department therefore endeavored to determine if coca leaves were to be included, if opium smoking was to be legalized, and if the monopoly included control of the importation of manufactured drugs.[9] Concern about the monopoly by the United States proved to be premature when the Ministry of Foreign Affairs informed Ambassador R. Henry Norweb that no plan to create a monopoly was then under consideration.[10]

In sum, Washington did not try to exert direct influence over the course of drug policy in Peru in the late 1930s, remaining content to receive information about government activities. Coca chewing constituted a domestic phenomenon unresponsive as always to external demands for change. Also, as a result of the war in Europe, the amount of Peruvian cocaine in illicit international channels after 1939 was insufficient to worsen drug problems in the United States. By 1940, Peru could control its own drug situation to an extent acceptable to American officials. Perhaps most important of all, the existence of the National Institute of Andean Biology seemed to promise an ultimate reassessment of the role of coca in Peruvian society.

Given the history of United States efforts as early as 1912 to induce Peru to adopt a strict drug control program, the reasons for diplomatic detachment on the eve of 1940 are not readily discernible. Several factors help to clarify the situation. Although it cannot be proven, it may be true, as the Bureau of Narcotics reported, that the flow of Peruvian cocaine slowed to a trickle in the late 1930s. If that actually occurred, then the coca-planting crisis and malaria epidemic of 1936 in the Indian sierra may have had more serious consequences than available evidence suggests.[11]

We should remember also that the Good Neighbor Policy in the latter half of the decade turned toward protecting the hemisphere against ideological and economic penetration by Nazi Germany and its allies. Beginning with President Roosevelt's speech at the Inter-American Conference for the Maintenance of Peace and War in December 1936 at Buenos Aires, the United States sought to create an environment in which the American republics would be, as the president declared, "wholly prepared to consult together for our mutual safety and our mutual good." Increasingly, the United States perceived the Nazi threat as imminent. By the Munich crisis in September 1938, repelling Nazi influence in the hemisphere became the primary objective of the Good Neighbor Policy. As Fredrick B. Pike has concluded, the policy had "as a conscious decision of its planners, taken on an interventionist aspect that bore some parallel to the sort of moral crusade that Woodrow Wilson had sought to wage in the Caribbean." The Declaration of Lima, issued in December 1938 at the close of the Eighth Pan-American Conference, and the Declaration of Panama of October 1939, further refined the consultative process and added, under the guise of reciprocity, to United States domination of hemispheric affairs. [12]

Although direct evidence is insufficient to prove the contention conclusively, one can argue reasonably that the holding of an inter-American conference in Lima in 1938 served United States objectives in several ways. Peru had consistently been wary of Germany's intentions in the Americas. With the exception of Argentina, the conferees at Lima went a long way toward uniting the American republics against Nazi subversion. Common cause in the coming international ideological conflict had other important effects. Throughout much of Latin America, it strengthened the hold on power of conservative, even authoritarian governments. While the resulting stability no doubt contributed to hemispheric security, it also limited the scope of domestic social programs. In Peru, limitations meant, first of all, virtual inattention to the needs of Indians, as was true of the regime of Oscar R. Benavides until he relinquished his hold on power at the end of 1939. His successor, Manuel Prado y Ugarteche, was more committed to the social integration of the Indian *communidades*. Prado, it should be noted, had the relative luxury of wartime prosperity within which to develop his Indian policy. The activities of the National Institute of Andean Biology in its earliest years should be seen in this light.[13] However indirectly, political stability therefore contributed to the attainment of American goals, whether in the larger sense of inter-American security or in the more restricted realm of antidrug policy.

Elsewhere in Latin America in the late 1930s, there was only intermittent activity against drugs. Argentina and Bolivia were urged to adopt stricter controls, but failed to do so. In fact, the Argentine province of Jujuy, attempting to regulate the commerce in coca, may have actually insured a plentiful supply of quality coca for its Indian laborers.[14] At the same time in Bolivia a debate was taking shape among medical and scientific researchers over the efficacy of coca use. Existing scientific findings tended to support el coqueo as a harmless activity. One dissenting report, however, stated that the League of Nations ought to recommend that coca usage be restricted solely to medical purposes. It also noted that claims of coca's ill effects were having no influence in curbing its use by the Indian population; coca chewing remained an integral part of Bolivian tradition. Then in an apparent contradiction of its major recommendation, the report recommended that it would be in Bolivia's interest to expand coca production in order to aid a sluggish economy and serve medical needs at the same time.[15]

Coca chewing was even advocated as a social good. Dr. German Orosco asserted that coca use did not "provoke the euphoria, sexual excitement, or depression" that some critics claimed. He rejected, too, the argument that coca debilitated the Indian population physically and mentally. On the contrary, he insisted, coca chewing created a source of energy (which no expert denied), thus helping Indians who had to work in the highest reaches of the Andes.[16] By 1940 the government of Bolivia was considering the establishment of a coca monopoly, but ultimately decided against it because of fears of an attendant price increase on coca for domestic use.[17]

Unlike other South American countries, Uruguay alone had

strengthened its drug control program during the 1930s. A national monopoly was operating there by the autumn of 1937. The government and its licensees controlled the import, export, and distribution of all drugs, as well as the business operations of pharmacies and laboratories.[18]

Despite the lack of strict administrative controls, with the exception of coca chewing by Andean Indians the level of drug usage in South America remained low around 1940. Moreover, raw cocaine from Peru and Bolivia probably did not contribute much to the diminished illicit international trade. There did not exist, as previously indicated, sufficient reason for the United States to become as involved with drug control in South America as in Mexico. At least by implication, officials in Washington acknowledged the difference in the two situations. By the end of 1939 the United States had informed the Permanent Central Opium Board in Geneva that it would supply legitimate narcotic needs to South America since the presence of war in Europe had cut off the usual sources of supply. The United States would not have taken this step if narcotics from South America had been contributing to the drug problem in this country.[19]

Drugs in Central America posed a far greater threat. Governments there proved incapable, if not unwilling, to combat the continuous smuggling and intrigue. Throughout the 1930s illicit narcotic traffic was like a swollen river running northward to the United States. In Panama and the Canal Zone, for instance, large quantities of illegal drugs were continually being smuggled from Europe and the Far East. However much they tried, the Panamanians were not able to cope with the situation.[20] Heroin and marijuana were the drugs causing the most problems for U.S. Army and Canal Zone officials.[21]

The United States frequently tried to curb the flow of drugs out of Central America. Before its antismuggling vessels were withdrawn in 1936, the Coast Guard patrolled the southern coastal waters of this country. Thereafter, the government utilized other means, such as aircraft, to track smugglers on the sea and in the air. Smuggling aboard private planes presented the greatest obstacle to effective control after 1935. As Stuart Fuller told the Opium

Advisory Committee in 1938: "Aerial patrols operate regularly in the areas adjacent to the Mexican border. Sufficient additional aircraft are detailed to meet particular situations as they arise."[22] The implicit claim of success of the air patrols in Fuller's statement did not coincide with the reality of unchecked smuggling between Honduras and the United States. The first few years of the decade, it should be recalled, witnessed extensive illegal activity centering upon the machinations of José María Guillen Velez.[23]

As Guillen's intrigues became more irregular, other drug problems quickly appeared. The subsequent narrative and analysis revolves around an exposition of the major impediments to effective drug control in the middle to late 1930s. The identifiable obstacles are the following: the lack of implementation of international controls; the economic and political priorities of the government of Tiburcio Carías Andino; the limited power of the United States to reduce illicit drug traffic from Honduras during the decade; and the unreliability of information on illicit usage and commerce.

Unlike Mexico and South America, the situation in Honduras was anarchic, the possibilities for smuggling extreme; negligible counterforce existed to overcome these obstacles. With no possibility for cooperative, preventive action, the United States could only respond to conditions in Honduras belatedly and with little effect.

As early as June 1933 the United States Treasury Department began to look into the activities of Raymond J. Kennett, who was serving as manager of the La Ceiba (Honduras) branch of a United States firm, the Huber-Honduras Company. Narcotic agents arrested Kennett in New Orleans after buying illegal drugs from him. The Huber company was evidently acting as an intermediary in the narcotic pipeline from Germany to North America, although actual complicity was never proved. The Treasury Department felt that the operation could not be carried on as successfully as it was without the involvement of prominent Hondurans.[24]

A representative of the United States in La Ceiba, Lawrence Higgins, told his superiors that the head of the firm, Edwin E. Huber, a United States citizen, was "a thoroughly disreputable character" acting in the guise of a modestly successful but honest businessman. Higgins claimed that Huber had supplied guns and ammunition to the rebel leader Augusto Sandino in Nicaragua and had personally supervised the shipment of materiel from El Salvador. Narcotic smuggling purportedly originated, Higgins maintained, from the company's offices in San Salvador and Tegucigalpa. Higgins also believed that Huber might have fled the United States as a result of an undisclosed law violation.[25] Upon learning of Kennett's arrest, Huber showed surprise and expressed disappointment in his employee. Huber's role in the illicit traffic remains uncertain, but the reaction of Vice Consul Warren Stewart to the situation accurately depicted the state of affairs in Honduras. "There is no doubt in my mind," he said, "that La Ceiba is a distributing point for narcotics of all kinds."[26]

United States antismuggling efforts alone could not be successful in Honduras. Customs agents at this time were experiencing trouble in detecting illegal drug shipments; traffickers often smuggled their wares to the United States in bales of returned merchandise. This ruse worked because customs inspectors were not likely to scrutinize returned and presumably unopened goods.[27]

By March 1934 Kennett had returned to Honduras after serving a brief jail sentence in New Orleans. The State Department requested the American minister there, Julius Lay, to submit reports about any conceivable smuggling operations involving Kennett.[28] Lay was unable to link Kennett, however, to the excessive drug shipments to Honduras reported by the League of Nations. As always, accurate information on narcotics was difficult to obtain. Lay blamed official corruption for making his task so arduous, and lamented the lack of domestic narcotic regulations.[29]

Kennett next was implicated temporarily in the July 1935 murder of Dr. Francisco Sánchez. Sánchez had refused to forge import certificates and had threatened to expose the involvement of several government officials in the narcotics trade. Allegedly involved in the smuggling operations were General Abraham Williams, Honduran Vice President and Minister of Government, who by the end of 1936 would be serving as Director of Public Health; and Vicente Williams, the Honduran Consul General at New Orleans. Two other members of the group reportedly had made numerous trips between Honduras and New Orleans: Guy R. Maloney, a self-styled soldier of fortune, and Isidore Slobotsky of the Star Furniture Company of New Orleans. Also involved with the group were Lowell Yerex, owner of the cargo airline Transportes Aéreos Centro-Americanos (TACA), and Kennett, who had gone to work for Yerex after severing his connection with the Huber brothers.[30] None of the six was arrested and charged at the time of the killing.

Soon thereafter the State Department asked its Central American representatives to watch Kennett's movements more closely. The surveillance was to last for thirty days beginning on October 1. Kennett spent two weeks in Guatemala trying to conclude a business deal whereby TACA would assume control of the Guatemalan national airline, Compañía Nacional de Aviación.[31] By the end of the month, after apparently failing in his mission, he had met with Yerex in Mexico City. From there he returned to Guatemala by way of Tegucigalpa. Following a brief stop in Guatemala he was off again, this time to Managua, Nicaragua. By then the State Department ordered the surveillance continued into December. But the rewards of the supervision were negligible. Washington's representatives had limited resources with which to uncover any clandestine purpose for Kennett's travels.[32]

Even as Kennett's movements were being charted, the State Department was still attempting to locate the large quantities of narcotics Guillen Velez imported a few years earlier. Customs agents had seized some of the contraband as it reached the United States, but many kilograms of morphine remained unaccounted for. The legation in Tegucigalpa gave up hope of uncovering additional quantities of morphine until after the national elections scheduled for October 1936. Foreign Minister Antonio Bermúdez disclaimed all official responsibility for his government, pointing out that Guillen received the drugs in the final days of the administration of Vicente Mejía Colindres, who left office in February 1933. Still missing, as it turned out, were twenty-four kilograms each of heroin, morphine, and cocaine.[33] Without the help of the Honduran government the United States had only a limited ability to act in this situation. To officials in Washington, Bermúdez's explanation must have seemed disingenuous, a validation of the various charges of government corruption. For his part, the foreign minister may have been depicting accurately conditions his government was powerless to change.

In any event, drug smuggling continued and details regarding some of the alleged participants became clearer. In September 1935, suspicion surrounding the participation of Yerex, Kennett, and the others in the murder of Dr. Sánchez had been removed following the arrest of several men in connection with a seizure of drugs in New Orleans.[34] Soon thereafter it was learned that Kennett had received a reduced sentence on his drug law violation through the intercession of Guy Maloney, now described as a former New Orleans police chief. After drifting south from the states, Maloney worked as the Honduran government's arsenal inspector. Yerex cast further suspicion on himself when it was learned that he had been in New Orleans at the time of Kennett's trial and had asked Maloney to intercede. Moreover, Yerex's reputed wealth could not have been based upon profits from TACA's business, for the airline had only been operating since 1932. Kennett, it is worth noting, became TACA's traffic manager upon his release from jail. Central American drug traffic in the mid-thirties often proceeded from contacts in Nicaragua and El Salvador to the United States after passing through the transit points of La Ceiba and Puerto Cortés, Honduras. The suspected receiver for many of the illicit shipments in New Orleans was Isidore Slobotsky, the local TACA agent.[35]

Authorities in Washington launched an investigation in December trying to clarify the seeming complicity of Yerex and his associates in the smuggling business. Yerex somehow learned of the inquiries and protested that he had hired Kennett "to give him another chance." As the investigation continued, Yerex reportedly visited a Captain d'Arcy, the skipper of a vessel believed to be transporting narcotics from Central America. Just after Yerex's visit, d'Arcy's ship left Honduras for New Orleans. This portion of the investigation uncovered no evidence conclusively substantiating the involvement of Yerex or others in smuggling operations.

Even verifiable information disclosed little about the illegal trade in narcotics. Specifically, Yerex and Slobotsky had conferred several times in New Orleans between 1933 and 1936. Since Slobotsky served as TACA agent there, the talks were not unusual in themselves. Yet, according to the government's investigation, the Star Furniture Store did not appear to conduct a profitable business. In March 1936, the final month of the investigation, the store served only a few customers in person. Outgoing mail business was brisk and there was a large amount of incoming mail, especially from TACA in Honduras. What made the situation peculiar for a mail order house, if that term fairly describes the Star Furniture Store, was that the owner did not advertise his business in the local papers.[36] Despite what was known or could be reasonably suspected about the link between TACA and smuggling, the investigation made little headway. In fact, the State Department ordered all surveillance of the TACA group curtailed for a time.[37] The resources of the United States government in 1936 were simply not sufficient to cope with illegal narcotic activity in Central America.

Another reminder of the limits of American ability to alter conditions in Honduras reappeared that same year. In March, José María Guillen Velez led an invasion in an abortive attempt to prevent the Constitutional Assembly from meeting. The Assembly was preparing to consider a new constitution which, among other things, extended the term of President Carías to January 1943. (The politics of *continuismo* were later employed to keep Carías in power until 1949.) The security of tenure in office provided an atmosphere of stability out of which Carías could pursue his primary political goal: domestic peace through suppression of revolutionary discord. This objective placed Carías in line with the evolving security emphasis of the Good Neighbor Policy. Testifying as it were to this congruence was the monitoring by United States representatives of suspected anti-Carías activity in 1936 and 1937.

After Guillen's invasion failed, he fled to the United States seeking support for future intrigues. Guillen surfaced in Tampa on November 21, 1936, where customs officials interrogated him, searched his luggage, and subsequently shadowed his movements. At one point it was learned that Guillen hoped to obtain rifles to use in another coup attempt planned for early 1937.[38]

Guillen soon left Florida for New Orleans where he stayed only briefly before leaving for Progreso, Mexico on January 9, 1937. H. S. Creighton, the chief customs agent in Texas, believed that Guillen wished to trade illicit drugs for guns and ammunition. Creighton may have been right. The Mexican government soon seized an ammunition and gun cache on a ship anchored near the island of Cozumel. This setback ended Guillen's revolutionary dreams. As noted earlier, the State Department discovered that Guillen would have become acting president of Honduras if rebel forces had succeeded in ousting the Carías government.[39]

As the Guillen affair was ending, the Bureau of Narcotics acquired information suggesting that a Honduran diplomat was smuggling narcotics into Panama on TACA planes. The source also claimed that President Carías Andino authorized the operation.[40] These allegations remained unverified, but earned for TACA earlier suspicions about its smuggling activities. Kennett, too, resurfaced as a key figure. Lowell Yerex apparently paid Kennett only $300 per month, but Kennett lived more luxuriously than such a salary warranted. His business endeavors included substantial transactions on the New York Stock Exchange. This discovery led customs and narcotics officials to inspect his bank records in Cincinnati, Ohio; but, as before, no conclusive evidence of questionable activity turned up.[41]

Another cloud of suspicion appeared over TACA in April when Harold A. White, vice president and general manager since the airline's inception, resigned alleging TACA's involvement in the illegal drug trade. White promised further revelations upon his return to the states. Arriving in Los Angeles he told customs agent Rae Vaeder that Yerex had forced him to sell his TACA stock. White also named Kennett as prominently connected with drug smuggling, along with Captain d'Arcy, Slobotsky, Maloney, and Yerex.[42]

White had scant factual support for his charges, however. Suspicion surrounding Yerex and his associates again subsided temporarily. It later appeared that White's allegation may have arisen out of personal pique against Yerex over the forced sale of White's TACA stock. By April 1938 White wanted to return to his former, increasingly profitable firm. Thus he shared Yerex's wish to clear his airline's name. In fact, Yerex went as far as to suggest that the Department of State send an undercover agent to work in TACA offices. In sum, United States officials had made no progress in their effort to detect the source of drugs smuggled from Honduras. They could not rely upon White's information or allegations, one of which claimed that TACA's competitors were behind the stories linking the airline with drugs.[43]

An examination of the information we have may better explain White's actions. First, White's association with TACA from its inception is clear. Second, TACA's support for President Carías since his election in 1932 is also a matter of record (see n. 30). Third, the participation of United States citizens in counterrevolutionary activity is documented, too. Fourth, as of November 1937, Harold A. White, formerly of TACA, had replaced another American national as the director of the Escuela Militar de Aviación.[44] Given the previously close relationship between the Honduran government and various TACA personnel, all of this casts doubt on the credibility of the reputed disaffection between White and Yerex. It also suggests that President Carías was more in control of Honduran domestic affairs than was apparent to foreign observers.

The troublesome affair seemed about to reach a conclusion in June 1938. Yerex and White met with John W. Bulkley of the Customs Agency Service and George A. Morlock of the Division of Far Eastern Affairs in the State Department. At the meeting Yerex discounted Slobotsky's complicity in drug smuggling, claiming that Slobotsky did not need the money. Yerex also said that he possessed no information implicating Kennett in any illicit activity. Yerex further noted that he worked in the same office with Kennett, but would not hesitate to dismiss him from TACA if incriminating evidence appeared. Bulkley, in turn, told Yerex that the Customs Agency Service could not use a secret agent to investigate TACA in Honduras. Customs officials did not favor such a course of action. Even if they had, approval from the Carías government for the presence of the agent would have been doubtful. Minimizing the need for an agent, Bulkley pointed out that no seizures of drugs emanating from Honduras had occurred recently.[45]

Bulkley's logic followed that of other officials in the United States at the time. That is, when smuggling operations were uncovered and reported by the Bureau of Narcotics, the government would claim success in its endeavors. Conversely, what they did not find did not exist, at least not to an appreciable extent. In the case of TACA, however, the burden of the evidence, reliable as well as alleged, seemed to indicate a close relationship between the airline and illicit drug commerce. TACA's actual complicity may be beside the point.

"Chaotic" seems to be the best term to describe the drug control situation in Central America in the 1930s. Without a large, multi-national antidrug effort, legally constituted authorities were at a great disadvantage. For reasons discussed in earlier chapters, Harry J. Anslinger and his colleagues had difficulty admitting the limitations of their particular style of drug control. The accommodation with Yerex that came out of the June meeting may be seen as a practical, if disingenuous way of handling a situation which remained fundamentally unchanged.

As a result of the meeting, the Treasury Department promised to halt all surveillance of Yerex's activities whenever he came to the

United States. Also, the State Department agreed to refrain from giving an unfavorable impression about TACA in Central America.[46] The decisions in Washington helped to strengthen further the Carías regime. The government needed the facilities of TACA in order to maintain the domestic economy at an acceptable level. By 1939, statistics were encouraging. Exports stood at $9.9 million, far below the 1929 level but $2.5 million above the previous year. It was also the first year since the start of the depression that exports exceeded imports. Notably, trade with the Axis powers in 1939 accounted for less than 2.5 percent of all Honduran exports, and less than 18 percent of all imports. By then, as Alton Frye has pointed out, Nazi Germany was questioning the efficacy of its trade with Central America. President Carías, it seems, was keeping his 1936 pledge to strengthen Honduran ties with the United States. In a related context, William K. Jackson, vice-president of the United Fruit Company, summed up the situation: "The greater the development of our trade relations with Latin America, the lesser will be their [sic] dependence and ours upon the whims of some European dictatorial ruler."[47]

Subsequent to the talks with Bulkley and Morlock, Yerex evidently decided to sever connections with Kennett. The split was slow in coming despite reports that Eugene LeBaron, long associated with the United Fruit Company, would assume Kennett's duties with TACA.[48] The change promised to be an important one for the airline. On March 13, 1939, Nicaragua signed a ten-year contract with TACA for cargo service. TACA also held concessions in Guatemala, El Salvador, and, of course, Honduras. The transaction therefore signified a notable gain for TACA in its acrimonious competition with Pan-American Airways for shipping business in Central America. The agreement contained a crucial proviso, though. As the *New York Times* reported: "The contract can be canceled because of smuggling, failure to maintain schedules, or transporting war materials for revolutionists."[49] Kennett's continuing employment with TACA would seem to have made the company's financial future unnecessarily risky.

Kennett was still working for TACA late in the year as head of a branch office in Costa Rica.[50] As had been the case for some time, the burden of proof fell on Yerex to demonstrate that his airline was not involved in the smuggling trade. A meeting between Bulkley, Stuart J. Fuller, and Eugene LeBaron, then serving as TACA's general counsel, did not help matters. In the course of the discussion LeBaron mentioned that Kennett's stay in jail for the narcotic law violation in New Orleans had been just one day and that he had paid a fine of five dollars. The usual jail term for a similar offense in Louisiana in the early 1930s was five years. Fuller subsequently told LeBaron that it was TACA's responsibility alone to alter its poor image. The State Department would lend no assistance because of the airline's questionable record throughout the decade. Fuller said that he doubted any change would take place as long as Kennett stayed on the payroll. LeBaron responded that Kennett did not pose a problem. On the contrary, El Salvador had declared him an unwelcome visitor and suspicion about the link between TACA and smuggling prevented the expansion of business to Panama. LeBaron made no promises, but said he would speak to Yerex about Kennett.[51]

In July 1940, seven months later, LeBaron notified Fuller that TACA had finally broken all ties with Kennett. The airline was prospering greatly in the Central American cargo business by that time. After nearly seven years of attempting to uncover Kennett's role, if any, in the illicit drug trade, United States officials had little to show for their efforts.[52] Information about Kennett consisted of speculation and largely unverifiable allegations. Suspicion surrounding his activities tainted the reputations of his business associates, perhaps with justification. Available evidence, however, does not support any verifiable conclusions about the relationship between Kennett, TACA, and smuggling. What is clearly discernible from the entire episode is the difficulty United States officials faced in promoting effective narcotic control abroad. Policymakers in Washington did not possess the means to bring to Honduras the style of control they desired. Yet it was difficult for these ardent men to acknowledge the limits of their own power. Harry Anslinger, Stuart Fuller, and their colleagues tended to ignore the bureaucratic, diplomatic, cultural, and even economic obstacles preventing the realization of their goals.

In Mexico, for instance, where promises far exceeded performance, administrative adoption of strict antidrug regulations did not guarantee abatement of domestic drug problems nor impede smuggling across the border to the United States. In South America only Uruguay appeared to have much success in adopting controls. Peru and Bolivia found cultural and economic considera-

tions compelling reasons to institute controls on the coca leaf and
its uses with great circumspection. Honduras (and to a lesser extent
Panama) served, willingly it often appeared, as an entrepôt for the
illicit drug trade.[53] The chaotic situation there precluded the use
of diplomacy to bring about the government's commitment to
stricter regulation. It also seems apparent that the international
drug control effort held little meaning for Latin America by the late
1930s. As for the United States, Anslinger's bureau may have dealt
effectively with domestic drug usage (although claims of large
reductions in the ranks of addicts should be accepted with reservations). On the hemispheric level, the same attitude which
seemed successful at home actually impaired the furtherance of
controls. Ironically, by 1940 the bureaucratic structure which revi-
talized United States policy a decade earlier was virtually powerless to resolve problems with drugs elsewhere in the Americas.
One result of this situation was that smugglers, perhaps Kennett
and TACA, engaged in their activities virtually untouched by government action.

  By way of comparison, it is worth noting that obstacles similar to
those encountered in Honduras existed in Asia as well during the
late 1930s. The United States response was more direct, however.
Time and again the State Department, and especially Stuart J.
Fuller, condemned the complicity of the Japanese in illicit opium
activity in China.[54] And just as often, it seems, the Japanese
protested the accusations, arguing that Japan genuinely desired to
suppress the use of opium.[55] The situation was worst in Manchuria,
Jehol, and the portions of north China under Japanese military
control. Fuller believed that the actions of the Japanese served to
undermine a serious effort on the part of the Chinese central
government to abolish opium poppy cultivation and suppress opium smoking. The matter concerned the United States because at
that time conditions in the Far East, more so than in Latin America, held the key to successful international narcotic control—or so
officials believed. There is reason to suspect, however, that prominent Chinese were competing with the Japanese for the lucrative
rewards of the opium trade more than they were trying to eliminate the trade.[56]

  As was the case in Honduras, getting accurate information on
antinarcotic activity proved difficult. The United States even considered paying informers for desired information because of the

obfuscation of the Foreign Office,[57] which consistently denied the existence of an authorized traffic in opiates in Japanese-controlled territory. Officials in Washington were therefore left to their own devices, meaning unilateral action taken close to home. Beginning around 1938 the Customs Agency Service gave special attention to Japanese vessels in American ports; and the Coast Guard began trailing ships under suspicion, searching some thoroughly and imposing heavy fines on those caught with illicit narcotics. Summing up the situation in 1940, Stanley K. Hornbeck wrote with great understatement: "Japanese laws for the control of narcotic drugs leave much to be desired. . . ."[58]

If smuggling from Honduras or the Far East to the United States receded around 1940, it happened more because of the European war than as a result of the efforts of officials in Washington. To their dismay these officials would realize within a few years that the war brought only a temporary relief, not a curtailing, of drug problems. In fact, the years from the mid-thirties to the end of the decade offered a preview, a window on the future as it were, of the coming struggle to control narcotics. What could not have been foreseen was the increasing complexity of the situation after World War II. In one sense the United States had been right about drug control ever since its delegation walked out of the Second Geneva Opium Conference in 1925: without limitation at the source, the cycle of raw materials ultimately supplying the illicit traffic, and thus creating a demand for additional drugs, would continue indefinitely. The failure of Honduras to adopt a program of drug control during the 1930s shows how deceptively simple yet unattainable that goal actually was.[59]

When a phenomenon such as smuggling takes on the immediacy it acquired by 1940 because of attendant social problems, it is easy to obscure or forget the larger historical lens through which it can be viewed. However odious smuggling may be to societies that relegate virtually to taboo status the nonscientific or nonmedical use of drugs, what is actually occurring is competition between the majority culture on the one hand and an unapproved subculture on the other. Throughout the history of Central America, as exemplified by the Honduran experience of the 1930s, smuggling has played a prominent role in that competition—a fact which United States narcotic foreign policy could scarcely affect in any event.

8 World War II and After: Patterns of Drug Control

The Second World War only partly changed the drug problems in the Americas. To a large extent, the war brought to a halt the influx through Central America of manufactured narcotics from Europe and the Far East. This development unfortunately gave rise to a formidable hemispheric commerce in proscribed drugs, originating primarily in Mexico, but also in parts of South America. On the other hand, the war did little to eradicate the narcotic-related problems that plagued American governments domestically. They remained much the same as before. In several instances, though, a genuine commitment to ameliorate these difficulties seemed to emerge; resultant action might thereby minimize their corollary impact on the inter-American narcotic situation. By the end of the war, this commitment seemed particularly evident in Peru, and perhaps in Mexico as well. Yet Mexico not only had former difficulties to face, which the war compounded, but also new ones, including unprecedented opium poppy cultivation. Other countries, too, had unfamiliar experiences with narcotics. The case of Argentina, suspected in Washington of being pro-Axis, offers an appropriate point of departure for a discussion of wartime drug control in the Americas.

At the inter-American conference at Rio de Janeiro in January 1942, the Argentines balked at signing an agreement committing them to active opposition of Axis interests in the Western Hemisphere. The impression the proposed agreement gave was that in the event of war between the Axis and any American state the other American nations would be compelled to declare war. Argentina's leaders refused to make such an open-ended commitment.[1]

Soon after the Rio Conference, the State Department inquired of Norman Armour, its ambassador in Buenos Aires, whether the Argentine government had excepted cocaine from a general decree prohibiting the export or reexport of all drugs. Officials in Washington had reason to believe that the exception was made because of Axis needs for the drug as an anesthetic. The State Department felt that perhaps twelve hundred kilograms of raw cocaine annually reached the Axis nations after being smuggled out of Peru and routed through Argentina.[2] Armour confirmed the department's suspicions about the export of cocaine. In fact, Argentina seemed willing to serve as the primary source of narcotics for the Axis powers. It was also learned that several firms in Buenos Aires had received government permission to manufacture opiates. Subsequently, in August 1942, commercial attaché Thomas L. Hughes reported the planting of a large opium poppy crop.[3] Later that year Washington learned that a government decree had created a factory system for the production of narcotics.[4]

By mid-1943 it was evident that the entire poppy crop for the previous year had failed as a result of improper planting techniques and a drought in the planting area. Some time before the failure was revealed, Bureau of Narcotics Commissioner Harry Anslinger became interested in the production of opiates in Argentina. In a letter to N. F. Peterson, a vice president of Hoffman–La Roche, Inc., the United States parent company of one of the poppy producing firms, Productos Roche, S.A., Anslinger warned that "if narcotic drugs produced as a result of those plantings should, through any fault or negligence on the part of your corporation, its agents, or subsidiaries, find their way into illicit traffic, this Government might be forced to take action against your corporation."[5]

Anslinger's admonition had the desired effect. Productos Roche abandoned local morphine manufacture and made plans to sell its opium crop. But even if Productos Roche stopped growing narcotics, similar firms in Argentina and Chile were prepared to take its place. Ambassador Claude G. Bowers in Santiago commented that the Chilean company, Drogas Botanicas, which might get involved in the narcotic commerce, was "lacking in a sense of social responsibility."[6] And in Argentina, Productos Roche went ahead and harvested its opium crop for 1943 despite some reports that it might be destroyed.[7]

Members of the embassy in Buenos Aires felt that if someone from the American Chamber of Commerce there would supervise the activity, Productos Roche might be convinced to destroy its opium crop. The problem was how to avoid any hint of United States involvement in the company's affairs. If possible, Washington desired to have its way regarding the poppies without straining further relations with Buenos Aires.[8] Reluctance by the American Chamber of Commerce about supervising the destruction of opium poppies made this goal difficult to attain. Armour suggested an alternative plan to his superiors. Roy Barnes, identified only as a "reliable American," would undertake the supervision; but if questioned by local officials Barnes would follow instructions and disavow any connection with the embassy or with the American Chamber of Commerce.

This scheme could not be carried out either. In Armour's words, "a delicate situation" was created. The ambassador discovered that Hoffman–La Roche, Inc. had cabled Productos Roche the following message: "Commissioner of Narcotics has now appointed Roy Barnes . . . please contact immediately." Armour assumed that Argentine censors made a copy of the cable; thus he feared that the government would halt all crop destruction. Consequently, Barnes was advised not to go ahead with the supervision. Despite the high prices other firms in Argentina and Chile were willing to pay for the poppies, Armour still hoped that the crop would not be processed into opiates.[9] Hoffman–La Roche ultimately eased the anxiety in Washington about its role in the narcotics trade with the Axis when it decided to have the harvested crop consigned to its headquarters in Nutley, New Jersey. By September 1944 the harvest was on its way to the United States despite the lack of the requisite authorization certificate from Anslinger.[10]

In retrospect, fears of Argentine-grown narcotics either supplying the Axis or fueling the illicit inter-American trade seem to have been warranted. A fortunate combination of circumstances managed to allay those fears. Poppy cultivation apparently failed during the years when shipments might have reached the Axis powers more easily than later in the war. This crop loss also limited the likelihood of smuggling to the United States. Moreover, Washington did not directly pressure the government in Buenos Aires to halt the growing of opium. Diplomatic overtures to that effect would probably have worsened relations between the two countries. Instead, as State Department files show, the United States concentrated its efforts on the one firm having a large measure of success with its narcotic operations. Whether moved by threats, the course of the war, or other considerations, Productos Roche ultimately complied with United States wishes to curtail its opium activities.

The war necessarily narrowed the scope of Argentina's drug market; yet, domestic consumption remained much the same as before the war. Farm hands and other laborers in the Andes continued to consume large quantities of coca leaves. This was true as well in Colombia, Bolivia, and Peru. The cultural tradition of el coqueo held an importance for many South Americans which neither a war nor the exhortations of the United States and the League of Nations combined could overcome. It was believed that much of the Colombian population chewed coca regularly, that half of all Bolivians were coqueros, and that coca was used by more than three million Peruvians.[11] One observer, remarking on what she saw as conditions of physical and moral degeneracy, noted: "Coca, alcohol, and syphilis ride together, a morbid trio of horsemen stalking the Andes." This exaggerated declaration, obscured the real, if transitory, changes in the quality of life for Peru's Indians during the war. Tradition and the demands of mining production ultimately precluded lasting social change for the Indian population.[12]

Peru, it should be recalled, had tried occasionally but without much resolve to restrict coca production and use. Consumption of coca leaves may have increased as much as 40 percent between 1930 and the mid-1940s.[13] In 1929 President Augusto B. Leguía had considered suppressing coca use but only succeeded in eliciting numerous testimonials favorable to coca. Leguía had said:

> Cocaine and its derivatives are of vast medical usefulness, but when human weakness seeks a refuge in its stupefying force, then it constitutes a danger which much be combatted energetically. In our country coca is a toxin for millions of people; moved by high human considerations and by compelling national exigencies I am thinking of going to the government coca market, to preserve its benefits but to cut off or at least restrict the evils it occasions.[14]

Intense opposition and his ouster from power nullified Leguía's intentions. Coca consumption continued, as did production for cocaine manufacturing despite a regulation in December 1939 by the Ministry of Public Health, Labor, and Social Welfare to suspend the granting of new factory licenses for production. [15] The presence of coca and cocaine was so unalterable in Peru that an observation in colonial times by the administrator Juan Matienzo de Peralta still seemed valid: "If there were no coca there would be no Peru."[16]

If the war had no effect upon the domestic use of coca, it nonetheless gave Peru a crucial role in the United States–led drive for better hemispheric drug control. Officials in Washington hoped that the government in Lima would regulate carefully all exports of drugs. In the spring of 1941 nearly 1,000 kilos of refined 90 percent pure cocaine became available. Previously, Germany's Lufthansa Airline had shipped large amounts of cocaine to Brazil, and from there to Germany and Italy. Peru, though, cancelled the Lufthansa concession.

The State Department, after learning of the existence of the cocaine, wanted to have a voice in its disposal. An embassy counselor in Lima feared that "with the laxity in the enforcement of narcotic regulations in this country it is probable that this cocaine may find its way into the illicit narcotics traffic." The United States, however, could not legally import refined cocaine, but it was felt that the Soviet Union might purchase the 1,000 kilos.[17] To compound matters, Peru and Russia did not formally recognize each other so the United States would have to serve as an intermediary in any transaction. The counselor, Joseph McGurk, feared that Russia would not need all the cocaine and that considerable quantities might end up in Axis hands. Great Britain also expressed concern about this possibility and offered to buy some of the cocaine. Since the British doubted that Peru would sell the cocaine for sterling, London asked the United States to purchase it under the Lend-Lease program. [18] This arrangement for disposal of the cocaine seemed a workable one. In November, Anslinger alerted the State Department that National Defense Headquarters, in connection with Lend-Lease, wanted 950 kilograms of cocaine for the Soviets. Anslinger suggested that the Office of Price Management purchase the requisite amount from Peru. The State Department ordered the request to be complied with discreetly so as not to encourage increased production and manufacture.[19]

In a related development some months earlier, Peru and Britain reached an agreement to control and restrict cocaine exports unless Washington sought an export increase.[20] Subsequently, a regulation took effect in Peru requiring cocaine processors to deposit monthly production figures with public health officials. This tactic was intended to bring under control the commerce in cocaine.[21] Real control, as most officials realized, remained impossible without production restrictions. Moreover, the accord with the British and the diplomatic activities of the United States evidently did not lessen Peru's willingness to sell cocaine to all customers. In the days shortly after the attack on Pearl Harbor, State Department personnel in Lima reported a Japanese request for amounts of cocaine similar to those promised to Russia. For a time the attack in the Pacific did not seem to foreclose the possibility of completing the deal with Japan.[22] And, as late as March 1942, the State Department feared that some Peruvian cocaine might still be reaching Germany.[23]

Soon thereafter the Division of American Republics composed a policy statement on Peruvian cocaine, the international market, and illegal trade:

> Unless Peru betters its record by conforming to the terms of international agreements which it has signed and takes drastic and effective steps to eliminate the illegal trade, the United States is prepared to take all measures necessary to produce the desired result, including cutting Peru off from sources of narcotic drugs and stopping its purchase of coca leaves.

The United States, which had recently imported at least 75 percent of Peru's legitimate coca leaf export crop, would carry out its threat by resuming coca planting in Puerto Rico "where the production has been eliminated to give Peru its market."[24]

In addition, Peru became part of the wartime hemispheric effort to control opium. Noting that an international surplus existed, Herbert Gaston of the Treasury Department suggested to the State Department that its representatives in Peru recommend the destruction of opium crops and discourage future planting. In a comment on this proposal, George Morlock observed that Senator Walter George of Alabama had introduced a bill in Congress providing for government controls on contemplated poppy planting in the United States. Morlock had difficulty reconciling the suggestion with wartime federal policy concerning the planting of poppies in this country. In his words, he and Anslinger agreed that "we should not make such a request" of Peru.[25]

Despite Morlock's misgivings, Ambassador R. Henry Norweb in Lima was instructed to try to discourage opium planting and cultivation. He was told to call attention to an executive decree of February 1940 restricting poppy growth. The ambassador's instructions ignored the George bill and merely noted that the United States had a three-year supply of opium available. Norweb learned later that a Supreme Resolution of the Peruvian Congress in May 1941, which abolished the prohibition on poppy cultivation but placed guidelines on future production, had supplanted the previous year's executive decree.[26]

The director of Peru's narcotics bureau met with commercial attaché Julian Greenup to discuss the situation. Greenup was informed that Peru had trouble controlling illegal traffic in opium because of the lucrative rewards resulting from smuggling. The director sought advice from the Federal Bureau of Narcotics. At this time officials in Washington doubted that Peru wanted to restrict poppy growth. A firm in Lima, Sociedad Anónima Fausto Piaggio, without proper authorization had offered to supply manufacturers in the United States with raw opium. This action had further increased official skepticism.[27] Constantino J. Carvallo, minister of public health, labor, and social welfare, tried to minimize these doubts. He declared that the firm in question did not possess any opium. He also said that Peru did not permit the production of raw opium for export, but only for supplying domestic medical needs. Anslinger apparently accepted this explanation since he continued to allow businesses in the United States to export all requested medicinal drugs to Peru, except morphine.[28] (World War II had an adverse effect upon the ability of some American republics to maintain an adequate supply of medical drugs. At the Eleventh Pan-American Health Conference held in Rio de Janeiro in September 1942, for example, the conferees adopted a recommendation exhorting the production of drugs in short supply. Given the level of production and over-supply existing in some nations, all shortages could be covered.[29])

In his report on the health conference, Greenup included details of a meeting with Peru's new public health director, César Gordillo Zuleta, who had reported that efforts at opium cultivation had generally failed. Only in the Huaura River region had cultivation succeeded. Gordillo Zuleta further told Greenup that if the demands of the war resulted in an undersupply of opium, he would not object to the establishment of an opium industry under the supervision of the Public Health Ministry.[30] State Department response to this information again sought to discourage poppy production. As George Morlock put it, the Bureau of Narcotics, the Board of Economic Welfare, and the State Department ought to "do all possible to prevent the production of opium in Peru for reasons of policy."[31] The primary consideration remained the omnipresent fear of increased illicit traffic in the hemisphere.

Perhaps the most effective way for Peru to prevent its opium from increasing the supply of illicit narcotics was through strict control over poppy cultivation and distribution of opiates. Such action would entail close supervision of the existing stocks of opium. Trying to supply a reason for better control, Anslinger let it be known that he would not issue certificates for the importation of Peruvian opium as long as the United States possessed supplies sufficient to satisfy its own needs.[32] The government in Lima, indicating a readiness to pursue a stricter policy, denied one firm's request in March 1943 to begin cultivation.[33] At the same time the United States continued to allow the export of badly needed narcotics for medical purposes. By mid-1943 Peru did not have enough morphine for treatment of cancer patients. Acting upon a request, Anslinger cabled Gordillo Zuleta that he would issue the export authorizations.[34]

A cooperative relationship between Lima and Washington had begun to emerge. Peru was moving toward the adoption of stricter controls over the production and distribution of opiates and the United States was providing indirect assistance, exporting the quantities of drugs needed by Peru for medical purposes. An example of the spirit of cooperation came at the end of 1943 when the United States halted codeine exports because the drug reportedly was not prescription-controlled. Yet Peru had nearly exhausted its supply. When Anslinger became convinced that codeine was handled through medical prescription, he quickly approved export permits.[35]

Peru was engaging in an antinarcotic effort which—though it did not match United States standards of strictness—must have pleased officials in Washington. A Peruvian decree in November 1943 required all cocaine producers to sell to the government stocks exceeding a one year's supply. The next spring the government even seriously considered the creation of a state monopoly to control cocaine. But there were obstacles. Eight or ten producers were maintaining their operations and did not want their permits revoked. They argued that they were performing a service by stockpiling cocaine during periods when there was an abundant coca leaf harvest. Still, the government's rationale for monopoly was that authorities were having to rely on the honesty of these producers to provide production statistics which the government could not verify. Despite this, the monopoly did not come into existence during the war.[36]

Officials in Washington would have preferred some form of limitation at the source rather than a monopoly. But if there had to be one, a state monopoly for the production and sale of coca leaves, and not cocaine, would be preferable. Extensive supervision of coca cultivation instead of cocaine production was unlikely though. Despite the increased government activity resulting from wartime exigencies, the enforcement of Peruvian drug laws was not uniform through the mid-forties. Violators, especially drug sellers, often received lenient treatment. Near the end of the war a change in policy may have been in the offing. A key official in Peru's narcotics bureau told Julian Greenup that Peruvian authorities regretted the lack of a mandatory sentence for drug traffickers. But no evidence suggests that any changes were forthcoming.[37]

Drug problems in Mexico had always posed more difficulties for the United States than similar problems in the other Latin American states, for Mexico was after all a contiguous neighbor. Geographical proximity—and wartime—were not the only shaping elements of the relationship between the two countries. Also significant were political antagonisms originating at the time of the Mexican Revolution and the differing ways in which each society viewed drug use. But Mexico's renewed antidrug commitment, arising out of the discussions in Washington in May 1940 between United States and Mexican officials, had helped to minimize these difficulties. As administrations in Mexico changed from that of

Cárdenas to Ávila Camacho, Anslinger, H. S. Creighton, and the others most concerned with the situation could only wait and see if the level of cooperation would remain the same.

Several indications appeared late in the year suggesting that their hopes would not be realized. In December, Creighton asked for and received permission from his superiors to resume the practice of sending operatives into Mexico to aid in the tracking of drug smugglers.[38] At the same time, a scandal arose within Mexico's narcotic bureaucracy. *Excélsior* reported allegations of irregular practices in the health department, including high-level complicity in the drug trade. The arrest of an attorney, José Perdonio Benítez, helped narcotics police discover numerous forged authorizations for excessive drug imports. Large quantities of these drugs, it was believed, ended up in the illicit traffic.

Suspicion about the irregularities had surfaced in July when the League of Nations released statistics showing that Mexico was exceeding its import allotment for the year. Officials in the Federal District subsequently learned of a delivery of 150 grams of cocaine to Perdonio. Two men who had previously served in the government, Albert P. Léon as secretary general of public welfare and Francisco Bassols in the Office of Control of Medicine and Pharmacopoeia, denied granting the order for the delivery of the cocaine. The order had been questioned because the Department of Public Health employed a special form for all consignments over five grams. Perdonio refused to divulge how he obtained the required signatures. Following his arrest, the Department of Public Health ordered all suspicious narcotic imports halted and restricted the granting of import authorizations. As *Excélsior* reported, illegal purchases continued—on proper forms which had obviously been altered.[39]

In his defense, Léon declared that the order found in Perdonio's possession was false. The order was supposedly issued to Dr. Heberto Alcázar, former chief of the Federal Narcotics Service. Yet Léon claimed that a different name, that of a woman, appeared on the order stub found in the office where Bassols worked. He further declared his and Bassols's signatures on the order to be forgeries.[40] Alcázar, trying to clear his name, told his friends at the United States Consulate General that he had done nothing irregular. He concluded that someone wanted to discredit him and others formerly attached to the Department of Public Health. Alcázar felt that Pascual Sánchez Anaya, chief of the narcotics police, might be responsible. Sánchez had previously worked for Alcázar and ill feelings existed between the two. In fact, Alcázar thought that Sánchez might be a major participant in the illegal activities the narcotics police had uncovered.[41]

Allegations of complicity against Alcázar worried officials in the United States, for high-level corruption in the government would only serve to increase drug smuggling. Were the charges true, Anslinger and the State Department would be forced to conclude that the spirit and practice of cooperation which Jóse Siurob left behind was fraudulent. Against this background, customs agent Alvin Scharff visited the new public health director in mid-December. Dr. Victor Fernández Manero told Scharff that he intended to eliminate any illegal or questionable activities in his department. Fernández Manero admitted the potential seriousness of the scandal, but felt that the situation might provide its own remedy since a change in administrations and personnel was under way.[42] Significantly, the day after the Fernández-Scharff discussion, *Excélsior* printed a story entitled, "The Narcotics Traffic Scandal Increases." Perdonio Benítez had revealed information further implicating Alcázar in the illegal activity. He possessed a note naming Alcázar as a key figure in the scandal, and an agent of the narcotics police had reportedly verified the note's authenticity. To this charge Alcázar replied that a careful check of Department of Public Health records would remove all suspicion from him.[43]

As the year ended, the future course and effectiveness of narcotic control in Mexico seemed in question. Important officials in both the Cárdenas and Ávila Camacho administrations suffered from damaged reputations. Reports from several regions in the country indicated an increase in smuggling. In some border areas, for example, where vegetable farming had failed to produce a good income, opium poppies were being planted. Smuggling would naturally follow.[44]

One mitigating factor in this situation was the avowed desire of Fernández Manero for cooperation with the United States—the only way smuggling could be reduced.[45] Officials in Washington had no reason to question his sincerity, and rather hoped to bolster his commitment. Creighton arranged to go to Mexico City to talk with Fernández Manero about the illicit traffic, while the United States government, prompted by the uncertainty of the situation in Mexico, temporarily removed the narcotic agents operating there.[46] Discussions took place early in February. One topic was destruction of the opium crop. Creighton expressed disappointment at the continuing poppy cultivation in Sonora and Sinaloa. Yet both he and Fernández Manero knew that destruction was not possible without the assistance of local officials.[47] The Mexican public health director told Creighton that he intended to supervise crop destruction of opium and marijuana plants in Baja California later in the month.[48]

During the talks Creighton sought formal approval from the Ávila Camacho administration for the continued presence of United States drug agents in Mexico. All prior agreements had been informal. Creighton's translator William K. Ailshie, vice consul at Mexico City, favored formalization because of the uneven record of drug control in Mexico. "The Federal Narcotics Service in Mexico City," he said, "does not have facilities to prevent the cultivation of poppy and marijuana plants throughout the Republic or the manufacture of opium derivatives, not to mention the illegal introduction of narcotics into Mexico, chiefly from Japan."[49] The Mexicans soon agreed to formalization, but sought an official request from Washington.[50] Herbert S. Bursley of the State Department attached a handwritten note to the report on the talks. It read: "I think it unfortunate that this question was aired. The situation regarding our people going to Mexico was OK."[51] The United States therefore deemed a formal accord unwise, and Mexico did not insist upon one. Washington's reluctance did not greatly offend the Mexicans for the government named Dr. Zaragoza Cuellar García, new chief of the narcotics service, as correspondent with the United States for the exchange of narcotic information. His selection reinforced the informal arrangements first made in the 1930s.[52]

Throughout the year the United States continued the practice of sending agents into Mexico to investigate smuggling and other drug-related activities. Three special agents arrived at the height of antinarcotic efforts in the fall.[53] Discretion was in order. As George Morlock commented: "I said . . . that I thought Treasury should be very careful not to overrun Mexico with its agents."[54]

By early 1942 rumors of a government scandal subsided and cooperative efforts were moving ahead. Consul General William P. Blocker at Ciudad Juárez felt optimistic enough to report that "the traffic in narcotics as a whole has been sharply reduced."[55] But as Blocker knew, intermittent vigilance would never reduce the level of smuggling for more than a short time. To emphasize the need for continuing action, a meeting was held in the Customs Agency Service office in El Paso. Those in attendance included Blocker, Creighton, a customs agent for the El Paso region, and Antonio Bermúdez, the mayor of Ciudad Juárez, who was "strongly pro-American," as Blocker put it. Plans were discussed for the reduction of border smuggling. Blocker's report gave no details, but stated: "Results of the campaign will be reported to the Department when achieved."[56]

Narcotics problems in the state of Chihuahua were not the only ones confronting Mexico at the time. From Mazatlán in Sinaloa came reports of extensive opium growing. Some of the harvested crop found its way into the United States. In fact, several state officials were suspected of reaping large rewards from poppy cultivation and smuggling, while concurrently implementing the national antinarcotic policy by destroying the fields of their competitors. Creighton, who had left his post in Texas to become the Treasury Department's special representative in Mexico City, met with the governor of Sinaloa, Rudolfo Loaiza. The governor told Creighton that stamping out the opium industry would be impossible since opium had nearly become the sole means of support throughout the state. Acreage under cultivation was constantly increasing, a fact noted by the Bureau of Narcotics in its annual report for 1942.[57]

Loaiza did not depict an entirely depressing situation for Creighton. He offered three suggestions for reducing the opium traffic. Federal troops, including cavalry, might help supervise poppy destruction. Also, health department agents could work more closely with state and local officials. Finally, improved roads and lines of communication might help limit additional cultivation. As a substitute for the revenue derived from poppy production, Loaiza suggested that the state build up its mining industry. Creighton hoped that agricultural crops would be planted even though opium poppy cultivation was more lucrative.[58]

Some destruction of poppies took place in January, March, and April, observed by special Treasury Department employee Salvador Peña.[59] He disputed Mexico's contention that one-third to one-half of the crop had been destroyed, for he believed that numerous fields had been harvested before being burned. Also, the destruction occurred only in Sinaloa—not in Durango, Sonora, and Chihuahua where it was needed as well. (Sonora reportedly served as an important staging area for the smuggling of drugs into the United States.[60])

Creighton shared Peña's doubts.[61] In a related, intriguing development a proposal emerged, probably from one of Treasury's men in Mexico, advocating that the United States purchase the Mexican opium crop. Although he felt the proposal might offer a way to combat smuggling, Creighton played down the idea in a report to his superiors.[62] United States opium supplies were sufficient and any purchases might encourage additional, unwanted planting of poppies.

Throughout the year Mexico requested assistance combating illegal drug traffic. In October Mayor Bermúdez complained about the inadequacy of prior aid and asked for additional agents. Morlock, joined by other federal officials in the belief that smuggling around El Paso was increasing, approved the request.[63] Some results were achieved when in December eight traffickers were arrested and eight pounds of opium confiscated.[64]

The campaign against border smuggling of opiates and marijuana continued into 1943. At a meeting in Washington with state and treasury department officials Fernández Manero revealed that Ávila Camacho had directed the governors of Sonora and Sinaloa to suppress poppy cultivation in their states. Fernández imprudently asserted that cultivation had therefore ceased.[65] Within a month the State Department notified Josephus Daniels's replacement, George S. Messersmith, that conditions near Mazatlán were worsening. "The illicit traffic in narcotic drugs between Mexico and the United States has increased considerably since 1940," a cable read, "and unless checked will probably become as large as formerly existing between the Far East and the United States."

Treasury Department estimations that Mexico's opium production for 1943 would reach sixty tons, or three times greater than 1942, underlined the urgency of the message. The cable emphasized the need to suppress production. Messersmith was instructed was to find out if Mexico desired additional assistance. The cable also contained the prospect of unpopular, unilateral action: if excessive production continued, border guards would have to search all incoming vehicles and travelers from Mexico.[66]

Creighton went to Washington to discuss the situation with Bulkley and Morlock. He told them that Chinese nationals began opium production around 1925, but that Mexicans now controlled over 90 percent of the operations. In his opinion, Loaiza was not making a genuine effort in Sinaloa to restrict production. Creighton even suspected that United States funds marked for antinarcotic assistance were ending up in the pockets of smugglers. (The amount of aid had risen from 20,000 pesos in 1942 to 250,000 pesos the next year.)

Creighton also had unsubstantiated evidence that denied Fernández Manero's antinarcotic commitment. While serving as governor of the gulf coast state of Chiapas in southeastern Mexico, Fernández Manero amassed a personal fortune of between two and three million pesos. At that time he maintained a close relationship with Loaiza. The coincidence seemed important to Creighton. Closing the discussion, he regretted that he had no remedial suggestions. He doubted the likelihood of enhanced collaboration against narcotics with Mexico despite his belief in the good intentions of Ávila Camacho. Morlock could only add that if conditions worsened, as was probable, the United States would issue a formal protest to the Mexican government. [67]

Subsequent reports from Mexico were not encouraging. Herbert Bursley, now embassy counselor, alerted Washington that another inspection trip would be made to the northern states. He hoped to send an observer even though he doubted the trip would be a success. Questioning the sincerity of the commitment behind the trip, Bursely suggested that it was being staged to relieve pressure on Fernández Manero from Mexican newspapers and the United States embassy. After the trip Messersmith concluded that "while some poppy fields have been destroyed, nothing of importance has been done, however, to prevent cultivation or to destroy growing poppies." [68] Not surprisingly, the fall plantings in Sinaloa were reported to be the largest yet.[69]

To officials in the United States, relations with Mexico over narcotics seemed destined to follow a pattern of conference, promises, and nonperformance, as the Bureau of Narcotics annual report for 1943 reveals. Had José Siurob remained in office after 1940 that record would probably not have differed. The pattern recurred in March 1944 when the Mexican government requested a meeting in Mexico with top-level officials from Washington.[70] After this particular gathering Messersmith expressed the frustration his colleagues and predecessors had long felt. He believed that at the highest level the administration wished to cooperate with the United States and genuinely committed itself to halting poppy growth near the northern border. As before, drug agents were welcome on trips into poppy country.

Sidney Kennedy, Creighton's replacement upon the latter's retirement, was also present at the meeting of narcotics officials. He thought that the United States should employ diplomatic protests to produce compliance by Mexico in antidrug activity. Yet diplomacy, as Kennedy discovered, could not overcome the problems which made effective control difficult. Dr. Gustavo Baz, minister of public health, elaborated. In the first place the government's antinarcotic program was poorly funded. Agents did not have sufficient funds to meet their own expenses, let alone to pay informers—a necessary practice. As a result agents were susceptible to bribes from drug merchants. Second, for several years the government had only enough manpower to send two agents to supervise crop destruction even though the United States share of the program's cost had risen steadily. Baz suggested that one more agent and a small increase in funds from Washington would enable Mexico to destroy 25 percent of the poppy fields. He intimated that the program might falter without additional funds.

The meeting concluded after one of Baz's subordinates presented a four-step plan to halt poppy growth. The measures included an educational campaign advocating the cultivation of agricultural crops, the withholding of public irrigation waters from lands with poppies, the forcible removal of opium growers from public lands, and the prosecution of selected growers as a warning to others. [71] The major drawback in the program as usual would be the difficulty of implementation.

An early test of Mexico's resolve to fulfill its antinarcotic pledges came in June. At the urging of Salvador Peña, a crop destruction expedition with twenty-three soldiers traveled to Durango. An inexplicable delay of one day alerted the growers to the coming raids. Upon arriving at the poppy fields, Mexican officials and the soldiers discovered local villages deserted and some of the fields burned. The soldiers made a superficial effort to destroy more fields; several soldiers assisted with the burning while the other twenty guarded against a surprise ambush. At the conclusion of the abortive expedition, the coordinator from Durango declared that another trip would not be made.[72] (See Appendix.) If Mexico, like Peru, actually desired to join with the United States in controlling the flow of illicit narcotics in the Americas, its efforts met with little success. Federal administrators simply did not possess the capability to affect conditions in the major drug growing regions of the country.

Hemispheric drug control through 1945 became essentially an inter-American matter which reflected how the war halted international efforts. Just before the war a League of Nations mission traveled to Latin America hoping to influence governments there to adopt more comprehensive control programs. The League found that printing its documents in Spanish increased compliance with reporting procedures on the domestic drug situation. It was hoped that encouragement from Geneva might bring more efficient controls to those states plagued by serious drug problems. The mission visited twelve states including Argentina, Uruguay, Peru, Bolivia, and Mexico. Results of the trip gratified the League and seemed to offer the prospect of an intensive antidrug effort.[73]

As we have seen, the wartime history of drug control in Argentina, the Andean region, and Mexico thwarted this expectation. A postwar report on the extent of wartime drug traffic chronicled a vast illegal trade. Both the United States and Canada had seized large quantities of contraband raw opium originating in Mexico. From 1940 to mid-1946, a total of 428 kilograms of prepared opium, primarily from Mexico, was seized. That country, too, served as a principal supplier of morphine and adulterated heroin reaching the United States. On the other hand, the report minimized the extent of cocaine traffic. The stated reason was the preoccupation of Japan with the war, but that assertion should be tempered by Washington's concern with illicit cocaine emanating from the Andes. Finally, most of the marijuana confiscated in the hemisphere in the early 1940s came from Mexico.[74]

The war had several notable effects upon the illicit drug trade. When older, established channels for smuggling came under closer scrutiny than before, new ones opened. The International Labor Organization appealed for assistance by seamen's unions and received a favorable response. Had this and other methods of detection been largely effective, the flow of drugs would not have stopped. From Mexico, couriers often crossed the Rio Grande by wading or swimming and pushing their precious cargoes on rafts. Traditional European and Asian transfer points closed during the war. The risky, bustling romanticism associated with Marseilles and Hong Kong disappeared as drugs entered the United States after passing through less recognizable towns in Mexico and Central and South America.

As for the quality of drugs, the war evidently caused much adulteration of the opiates. The level of purity often did not reach 5 percent. Supply from the Americas, falling short of prewar international levels, drove prices higher. On the other hand, the war set off an increase in the smuggling of a cheaper substance, marijuana. By 1942 organized gangs were reportedly distributing it in the United States. The risks were great; the number of seizures rose appreciably for the next few years.[75] Anslinger and his colleagues tried to bring this situation under control by appealing, where possible, to Latin American governments to improve their own control programs. There was little the United States could do legislatively. One law which was passed, an opium poppy control measure, prohibited domestic poppy cultivation except under a special license allowing cultivation for medical and scientific purposes. The government issued no such licenses during the war.[76]

A sense emerged in Washington that the global conflict had done much to reduce the number of addicts in the United States. The Bureau of Narcotics saw this as a continuation of a prewar trend initiated by its tough policies and vigilance in enforcement. A United Nations report echoed this sentiment.[77] This feeling of success renewed the unresolvable controversy about the number of addicts. Apparently, the figure fell somewhere between 20,000, which would have been slightly more than one addict per 10,000 people, the bureau's estimated ratio, and 48,000, the number given by the Public Health Service in 1948. Anslinger termed the lower figure "an irreducible minimum."[78] The evidently low level of addiction prompted Congress in 1948 to consider closing the federal narcotic farms, but Anslinger succeeded in keeping them open.[79] As always the precise extent of addiction was not possible to calculate; methods remained unreliable and self-serving. It is clear, however, that the level fell during the war, barely increased for the next two years, and then began a steady rise.[80]

When this increase was beginning, the bureau seemed to be

searching for a scapegoat to blame. "There has always been a climate of public opinion which has favored the spread of narcotic addition," Anslinger declared.[81] He especially feared that undue publicity might tempt people into narcotic use:

> It has been our observation that direct propaganda on drugs, particularly to the youth, is likely to be dangerous, because it "advertises" the use of drugs for nonmedical purposes and stimulates curiosity on the part of persons who would not otherwise have become interested.

Abuse among youngsters resulted not from "ignorance of consequences but because they had learned too much about the effects of drugs."[82] As one of the guardians of public morality, the bureau liked to have it both ways: in the 1920s an educational campaign played a significant role in the passage of the Marihuana Tax Act; a decade later public awareness impeded realization of the bureau's goals.

Anslinger's tenacity in the fight against drugs was unrivaled. The New York *Herald Tribune* reported in 1948 that he carried at all times a leather-bound book containing the names of thousands of persons possibly involved in the illegal drug trade.[83] In a book he coauthored, *The Traffic in Narcotics,* Anslinger disparaged many of the articles on narcotics appearing in the press. He found the reporting inaccurate and misleading, and he denounced the use of sensationalism for the sake of sales. As always, nonbureau information was regarded with skepticism, no matter how sophisticated the research. The acrimonious controversy over the 1944 La Guardia report offers a prime example.[84]

The commissioner claimed that the report contributed to the atmosphere favoring drug experimentation. "The Bureau immediately detected the superficiality and hollowness of its findings and denounced it." In the eyes of the bureau the damage had been done. Potential users believed marijuana to be harmless.[85] This error, Anslinger would argue in 1951, started many young people on the road to heroin. "They started there," he said, "and graduated to heroin; they took the needle when the thrill of marihuana was gone."[86] This position effectively reversed the bureau's stand during the hearings on marijuana control fourteen years earlier. [87] The war and immediate postwar years saw a continuation of the scientific debate on the effects of marijuana. At the very least, the research findings raised additional doubts about the government's wholesale condemnation of the drug on scientific grounds.[88] For whatever reasons, bureaucratic inflexibility, social policy, or personal pique, Anslinger initiated no reassessment of the bureau's position. Instead he termed the La Guardia report "the favorite reference of the proselytor [*sic*] for narcotic-drugs use."[89]

The image of weak-willed victims succumbing to the lure of narcotics could not conceal Anslinger's contempt for addicts. He felt that 90 percent of them suffered from psychiatric disturbances, neuroses of some sort, or were socially maladjusted. "While there is no typical addict personality," he warned, "it is safe to say that there are numerous addiction prone people who could easily succumb to the drug habit."[90] (Had the commissioner chanced to read the memoirs of jazz saxophonist Milton "Mezz" Mezzrow, detailing in part the association of marijuana, opiates, and musicians, he no doubt would have felt his typology was confirmed.) Of the young people he tried to shield from the horrors of addiction, Anslinger, after detailing an abrupt rise in addiction from 1948 to 1952, remarked: "It is the considered judgment of the officials of the Bureau of Narcotics that this epidemic of narcotic addiction is primarily an extension of a widespread surge of juvenile delinquency." [91]

After the war the bureau did not consider the possibility that addicts could be treated to overcome addiction without being stigmatized as criminals. Reviving a modified form of the 1919–20 narcotic clinic plan offered one possible way of coping with addiction. Handled properly and adequately supervised by clinics, many drug users, depending upon the extent of their addiction, might have been able to withdraw from drug dependence or could have been maintained if withdrawal were not medically advisable, thus retaining a sense of personal dignity.

Yet, Commissioner Anslinger viewed ambulatory treatment suspiciously, not believing that addicts wanted to be relieved from their dependency. "The average drug addict who purports to undergo this treatment," he wrote in 1946, "will invariably seek other sources of supply as his dosage is reduced." [92] Later he took an even more inflexible stand against clinic dispensation plans, saying, "What is being sought under the guise of a solution appears to be a form of government subsidization of drug addiction—a plan as fantastic as it is amoral. If drug addiction is an evil habit—and who will say that it is not—it should be rooted out and destroyed."[93] As Bonnie and Whitebread have noted: "The punitive approach to narcotics use and dependence reached its zenith in the 1950s."[94]

Against this background of government indifference to the plight of addicts, the extent of addiction steadily rose. The Bureau of Narcotics admitted the existence of 60,000 addicts in 1954, but three years earlier the New York Mayor's Committee on Narcotics estimated a maximum figure of 90,000 in New York City alone. In a 1955 article on the feasibility of legalizing narcotic use, the authors condemned the high relapse rate of addicts formerly confined at the federal narcotic hospitals. They also quoted Rufus G. King, chairman of the Committee on Narcotics and Alcohol of the American Bar Association, on the government's difficulty in handling the nation's drug problems. King had said:

> All the billions our society has spent enforcing criminal measures against the addict have had the sole practical result of protecting the peddler's market, artificially inflating his prices and keeping his profits fantastically high. No other nation hounds its addicts as we do and no other nation faces anything remotely resembling our problem.[95]

Alfred R. Lindesmith, a longtime bureau critic, shared King's sentiments. He claimed that since the passage of the 1914 Harrison Narcotic Act considerable injustice had been done to the addict, the victim of addiction, and little done to punish the peddler, the perpetrator. He charged politicians with exploiting a national problem, saying "they point in alarm, they denounce—and they demand heavier and heavier penalties." The penalties fell upon victims, but "what politican bothers to rush to the defense of 'dope fiends?'" "The forgotten man has been the addict," Lindesmith concluded.[96]

It was within this psychological context, framed by the Bureau of Narcotics and decried by its critics, that postwar patterns of hemispheric and international drug control would be set. Prewar experiences had revealed the inability of the League of Nations to do much more than gather statistics, hold meetings, or threaten sanctions. The real antidrug battle would have to be waged by or between individual countries. During the war inter-American relations followed such a course to a previously unprecedented degree. The politics of drug control in the hemisphere became the counterpart of the contemptuous attitude of the bureau regarding addiction. Not only were individual addicts to be accorded harsh treatment, so too were recalcitrant governments, where possible, to be prodded into implementing drug control policies more in line with that followed by Washington. The practical limits of narcotic diplomacy, which were substantial, placed few restrictions on attitudinal changes advocating less ambivalence about drug usage.

The United States therefore supported any reassessment by Latin Americans of the role of drugs in society. There were two prominent examples in the 1940s of such an effort, one by an individual in Argentina, the other transpiring with government approval in Peru. In the first instance a leading narcotic expert, Dr. Pablo Osvaldo Wolff, published several papers on drugs, society, and criminal activity. He termed addictions "exaggerations or aberrations of normal human desires: the search for pleasure and the desire to avoid suffering." Taking a position which Argentina held as early as 1930, he declared that the state has a responsibility to provide treatment for addiction. Yet he supported as well a position similar to Washington's on the forced detention of addicts. If need be, he wrote, they should be detained against their will in treatment centers.[97]

On the relationship between narcotics and criminal activity, Wolff felt that crimes should be seen as "tendencias de reacción" to narcotics. Moreover, narcotic-related psychological alterations, however imperceptible, induced criminal tendencies. To support his conclusions he cited examples of certain drugs and what he judged to be their relation to crime. Morphine addicts rarely committed violent crimes, he felt, but the reverse was true for users of cocaine. About marijuana, he stated that "this drug is certainly more noxious than opium in that it brings on a resultant mental infirmity."[98] Wolff's views on drug abuse and related behavior closely approximated opinions then current in Washington. Anslinger often cited the doctor's work in the 1940s as evidence of hemispheric support for his bureau's drug control policies. In a foreword to a study by Wolff, *Marihuana in Latin America: The Threat It Constitutes*, the commissioner called the conclusions "completely impartial" and asserted that the author "convincingly refutes attempts made by the La Guardia Committee and others to minimize the deteriorating effects of marihuana."[99]

The other example appeared in 1947 with the publication of a major scientific study on the coca leaf and its effects, *Estudios Sobre La Coca y La Cocaina en el Perú*, by Carlos Gutiérrez-Noriega and Vicente Zapata Ortiz of the School of Medicine in Lima. Gutiérrez-Noriega was perhaps the leading international authority on the coca leaf. With the help of other colleagues at the School of Medicine the two men began the study in 1936 at a time when many Peruvians accepted coca as being indispensable for the well-being of the Indian population. The study's general conclusions denied the validity of such a belief on a scientific basis.[100]

More important, the study tried to uncover the extent of coca use and illuminate its physical and social effects upon Peruvians. The authors showed that not all coqueros were addicts. Perhaps 20 percent of them indulged chronically. Mental or physical deterioration was not pronounced among casual users, but it was felt that extensive coca chewing resulted in mental debility. The authors did not assert that this finding had yet become scientifically verifiable. Nonetheless, they noted that in central Peru for instance, women, who usually consumed less coca than men, seemed better able to handle mental activity.

Although some of their evidence appeared to be circumstantial and some conclusions merely informed conjecture, Gutiérrez-Noriega and Zapata Ortiz offered one dramatic conclusion. "In effect there exists," they stated, "a significant *correlation between the rate of illiteracy and other manifestations of social retardation and the consumption of coca*."[101] They stressed their belief that as many as 80 percent of the male Indians in the Andes were illiterate, a higher percentage than among coastal Indians. They attributed this level of *analfabetismo* to both the use of coca and the sociocultural tradition encouraging el coqueo. Illiteracy also seemed less prevalent among Indians showing a high degree of acculturation. The acquisiton of Spanish customs in place of Indian traditions may have helped to break the dependency upon coca. It would not be the final word on the subject, but *Estudios Sobre La Coca y La Cocaina en el Perú* surpassed all prior efforts to present a comprehensive portrayal of coca use. The authors gave the impression that the consumption of coca had long been employed by governing elites to maintain a rigid societal hierarchy and literal division of labor between the Indians and those of Spanish descent in Peru. This conclusion has been reinforced by the thorough research of Thomas M. Davies, Jr., into the ill-considered and often insincere legislative efforts to integrate Indians into Peruvian national life in the first half of the twentieth century.[102]

The work of Wolff and the Peruvians did not, of course, condemn the use of drugs in the same legalistic or moral fashion as in the United States. Their efforts did encompass, though, the underlying assumption that drugs posed a threat to the well-being of individuals and society as a whole. Ambivalence or historical tolerance regarding drug use might in time give way to social policies in Latin American nations similar to antinarcotic attitudes prevalent in the United States. Such was not the case in the 1940s. Developments in attitude or policy during the decade reflected more than anything else the undeveloped state of antinarcotic activity then existing in most of Latin America.

If officials in Washington were inclined to employ bilateral diplomacy in preference to international gatherings to achieve their goals, they still needed the administrative services the world agencies provided. The fortunes of war, as it were, resulted in the United States exercising closer supervision, and perhaps control, over the operations of those agencies than ever before. In 1940 the records and key personnel of the Permanent Central Opium Board and the Drug Supervisory Body moved to this country. These two agencies were able to continue their statistical work establishing international narcotic needs. In 1942 and 1943 Anslinger persuaded the Netherlands and Great Britain to promise to halt government monopolies for opium smoking in their Pacific territories when control was regained from Japan. In July 1945, France announced a similar policy for Indo-China.

The United States Congress in 1944 passed the so-called Judd Resolution, introduced by Representative Walter Judd of Minnesota, authorizing the president to implore opium-producing countries to limit cultivation to medical and scientific needs. The State Department sent entreaties to Great Britain for Burma and India, to China, Iran, Russia, Turkey, Yugoslavia, and Mexico. Among the replies was Mexico's in May 1945 pledging unlimited cooperation with Washington's request.[103]

With the inception of the United Nations, the antinarcotic functions of the League transferred to the new organization. Herbert L. May of the PCOB paved the way at San Francisco in April 1945 for a smooth transition of his agency, the Drug Supervisory Body, and the Opium Advisory Committee to the United Nations.[104] The United States delegation supported this move; in December at London the Preparatory Commission of the United Nations recommended the creation of a Commission on Narcotic Drugs under the Economic and Social Council.[105] This step was taken in February 1946. The duties of the new commission included the preparation of a convention designed to curtail world opium production, an offshoot of the Judd Resolution.[106] Progress on opium control did not soon occur. The first two sessions of the Commission on Narcotic Drugs in 1946 and 1947 dealt primarily with organizational matters. The commission did manage, however, to draw up and submit to individual nations a questionnaire modeled on the Judd Resolution. At the same time it was reported that Argentina and Chile were again trying to grow opium poppies.[107]

The production and manufacture of illicit drugs continued apace while the Commission on Narcotic Drugs was being organized. The commission quickly became convinced of the need to limit the cultivation of raw narcotic materials—virtually an impossible task as we have seen. There did exist some basis for hope, however. At the second session of the commission, the government of Peru requested that a commission of inquiry be sent to Peru to study the medical and socioeconomic effects of restricted coca leaf production. (The findings of the inquiry will be mentioned in the epilogue.) At the time, the commission believed that coca chewing constituted a serious problem not only in Peru, but also in Bolivia and parts of Argentina, Chile, Colombia, and Ecuador. Directly related, of course, to coca production was the international traffic in illicit cocaine about which the Bureau of Narcotics reported in 1948: "The increase in cocaine seizures is extremely disturbing. . . . Cocaine is available in large quantities in Peru, Chile, and Bolivia and . . . American seamen are smuggling it regularly to the United States."[108] The action of Peru presented the hope of controlling the situation to some extent.

There existed far less optimism when the discussion turned to limiting opium poppy production either in the Middle East or Mexico. In March 1948, the *St. Louis Post-Dispatch* reported the existence of more than ten thousand poppy fields in Mexico. These fields probably supplied over one-half the opium, morphine, and heroin smuggled into the United States. Commenting on the situation, Anslinger declared:

> If the Mexican Government does not take action, the situation will become worse. They [*sic*] seem to take the position the American Government is equally at fault because we allow the gangsters to go down there and buy opium. But as a matter of fact, our evidence shows that it is the Mexicans who are promoting it. In fact, Mexicans in very high circles have already been arrested.

Only the state of Sonora, the *Post-Dispatch* asserted, had tried to cooperate with the United States in antiopium activity after the war.[109]

The United States had filed a formal protest on July 30, 1947 with the Economic and Social Council over Mexico's inactivity. Showing a weakness much like that of the League of Nations, the Commission on Narcotic Drugs passed but suspended, pending a report on conditions in Mexico, a resolution requesting the Mexican government to restrict poppy cultivation. Anslinger had no reason to be optimistic about the chances of limitation. Initial reports of success in the eradication campaign of 1947 proved to be exaggerated. Subsequent confidential reports, including a memorandum written by Treasury agent D. G. DeLagrave, found that the campaign measures "even had they been carried out in their entirety . . . would have proved inadequate."[110]

The situation was truly serious. Illicit opium shipments from Mexico at the time reportedly equalled the combined amount reaching the United States from India, Turkey, and Iran. The domestic market, with an increase in addiction serving as a grim barometer, seemed ready to absorb additional opiates. Formal statements of protest soon gave way to renewed efforts at cooperation. The Mexican government issued a decree providing heavier penalties for those trafficking in drugs. In turn, the United States indefinitely postponed action on its protest to the Economic and Social Council.[111]

Wartime diplomacy had clearly failed to eliminate smuggling; the war had been responsible for whatever success there was against the illicit traffic. Postwar conditions at home and abroad frustrated and embarrassed the Bureau of Narcotics.[112] The drug control policies of the United States may have therefore become little more than a chimera, but that determination would be left for others to decide after Harry Anslinger concluded his government service in 1962. Meanwhile, the Bureau of Narcotics would continue, in fulfillment of its bureaucratic function, to help formulate domestic and foreign drug policy. In so doing, the bureau had an unquestioned and considerable role to play.

9   "The Horror and Damnation of Poor Little Human Flies"

> He said, "Please don't think me impertinent, but you do suffer rather, don't you?"
> I said, "Yes, it hurts like hell and is hurting at this minute."
> He sipped a glass of milk and said, "You know, whiskey won't help you."
> I said, "There is nothing that can help me."
> His faded eyes came alight. He said, "Oh, indeed there is. Let us see, it is four o'clock—another fifteen minutes. Oh, yes, there is something which helps!"

Thus the journalist Walter Duranty found opium, giving himself to its allure, its nightmare.[1]

The international movement to control the use of narcotics began, not as a response to any perceptible opiate-induced decline of Western Civilization, but as an effort to infuse Western social and cultural mores into the Far East, the area of extraterritoriality, of European and American protectorates and colonies. Early in the twentieth century no country desired the success of the movement more than the United States. Its perceived mission of moral reform was intended to work well as the companion of political tutelage.

Three overlapping phases marked the involvement of the United States government in narcotics control activity during the period under consideration in this study. During the first phase, which lasted barely into the 1920s, social and political reformers involved themselves in a humanitarian crusade to save others from their weaknesses. The reformers, led by such persons as Bishop Charles H. Brent, Hamilton Wright, and his wife, Elizabeth Washburn Wright, assumed that the abuse of drugs should and could be overcome. The international means to bring about control seemed simple. Moral suasion would be used to encourage narcotic-producing nations to curtail those practices. Ideally, all interested countries would assemble at international meetings to devise formulas for effective drug control. In this way illicit drugs would be kept away from America's shores. The results of the first few meetings held at Shanghai and The Hague revealed the complexities involved in achieving adequate restrictions.

Just as the international antinarcotic movement was getting started, United States officials became increasingly aware of the drug situation at home. Viewing drug usage as a serious social problem, federal and state officials along with private citizens expressed alarm at the apparently high incidence of drug abuse in the nation. As a consequence, they naturally considered adopting legislative controls. Some of the demands for domestic drug control were racially motivated, particularly those emanating from the South, but most followed the humanitarian bent then characteristic of the international movement. Indeed, it seemed possible in the age of progressivism that treatment for addiction might emphasize either cure or maintenance, depending upon an addict's individual needs. The work of Dr. Charles E. Terry in Jacksonville, Florida, and Lucius Polk Brown in Tennessee serve as two prominent examples of the era's faith in solutions for even the most troublesome social problems.[2]

The legal device employed to restrict drug usage in the United States, the Harrison Narcotic Law of 1914, signified the coming of the second phase of antinarcotic activity. Not until the end of the decade would its momentous impact become evident. The law established certain administrative duties for physicians, druggists, and the government that led to the creation of a drug law bureaucracy, first under the auspices of the Bureau of Internal Revenue and later as part of the Prohibition Unit. With the help of two Supreme Court rulings in 1919 routine clerical duties gradually expanded into punitive and restrictive enforcement operations.

A fundamental change in medical and moral assumptions about the nature of drug addiction accompanied the growth of the enforcement bureaucracy. Addicts quickly came to be viewed as society's dregs, breeding crime and perpetuating an illicit, underground drug trade. Federal officials never considered that such conditions might have resulted from the way in which the government enforced the Harrison law. It serves no instructive purpose, however, to condemn public officials for sharing the biases of the times in which they lived. For all its beneficent aspects, the progressive spirit included a substantial measure of intolerance toward cultural dissimilarities—especially one like drug usage which seemed to threaten the social fabric of the country. The final effort to soothe humanely the travail of addiction disappeared with the demise of the temporary experiment with narcotic clinics in 1919–20. Officially, drug usage had become a chronic national affliction not to be readily overcome. It might be deterred partially—as the Public Health Service came to believe—by legislation treating addiction as a criminal offense, not a disease. The antidrug program that was evolving in the United States must be described as one of coercive social control, bolstered in part by overtones of class, and, to a degree, racial discrimination.

During the 1920s policymakers in Washington tried without success to extend the practical dimensions of their philosophy to the world arena. At annual meetings of the Opium Advisory Committee of the League of Nations and at the Second Geneva Opium Conference in 1925, American delegations announced that they would accept nothing less than binding agreements for limitation at the source. No drug-producing or -manufacturing nation was prepared to accept such a position at that time. The United States therefore lost influence over others and, until 1931, forsook the opportunity to assume leadership in the international movement. Officials in Washington soon realized their mistake and tried to rebuild the broken ties with the world community. The self-righteousness characteristic of the first two phases of the American effort to control drugs, an attitude shared by both social reformers and government authorities in their antidrug endeavors, impeded the adoption, and at times even the consideration of realistic controls.

By 1930 a change was at hand. The bureaucratic structure of domestic drug control needed revitalization. A scandal at the highest level of the Narcotic Control Division hierarchy embarrassed the government, seriously damaging the credibility of its struggle against drugs. The creation of the Federal Bureau of Narcotics and the appointment of Harry J. Anslinger as Commissioner of Narcotics soon healed the wound. These two actions also initiated the third phase of the American campaign against drugs, a phase marked more by pragmatic accommodation with other nations than by its residual air of moral superiority.

The United States thus revived at a single stroke its deteriorating position at home and abroad. The Bureau of Narcotics took charge of both foreign and domestic drug policy, thereby diminishing prior congressional influence over policy. Internationally the government began to work for incremental progress in the effort to limit the trade in narcotics to medical and scientific necessities. Even so there is only so much international agreements can achieve. Kettil Bruun, Lynn Pan, and Ingemar Rexed, international experts on drugs and alcohol, have reminded us:

> A treaty should ideally be an instrument of some duration, and this militates against setting forth of a very specific set of goals in the treaty itself. Moreover, its international character behooves it to avoid goals that have relevance for only a single nation. That the dual goals of ensuring medical/scientific availability and preventing other kinds of use are not always commensurable makes it all the more difficult to set specific objectives.[3]

Hoping to minimize the delay and compromise that inevitably define the limits of multilateral accords, the United States employed direct and indirect contacts with other nations to try to bring them into closer conformity with Washington's position on drug control.

At home the Federal Bureau of Narcotics brought a previously unknown efficiency to drug law enforcement. In doing so the bureau created a self-perpetuating need for its existence. Addiction continued to be portrayed as a social contagion, a matter to be treated only secondarily as a medical problem. It is unfortunate that when the United States had to restructure the bureaucracy enforcing drug laws, it did not reconsider as well the assumptions underlying the laws. Had this reevaluation occurred the federal narcotic farms might have been more successful at rehabilitating addicts.

Ever since the closure of the narcotic clinics a need existed for federal treatment centers. In 1928 nearly one-third of the seventy-seven hundred inmates in federal prisons had been convicted of Harrison law violations. Congressman Stephen G. Porter spoke of the need for federal centers as early as 1923. A bill he sponsored creating two facilities became law in January 1929. In debate on the bill, the farms were termed separate prisons for addicts. The Surgeon General of the Public Health Service, the official in charge of the institutions, opposed their creation. The bill passed, though, and the first facility opened in Lexington, Kentucky in 1935, the other in Fort Worth, Texas three years later.[4]

The Bureau of Narcotics closely scrutinized the operation of the farms. No likelihood existed therefore that the United States would alter its attitude on addicts and addiction. Although bureaucracies tend to perpetuate themselves, thus disallowing an examination of the assumptions underlying their existence and practices, the officials in charge can attempt to make their organizations more responsive to the needs of those with whom they deal. This did not happen while Harry J. Anslinger served as the head of the Bureau of Narcotics. As David F. Musto has written:

> There is no evidence that during Anslinger's tenure as commissioner he ever changed his mind that the most effective way of gaining public compliance with a law regulating a dangerous drug was a policy of high fines and severe mandatory prison sentences for first time convictions.[5]

While United States drug policy evolved into the form it assumed in the 1930s, Latin America was first being introduced to the idea of drug control. The government in Washington encouraged nations there to initiate antidrug programs of their own. At no time after the early 1900s, it should be recalled, did the United States not consider internationalizing its control policies, whether such action sprung from humanitarian concerns or took a more restrictive, coercive form. Drug control in the early twentieth century remained a phenomenon peculiar to Western, Anglicized cultures desirous of regulating individual social behavior. As a result, the United States among other nations defined drug use as an unacceptable vice. Not surprisingly, that perspective minimized the divergent cultural experience of other countries with drugs.

As we have seen, Latin America possessed a deeply rooted tradition of drug and alcohol use. For example, R. C. Padden has termed alcohol in Mexico an "anodyne against the pain of existence." Montezuma the Elder outlawed its use in the early 1500s, but his action failed to halt consumption even under the threat of a death penalty for public drunkenness.[6] Indians in Mexico began using peyote prior to the eighteenth century[7]—and perhaps marijuana as well, but that is less certain. Coca leaf chewing in the Andes originated long before contact with Europeans. The royal family and nobles of the Inca Empire reserved to themselves the right to chew coca, but after the conquest el coqueo pervaded all segments of the native population. Intermittent Spanish efforts to outlaw coca proved largely unsuccessful. Coca provided substantial alimentary support for the development of Peru's economy in addition to its religious significance.[8]

This heritage favoring the use of stimulants and intoxicating beverages of one kind or another prevented most Latin American countries from legislating other than rudimentary drug controls before 1930. As Terry and Pellens cogently wrote in a related context: "The enormity [sic] of such a task is patent but its significance is perhaps too often lost by those who in their zeal for reform have made ill-considered and unwarranted attacks on the customs and policies of other nations."[9] At the urging of the United States, Peru took a hesitant step toward applying controls on the coca leaf envisioned by the 1912 Hague Convention, but drew back. Mexico, too, received encouragement from Washington to adopt drug controls. Various actions were taken, especially after 1920, but enforcement of antidrug measures was irregular and achievements were few.

Latin American nations could not completely ignore, however, the insistent entreaties of the international control movement. Thus many nations signed the several conventions agreed upon before 1931 at The Hague and Geneva; some of them also occasionally submitted annual reports to the Opium Advisory Commitee. Nonetheless, Latin American performance in the antidrug campaign remained perfunctory at best. For its part, the United States, burdened by inflexibility, had little power to improve or influence the record of activity there. Diplomatic overtures during the 1920s did not accomplish much. Latin American governments for the most part were not concerned with drug regulation. In some regions drugs posed no problems. In other areas, such as Mexico and Central America, emerging difficulties were minimized; elsewhere, especially in the Andes, the enjoyment of coca was an integral part of Indian culture and could not be eliminated, even had the commitment to do so existed.

A change in attitude first appeared at the time of the 1931 Geneva conference. Uruguay put into effect the strongest drug control program in South America, and Mexico adopted several regulatory measures on its own and in concert with the United

States. Yet the signals indicating a general shift in position were rarely transformed into restrictive policies. Governments would sign an agreement, then defeat its purpose through reservations— as Bolivia and Peru did with coca leaf controls.

Few Latin American states considered adopting and enforcing strong antidrug policies until the United States expressed concern over the local situation. After 1936 the United States increasingly subordinated the promotion of comprehensive drug controls to the more important quest for inter-American security. For some nations, such as Honduras, domestic political considerations took precedence over the adoption of effective controls. Only in its relations with Mexico prior to 1940 could Washington find much satisfaction. (Uruguay evidently acted on its own initiative.) This singular achievement disappeared by the end of the Second World War, however. The war compounded drug problems in crucial Latin American areas, particularly Mexico. Whatever determination there existed to enhance antinarcotic activity was generally thwarted. Not until after the war, with the creation of the United Nations Commission on Narcotic Drugs, did most nations in Latin America consider adopting drug control policies similar to those in effect in other countries.[10]

In the Andean nations and Mexico where the United States most strongly desired the adoption of controls, cultural resistance presented a formidable obstacle to change, thereby stalemating plans to extend throughout the hemisphere American-style antidrug principles and policies. Moreover, Latin American reluctance to alter narcotic policies held important implications. The reluctance, in effect, questioned the validity of the assumptions upon which Washington's control philosophy was based. Despite the efforts of the Bureau of Narcotics and the State Department, addiction at home steadily increased and illicit traffic flourished in the aftermath of war.

By the late 1940s a reconsideration of the relationship of the federal government to drugs and to those who use them was in order. Addicts needed to be reintegrated into American society. Had this transformation in attitude and policy taken place, the United States would have better understood the impediments to drug control in the Americas. But no reconsideration occurred. United States policy continued to emphasize the threat of drugs to American citizens without sufficient appreciation of the drug situation in Latin American states. As such, the actions of narcotic officials led by Harry J. Anslinger obscured as they had since 1930 the narrow line between diplomacy and intervention in the internal affairs of other nations. The postwar international control movement, dominated as it was by the United States, was powerless to attune American policy to the realities of the situation.

The most unfortunate consequence of the intractability of United States policy was that in the first two decades after the war there continued what Walter Duranty termed "the horror and damnation of poor little human flies"—individuals trapped in the double web of addiction and government contempt.[11]

Epilogue:
The Limits of Flexibility

Drug dependence became one of the most visible social maladies in the Americas during the 1970s. At the start of the decade a heroin epidemic plagued the United States. A torrent of Mexican and, to a lesser degree, Colombian marijuana flooded the country, and smuggling offered to many the maleficent lure of fabulous wealth and deadly violence. As if in counterpoint, Latin American nations recognized as never before the enormity of social problems connected with drugs.

Available evidence does not permit a comprehensive, let alone accurate, exposition of conditions in the hemisphere from 1948 to the present. One example serves to make the point. That unprecedented amounts of cocaine were produced for illicit consumption in the 1970s is indisputable. But what of the years before 1970? If measured by quantities seized, cocaine was not an overly popular drug. Nonetheless, records of the Department of State and the annual reports of the Bureau of Narcotics suggest its relatively consistent appeal. From 1947 to 1960, cocaine reached the United States from points of origin in Peru, Bolivia, Chile, Colombia, and Ecuador. The illicit traffic began increasing soon after the end of the war, supplied primarily by illegal cocaine factories near Huánuco and Tingo María, Peru. An attempt on the part of the government in Lima to control production through the licensing of factories proved unsuccesssful. The traffic apparently declined between 1952 and 1955, but grew steadily thereafter. However, public preference for marijuana in the United States early in the 1960s dwarfed the demand for cocaine.[1]

The efficacy of efforts at cocaine control remains uncertain. The sending of the Commission of Inquiry on the Coca Leaf to Bolivia and Peru in 1949 indicated an unaccustomed interest in possible controls on coca leaf production. Yet the findings of the Commission of Inquiry and the reactions of Peru and Bolivia, especially, reinforced the adage that the more things change the more they remain the same. The commission found that "coca leaf chewing has harmful effects," and that the "dangerous habit" resulted from "unfavorable social and economic factors." A solution would consist of "improving the living conditions of the populations concerned; and initiating simultaneously a governmental policy to limit the production, control distribution, and eradicate the habit." Peru and Bolivia dissented in part, arguing that the presumed negative effects of el coqueo had not been established scientifically.[2]

The continuing debate over the effects of el coqueo in the pages of *América Indígena* mirrored governmental ambivalence. Carlos Monge Medrano, then serving as the director of the Peruvian Indian Institute, defended coca chewing as necessary for Indian life in the upper reaches of the Andes. He argued that the need to chew coca leaves decreased the nearer Indians lived to sea level. In opposition, C. A. Ricketts dismissed the views of Monge as merely personal opinions, arguing instead along similar lines to those put forth by the Commission of Inquiry. The debate, of course, had no immediate resolution. What remained abundantly clear was that the annual production of Peruvian coca leaves yielded over seventy-one tons of cocaine at a time when the legitimate international demand did not exceed five tons per year.[3]

One positive development for drug control prior to 1970 was the work of the United Nations Commission on Narcotic Drugs. Whereas unrealistic expectations impaired the work of the Opium Advisory Committee of the League of Nations, similarly vain hopes did not compromise the commission. Despite, or perhaps because of the domination of the United States over its activities, the commission dealt efficiently with administrative and technical matters. It also oversaw the adoption in 1961 of the Single Convention on Narcotic Drugs, an international agreement that replaced all prior accords except the weak 1936 convention for the suppression of illicit traffic. Moreover, the commission worked well with other agencies in promoting drug control, especially the World Health

Organization, which emphasizes the treatment of addiction as the most efficacious means of control.[4]

Other developments had diverse effects upon conditions in the Americas in the 1970s. In their entirety they reveal new obstacles in the path of effective control and demonstrate as well the persistence of older, familiar impediments. First of all, the American narcotics bureaucracy underwent considerable change at the highest levels after Harry J. Anslinger retired in 1962. The Federal Bureau of Narcotics and the Bureau of Drug Abuse Control (formerly under the jurisdiction of the Department of Health, Education, and Welfare) were merged in 1968 to form the Bureau of Narcotics and Dangerous Drugs within the Justice Department (BNDD), with John Ingersoll as director. As with the creation of the old bureau in 1930, a scandal occurred simultaneously involving federal drug agents working out of the New York office. This time there was no Anslinger to placate the agency's critics.

What next transpired portrays a fairly consistent picture of minor scandals, indicative of administrative disorder. Displeased with the domestic operations of the BNDD, which concentrated more upon tracking international smugglers than apprehending street peddlers, the administration of Richard M. Nixon created the Office of Drug Abuse in 1972. It was combined the following year with BNDD to form the Drug Enforcement Administration (DEA). Almost from its inception, congressional critics of DEA charged it with mismanagement.[5] It remains for agents in the field, until recently in occasional competition with Customs Agency personnel, to enforce policy directives emanating from Washington. Despite a serious scandal in its own Office of Drug Abuse Policy, the administration of Jimmy Carter finally brought a semblance of order to the nation's narcotic bureaucracy.

Even before the creation of the DEA, United States officials had a serious situation to contend with in the hemisphere. Starting in the late 1940s illicit traffic in opiates and marijuana flowed in ever-growing amounts from Mexico to the United States. Most alarming of all was the endless supply of heroin. In addition to Mexico, the primary sources of supply by 1970 were Turkey and the Golden Triangle of Southeast Asia. The following statistic shows the epidemic proportions of the problem: officials believed that at least one-fourth of the estimated one million users were addicts.

With corruption at the enforcement level at home and abroad impairing the effectiveness of activity against heroin, the only logical action became limitation at the source. Seizure of drugs in transit along routes from Turkey through the Mediterranean and France, from Southeast Asia to the West Coast, and north from Mexico had failed. Accordingly, the United States promoted the creation of the United Nations Fund for Drug Abuse Control as an educational tool in the fight against opium. Far more important was the decision of the government of Turkey to prohibit the cultivation of opium poppies starting in the fall of 1972. For the first time the United States committed itself also to pledging considerable financial support to the antidrug efforts of other countries. This decision along with Turkey's action effectively severed the notorious "French Connection."[6]

The years 1968 and 1969 set the tone for recent inter-American activity against drugs. Whatever its domestic shortcomings, the decision of the Bureau of Narcotics and Dangerous Drugs to concentrate upon the international traffic was of signal importance. Ironically, the effort to arrest major smugglers, or *traficantes*, began with an ill-conceived program in September 1969 at the Mexican border, Operation Intercept. This deliberate attempt to place economic pressure upon Mexico for its poor antidrug record was soon transformed into Operation Cooperation. In the wake of Intercept, which cost $30 million in its three weeks, officials designed a program of material and financial assistance for the purposes of crop contamination or eradication. Aid took the form of helicopters, automatic weapons, money ($11.6 million in Fiscal Year 1975), DEA agents for the training of Mexican enforcement personnel, and herbicides and defoliants.[7] Limitation at the source had come to the Americas.

The long-awaited program entailed substantial commitments on both sides of the Rio Grande. Mexico officially acknowledged that it served as a major source of heroin and marijuana. So much so that with the suspension of opium planting in Turkey, Mexican heroin was filling between 80 and 90 percent of the North American demand—almost a 70 percent increase from 1971 to 1975. In order to curb the production and flow of heroin, Mexico needed more money, men, and materiel than the annual $10 million in assistance from the United States was able to fund. This interruption of illicit traffic probably accounted for no more than 10 percent of the total trade, a figure that Congressman Lester L. Wolff of the Select Committee on Narcotics Abuse and Control termed "ludicrous."[8]

President Gerald R. Ford called for a stronger antidrug effort, a sentiment echoed by his successor. The increasing number of deaths of drug agents in Mexico underscored the need for more effective action and assistance. An enhanced program of assistance allowed Mexico in 1976–77 to turn almost exclusively to the use of herbicides for the destruction of opium poppy fields. If the results were impressive, based upon a rise in the street price of greatly adulterated heroin, the costs were high. Mexico was spending perhaps $35 million per year in its war on drugs; and at least twenty-two field agents were killed in 1976.[9] Smuggling and violence would not readily be separated.

Even as success came to the Mexican–United States antidrug efforts, the admonition in 1977 of Dr. Peter G. Bourne, head of the White House Office of Drug Abuse Policy, realistically appraised the situation: "I don't think we ought to be overly optimistic. I don't think we're going to eradicate opium cultivation." Bourne and other officials knew well that when the heroin empire of a major traficante fell apart, as did that of Fred Gómez Carrasco in 1974, other traficantes were waiting to take his place in a climate still conducive to smuggling. During the decade illicit cultivation spread throughout Mexico, far beyond its prior concentration in the northwestern states. The unholy trio of smuggling, foreign money, and threats of violence often provided sufficient inducement for local officials to ignore the heroin trade.[10]

Nonetheless, there was marked progress in the war against drugs. In Mexico, a new agency, the Centros de Integración Juvenil, dealt with the problems of young addicts. In the United States, officials in the Carter administration saw continuing adulteration and rising prices force numerous Americans to give up their heroin habits. Concomitantly, overdose deaths declined by 40 percent for 1977–78. Hoping to keep opium production at diminished levels, the Mexican government began to study alternative income programs for the remote, often impoverished areas where poppies were grown.[11]

Some uncertainty remains, however, about the Mexican antidrug commitment of the late 1970s. President José López Portillo at various times appointed or otherwise employed in important ca-

pacities individuals allegedly connected with smuggling operations. Moreover, the extent of collaboration with United States
personnel in Mexico dropped to its lowest level since DEA agents
first began observing opium and marijuana destruction in 1975.
Reluctance to have the agents accompany the expeditions may
have stemmed more from the furor in the United States over the
use of paraquat on marijuana than from a diminution of Mexico's
commitment to limitation at the source.[12] A paraquat scare lasted
from March through August 1978 and resulted in the so-called
Percy Amendment (named after Sen. Charles Percy, Rep., Ill.) to
the International Security Assistance Act of 1961. The amendment
prohibited the government from providing assistance for any program of marijuana eradication involving a herbicide, if the use of
the herbicide "is likely to cause serious harm to the health of
persons who may use or consume the sprayed marijuana" unless a
marker is used which will "clearly and readily warn potential users"
of the herbicide.

Secretary of Health, Education, and Welfare Joseph A. Califano
announced on August 2, 1979 that marijuana sprayed by paraquat
was likely to prove harmful to those who in some way consumed
the contaminated substance. Some drug officials believed that the
secretary's determination, which was based upon questionable evidence, would effectively cut off the funds provided Mexico to assist
in the eradication of marijuana and opium poppies. It seemed of
little consequence that none of the funding was specifically directed for the purchase of paraquat that Mexico obtained with its
own funds from ICI Ltd. in Great Britain. The Department of
State interpreted the amendment broadly enough so that assistance
continued without interruption. Also, Senator Percy clarified his
amendment with another, attached to the International Security
Assistance Act of 1979, which, while still prohibiting the use of
United States funds for paraquat, is consistent with the interpretation of the Department of State.[13]

The upshot of the controversy, however, was that the government of López Portillo began to doubt the seriousness of the
United States commitment to a comprehensive drug control program. In the words of Ralph Saucedo, a DEA official: "The Mexicans have been, in the area of eradication, very constant." In fact,
the government of Mexico in 1976 jailed 4,500 heads of household
from the state of Sinaloa as part of the eradication campaign, an

action which damaged for some time the entire economy of the state. Based upon the apparently uncompromising nature of their eradication program, Mexican drug officials view with suspicion the tolerance of the marijuana lobby exhibited by some authorities in Washington.[14]

In one sense, the uncertainty on each side of the Rio Grande about the credibility of antidrug fervor on the other side matters little. The flow of drugs will continue. As one observer has concluded: "Short of closing the border and patrolling it with thousands of law enforcement officers, there is little hope of ending the drug traffic as long as the demand exists in the United States."[15]

Not all of the drug problems in the Americas during the 1970s originated in Mexico. For example, the practice by Paraguay's General Alfredo Stroessner of providing a home for some of the most notorious individuals engaged in the illicit international trade also proved troublesome. Further, several nations which had previously served primarily as transfer points for drugs grown or manufactured elsewhere either began or greatly increased the cultivation of opium poppies and marijuana. Another, Colombia, became more involved than ever in the cocaine and marijuana traffic.[16]

In the first fifteen years after the Second World War, the annual reports of the Bureau of Narcotics only once referred to Colombia by name as a source of illicit cocaine, emphasizing instead the cultivation of coca leaves in Bolivia and Peru, and the refining of cocaine and its export out of South America from those countries and Ecuador and Chile.[17] From the late 1960s to the mid-1970s, the Colombian cocaine trade boomed. Colombia grew coca and refined cocaine for the trade, while also producing high-grade marijuana for the North American market. Coca paste was refined into cocaine hydrochloride in Bogotá, Cali, and Medellin, then exported north through the Caribbean—particularly via Costa Rica. Guajira Peninsula in northeast Colombia served as the major staging area for drug exportation. In the words of DEA agent Octavio González in Bogotá in 1975: "The area is controlled by Indians and there is little local law enforcement."[18]

United States aid to Colombia could not produce results comparable to those achieved in Mexico. The House Select Committee on Narcotics Abuse and Control (established in 1976) termed Colombia "the single most important staging point for cocaine destined to the United States." Antidrug programs had to contend with "endemic corruption" and the "irresistible" attraction of bribes to local officials.[19] Financial assistance totaled $800,000 in Fiscal Year 1977. The Department of State developed a long-term assistance program similar to the one previously devised for Mexico. Colombia responded legislatively by enacting four separate antidrug laws by the end of 1977.[20] Successful enforcement of the laws remained, as always in the fight against drugs, an entirely separate matter.

By the end of the decade accomplishments were few. The Select Committee on Narcotics Abuse found a "genuine commitment" on the part of the government of Julio César Turbay Ayala to combat the problem, which must have seemed like a hydra to Colombian officials. One of the major aspects of the problem was the contribution of the drug business to the national economy. Although boosting the rate of inflation to more than 25 percent, the dollar value of the drug trade—by adding $1 billion to the economy in 1979—surpassed the value of coffee exports. It is worth noting that the per capita income of Colombia was $674 in 1977. The marijuana trade alone reportedly supported forty thousand families. The burgeoning of marijuana cultivation directly resulted from North American demands for cannabis uncontaminated by paraquat. So lucrative was the trade that numerous reports of official corruption, extending even to Turbay Ayala, began reaching Washington. Fears of continued smuggling and attendant corruption could not have been allayed when a policy-study group in Bogotá, the National Association of Financial Institutions, proposed the legalization and taxation of marijuana.[21]

The United States revised its aid program in an attempt to combat the seemingly intractable conditions. Colombia received approximately $16 million in assistance for fiscal years 1979 and 1980, an enormous increase in a short period of time. This amount compared favorably with the level of assistance to Mexico. Along with the training of enforcement personnel, funds were provided for the purchase of helicopters, patrol vessels, and radar. It remained to be seen whether the assistance would help Colombia appreciably reduce the northward flow of drugs. Ralph Saucedo captured the essence of the situation. Colombia, he observed, "has much less control, actual control of its territory than does Mexico . . . from the point of view of enforcement." Or as Mathea Falco, senior adviser on narcotics in the State Department, told the

House Subcommittee on Inter-American Affairs: "I fear that the solutions are not overnight solutions."[22]

Conditions in Bolivia and Peru warranted a similar conclusion. An Inter-American Consultative Group on Coca Leaf Problems met in Lima in 1964, but the deliberations failed to reach an agreement concerning reduced cultivation. Bolivia would not sign the Single Convention on Narcotic Drugs until 1975; and Peru, although a signatory power, stipulated that a twenty-five-year period might be needed before reduction was undertaken. The establishment of the National Coca Monopoly in 1969 brought no substantive change in the situation. No more helpful were the social policies of the government of Fernando Belaúnde Terry, which held power from 1963 to 1968. Public spending extended political patronage at the expense of social reform.[23] Nor did the seizure of power by the revolutionary government of Juan Velasco Alvarado offer hope for increased anticoca activity. Several months before Velasco was overthrown, an unnamed United States official lamented: "The Peruvian Government has no unified policy on coca."[24]

Routes taken by coca paste or cocaine out of the Andes were generally well known, especially through Panama and the Caribbean, but interception proved no easier than at any other time. Until the fall of the Allende government, Chile served as a principal refining center. That situation apparently changed under the military junta. Clandestine labs also operated in Ecuador and Argentina. Through the mid-1970s, Latin Americans, including expatriate Cubans, reportedly controlled the inter-American cocaine trade. Perhaps as many as twenty metric tons of Andean cocaine supplied North American demands in 1976.[25]

As in the cases of Colombia and Mexico, United States officials devised a long-term program of direct antidrug assistance. Secretary of State Henry A. Kissinger discussed coca controls and alternative agricultural programs on a trip to Bolivia in June 1976. DEA personnel were provided to train local officials; and Bolivia, Peru, and Ecuador received more than $3 million in aid during Fiscal Year 1977. Officials in Washington did not delude themselves, however, into believing that greater assistance and stronger anticoca commitments on the part of Andean governments would soon produce desired results. As Commssioner of Customs Vernon D. Acree declared in a related context in 1976: "The level of smuggling of narcotics has continued almost unabated. . . . Smuggling has become highly organized . . . Interdiction has become, of course, corespondingly more difficult . . ."[26]

Regulatory efforts by Bolivia and Peru met with little success in the short term. In 1977 Bolivia initiated a program to limit coca cultivation to quantities needed for legitimate daily use. New regulations mandated the registration of growers and prohibited new cultivation. The government also considered implementing a crop substitution program. The following year, a new drug law in Peru forbade expanded coca plantings and required the conversion of unspecified large fields to other crops by the early 1980s. Conversion would depend upon the availability of acceptable economic alternatives, an unlikely occurrence at best. Commenting upon the situation in the late 1960s in Bolivia and Peru, a United Nations official offered a seemingly timeless observation: "You need a terrific social upheaval first. The coca bush is the only cash crop [of the Andean Indians], and until the social and economic position improves, there will be no change." [27] As was apparent throughout the next decade, political instability in both Bolivia and Peru did not offer the kind of social change the official had in mind.

The Select Committe on Narcotics Abuse underscored the difficulty of implementing controls on coca in its report on a study mission to South America. Whether for reasons of political turmoil, poverty, tradition, corruption, or a combination thereof, the committee concluded, the control of coca seemed beyond the ability of Peru and Bolivia. Far too many Indians remained far too dependent upon coca for their livelihood. As a cash crop, coca could be harvested three to four times per year. Growers in traditional planting areas, Yungas and Chapare in Bolivia and Cuzco and Huánuco in Peru, would ignore orders for eradication or substantial limitations on cultivation.[28]

Thus, historical obstacles to coca leaf control once more were preventing a comprehensive campaign against cocaine in the Americas. The nature of assistance to Bolivia and Peru for coca control in the late 1970s reflected a realistic appraisal of the situation on the part of policymakers in Washington. The four DEA agents assigned to Peru were stationed in Lima rather than throughout the country as in Mexico. Little could have been accomplished in the growing regions. Moreover, the Department of State virtually eliminated financial assistance to Bolivia and Peru for the development of a crop substitution program. It did not believe that income substitution could overcome the growers' satisfaction in cultivating coca. Nor was incarceration the answer. "We do not want to punish the growers," said one Department of State official. "We do not want them to go to jail."[29] In the short term, policy options were virtually nonexistent.

Additional remarks are in order concerning Peru, Bolivia, and the prospect of coca controls. Peruvian coca provides the basis for between 60 and 75 percent of the cocaine refined in South America. In the departments where coca is grown, the economy depends upon the commerce in coca leaves. In some instances, Indian laborers in the Andes may still be paid in part with a ration of coca leaves. As long as coca is grown, it will be chewed, traded, and exported for traditional purposes be they cultural, economic, or illicit.[30]

The government of Peru recognizes the connection between el coqueo and the international traffic in cocaine, and acknowledges the difficulty of altering the situation. As Alejandro Costa, head of the National Coca Monopoly, remarked in 1976: "We have in mind the slow and gradual elimination of the habit of chewing. It will take massive education and a long time."[31]

What is not so apparent, either in Costa's observation or in the anticoca programs of the 1970s, is a recognition of the need to transcend the cultural and social separation that still pervades Peruvian society. Even if the will exists to end the disparagement of Indian culture, such a commitment remains open to question despite the success of the revolutionary government in virtually eliminating the hacienda system. The means to bring about so fundamental a change are not presently available. The global recession of the early 1970s had a debilitating effect on the national economy. The foreign debt grew to staggering proportions, thereby reducing social spending to a minimum and making Peru, in the words of Stephen Kinzer, "a ward of the international banking system."[32] In this unhappy situation, the promotion of cultural changes that might lead to controls on coca is out of the question.

The government of Bolivia is no more likely to control coca grown for the cocaine trade. On July 17, 1980, the Bolivian army under the leadership of Gen. Luis García Meza Tejada seized power from the transitional government of Lydia Gueiler Tejada. Gueiler was scheduled to turn over power to an individual named by the national congress on August 4. That individual was likely to be Hernán Siles Zuazo, who had won a plurality in nationwide voting on June 29. García Meza claimed to be resisting a "Communist assault" on Bolivian institutions.[33]

What actually seems to have occurred was a "cocaine coup." In 1979, a few Bolivians may have earned as much as $500 million from the cocaine trade. Included among that number were prominent officials in the García Meza government, especially Col. Luis Arce Gómez, the interior minister and chief of security. In response to the coup, the United States recalled its ambassador, Marvin Weissman, for consultation and expressed "extreme disapproval" of the takeover. Subsequently, the Department of State cancelled economic aid projects, military assistance, and, on August 13, terminated its drug-related assistance. The Permanent Council of the Organization of American States, acting on a resolution sponsored by the other members of the Andean Common Market—Venezuela, Colombia, Ecuador, and Peru—deplored the coup and demanded an inquiry into alleged human rights violations by the junta.[34]

The severity of repression led one journalist to term the García Meza government "Bolivia's most repressive regime in this century." Its hold on power was buttressed by a promise of more than $200 million in economic and military assistance from Argentina, plus the support of right-wing regimes in Brazil, Paraguay, Uruguay, and Chile. In such an atmosphere, suppression of the cocaine trade, which the generals may have feared from a civilian government, was impossible. "Cocaine," noted an editorial in the *Washington Post*, " . . . has become Bolivia's largest export earner. Peasants can make more money growing coca leaves than coffee beans."

By June 1981 the Bolivian government was about to undergo another change. García Meza had tried and failed to improve relations with the United States. Neither the ouster from the government in February of Arce Gómez and the minister of education, Ariel Coca (because of their association with the cocaine trade), nor the initiation of an anticocaine campaign (which was met with skepticism in Washington), induced the administration of President Ronald Reagan to restore economic and military assistance or to resume a diplomatic presence in La Paz. Three abortive, right-wing coup attempts in May, behind which may have loomed the figure of Arce Gómez, then increasingly popular with the Argentines, prompted García Meza to announce that he would step down as president and commander of the army no later than August 6.[35]

At length, the record of inter-American drug control during the 1970s, when examined on a country-by-country basis, can only be judged a partially encouraging one. More than ever before, governments throughout the hemisphere pledged to the struggle against drugs their nations' financial and material resources as willingly as they professed their good intentions. In the forefront of the struggle as always, United States officials had to be pleased with certain developments. Mexico, with its own resources and $90 million in aid from the United States during the decade, was winning the war against heroin and perhaps marijuana as well. Colombia appeared to be holding its own against the traffic in cocaine, but seemed less able to reduce the flow of marijuana. President Turbay Ayala first employed the national police in the latter effort, then called on the army for assistance, and, in the summer of 1980, turned again to the national police.[36] For a time, even Bolivia and Peru helped foster an atmosphere of rising expectations by considering seriously for the first time programs to reduce coca leaf cultivation.

Other developments were far less promising. García Meza's coup in Bolivia was only the most visible. The cultivation of coca leaves continued to expand, perhaps by as much as 20 percent each year. In Peru, it remained to be seen whether the government of Fernando Belaúnde Terry, who returned to power after an absence of twelve years, would attempt to control the situation there.[37] Even if cultivation restrictions were possible in the Peruvian highlands, other areas, such as northwestern Brazil, were beginning to pose similar problems.[38] Moreover, the illicit traffic in all drugs was more structured in 1980 than it had been since the early 1970s. According to one official in the DEA, the great amount of money involved made it more difficult to control than ever.[39]

The future of effective controls was threatened further by the ominous resurgence of the heroin trade from Iran, Pakistan, and Afghanistan that was inundating Western Europe by the end of 1979 and beginning to reach the United States. The head of the DEA, Peter B. Bensinger, placed the level of purity at 20 percent, an incredible increase over the 3.5 percent purity of Mexican heroin. Iranians reportedly harvested fifteen hundred tons of raw opium in 1979, one hundred times the size of the Mexican crop.[40] With this influx of heroin, including perhaps renewed supplies from Mexico, addiction in the United States is already climbing, reversing a five-year downward trend. The Iranian revolution and the Soviet occupation of Afghanistan with its resulting unrest in Pakistan did not augur well for any improvement in conditions.

The situation cannot prove anything else but bitterly ironic, frustrating, and disappointing for drug control officials in the United States. During the 1970s their efforts resulted in the virtual elimination of opium traffic from Turkey and its curtailment from the Golden Triangle of Southeast Asia. Mexico's accomplishments have been noted in detail. What was emerging in the struggle against opium, marijuana, and cocaine was an international willingness to attempt limitation at the source. At the same time, American officials were responding to conditions in Latin America in ways that promised a previously unknown measure of success. No longer did they cling to the belief, too long evident in hemispheric narcotic relations, that an efficient bureaucracy (in Washington) could effectively manage, and thereby overcome, drug-related societal problems wherever they existed.

First of all, United States officials recognized the limits of their ability to alter conditions unilaterally. Operation Intercept taught them an important lesson. This recognition of limited power provided the basis for a more coordinated drug bureaucracy at home while allowing the bureaucracy to work with international agencies, such as the United Nations Fund for Drug Abuse Control, without unrealistic expectations of immediate success.

Second, officials in Washington appreciated as never before the existence of domestic drug problems in Latin America. Only by assisting other nations in their struggle against drugs could the United States expect more than ephemeral success at home. The increase in financial and material aid at mid-decade illustrates well this nascent understanding of the need for reciprocity in drug control activity. In short, these two changes in policy allowed American authorities to develop a flexible program of assistance that took into account the complex nature of the problems to be overcome.

As I have suggested throughout this study, drug control cannot succeed if officials remain ignorant of the historical or cultural reasons for the presence of drugs in society. Nor can drug control be understood in isolation from contemporaneous occurrences. That is, however flexible United States drug policy has become, effective control over drugs may remain an elusive quest. Drug dependence seems endemic in modern technological societies. Moreover, financial rewards continue to outweigh the risks for those who provide drugs, whether one lives a subsistence existence somewhere in Latin America or revels in the life-style successful drug dealing inevitably provides.

These considerations cast doubt on the likelihood of a resolution in the war between drugs and society. Limitation at the source, long viewed with confidence as the ultimate solution to the drug problem, now seems unattainable. The necessary income support programs will entail enormous costs. No legislature, in the United States or elsewhere, will shoulder such a fiscal burden willingly. It seems certain that in the absence of effective controls on chronic inflation, the United States will be forced to reduce the inter-American assistance programs of the late 1970s. In the aftermath of budgetary retrenchment, drug dependence will again increase.

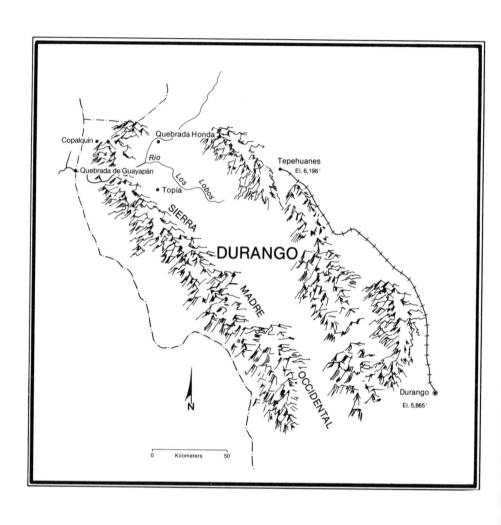

Copalquin •

Quebrada Honda
•

Tepehuanes
• El. 6,198'

Río
• Quebrada de Guayapán

Los

Lobos

• Topia

SIERRA

DURANGO

MADRE

OCCIDENTAL

Durango ◉
El. 5,865'

N

0   Kilometers   50

Appendix:
Opium Poppy Destruction
in Mexico, 1944

No. 942

AMERICAN CONSULATE
Durango, Durango, Mexico, June 27, 1944

AIR MAIL
STRICTLY CONFIDENTIAL
Subject: Opium Poppy Fields in State of Durango Destroyed.
The Honorable
The Secretary of State,
Washington.

Sir:

I have the honor to transmit herewith copies, with translation, of a report of the destruction, under the supervision of the Servicios Sanitarios Coordinados (Public Health Service) of Durango, accompanied by kodak photographs, of the poppy fields and the work of destruction being carried on by the Federal troops and the men employed to assist in the work.

The poppy plantings mentioned in the enclosed reports are located at the villages of METATES, QUEBRADA HONDA, and

FRESNO which places are three days by horseback almost due west from Tepehuanes, the end of the railway line extending from Durango to Tepehuanes. These places are situated to the right of a line drawn from Topia to Copalquin, Durango, and about half way between those places. These villages are located in the heart of the Sierra Madre mountains and are very difficult to reach. In fact the only manner of reaching these villages is by horse or mule back. The people in that section of this state are quite uneducated and uncultured and whose [sic] standard of living is very low. It will be noted from the reports transmitted herewith that the poppy plantings were on small parcels of land. This is due to the fact that the amount of tillable land in that secluded part of the state is in small tracts located in small valleys between mountains. The pictures accompanying this report will give a better idea of the terrain in that section of the state.

The expedition covered by the enclosed report was made as a result of representations made to the local Servicios Sanitarios Coordinados by Mr. Salvador C. PENA, Treasury Representative assigned to the American Embassy, Mexico, D.F. The originals of the documents enclosed herewith were delivered to this Consulate by Dr. Casimiro VALLADARES PINEDA, Chief of the Servicios Sanitarios Coordinados, Durango, and this office transmitted them to the Treasury Representative mentioned through the Embassy.

It will be noted from the report submitted by Inspectors Juan Francisco CURIEL and Miguel Onesimo CALDERON that the 10th Military Zone, with headquarters in the city of Durango ordered Lieutenant Colonel of Cavalry Romulo Soto BURCIAGA, stationed at Tepehuanes, to accompany the inspectors designated by Servicios Sanitarios Coordinados, Juan Francisco Curiel and his assistant, Miguel Onesimo Calderon, to the region where it was reported there were plantings of poppy for the purpose of destroying them. Lieutenant Colonel Burciaga took a squad of 23 soldiers with him. It will be noted further from the report that there was a delay of one day in the expedition getting started from Tepehuanes. Whether the pretext offered for the delay was legitimate or not it is not known, but it is stated in the report that the people of these villages had been notified two days previous to their arrival that government employees were on their way. Although it cannot be verified, it is not improbable that the poppy growers were informed from Durango of the pending arrival of forces to destroy their fields prior to the time the inspector and his assistant departed from this city.

It will also be noted that the report of the inspector mentions a lack of cooperation on the part of the people along the trail to their destination, and upon their arrival at the villages mentioned they were almost depopulated. Although statements were taken from several persons, including principally women, but one individual, Ramon GAMIZ, was arrested and brought into Durango.

The enclosed photographs will show that but one or two soldiers assisted in the destruction of the poppy fields. Doctor Casimiro Valladares Pineda explained that the reason so few troops assisted in the destruction of these plantings was because the balance of the squad was guarding those who were working in order to prevent the natives from ambushing them. Doctor Valladares stated further that the reason that some of the women whose lands were planted to poppy were not arrested and brought into Durango was because Lieutenant Colonel Burciaga was afraid that if he arrested these women the natives would ambush the troops along the trail. Doctor Valladares further stated that his inspector and assistant informed him that they would not make another trip to that section. They are afraid that some of those whose poppy fields were destroyed may come into Durango and assassinate them. The Doctor further stated that if he is ordered to send inspectors to that section again to destroy poppy plantations, he will ask the Federal Government to send inspectors from Mexico City for that special purpose, so that his local inspectors will not be subject to the possibilities of being murdered in the city of Durango.

The EXCELSIOR, one of the principal Mexico City dailies, published an article a short time ago to the effect that Governor Rodolfo LOAIZA, of the State of Sinaloa, which [sic] occurred in Mazatlan, Sinaloa, Mexico, during the Carnival last Feburary was assassinated by individuals belonging to a ring handling opium grown in the State of Sinaloa in the vicinity of Badiraguato who claim that Governor Loaiza double crossed them. That notice published in the paper has created even a greater fear in the minds of the local inspectors of the Servicios Sanitarios Coordinados.

The area visited by the inspectors making the enclosed report to the Chief of Servicios Sanitarios Coordinados is but a few miles in extent, and since the terrain of the entire western part of this State is practically the same as that in which opium poppy was being grown, and as considerable plantings of this poppy have been destroyed in the vicinity of Badiraguato, Sinaloa, located to the west of the plantings in this State, and since that section is quite isolated, it is not improbable that there may be other plantings in that district which have not been reported.

It is difficult to arrive from the report of Doctor Valladares at the exact acreage of poppy planting destroyed by the inspectors, but it appears that the acreage destroyed, and already harvested prior to their arrival, amounted to approximately 232 hectares (1 hectare equals 2.47 acres), or 573.04 acres which is quite a sizeable acreage planted to this drug producing plant.

It will be noted from some of the enclosed reports that a part of the poppy plantings visited by the inspectors mentioned above had already been harvested when the inspectors arrived. It has been learned that opium poppy is planted in the district around Metates during the month of October. In order to prevent plantings from maturing it appears necessary that authorities visit that section three times a year; one time in December after the plants planted then have had time to come up and begin growing; another time in February so as to destroy a second planting; and another time during the latter part of April in order to destroy any fields which may have been missed on the two previous trips.

This Consulate has been informed through the correspondent which first reported the existence of opium poppy to the Federal Health Department, Mexico City, whose name is mentioned in Doctor Valladares' report, that a Major Gorgonio ACUNA, assigned to the 9th Military Zone with headquarters at Culiacan, Sinaloa, and who is a native of Metates, is the go-between for the growers and the purchasers for the opium which finds an outlet on the west coast. It was further reported that Major Acuna is associated with an American, name not known, who purchases for 1,000 pesos per kilogram (1 kilogram equals 2.2046 pounds) all the opium which finds an outlet to the west coast, and that this American smuggles the opium into Los Angeles. As stated above, the name of this American is not known, but it is reported that Major Gorgonio Acuna acts as his go-between with the producers, so he can disclose the name of this party, if he can be made to talk. It is also reported that this American visits Mazatlan quite frequently. It is further reported that he advances money to the producers of opium in Sinaloa and Durango with which to clear additional lands for planting to poppy. It appears that a part of the opium produced in the district mentioned finds its way to the United States through Guanacevi, Durango; Parral, Chihuahua; and El Paso, Texas.

It is believed that the enclosed copies of reports submitted by the inspector of Servicios Sanitarios Coordinados present conclusive evidence that opium poppy has been cultivated on a somewhat extensive scale in the immediate district visited, but that but little real effort was made to break up the ring of producers. Due to the fact that it was late in the season when these officials visited that district, a part of the crop had already been harvested. The fact that the growers were tipped off two days before the arrival of these authorities indicates that they have lookouts in Tepehuanes, and quite possibly in the city of Durango in the same office to which these inspectors pertain.

As a precaution for greater safety, this report is being forwarded to the American Embassy, Mexico, D.F. for transmission by that office to the Department by courier.

Respectfully yours,

E. W. Eaton
American Vice Consul

Notes

Preface

1. H. Wayne Morgan, ed., *Yesterday's Addicts: American Society and Drug Abuse, 1865–1920* (Norman: University of Oklahoma Press, 1974), introduction. Also useful in this regard is Arnold Jaffe, "Addiction Reform in the Progressive Age: Scientific and Social Response to Drug Dependence in the United States, 1870–1930" (Ph.D. diss., University of Kentucky, 1977), especially Part II, "Control and Its Achievement" (hereafter cited as Jaffe, "Addiction Reform").

2. Sidney W. Mintz, "History and Anthropology: A Brief Reprise," in *Race and Slavery in the Western Hemisphere: Quantitative Studies,* ed. Stanley L. Engerman and Eugene D. Genovese (Princeton: Princeton University Press, 1975), pp. 477–94, especially pp. 484–85.

3. "The Colombian Connection," *Time,* January 29, 1979, pp. 22–26, 28–29; Robert F. Jones, "Powerboat Racing Has Gone to Pot," *Sports Illustrated,* April 9, 1979, pp. 28–30, 33; Carl Hiaasen and Al Messerschmidt, "Cocaine Killers," *Rolling Stone,* September 20, 1979, pp. 82–85; *Wall Street Journal,* November 20, 1978.

4. Kettil Bruun, Lynn Pan, Ingemar Rexed, *The Gentleman's Club: International Control of Drugs and Alcohol* (Chicago: University of Chicago Press, 1975), p. 16 (hereafter cited as Bruun, Pan, and Rexed, *Gentleman's Club*).

Chapter 1: Culture and Bureaucracy

1. Don S. Kirschner, "The Ambiguous Legacy: Social Justice and Social Control in the Progressive Era," *Historical Reflections,* 2 (Summer 1975), pp. 71, 73 (hereafter cited as Kirschner, "Ambiguous Legacy").

2. Clifford Geertz, *The Interpretation of Cultures* (New York: Basic Books, 1973), pp. 5, 10, 14, 17; on p. 24 Geertz observes: "The whole point of a semiotic approach to culture is . . . to aid us in gaining access to the conceptual world in which our subjects live so that we can, in some extended sense of the term, converse with them."

3. Ibid., pp. 44–46, 49, 52.

4. Sidney W. Mintz, "Foreword," in *Afro-American Anthropology: Contemporary Perspectives,* ed. Norman E. Whitten, Jr. and John F. Szwed (New York: The Free Press, 1970), pp. 9–10.

5. Herbert G. Gutman, *Work, Culture, and Society in Industrializing America: Essays in American Working Class and Social History* (New York: Alfred A. Knopf, 1976), pp. 18, 66 (hereafter cited as Gutman, *Work, Culture, and Society*).

6. Mariano Picón-Salas, *A Cultural History of Spanish America: From Conquest to Independence*, trans. Irving A. Leonard (Berkeley and Los Angeles: University of California Press, 1971), pp. xv–xvi, 18, 24, 49–50. On social standing, see Magnus Mörner, *Race Mixture in the History of Latin America* (Boston: Little, Brown and Company, 1967), pp. 60–61; and more generally, Eric R. Wolf and Edward C. Hansen, *The Human Condition in Latin America* (New York: Oxford University Press, 1972), pp. 22, 25–27.

7. Miguel Leon-Portilla, ed., *The Broken Spears: The Aztec Account of the Conquest of Mexico* (Boston: Beacon Press, 1962), p. xxiv; R. C. Padden, *The Hummingbird and the Hawk: Conquest and Sovereignty in the Valley of Mexico, 1503–1541* (Columbus: Ohio State University Press, 1967), pp. 17–18, 58, 81, 94–95, 98–99 (hereafter cited as Padden, *Hummingbird and the Hawk*); Jacques Soustelle, *Daily Life of the Aztecs on the Eve of the Spanish Conquest*, trans. Patrick O'Brian (New York: The Macmillan Company, 1962), pp. 54, 143 (hereafter cited as Soustelle, *Daily Life of the Aztecs*).

8. Padden, *Hummingbird and the Hawk*, pp. 26, 134, 227–29; Eric Wolf, *Sons of the Shaking Earth: The People of Mexico and Guatemala— Their Land, History and Culture* (Chicago: University of Chicago Press, 1959), pp. 171–72, 199 (hereafter cited as Wolf, *Sons of the Shaking Earth*).

9. Alfred Métraux, *The History of the Incas*, trans. George Ordish (New York: Schocken Books, 1969), pp. 61, 93, 97–98 (hereafter cited as Métraux, *History of the Incas*); W. Golden Mortimer, M.D., *History of Coca: "The Divine Plant" of the Incas*, ed. Michael Horowitz (San Francisco: And/Or Press, 1974), pp. 6, 46, 58, 65 (hereafter cited as Mortimer, *History of Coca*); Wolf, *Sons of the Shaking Earth*, p. 137.

10. Victor Wolfgang von Hagen, ed., *The Incas of Pedro de Cieza de León*, trans. Harriet de Onis (Norman: University of Oklahoma Press, 1959), p. 260 (hereafter cited as von Hagen, ed., *The Incas*); James Lockhart, *Spanish Peru, 1532–1560: A Colonial Society* (Madison: University of Wisconsin Press, 1968), p. 25 (hereafter cited as Lockhart, *Spanish Peru*); and Mortimer, *History of Coca*, pp. 9, 107.

11. Lockhart, *Spanish Peru*, pp. 200, 205–210, 215; Métraux, *History of the Incas*, pp. 164, 166, 177. Official Spanish statistics show a decline in the Indian population from 1.5 million in 1561 to six hundred thousand in 1796.

12. Lockhart, *Spanish Peru*, p. 9.

13. Philip Wayne Powell, *Soldiers, Indians, and Silver: North America's First Frontier War*, rev. ed. (Tempe: Arizona State University Press, 1975), chaps. 1, 11, 12; Wolf, *Sons of the Shaking Earth*, pp. 9, 192; François Chevalier, *Land and Society in Colonial Mexico: The Great Hacienda*, trans. Alvin Eustis (Berkeley and Los Angeles: University of California Press, 1963), pp. 14, 38–42 (hereafter cited as Chevalier, *Land and Society*).

14. Chevalier, *Land and Society*, pp. 68–69, 142–43, 200.

15. Ibid., pp. 288, 309.

16. Edward H. Spicer, "Yaqui," in *Perspectives in American Indian Cultural Change*, ed. Edward H. Spicer (Chicago: University of Chicago Press, 1961), pp. 7–93 (hereafter cited as Spicer, "Yaqui"). The Yaquis were not, of course, the only Indians living in northwestern Mexico. Their singular history of near-autonomy from Spanish and subsequently Mexican forms of government compels special mention. Unlike the Seris and the Tarahumaras, or the Mayos, Opatas, and Pimas, the Yaquis clung to their own forms of cultural, religious, and societal organization. Even the trial of deportation could not extinguish Yaqui autonomy. Yet, when some of the remaining Yaquis returned home during and after the revolutionary decade, they found in their communities competing governmental organizations that virtually ignored the more democratic Yaqui forms. Inevitably, further alienation from the mainstream of Mexican political life was the result. Edward H. Spicer, *Cycles of Conquest: The Impact of Spain, Mexico, and the United States on the Indians of the*

Southwest, 1533–1960 (Tucson: University of Arizona Press, 1962), pp. 395–405; cf. Salomé Hernández, "Innocence or Guilt? Mexico's Arrest of the Yaquis, 1899–1909," *Journal of the West*, 14 (October 1975), pp. 15–26.

17. Descriptions of living conditions and social structure in Mexico on the eve of the twentieth century can be found in Wolf, *Sons of the Shaking Earth*, pp. 213, 238–45; and Jan Bazant, *A Concise History of Mexico from Hidalgo to Cardenas, 1805–1940* (Cambridge: At the University Press, 1977), pp. 39, 59, 65, 73–75, 127, and 128 for the quotation (hereafter cited as Bazant, *Concise History of Mexico*).

18. Lockhart, *Spanish Peru*, pp. 11, 25, 33, and 206–8 for details of the mita system; Thomas M. Davies, Jr., *Indian Integration in Peru: A Half-Century of Experience, 1900–1948* (Lincoln: University of Nebraska Press, 1974), chap. 1 (hereafter cited as Davies, *Indian Integration in Peru*).

19. Helpful in my analysis has been the important essay, George M. Fredrickson and Christopher Lasch, "Resistance to Slavery," *Civil War History*, 13 (December 1967), pp. 315–29.

20. Both Chevalier, *Land and Society*, p. 14 and Soustelle, *Daily Life of the Aztecs*, pp. 155, 218 tell of the accustomed use of peyote.

21. Spicer, "Yaqui," passim; useful, too, for this discussion have been Bazant, *Concise History of Mexico*, and James W. Wilkie, *The Mexican Revolution: Federal Expenditure and Social Change since 1910*, 2nd rev. ed. (Berkeley and Los Angeles: University of California Press, 1970) (hereafter cited as Wilkie, *The Mexican Revolution*).

22. Generally, see Wolf, *Sons of the Shaking Earth*, pp. 188, 201; and Chevalier, *Land and Society*, pp. 46–49.

23. Woodrow Borah, *Early Colonial Trade and Navigation between Mexico and Peru* (Berkeley and Los Angeles: University of California Press, 1954), pp. 63, 96, 112–14.

24. Ibid., pp. 116–27.

25. The quest for plunder also played a notable role in the early development of smuggling; see Kenneth R. Andrews, *The Spanish Caribbean: Trade and Plunder, 1530–1630* (New Haven: Yale University Press, 1978).

26. Ibid., pp. 74–80.

27. Murdo J. MacLeod, *Spanish Central America: A Socioeconomic History, 1520–1720* (Berkeley and Los Angeles: University of California Press, 1973), pp. 41, 44–47, 61, 73–74, 85, 96–97, 133–34, and 142 for the quotation (hereafter cited as MacLeod, *Spanish Central America*).

28. Ibid., pp. 165–67, 208, 220–25, 228.

29. Ibid., part 3.

30. Carlos Gutiérrez-Noriega, "El Hábito de la Coca en Sud América," *América Indígena*, XII (abril de 1952), pp. 111–12 (hereafter cited as Gutiérrez-Noriega, "El Hábito de la Coca"); Dr. German Orosco, "El alma de la humilde hoja del indio dominó el refinamiento del blanco," *Revista Geographica Americana*, XVI (septiembre de 1941), p. 149 (hereafter cited as Orosco, "El alma de la humilde hoja"); Carlos Gutiérrez-Noriega y Vicente Zapata Ortiz, *Estudios Sobre La Coca y La Cocaina en el Perú* (Lima: Ministerio de Educación Publica, 1947), p. 17 (hereafter cited as Gutiérrez-Noriega y Zapata Ortiz, *Estudios Sobre La Coca*); Elsa Dell'Occhio, "La coca, el cocaísmo y los problemas de la hora presenta," *Runa: Archivo Para Las Ciencias Del Hombre*, II (1949), p. 192 (hereafter cited as Dell'Occhio, "La coca, el cocaísmo"); von Hagen, ed., *The Incas,*, p. 259. The preparation of coca for chewing is often meticulous. In Peru, leaves are mixed with an alkaline substance of pot ash or unslaked lime. In Colombia, the preparation for el coqueo, called *mambeo*, entails boiling lime rock from mineral beds to obtain a paste which is then dissolved in a water solution. Ash is added; the entire preparation is cooled, wrapped in a leaf, and buried for several days to insure good quality for chewing. See Carlos Gutiérrez-Noriega, "El Hábito de la Coca en el Perú," *América Indígena*, IX (abril de 1949), p. 147 (hereafter cited as Gutiérrez-Noriega, "El Hábito de la Coca en el Perú"); Jorge Bejarano,

"El Cocaísmo en Colombia," *América Indígena*, V (enero de 1945), 14; and von Hagen, ed., *The Incas*, p. 259.

31. Luis A. Léon, "Historia y Extinción del Cocaísmo en el Ecuador," *América Indígena*, XII (enero de 1952), pp. 9–12, 15–26 (hereafter cited as Léon, "Historia y Extinción del Cocaísmo").

32. Gutiérrez-Noriega y Zapata Ortiz, *Estudios Sobre La Coca*, pp. 21–28; Gutiérrez-Noriega, "El Hábito de la Coca en el Perú," pp. 144–45; for additional information on coca use at the time of the Spanish conquest, see Léon, "Historia y Extinción del Cocaísmo," pp. 13–14; José Marroquin, "Cocaísmo entre los indigenos peruanos," *Boletín de Identificación y Policia Tecnica, Lima* (julio–agosto de 1945), pp. 69–70 (hereafter cited as Marroquin, "Cocaísmo"); Lockhart, *Spanish Peru*, pp. 139, 146.

33. Gutiérrez-Noriega, "El Hábito de la Coca," p. 112; Gutiérrez-Noriega y Zapata Ortiz, *Estudios Sobre La Coca*, p. 17; Dell'Occhio, "La coca, el cocaísmo," pp. 192–93; for coca usage in Colombia, see Luis Duque Gómez, "Notas Sobre el Cocaísmo en Colombia," *Boletín de Arqueologia*, I (septiembre-octubre de 1945), p. 445 (hereafter cited as Duque Gómez, "Notas Sobre el Cocaísmo"); José Perez de Barradas, "Antiguedad del uso de la coca en Colombia," *Academia Colombiana de Ciencias Exactas, Fisicas, y Naturales, Revista. Bogotá*, III (enero–abril de 1940), pp. 323–24 (hereafter cited as Perez de Barradas, "Antiguedad del uso de la coca"); for coca in Bolivia, see F. E. Class, "The Sacred Coca Plant," *Pan-American Magazine*, December 1922, pp. 198–99 (hereafter cited as Class, "The Sacred Coca Plant"); *El Diario* (La Paz), "La industria y comercio de la coca en Bolivia," *Boletín Comercial y Minero. La Paz*, 15 de junio de 1938, p. 37 (hereafter cited as *El Diario* (La Paz), "La industria y comercio de la coca en Bolivia").

34. For the continuing usage of coca in a ritualistic context, see Marroquin, "Cocaísmo," p. 70; Perez de Barradas, "Antiguedad del uso de la coca," p. 326; Mortimer, *History of Coca*, p. 73; for the role of coca in mitigating the living conditions of Andean Indians, see S. F. Blake, "The 'Divine Plant' of the Incas," *Agriculture in the Americas*, III (June 1943), p. 143; Duque Gómez, "Notas Sobre el Cocaísmo," pp. 445–51; Julio César Perez, "El Problema Social de la Coca en Bolivia," *Protección Social. La Paz*, agosto de 1942, p. 31; for the use of alcohol in Ecuador, see Victor Gabriel Garcés, "El Indio Ecuatoriano y la Coca," *América Indígena*, V (octubre de 1945), pp. 188–92; Orosco, "El alma de la humilde hoja," p. 151; the religious aspect of el coqueo is explored in Richard T. Martin, "The Role of Coca in the History, Religion, and Medicine of South American Indians," in *The Coca Leaf and Cocaine Papers*, ed. George Andrews and David Solomon (New York: Harcourt Brace Jovanovich, 1975), pp. 20–37.

35. Leopoldo Salazar Viniegra, "El Mito de la Marijuana," *Criminalia. México* (diciembre de 1938), p. 207 (hereafter cited as Salazar Viniegra, "El Mito de la Marijuana"); F[rancisco] Guerra y H. Olivera, *Las Plantas Fantásticas de México* (México, D.F.: Imprenta del Diario Español, 1954), pp. 15–16; Dr. H. Jardines Carrion, "La Marihuana en América," *Revista Farmaceutica de Cuba*, 29 (junio de 1951), p. 34 which suggests that marijuana may have reached the Americas as early as 1521; for marijuana usage in the United States, see Howard S. Becker, *Outsiders: Studies in the Sociology of Deviance* (New York: The Free Press of Glencoe, 1963), p. 135 (hereafter cited as Becker, *Outsiders*); United States. Federal Narcotics Control Board, *The Traffic in Opium and Other Dangerous Drugs for the Year Ended December 31, 1929* (Washington, D.C.: Government Printing Office, 1930), p. 15 (hereafter cited as Federal Narcotics Control Board, *Traffic in Opium [year]*); Richard J. Bonnie and Charles H. Whitebread II, *The Marihuana Conviction: A History of Marihuana Prohibition in the United States* (Charlottesville: University Press of Virginia, 1974), p. 5 (hereafter cited as Bonnie and Whitebread, *The Marihuana Conviction*).

36. Although smuggling had not ceased, it is not immediately pertinent to the present discussion.

37. David F. Musto, M.D., *The American Disease: Origins of Narcotic Control* (New

Haven: Yale University Press, 1973), chap. 1 offers a good description of pre-1900 drug usage (hereafter cited as Musto, *The American Disease*).

38. Norman H. Clark, *Deliver Us from Evil: An Interpretation of American Prohibition* (New York: W. W. Norton & Company, 1976), pp. 23, 218 (hereafter cited as Clark, *Deliver Us from Evil*); James H. Young, *The Toadstool Millionaires: A Social History of Patent Medicines in America before Federal Regulation* (Princeton: Princeton University Press, 1961), pp. 68–69, 221–22, 244, 247.

39. Charles E. Terry, M.D., and Mildred Pellens, *The Opium Problem* (New York: The Bureau of Social Hygiene, 1928), pp. 5, 67–69, 89–90 (hereafter cited as Terry and Pellens, *The Opium Problem*).

40. For the relationship between cocaine and addiction, see Lawrence Kolb and A. G. DuMez, "The Prevalence and Trend of Drug Addiction in the United States and the Factors Influencing It," *Public Health Reports*, May 23, 1924, p. 1198 (hereafter cited as Kolb and DuMez, "The Prevalence and Trend of Drug Addiction"); for heroin, see Troy Duster, *The Legislation of Morality: Law, Drugs, and Moral Judgment* (New York: The Free Press, 1970), pp. 3, 8 (hereafter cited as Duster, *The Legislation of Morality*); Terry and Pellens, *The Opium Problem*,, pp. 76, 82–83; Alfred W. McCoy, with Cathleen B. Read and Leonard P. Adams II, *The Politics of Heroin in Southeast Asia* (New York: Harper & Row, 1972), pp. 3–5; for marijuana, see Bonnie and Whitebread, *The Marihuana Conviction*, pp. 1, 4.

41. Arnold H. Taylor, *American Diplomacy and the Narcotics Traffic, 1900–1939: A Study in International Humanitarian Reform* (Durham: Duke University Press, 1969), p. 47 (hereafter cited as Taylor, *American Diplomacy and the Narcotics Traffic*). For the broad range of addiction estimates prior to 1900, see Terry and Pellens, *The Opium Problem*, chap. 1 and pp. 469–75; Kolb and DuMez, "The Prevalence and Trend of Drug Addiction," pp. 1179–89, 1197; Alfred R. Lindesmith, *The Addict and the Law* (Bloomington: Indiana University Press, 1965), pp. 105–6 (hereafter cited as Lindesmith, *The Addict and the Law*); Rufus King, *The Drug Hang-Up: America's Fifty Year Folly* (New York: W. W. Norton & Company, 1972), p. 18 (hereafter cited as King, *The Drug Hang-Up*).

42. Clark, *Deliver Us from Evil*, pp. 2, 5.

43. Terry and Pellens, *The Opium Problem*, pp. 11, 68.

44. Clark, *Deliver Us from Evil*, pp. 220–21; cf. Terry and Pellens, *The Opium Problem*, pp. 807–8. For more on the range of ethnocentric responses to Chinese in America, see Stuart Creighton Miller, *The Unwelcome Immigrant: The American Image of the Chinese, 1785–1882* (Berkeley and Los Angeles: University of California Press, 1969); Elmer Clarence Sandmeyer, *The Anti-Chinese Movement in California* (Urbana: University of Illinois Press, 1973); Alexander Saxton, *The Indispensable Enemy: Labor and the Anti-Chinese Movement in California* (Berkeley and Los Angeles: University of California Press, 1971).

45. Musto, *The American Disease*, pp. 6–8, and 254 note 15 for the quotation—from the *New York Herald Tribune*, June 21, 1903.

46. Clark, *Deliver Us from Evil*, pp. 13, 27–31, 43. Even reliance upon the law was no guarantee that reformers could formulate effective means of drug control; Musto, *The American Disease*, pp. 16–19.

47. Clark, *Deliver Us from Evil*, pp. 10–11, 219–23. The historical literature pertaining to the many aspects of social reform and the creation of the welfare state is abundant; a representative sampling can be found in the works in the bibliography by John D. Buenker, Clarke A. Chambers, Allen F. Davis, Sidney Fine, Otis L. Graham, Jr., Roy Lubove, and Robert H. Wiebe.

48. Kirschner, "The Ambiguous Legacy," p. 77; Christopher Lasch, *The New Radicalism in America, 1889–1963: The Intellectual as a Social Type* (New York: Alfred A. Knopf, 1965), pp. 146–47, 161; idem, *The World of Nations: Reflections on American History, Politics, and Culture* (New York: Alfred A. Knopf, 1973), pp. 6, 16–17 (hereafter cited as Lasch, *The*

World of Nations); Kirschner, "The Ambiguous Legacy," p. 85 note 52 offers a perceptive critique of the Lasch thesis.

49. Especially see Taylor, *American Diplomacy and the Narcotics Traffic.*

50. Herbert L. May, "The International Control of Narcotic Drugs," *International Conciliation*, No. 441 (May 1948), pp. 308, 310, 314 (hereafter cited as May, "The International Control of Narcotic Drugs"); King, *The Drug Hang-Up*, pp. 10–11; Musto, *The American Disease*, pp. 26–28, 30.

51. May, "The International Control of Narcotic Drugs," pp. 308, 320–21; Taylor, *American Diplomacy and the Narcotics Traffic*, pp. 47, 54–55; Musto, *The American Disease*, pp. 31–37.

52. Taylor, *American Diplomacy and the Narcotics Traffic*, pp. 82–83, 87, 91, 96–120; May, "The International Control of Narcotic Drugs," pp. 321–23; Musto, *The American Disease*, pp. 37–39, 50–52. The protocol of cloture recommended further study of Indian hemp. The conferences of 1913 and 1914 dealt primarily with the implementation process for the 1912 convention.

53. Musto, *The American Disease*, pp. 40–45, 48, 54–61. Prominent among the studies of the origins of scientific management are Samuel P. Hays, *Conservation and the Gospel of Efficiency: The Progressive Conservation Movement, 1890–1920* (Cambridge: Harvard University Press, 1959), and Samuel Haber, *Efficiency and Uplift: Scientific Management in the Progressive Era, 1890–1920* (Chicago: University of Chicago Press, 1964). For the contents of the law, see United States. Statutes at Large, vol. 38, 63 Cong., 3 Sess., Part I, pp. 785–90.

54. Musto, *The American Disease*, pp. 97–120; cf. Terry and Pellens, *The Opium Problem*, p. 35 on the New York City clinic.

55. The estimates for the extent of addiction can be found in Kolb and DuMez, "The Prevalence and Trend of Drug Addiction," pp. 1180–84, 1188–89, 1198, 1200; Lindesmith, *The Addict and the Law*, pp. 99, 105, and 111 which contains a critique of Kolb and DuMez; *New York Times*, May 23, 1923, p. 32. The Special Committee of the Treasury Department, noting that estimates of addiction ranged between 200,000 and 4,000,000, placed the figure at approximately 1,000,000. The Special Committee feared that the extent of addiction would increase with the enforcement of prohibition laws. United States Treasury Department, *Traffic in Narcotic Drugs: Report of the Special Committee of Investigation Appointed March 25, 1918 by the Secretary of the Treasury*, June 1919 (Washington, D.C.: Government Printing Office, 1919), pp. 6–7, 20 for the quotation, and 21–22 (hereafter cited as Treasury Department, *Report of the Special Committee*). Compounding the scholar's problem of estimating the level of addiction is the later assertion of the Federal Bureau of Narcotics that every addict leads four other persons to a life with drugs during the years of his addiction.

56. Lindesmith, *The Addict and the Law*, p. 5; Duster, *The Legislation of Morality*, pp. 3, 9–12 with the quotation from the *American Journal of Clinical Medicine* on p. 11.

57. Musto, *The American Disease*, pp. 122–26.

58. The Treasury Department employed the tactic of adding an excise tax in addition to regulations promulgated under the Harrison Narcotic Law to discourage maintenance and further supervise the activities of doctors. For pertinent court cases, see *United States v. Doremus* (1919) 249 U.S. 86, and *Webb et al. v. United States* (1919) 249 U.S. 96. The subsequent case is *United States v. Behrman* (1922) 258 U.S. 280. Interpretive discussion is in Musto, *The American Disease*, pp. 129–32, 185; King, *The Drug Hang-Up*, pp. 21, 42–43; Duster, *The Legislation of Morality*, pp. 14–16; Lindesmith, *The Addict and the Law*, pp. 3–6; and Harry J. Anslinger and William F. Tompkins, *The Traffic in Narcotics* (New York: Funk and Wagnalls, 1953), p. 187 (hereafter cited as Anslinger and Tompkins, *The Traffic in Narcotics*). An additional Supreme Court decision, *Linder v. United States* (1925) 268 U.S. 5, can be interpreted as a moderate revision of the Webb ruling on

prescriptions. By that time, however, enforcement policies under the Harrison law prevented any revisions in practice.

59. The official history of the Bureau of Internal Revenue confirms the regulatory nature of the Harrison law as amended in the 1918 Revenue Act. Lawrence F. Schmeckebier and Francis X. A. Eble, *The Bureau of Internal Revenue: Its History, Activities, and Organization* (Baltimore: The Johns Hopkins Press, 1923), pp. 47–48, 56–57, 116–17 (hereafter cited as Schmeckebier and Eble, *The Bureau of Internal Revenue*). Amendments in the Revenue Act made it easier to identify those using drugs illegally. See also Musto, *The American Disease*, pp. 59–60, 135, 138–46, 305 note 68. The quotation from Commissioner Roper's report is in United States. Department of the Treasury, *Annual Report of the Commissioner of Internal Revenue for the Fiscal Year Ended June 30, 1920* (Washington, D.C.: Government Printing Office, 1920), pp. 33–34; the commissioner referred to the clinics as "temporary expedients." See also, idem, *Annual Report of the Commissioner of Internal Revenue for the Fiscal Year Ended June 30, 1919* (Washington, D.C.: Government Printing Office, 1919), p. 61.

60. An assessment of the narcotic clinics appearing long after they had closed implied that if the clinics had continued operating, many people would have flocked to them to obtain drugs. Anslinger and Tompkins, *The Traffic in Narcotics*, pp. 185–86; cf. Lindesmith, *The Addict and the Law*, p. 142; Musto, *The American Disease*, pp. 146–68.

61. Schmeckebier and Eble, *The Bureau of Internal Revenue*, pp. 61–62; the organizational structure of the Narcotic Division is described on pp. 168–69. Despite the effort to bring efficiency to drug law enforcement, organizational rivalry existed between the Narcotic Division and the Customs Service—the agency charged with halting smuggling. See Jaffe, "Addiction Reform," Part II, passim; Lawrence F. Schmeckebier, *The Customs Service: Its History, Activities, and Organization* (Baltimore: The Johns Hopkins Press, 1924), pp. 75–76. Most informative on the evolving nature of organizations and bureaucracies in the progressive years are Louis Galambos, "The Emerging Organizational Synthesis in Modern American History," *Business History Review*, 44 (Autumn 1970), pp. 279–90; and Robert H. Wiebe, *The Search for Order, 1877–1920* (New York: Hill and Wang, 1967). The scholarly conflict over the role of institutionalization in American history can be followed in David J. Rothman, *The Discovery of the Asylum: Social Order and Disorder in the New Republic* (Boston: Little, Brown and Company, 1971), pp. xiv–xix, 286, 290, 294–95. Rothman criticizes by implication the interpretations of Lasch, note 48 *supra*, and Michael B. Katz. "Origins of the Institutional State," *Marxist Perspectives*, 1 (Winter 1978), pp. 6–22, which is an important essay concerning in part the relationship between capitalism and modern institutions. An overview, useful for comparison, of the evolution of the organizational or bureaucratic state in Europe can be found in Charles S. Maier, *Recasting Bourgeois Europe: Stabilization in France, Germany, and Italy in the Decade afer World War I* (Princeton: Princeton University Press, 1975), pp. 3–15.

62. Theodore J. Lowi, *The End of Liberalism: Ideology, Policy, and the Crisis of Public Authority* (New York: W. W. Norton & Company, 1969), pp. 93–97. At length, the social and administrative implications of moral reform reinforce elite biases against subordinate groups that do not display a positive commitment to the perpetuation of the majority culture within a society; see Gutman, *Work, Culture, and Society*, pp. 69–72.

63. Musto, *The American Disease*, pp. 147, 318 notes 6 and 7; Lindesmith, *The Addict and the Law*, pp. 141–42; Terry and Pellens, *The Opium Problem*, pp. 49, 90–91; Treasury Department, *Report of the Special Committee*, p. 25.

64. Taylor, *American Diplomacy and the Narcotics Traffic*, pp. 106, 110.

65. Francis M. Huntington Wilson to Diplomatic Officers of the United States Accredited to the Governments of Latin America, April 15, 1912, National Archives, Records of the Department of State, Record Group 59, Decimal File 511.4A1/1282d (hereafter cited as RG 59 [decimal file]).

66. Harold Knowles to Secretary of State Philander C. Knox, June 27, 1912, RG 59 511.4A1/1310; Taylor, *American Diplomacy and the Narcotics Traffic*, p. 110. Some of the revenue in Peru from the sale of coca leaves from purchases in the United States—revenue which temporarily seemed threatened by increased coca plantings in British Malaysia and the Belgian Congo; Eduardo Higginson, "Memoria del Consulado General del Perú en Nueva York correspondiente el año 1912," *Anales de la Dirreción de Fomento*, no. 6 (junio de 1913), pp. 62–63; Carlos Larrabure y Correa, "Ensayos culturales de la coca en las colonias europeas," *Boletín de la Dirreción de Fomento*, año IX (noviembre de 1912), pp. 9–11.

67. Taylor, *American Diplomacy and the Narcotics Traffic*, pp. 111–14, 119.

68. May, "The International Control of Narcotic Drugs," p. 303.

69. A. J. Peters, Assistant Secretary of the Treasury, to Secretary of State Robert Lansing, enclosing a report from United States Customs Collector San Diego, February 2, 1916, RG 59 812.114 Narcotics/10; John B. Elliott to Lansing, December 11, 1918, RG 59 812.114 Narcotics/21; G. S. Quate, Deputy Collector of Customs, Calexico, California, to Elliott, Deputy Collector of Customs, Los Angeles, January 19, 1918, RG 59 812.114 Narcotics/22.

Chapter 2: The Road to Geneva

1. Musto, *The American Disease*; Taylor, *American Diplomacy and the Narcotics Traffic*.

2. Gary Dean Best, *The Politics of American Individualism: Herbert Hoover in Transition, 1918–1921* (Westport: Greenwood Press, 1975), pp. 93–94, 100, 178 (hereafter cited as Best, *The Politics of American Individualism*); Jordan A. Schwarz, "Hoover and Congress: Politics, Personality, and Perspective in the Presidency," in *The Hoover Presidency: A Reappraisal*, ed. Martin L. Fausold and George T. Mazuzan (Albany: State University of New York Press, 1974), p. 89 (hereafter cited as Schwarz, "Hoover and Congress" and *The Hoover Presidency*); Joan Hoff Wilson, *Herbert Hoover: Forgotten Progressive* (Boston: Little, Brown and Company, 1975), pp. 38, 55–56, 61 (hereafter cited as Wilson, *Herbert Hoover*); for the Hoover quotation, see David Burner, *Herbert Hoover: A Public Life* (New York: Alfred A. Knopf, 1979), p. 139 (hereafter cited as Burner, *Herbert Hoover*).

3. See Ellis W. Hawley, "Herbert Hoover, the Commerce Secretariat, and the Vision of an 'Associative State,' 1921–1928," *Journal of American History*, 61 (June 1974), pp. 116–40; Burner, *Herbert Hoover*, pp. 139, 171; Wilson, *Herbert Hoover*, p. 69.

4. Best, *The Politics of American Individualism*, p. 100; Burner, *Herbert Hoover*, pp. 140, 161.

5. An informed discussion of interest group politics relevant to Hoover's time can be found in Grant McConnell, *Private Power and American Democracy* (New York: Alfred A. Knopf, 1966), pp. 6–7, 50, 65–68 (hereafter cited as McConnell, *Private Power*); and see David W. Eakins, "The Origins of Corporate Liberal Policy Research, 1916–1922: The Political-Economic Expert and the Decline of Public Debate," in *Building the Organizational Society: Essays on Associational Activities in Modern America*, ed. Jerry Israel (New York: The Free Press, 1972), pp. 163–64, 166, 179 for an important critique of special interest liberalism and its antidemocratic tendencies (hereafter cited as Eakins, "Liberal Policy Research") and (*Building the Organizational Society*). More directly critical of Hoover's contributions to the development of public policy in America is Peri Ethan Arnold, "Herbert Hoover and the Continuity of American Public Policy," *Public Policy*, XX (Fall 1972), pp. 526, 543–44.

6. Wilson, *Herbert Hoover*, pp. 50, 61, 72, 84–86; Ellis W. Hawley, "Herbert Hoover and American Corporatism, 1929–1933," in *The Hoover Presidency*, pp. 103–5 (hereafter cited as Hawley, "Hoover and American Corporatism"); Schwarz, "Hoover and Congress," p. 89; Burner, *Herbert Hoover*, p. 161.

7. Schwarz, "Hoover and Congress," pp. 90–96; the standard interpretation of presidential-congressional relations in the 1920s is Emmet John Hughes, *The Living Presidency: The Resources and Dilemmas of the American Presidential Office* (New York: Coward, McCann & Geoghegan, 1973), pp. 63, 122, 209; cf. William H. Harbaugh, "The Republican Party, 1893–1932," in *History of U.S. Political Parties*, vol. 3, *1910–1945: From Square Deal to New Deal*, ed. Arthur M. Schlesinger, Jr. (New York: Chelsea House in association with R. R. Bowker, 1973), pp. 2070, 2106ff.

8. Best, *The Politics of American Individualism*, pp. 127–28; Burner, *Herbert Hoover*, pp. 157, 176; Wilson, *Herbert Hoover*, pp. 62, 92–93. On trade associations and the role of antitrust law as a controlling device, see Robert F. Himmelberg, *The Origins of the National Recovery Administration: Business, Government, and the Trade Association Issue, 1921–1933* (New York: Fordham University Press, 1976).

9. Robert K. Murray, *The Politics of Normalcy: Governmental Theory and Practice in the Harding–Coolidge Era* (New York: W. W. Norton & Company, 1973), pp. 83, 86–88, 93; the quotation is on p. 87 (hereafter cited as Murray, *The Politics of Normalcy*); cf. Eugene P. Trani and David L. Wilson, *The Presidency of Warren G. Harding* (Lawrence: The Regents Press of Kansas, 1977), pp. 79–81 (hereafter cited as Trani and Wilson, *Harding*).

10. Donald R. McCoy, *Calvin Coolidge: The Quiet President* (New York: The Macmillan Company, 1967), pp. 193–202, 235–36, 269–72.

11. Ibid., pp. 282–83.

12. Hawley, "Hoover and American Corporatism," pp. 108–9, 113–16, 119; Schwarz, "Hoover and Congress," pp. 99–100.

13. James G. Burrow, *AMA: Voice of American Medicine* (Baltimore: Johns Hopkins Press, 1963), pp. 27–66, 105–6, 132–64.

14. Ibid., pp. 168–70; Rosemary Stevens, *American Medicine and the Public Interest* (New Haven: Yale University Press, 1971), pp. 142–48.

15. *New York World*, February 22, 1921, as cited in Trani and Wilson, *Harding*, p. 115.

16. Best, *The Politics of American Individualism*, pp. 142, 147, 151. For a good review of Wilson's relations with Congress, see Melvyn P. Leffler, *The Elusive Quest: America's Pursuit of European Stability and French Security, 1919–1933* (Chapel Hill: University of North Carolina Press, 1979), chap. 1.

17. L. Ethan Ellis, *Republican Foreign Policy, 1921–1933* (New Brunswick: Rutgers University Press, 1968), p. 40.

18. Best, *The Politics of American Individualism*, p. 167; Trani and Wilson, *Harding*, pp. 109–10, 114–16; Kenneth J. Grieb, *The Latin American Policy of Warren G. Harding* (Fort Worth: Texas Christian University Press, 1976), p. 7 (hereafter cited as Grieb, *Latin American Policy*). Hughes and Hoover had a good working relationship. Despite the competition between their departments over commercial policy, which the reorganization of the Bureau of Foreign and Domestic Commerce brought under the jurisdiction of the Department of Commerce, the activities of the two were often complementary: see Joseph Brandes, *Herbert Hoover and Economic Diplomacy: Department of Commerce Policy, 1921–1928* (Pittsburgh: University of Pittsburgh Press, 1962); Burner, *Herbert Hoover*, p. 184; Wilson, *Herbert Hoover*, chap. 4 passim; cf. Joseph Tulchin, *The Aftermath of War: World War I and U.S. Policy Toward Latin America* (New York: New York University Press, 1971), pp. 108, 110–11 (hereafter cited as Tulchin, *Aftermath of War*).

19. Jerry Israel, "A Diplomatic Machine: Scientific Management in the Department of State, 1906–1924," in *Building the Organizational Society*, p. 189 (hereafter cited as Israel, "A Diplomatic Machine"); Warren Frederick Ilchman, *Professional Diplomacy in the United States, 1779–1939: A Study in Administrative History* (Chicago: University of Chicago Press, 1961), pp. 185–88. The standard sources on the modernization of the Foreign Service are Graham H. Stuart, *American Diplomatic and Consular Practice*, 2nd ed. (New York: Appleton-Century Crofts, 1952); and William Barnes and John Heath

Morgan, *The Foreign Service of the United States: Origins, Development, and Functions* (Washington, D.C.: Government Printing Office, 1961); cf. Richard Hume Werking, *The Master Architects: Building the United States Foreign Service, 1890–1913* (Lexington: University Press of Kentucky, 1977).

20. Martin Weil, *A Pretty Good Club: The Founding Fathers of the U.S. Foreign Service* (New York: W. W. Norton & Company, 1978). Chapters 1 and 2 best depict the elitism within the diplomatic corps. Hugh Wilson's remark is on p. 47. See also Waldo H. Heinrichs, Jr., "Bureaucracy and Professionalism in the Development of American Career Diplomacy," *Twentieth-Century American Foreign Policy*, ed. John Braeman, Robert H. Bremner, and David Brody (Columbus: Ohio State University Press, 1971), pp. 120–22, 126–27, 132–38, 145, 152–54, 172–79.

21. The literature on American economic foreign policy in the 1920s is vast. The seminal study is William Appleman Williams, "The Legend of Isolationism in the 1920's," *Science and Society*, XVIII (Winter 1954), pp. 1–20. See also works listed in the bibliography by Frank Charles Costigliola, Michael J. Hogan, Melvyn P. Leffler, Robert H. Van Meter, and Joan Hoff Wilson.

22. United States Congress. House of Representatives, Committee on Ways and Means, Report No. 852, *Importation and Exportation of Narcotic Drugs*, 67 Cong., 2 Sess., March 27, 1922 (Washington, D.C.: Government Printing Office, 1922), p. 6 (hereafter cited as House of Representatives, *Narcotic Drugs*). The Mellon quotation is in a letter, dated June 22, 1921, to Joseph W. Fordney, Chairman, Committee on Ways and Means, on pp. 19–20. Musto, *The American Disease*, pp. 189–90.

23. Again, the level of addiction remained essentially unknown, a function of the varying estimates mentioned in chapter 1, notes 41 and 55. For Levi G. Nutt's view of the extent of addiction, see Musto, *The American Disease*, pp. 189–90.

24. *United States v. Behrman* (1922) 258 U.S. 280; *Linder v. United States* (1925) 268 U.S. 5. See Musto, *The American Disease*, pp. 184–88 for a discussion of the rulings and their effects.

25. United States. Statutes at Large, vol. 42, 67 Cong., 2 Sess., Part I, pp. 596–98; House of Representatives, *Narcotic Drugs*, pp. 1,3, 6, 11. Some years later the AMA softened its opposition to the 1922 law. The efficiency that the Federal Narcotics Control Board was to bring may have been more apparent than real; the board may never have convened although its member departments did correspond. Musto, *The American Disease*, p. 197.

26. Bess Furman, in consultation with Ralph C. Williams, M.D., *A Profile of the United States Public Health Service, 1798–1948* (Washington, D.C.: Government Printing Office, 1973), chap. 12, especially pp. 283, 286, 304–5 (hereafter cited as Furman, *A Profile*).

27. Ibid., chap. 13.

28. Musto, *The American Disease*, pp. 141–44.

29. Denna Frank Fleming, *The United States and World Organization, 1920–1933* (Reprint ed., New York: AMS Press, 1966), pp. 60–64, 219–21 (hereafter cited as Fleming, *The United States and World Organization*). Joan Hoff Wilson has termed selective American involvement abroad during the 1920s "independent internationalism." That concept has application for narcotic foreign policy as well; Joan Hoff Wilson, *American Business and Foreign Policy, 1920–1933* (Lexington: University Press of Kentucky, 1971), pp. xvi–xvii, 26. One example of this phenomenon was Harding's support for American membership on the World Court; Murray, *The Politics of Normalcy*, pp. 96–97.

30. For a brief sketch of Mrs. Elizabeth Washburn Wright's career, see Taylor, *American Diplomacy and the Narcotics Traffic*, pp. 302–5.

31. May, "The International Control of Narcotic Drugs," 323; League of Nations, Report of the Advisory Committee on Traffic in Opium, *First Session, Geneva, May 2nd–5th, 1921* C. 28.M.157. XI. (Geneva, 1921), pp. 2, 4, 6.

32. Hughes to W. H. de Beaufort, June 18, 1921, RG 59 511.4A1/1580; Fleming, *The United States and World Organization*, pp. 65–66.

33. Memorandum by Edwin L. Neville to William Phillips, October 27, 1922, RG 59 511.4A1/1687; Hughes to President Warren G. Harding, November 25, 1922, RG 59 ibid.

34. Furman, *A Profile*, pp. 332–33, 342–43; Fleming, *The United States and World Organization*, pp. 64–65, 233–35.

35. Hughes to Mellon, December 14, 1922, RG 59 511.4A1/1707a.

36. Elizabeth Washburn Wright, "America at the Geneva Opium Conference," *The Outlook*, July 11, 1923, p. 361.

37. Taylor, *American Diplomacy and the Narcotics Traffic*, p. 157.

38. Ibid., pp. 157–59; Mrs. Elizabeth Washburn Wright to Undersecretary of State Phillips, February 7, 1923, RG 59 511.4A1/1751.

39. United States Congress. House of Representatives, Document No. 380, *The Traffic in Habit-Forming Narcotic Drugs: Hearings before the Committee on Foreign Affairs*, 68 Cong., 1 Sess., on H.J. Res. 195 "Authorizing an Appropriation for the Participation of the United States in Two International Conferences for the Control of Traffic in Habit-Forming Narcotic Drugs," February 21, 1924 (Washington, D.C.: Government Printing Office, 1924), p. 21 for Stephen G. Porter to Hughes, February 12, 1923 (hereafter cited as House of Representatives, *The Traffic in Drugs*).

40. Ibid., p. 49.

41. *New York Times*, May 3, 1923, p. 32; May 4, 1923, p. 17; and May 25, 1923, p. 3. For more on the instructions of the United States delegation, see United States. Department of State, *Papers Relating to the Foreign Relations of the United States, 1923*, 2 vols. (Washington, D.C.: Government Printing Office, 1938), I, pp. 97–103 (hereafter cited as *FRUS, [year]*). The cohesive, imposing presence of the delegation no doubt had a dramatic impact on the other experts gathered at Geneva; Fleming, *The United States and World Organization*, p. 224.

42. *New York Times*, June 2, 1923, p. 15.

43. Ibid., June 3, 1923, p. 5.

44. Taylor, *American Diplomacy and the Narcotics Traffic*, pp. 168–70.

45. League of Nations, Report of the Advisory Committee on Traffic in Opium, *Report on the Work of the Committee During Its Second Session, Held at Geneva from April 19th–29th, 1922* C. 233(1).1922.XI. (Geneva, 1922), pp. 1–3.

46. League of Nations, Advisory Committee on Traffic in Opium and Other Dangerous Drugs, *Report to the Council on the Work of the Fifth Session (May 24th to June 7th, 1923)* A.13.1923.XI. (Geneva, 1923), p. 12; idem, *Report to the Council on the Work of the Seventh Session, August 24th–31st, 1925* A.28.1925.XI. (Geneva, 1925), p. 9.

47. To write of the "revolutionary decade" seems appropriate, even though the Revolution would not become "institutionalized" for some time—both in the context of unfolding events in Mexico and in a historiographical sense. See the related discussion in John Womack, Jr., "The Mexican Economy During the Revolution, 1910–1920: Historiography and Analysis," *Marxist Perspectives*, 1 (Winter 1978), pp. 80–123.

48. Regarding the drug situation in Baja California, see Walter F. Boyle to Hughes, October 20, 1921, RG 59 312.1121/1; *Excélsior* (Mexico City), February 20, 1923.

49. For information on conditions in the Tijuana area around 1920, see John A. Price, *Tijuana: Urbanization in a Border Culture* (Notre Dame: University of Notre Dame Press, 1973), pp. 41–56 (hereafter cited as Price, *Tijuana*). On the governorship of Esteban Cantú, see also Mark T. Gilderhus, *Diplomacy and Revolution: U.S.–Mexican Relations under Wilson and Carranza* (Tucson: University of Arizona Press, 1977), pp. 72, 76–77; and Braulio Maldonado, *Baja California: Comentarios Politicos*, 2nd ed. (México, D.F.: B. Costa-Amic, 1960), pp. 59–63. On drug-related activity in the Tijuana area, see the report in note 48, *supra* in the Department of State files; and Price, *Tijuana*, pp. 32–35. The

persistence of drugs along the border to the present can be traced in Raul A. Fernandez, *The United States–Mexican Border: A Politico-Economic Profile* (Notre Dame: University of Notre Dame Press, 1977), pp. 125–27; Price, *Tijuana*, chaps. 5 and 6; Carlos Monsiváis, "The Culture of the Frontier: The Mexican Side," in *Views Across the Border: The United States and Mexico*, ed. Stanley R. Ross (Albuquerque: University of New Mexico Press, in cooperation with the Weatherhead Foundation, 1978), p. 61; and Stanley R. Ross, "Commentaries: Introduction," in *Views Across the Border: The United States and Mexico*, ed. Stanley R. Ross (Albuquerque: University of New Mexico Press, in cooperation with the Weatherhead Foundation, 1978), pp. 379–80.

50. For the two quotations, see Oscar J. Martinez, *Border Boom Town: Ciudad Juárez since 1848* (Austin: University of Texas Press, 1978), p. 57 (hereafter cited as Martinez, *Border Boom Town*). For continuing border difficulties with drugs, see John W. Dye to Hughes, February 23, 1923, RG 59 812.114 Narcotics/64.

51. On economic opportunities along the border, in general see Kenneth F. Johnson, *Mexican Democracy: A Critical View*, rev. ed. (New York: Praeger Publishers, 1978), preface, chap. 7 (hereafter cited as Johnson, *Mexican Democracy*); more specifically, see Martinez, *Border Boom Town*, pp. 3–37; and Francisco R. Almada, *La Revolución en el Estado de Chihuahua*, 2 vols. (Chihuahua: Biblioteca del Instituto Nacional de Estudios Historicos de la Revolución Mexicana, 1964), I, p. 55 (hereafter cited as Almada, *La Revolución en Chihuahua*).

52. Martinez, *Border Boom Town*, pp. 38–56. Much of the trade in arms ended up in the hands of Pancho Villa's *Division del Norte*, a diverse group of followers who helped Villa control the state of Chihuahua; Peter H. Smith, *Labyrinths of Power: Political Recruitment in Twentieth-Century Mexico* (Princeton: Princeton University Press, 1979), p. 34 (hereafter cited as Smith, *Labyrinths of Power*); John Womack, Jr., *Zapata and the Mexican Revolution* (New York: Random House, 1968), pp. 192–95 (hereafter cited as Womack, *Zapata*).

53. O. Gaylord Marsh, Progreso, to Hughes, February 12, 1923, RG 59 812.114 Narcotics/62.

54. *Boston Globe*, May 6, 1923; *Excélsior* (Mexico City), June 4, 1923; June 10, 1923; June 11, 1923; and June 15, 1923.

55. George T. Summerlin to Hughes, July 19, 1923, RG 59, 812.114 Narcotics/79; *Diario Oficial*, Mexico, July 28, 1923.

56. See, for example, the discussion in Womack, *Zapata*, pp. 357–75; Wilkie, *The Mexican Revolution*, pp. 57–59; and Frank R. Brandenburg, *The Making of Modern Mexico* (Englewood Cliffs: Prentice-Hall, 1964), pp. 52–62 (hereafter cited as Brandenburg, *Modern Mexico*); more generally, see Johnson, *Mexican Democracy*, pp. 20–37.

57. Pablo González Casanova, *Democracy in Mexico*, trans. Danielle Sati, 2nd ed. (New York: Oxford University Press, 1970), pp. 72–103 (hereafter cited as González Casanova, *Democracy in Mexico*); Gabriel A. Almond and Sidney Verba, *The Civic Culture: Political Attitudes and Democracy in Five Nations* (Princeton: Princeton University Press, 1963), p. 40. Charles C. Cumberland, *Mexico: the Struggle for Modernity* (New York: Oxford University Press, 1968), pp. 241–49. Johnson, *Mexican Democracy*, pp. 14, 20, emphasizes the paternalism and manipulation inherent in Mexican politics. Smith, *Labyrinths of Power*, pp. 49, 53–56 describes the limitations of pluralism. Whether alienated or not, a large segment of the Mexican population may remain uninvolved politically. See Richard R. Fagen and William S. Tuohy, *Politics and Privilege in a Mexican City* (Stanford: Stanford University Press, 1972), pp. 158–72.

58. González Casanova, *Democracy in Mexico*, pp. 127–34.

59. Johnson, *Mexican Democracy*, chap. 3 argues that the caudillo phenomenon still pervades Mexican presidential politics. For a discussion pertinent to presidential power and authority immediately after the revolutionary decade, see González Casanova, *Democ-*

racy in Mexico, p. 31; and Wilkie, *The Mexican Revolution,* pp. 17, 19–21, 30–39 for an emphasis on fiscal authority.

60. Frederick C. Turner, *The Dynamic of Mexican Nationalism* (Chapel Hill: University of North Carolina Press, 1968), pp. 3–21. Turner later seems to qualify his claims regarding the pervasiveness of nationalism (see pp. 144–55, 170–79).

61. Johnson, *Mexican Democracy,* pp. 14, 21.

62. Three classic treatments of agrarian reform are Eyler N. Simpson, *The Ejido: Mexico's Way Out* (Chapel Hill: University of North Carolina Press, 1937); Frank Tannenbaum, *The Mexican Agrarian Revolution* (Washington, D.C.: The Brookings Institution, 1929); and Nathan L. Whetten, *Rural Mexico* (Chicago: University of Chicago Press, 1948). A superb analysis of land reform and the ejido is John Hamilton McNeely, "The Politics and Development of the Mexican Land Program" (Ph.D. diss., University of Texas, 1958), pp. 24, 28–29, 34–35, 40–46, 68 (hereafter cited as McNeely, "The Mexican Land Program"). See also Smith, *Labyrinths of Power,* pp. 28–37; and Centro de Investigaciones Agrarias [Sergio Reyes Osorio et al.], *Estructura Agraria y Desarrollo Agrícola en México: Estudio Sobre Las Relaciones entro La Tierra y El Desarrollo Agrícola de México* (México, D.F.: Fondo de Cultura Económica, 1974), pp. 15–16, 23–24. Once again in a consideration of land and Mexico, the case of the Yaqui Indians and the threat to their landholdings by the imposition of an alien socioeconomic system is instructive. See McNeely, "The Mexican Land Program," pp. 86–96. As McNeely concludes on p. 96: "Thus, new *caciques* arose from the Revolution to replace the old ones." That the ejido might serve nonprogressive objectives was apparent even before the Mexican Revolution; see Almada, *La Revolución en Chihuahua,* I. pp. 56, 61.

63. Smith, *Labyrinths of Power,* p. 40; Roger D. Hansen, *The Politics of Mexican Development* (Baltimore: The Johns Hopkins Press, 1971), p. 27 (hereafter cited as Hansen, *Mexican Development*); Wilkie, *The Mexican Revolution,* pp. 218–19. The war indeed had a devastating effect on Sonora. For a suggestive, though incomplete portrait of Sonora in the revolutionary decade, see Eduardo W. Villa, *Compendio de Historia del Estado de Sonora* (México, D.F.: Editorial "Patri Nueva," 1937), pp. 474–76, 480.

64. Hansen, *Mexican Development,* pp. 29, 32, 40, 60; Clark W. Reynolds, *The Mexican Economy: Twentieth-Century Structure and Growth* (New Haven: Yale University Press, 1970), pp. 102–7 (hereafter cited as Reynolds, *The Mexican Economy*). Even with reform under Lázaro Cárdenas, class lines remained intact; Hansen *Mexican Development,* chap. 4.

65. On education, see Smith, *Labyrinths of Power,* pp. 45–46; Wilkie, *The Mexican Revolution,* pp. 208–9. Even today, higher education has not become an avenue of extensive social and economic mobility; Smith, *Labyrinths of Power,* pp. 46–49. On income distribution, see Hansen, *Mexican Development,* passim; Smith, *Labyrinths of Power,* pp. 44–45; Reynolds, *The Mexican Economy,* pp. 71–75. Concerning the general level of poverty, see Wilkie, *The Mexican Revolution,* chap. 9, especially the charts on pp. 234, 236.

66. Wilkie, *The Mexican Revolution,* pp. 215–22.

67. Smith, *Labyrinths of Power,* pp. 60–62; Woodrow Borah, "Discontinuity and Continuity in Mexican History," *Pacific Historical Review,* 48 (February 1979), pp. 22–24. For more on the persistent dichotomy between progress and socioeconomic inequalities in Mexico, see Reynolds, *The Mexican Economy;* Merilee Serrill Grindle, *Bureaucrats, Politicans, and Peasants in Mexico* (Berkeley and Los Angeles: University of California Press, 1977); Wayne A. Cornelius, *Politics and the Migrant Poor in Mexico City* (Stanford: Stanford University Press, 1975); and Susan Eckstein, *The Poverty of Revolution: The State and Urban Poor in Mexico* (Princeton: Princeton University Press, 1977).

68. A sampling of more traditional views of the campesino can be found in Brandenburg, *Modern Mexico,* pp. 38–39; Rodolfo Stavenhagen, "Social Aspects of Agrarian Structure in

Mexico," in *Agrarian Problems and Peasant Movements in Latin America,* ed. Rodolfo Stavenhagen (New York: Anchor Books, 1970), pp. 227–28; and, more generally, see idem, *Les classes sociales dans les sociétés agraires* (Paris: Editions Anthropos, 1969), pp. 112–13, 117–22.

69. The present discussion of the process of cultural change and the threat it often constitutes to an established way of life follows closely the related discussion in chapter one. The analysis here is based upon Arnold J. Bauer, "Rural Workers in Spanish America: Problems of Peonage and Oppression," *Hispanic American Historical Review,* 59 (February 1979), pp. 34–63. See also note 67.

70. Womack, *Zapata,* pp. 192–94, 219–23; cf. Almada, *La Revolución en Chihuahua,* II, p. 147.

71. *FRUS, 1916* (Washington, D.C.: Government Printing Office, 1925), p. 465; Womack, *Zapata,* pp. 192–93; Friedrich Katz, "Pancho Villa and the Attack on Columbus, New Mexico," *American Historical Review,* 83 (February 1978), pp. 101–30, especially 107–8, 117, 124–25. Villa believed that Carranza had reached an agreement with Wilson under which the United States would treat Mexico as a virtual protectorate. And see Almada, *La Revolución en Chihuahua,* II. pp. 257–59.

72. Haldeen Braddy, *Cock of the Walk: The Legend of Pancho Villa* (Port Washington, N.Y.: Kennikat Press, [1955], 1970), pp. 113, 119–20, 149; John Reed, *Insurgent Mexico* (1914; reprint ed.; New York: International Publishers, 1969), p. 179 for indirect evidence; William Wolf, "Uncle Sam Fights a New Drug Menace . . . Marihuana," *Popular Science,* May 1936, pp. 119–20 (hereafter cited as Wolf, "Uncle Sam Fights a New Drug Menace").

73. Citizens of Yuma, Arizona, to Hughes, September 27, 1924, RG 59 711.129/13.

74. Henry E. Dobyns and Paul L. Doughty, *Peru: A Cultural History* (New York: Oxford University Press, 1976), p. 210 (hereafter cited as Dobyns and Doughty, *Peru*).

75. Leguía is quoted in James C. Carey, *Peru and the United States, 1900–1962* (Notre Dame: University of Notre Dame Press, 1964), p. 42 (hereafter cited as Carey, *Peru and the United States*). For Leguía's background, see Jorge Basadre, *Historia de la República del Perú,* 5th ed., rev. and enl., 10 vols. (Lima: Ediciones "Historia," 1961-64), VIII, p. 3553 (hereafter cited as Basadre, *Historia del Perú*); Carey, *Peru and the United States,* p. 23 note 11. Information on the coalition supporting Leguía in 1919 in Basadre, *Historia del Perú,* VIII, pp. 3929–32; Fredrick B. Pike, *The Modern History of Peru* (New York: Frederick A. Praeger, 1967), p. 218 (hereafter cited as Pike, *The Modern History of Peru*). On democracy in Peru, see Dobyns and Doughty, *Peru,* p. 207; Pike, *The Modern History of Peru,* pp. 246–49; Carey, *Peru and the United States,* pp. 7, 36.

76. Dobyns and Doughty, *Peru,* p. 211; Davies, *Indian Integration in Peru,* pp. 45, 56–58; Carey, *Peru and the United States,* pp. 26–27; Fredrick B. Pike, *The United States and the Andean Republics: Peru, Bolivia, and Ecuador* (Cambridge: Harvard University Press, 1977), pp. 148, 172 (hereafter cited as Pike, *The Andean Republics*).

77. Dobyns and Doughty, *Peru,* pp. 216–20; Pike, *The Modern History of Peru,* pp. 227, 229; Carey, *Peru and the United States,* pp. 32–35, 51–80 concerning foreign economic influence in Peru; and Pike, *The Andean Republics,* pp. 192–95. On economic aspects of Leguía's social policy, see Basadre, *Historia del Perú,* IX, pp. 4127–31; Carey, *Peru and the United States,* passim.

78. Davies, *Indian Integration in Peru,* pp. 69, 73, 75–80; Basadre, *Historia del Perú,* IX, pp. 4191–92.

79. On *la vialidad,* see Dobyns and Doughty, *Peru,* pp. 221–22; Davies, *Indian Integration in Peru,* pp. 82–85; Basadre, *Historia del Perú,* IX, pp. 4143–47.

80. Pike, *The Modern History of Peru,* pp. 221–22; Basadre, *Historia del Perú,* IX, pp. 4190–93; for information on an analogous situation in Bolivia, see Pike, *The Andean Republics,* p. 187.

81. Dobyns and Doughty, *Peru,* p. 223; Davies, *Indian Integration in Peru,* pp. 89–93;

Pike, *The Modern History of Peru*, pp. 219–21, and 233 for a statement of the anti-oncenia goals of the indigenistas.

82. For the 1921 decree, see Frederick A. Sterling to Hughes, April 14, 1923, RG 59 811.114N16/107; for the March 1923 decree, Sterling to Hughes, March 23, 1923, RG 59 823.114 Narcotics/5; and Sterling to Hughes, July 17, 1922, RG 59 800.114/371.

83. *Christian Science Monitor*, August 12, 1922; Sterling to Hughes, April 14, 1923, RG 59 811.114N16/107.

84. C. Harvey Gardiner, *The Japanese and Peru, 1873–1973* (Albuquerque: University of New Mexico Press, 1975), pp. 22–37, 47–48, 61–67. It was not unusual for Japanese laborers to help harvest the coca leaf crop.

85. Sterling to Hughes, April 14, 1923, RG 59 823.114 Narcotics/6; Carey, *Peru and the United States*, chap. 3, especially p. 49.

86. Class, "The Sacred Coca Plant," p. 298; Jesse S. Cottrell to Hughes, February 26, 1924, RG 59 824.114 Liquors/3. Bolivian coca from the Yungas area was less accessible to cocaine exporters than that of Peru; Weston LaBarre, "The Aymara Indians of the Lake Titicaca Plateau, Bolivia," *American Anthropologist*, 50 (January 1948), pp. 67–70. More generally, see Harold Osborne, *Indians of the Andes: Aymaras and Quechuas* (Cambridge: Harvard University Press, 1952), pp. 206–9, 237–51.

87. Henry Fletcher to Hughes, April 29, 1923, RG 59 511.4A1/1814; *FRUS, 1923*, I, pp. 287–92; Grieb, *Latin American Policy*, pp. 129–43, 177–91; Tulchin, *Aftermath of War*, pp. 79–83, 91–98, 103–4; and Pike, *The Andean Republics*, pp. 201–2, 237 for the negative reaction in Latin America to aspects of United States boundary dispute diplomacy.

88. Taylor, *American Diplomacy and the Narcotics Traffic*, pp. 171–75.

89. Ibid., pp. 176–77.

90. "Coca Leaves and Cocaine," *Pan-American Magazine*, May–June 1922, pp. 2–3; Department of State to C. E. Guyant, Callao-Lima, January 30, 1924, RG 59 811.114N16/373b; Guyant to Hughes, February 6, 1924, RG 59 811.114N16/418; Hughes to the American Embassy, Lima, September 11, 1924, RG 59 511.4A2/90a.

91. On cultivation in Bolivia, see Cottrell to Hughes, February 19, 1924, RG 59 824.114 Narcotics/3; W. Russell Baker to Hughes, September 19, 1924, RG 59 511.4A2/106; League of Nations, Advisory Committee on Traffic in Opium and Other Dangerous Drugs, *Report to the Council on the Work of the Sixth Session, August 4th–14th, 1924* A.32.1924.XI. (Geneva, 1924), p. 2.

92. Summerlin to Hughes, June 16, 1923, RG 59 812.114 Narcotics/75; Summerlin to Hughes, October 6, 1924, RG 59 511.4A1/1931; *Diario Oficial*, Mexico, July 28, 1923. For the decree of January 1925, see H. F. A. Schoenfeld to Hughes, January 21, 1925, RG 59 812.114 Narcotics/95; Schoenfeld to Secretary of State Frank B. Kellogg, August 17, 1925, RG 59 812.114 Narcotics/104. The decree included cocaine and was later amended to include marijuana; *New York Times*, February 7, 1925, p. 3.

93. House of Representatives, *The Traffic in Drugs*, passim; Taylor, *American Diplomacy and the Narcotics Traffic*, pp. 183–85; Pinkney Tuck, from Stephen G. Porter, to Hughes, February 1, 1925, RG 59 511.4A2/263; League of Nations, *Records of the Second Opium Conference, Geneva, November 17, 1924 to February 19th, 1925* C.760.M.260.1924.XI. (Geneva, 1925), I, "Plenary Meetings: Text of the Debates," pp. 201–4, 206–7 (hereafter cited as League of Nations, *Records of the Second Opium Conference*); and *New York Times*, February 7, 1925, pp. 1, 3.

94. League of Nations, *Records of the Second Opium Conference*, I, pp. 13, 63–64, 90; League of Nations, Advisory Committee on Traffic in Opium and Other Dangerous Drugs, *Minutes of the Sixth Session, Geneva, August 4th–14th, 1924* C.397.M.146.1924.XI. (Geneva, 1924), Annex 12: "Observations of the Bolivian Government regarding the Proposal to Restrict the Cultivation of Coca," 105; League of Nations, *Records of the Second Opium Conference*, II, "Meetings of the Committees and Subcommittees: Minutes of Sub-Com-

mittee C, Geneva, November 29, 1924 to January 30, 1925," pp. 227–29. In debate, Pinto-Escalier suggested indirectly that it was Peruvian rather than Bolivian coca which ended up in the hands of illicit cocaine manufacturers.

95. Taylor, *American Diplomacy and the Narcotics Traffic*, pp. 209–10.

96. Moshar-ol-Molk, Persian Minister for Foreign Affairs, to W. Smith Murray, Chargé d'Affaires, Teheran, September 30, 1924, RG 59 511.4A2/128.

Chapter 3: Rebuilding the Politics of Drug Control

1. Taylor, *American Diplomacy and the Narcotics Traffic*, pp. 201–2; Musto, *The American Disease*, p. 203; and William O. Walker III, "The Politics of Drug Control: The United States and Latin America, 1900–1945" (Ph.D. diss., University of California, Santa Barbara, 1974), pp. 72–75 for an example of the power Porter held over the course of the nation's drug policy (hereafter cited as Walker, "The Politics of Drug Control").

2. Taylor, *American Diplomacy and the Narcotics Traffic*, p. 219; Oral History Research Office, Butler Library, Columbia University, *The Reminiscences of Herbert L. May*, p. 36 (hereafter cited as *The Reminiscences of Herbert L. May*,).

3. Taylor, *American Diplomacy and the Narcotics Traffic*, pp. 213, 223–24. At the time, European pharmaceutical firms served as the major suppliers of illicit manufactured drugs, further convincing United States officials that limitation at the source was the only effective solution to international drug problems; Bruun, Pan, and Rexed, *The Gentleman's Club*, pp. 223–25.

4. *The Reminiscences of Herbert L. May*, p. 33.

5. Memorandum of a "Conversation between Representative Stephen G. Porter and Dr. Rupert Blue with Mr. Clark, Mr. Johnson, and Mr. Caldwell," September 24, 1928, RG 59 511.4A2A/9.5; Conversation, September 24, 1928, on "Invitation to the United States to Participate with the Council of the League in Electing the Permanent Central Board Provided for by the Geneva Opium Convention," in Library of Congress, Nelson Trusler Johnson Papers, Box 48, "Memoranda of Conversations, 1927–1928" (hereafter cited as Johnson Papers).

6. Conversation, September 24, 1928, Johnson Papers, Box 48.

7. Memorandum by Stuart J. Fuller to Pierrepont Moffat, September 5, 1933, RG 59 511.4A2A/300; *The Reminiscences of Herbert L. May*, p. 34; Taylor, *American Diplomacy and the Narcotics Traffic*, p. 223; Musto, *The American Disease*, pp. 203–4.

8. Conversation with Herbert L. May, December 20, 1928, Johnson Papers, Box 48; and see *The Reminiscences of Herbert L. May*, pp. 50, 57–58 for May's assessment of the Department of State officials with whom he worked while serving on the Permanent Central Opium Board.

9. May, "The International Control of Narcotic Drugs," p. 329; James E. Sheridan, *China in Disintegration: The Republican Era in Chinese History, 1912–1949* (New York: The Free Press, 1975), pp. 102–3; Jonathan Marshall, "Opium and the Politics of Gangster-ism in Nationalist China, 1927–1945," *Bulletin of Concerned Asian Scholars*, 8 (July–September 1976), pp. 19–20 (hereafter cited as Marshall, "Opium and the Politics of Gangsterism").

10. Mrs. Hamilton Wright to Kellogg, March 15, 1928, RG 59 511.4A2/568.

11. Memorandum by Johnson of a conversation with Mrs. Wright, July 7, 1926, RG 59 500.C1197/18.

12. Mrs. Wright to Johnson, January 25, 1928, RG 59 511.4A2/563.

13. Johnson to Kellogg, January 27, 1928, RG 59 511.4A2/564; Kellogg to Charles Evans Hughes, Chairman of the United States Delegation to the Sixth International Conference of American States, February 4, 1928, RG 59 511.4A2/563.

14. Class, "The Sacred Coca Plant," pp. 297–300; "Drug Curse is Pall on Roof of World," *Popular Mechanics*, February 1924, pp. 248–49.

15. Cottrell to Kellogg, February 14, 1927, RG 59 800.114N16/112; Frederick P. Hibbard to Secretary of State Henry L. Stimson, August 30, 1929, RG 59 800.114N16/375.

16. Federal Narcotics Control Board, *Traffic in Opium, 1927* (Washington, D.C.: Government Printing Office, 1927), p. 5; United States Legation (La Paz) to the Department of State for the Division of Far Eastern Affairs, February 10, 1932, RG 59 824.114 Narcotics/14; "Nueva Legislación," *Boletín de la Oficina Sanitaria Panamericana*, 9 (marzo de 1934), p. 347 (hereafter cited as *Boletín OSP*).

17. Drs. Sebastían Lorente y Baltazar Caravedo, "Bases Fundamentales para la Organización de la Defensa Social contra la Toxicomanía," *Boletín OSP*, 7 (enero de 1928), pp. 193–94.

18. Ibid., pp. 195–97. Pike, *The Modern History of Peru*, pp. 246–49.

19. Richmond P. Hobson to Stimson, September 6, 1930, RG 59 511,4A7/12; R. Norris Shreve to Stimson, November 3, 1930, RG 59 823.114 Narcotics/19; Stanley K. Hornbeck to Shreve, November 24, 1930, RG 59 823.114 Narcotics/20; Memorandum by Fuller, November 28, 1930, RG 59, 823.114 Narcotics/22.

20. *El Comercio* (Lima), January 22, 1932; Seymour Lowman, Assistant Secretary of the Treasury, to Fuller, September 6, 1932, RG 59 823.114 Narcotics/50.

21. For Colombia, see Lester L. Schnare to Hughes, May 8, 1924, RG 59 811.114N16/515; for Chile, see Francis Fisher Kane, "Coca-chewing," *The Survey*, June 15, 1927, p. 347.

22. El Consejo Nacional de Higiene, "La Higiene en el Uruguay," *Boletín OSP*, 7 (junio de 1928), p. 673; League of Nations, Advisory Committee on Traffic in Opium and Other Dangerous Drugs, *Report to the Council on the Work of the Thirteenth Session, held at Geneva from January 20th to February 14th, 1930* C. 138.M.51.1930.XI. (Geneva 1930), p. 12 (hereafter cited as League of Nations, *Report to the Council on the Work of the Thirteenth Session*).

23. Hoffman Philip to Hughes, November 21, 1923, RG 59 833.114 Narcotics/5.

24. J. Butler Wright to Stimson, March 17, 1932, RG 59 833.114 Narcotics/28 summarizing a letter from the Montevideo chief of police to the minister of the interior.

25. James R. Sheffield to Kellogg, January 7, 1927, RG 59 800.114N16/88; Dwight W. Morrow to Kellogg, December 10, 1927, RG 59 800.114N16/310.

26. *El Universal* (Mexico City), September 16, 1929; "Nueva Legislación," *Boletín OSP*, 8 (diciembre de 1929), 1422.

27. Henry C. A. Damm to Kellogg, May 12, 1926, RG 59 812.114 Narcotics/108; Frank Bohr to Kellogg, May 4, 1927, RG 59, 812,114 Narcotics/116; Department of State to United States Consuls in Mexico, October 14, 1927, RG 59 812.114 Narcotics/122.

28. Bohr to Kellogg, March 14, 1927, RG 59 812.00/28281. Were the activities of the Chinese actually being tolerated by the local Mexican citizenry, such an occurrence marked an unusual accommodation between the two peoples. See, for example, *FRUS, 1916*, pp. 617–22; more specifically, concerning Chinese exclusion from areas producing opium poppies, see William A. Smale, Ensenada, to Secretary of State Cordell Hull, June 12, 1933, RG 59 812.504/1402.

29. H. H. Leonard to Stimson, September 23, 1930, RG 590 812.114 Narcotics/160.

30. For Ciudad Juárez, see Consul John Dye, Report on Political Conditions, April 1927, RG 59 812.00/28379; for Laredo, see *New York Times*, February 26, 1928, III, p. 2.

31. See chapter 2, note 73.

32. Secretary of the Treasury Andrew W. Mellon to Hughes, December 18, 1924, RG 59 711.129/16; Sheffield to Kellogg, March 31, 1925, RG 59 711.129/27; Sheffield to Kellogg, April 1, 1925, RG 59 711.129/27; William R. Vallance, Office of the Solicitor of the State Department, to Wilbur J. Carr, May 20, 1925, RG 59 711.129/72.

33. Dye to Kellogg, April 24, 1925, RG 59 711.129/51; Leighton Hope, Ensenada, to Kellogg, April 23, 1925, RG 59 711.129/59.

34. Sheffield to Kellogg, December 29, 1925, RG 59 711.129/109; see the text of the treaty in United States Treaty Series, No. 732, *Convention between the United States and*

Mexico to Prevent Smuggling and for Certain Other Objects (Washington, D.C.: Government Printing Office, 1926); for a similar pact with Cuba, see United States Treaty Series, No. 739, *Convention between the United States and Cuba to Prevent Smuggling* (Washington, D.C.: Government Printing Office, 1926).

35. *FRUS, 1927*, 3 vols. (Washington, D.C.: Government Printing Office, 1942), III, pp. 230–31; Memorandum by Kellogg of a Conversation with the British Ambassador Regarding the Situation in Mexico, March 23, 1927, RG 59 711.12/1030. Two years earlier, Kellogg, who looked askance at the Mexican Revolution, remarked publicly in relation to conditions in Mexico that the "Mexican Government is now on trial before the world." Graham H. Stuart, *The Department on State: A History of Its Organization, Procedure, and Personnel* (New York: The Macmillan Company, 1949), pp. 283–84; for a fuller description of Kellogg's Mexican policy, see L. Ethan Ellis, *Frank B. Kellogg and American Foreign Relations, 1925–1929* (New Brunswick: Rutgers University Press, 1961), pp. 23–27.

36. John Dye, Report on Political Conditions, April 1927, RG 59 812.00/28379.

37. William P. Blocker to Stimson, April 23, 1931, RG 59 812.114 Narcotics/163.

38. *FRUS, 1928*, 3 vols. (Washington, D.C.: Government Printing Office, 1942–43), I, pp. 444–49; League of Nations, Advisory Committee on Traffic in Opium and Other Dangerous Drugs, *Report to the Council on the Work of the Tenth Session, Geneva, September 28th to October 8th, 1927* C.521.M.179.1927.XI. (Geneva, 1927), p. 9. More generally, see Sumner Welles, *The Time for Decision* (New York: Harper & Brothers, 1944), pp. 188–89 (hereafter cited as Welles, *The Time for Decision*); Alexander DeConde, *Herbert Hoover's Latin-American Policy* (Stanford: Stanford University Press, 1951), pp. 10–12.

39. Conversation with Mrs. Wright, January 18, 1928, Johnson Papers, Box 48.

40. Mrs. Wright to Kellogg, March 15, 1928, RG 59 511.4A2/569.

41. Memorandum by Johnson to Kellogg, March 10, 1928, RG 59 511.4A2/569.

42. Taylor, *American Diplomacy and the Narcotics Traffic*, p. 214; on p. 215, Taylor writes of Porter: "It is fairly safe to assume that had the chairman of the American delegation in 1925 been one who was free of anti-League bias, the suggestion that the delegation withdraw would not have risen."

43. Ibid., pp. 230–32. League of Nations, *Report to the Council on the Work of the Thirteenth Session*, pp. 8–9; League of Nations, *Traffic in Opium and Other Dangerous Drugs, Report of the Fifth Committee to the Assembly* A.86.1929,XI. (Geneva, 1929), pp. 4–5.

44. Memorandum by John Kenneth Caldwell to Johnson, October 8, 1929, RG 59 511.4A6/1.5

45. Stimson to Porter, October 14, 1929, RG 59 511.4A6/2; Caldwell's "Memorandum of a Conference held in the Office of the Honorable Stephen G. Porter on October 16,1929," October 18, 1929, RG 59 511.4A6/5.

46. Memorandum by Caldwell of a conversation, November 4, 1929, with Stanley K. Hornbeck, Herbert L. May, and Mrs. Helen H. Moorehead, November 4, 1929, RG 59 511.4A6/6.

47. Caldwell to Johnson, November 8, 1929, RG 511.4A6/14.

48. Memorandum by Caldwell of a conversation with Porter, December 14, 1929, RG 59 811.114N16/1718.5.

49. Taylor, *American Diplomacy and the Narcotics Traffic*, p. 235; for more information on American opposition to cartel arrangements, see Memorandum by Caldwell to Joseph P. Cotton, March 21, 1930, RG 59 511.4A6/46.

50. Taylor, *American Diplomacy and the Narcotics Traffic*, pp. 236–37; *FRUS, 1931*, 3 vols. (Washington, D.C.: Government Printing Office, 1946), I, pp. 649–50.

51. *FRUS, 1931*, I, pp. 650–52 for Stimson's letter to Hoover.

52. Taylor, *American Diplomacy and the Narcotics Traffic*, p. 241

53. House of Representatives, *Narcotic Drugs,* pp. 1, 3, 6, 11; Laurence F. Schmecke-bier, *The Bureau of Prohibition: Its History, Activities, and Organization* (Washington, D.C.: The Brookings Institution, 1929), pp. 3, 136–41.

54. Harry Cohen, M.D., to Stimson, May 27, 1929, RG 59 800.114N16/351. Terry and Pellens wrote that opium use was still widespread at the time; Terry and Pellens, *The Opium Problem,* p. 53.

55. Caldwell's Memorandum of a Conference held in the Office of Mr. Lowman, Assistant Secretary of the Treasury, April 11, 1929, RG 59 811.114N16–Porter Bill/1.

56. Caldwell's Memorandum of a Conference held in the Office of Mr. Lowman, Assistant Secretary of the Treasury, April 13, 1929 [dated April 15, 1929], RG 59, 811.114N16–Porter Bill/2.

57. Furman, *A Profile,* pp. 364-65; Cohen to Stimson, May 27, 1929, RG 59 800.114N16/351 (emphasis in original).

58. Memorandum from Caldwell to Cotton, March 5, 1930, RG 59 811.114N16-Porter Bill/22; United States Congress. House of Representatives, *Hearings before the Committee on Ways and Means,* 71 Cong. 2 Sess., on HR 10,561, "A Bill to Create in the Treasury Department a Bureau of Narcotics and for Other Purposes," March 7 and 8, 1930 (Washington, D.C.: Government Printing Office, 1930), pp. 43–44 (hereafter cited as House of Representatives, "Bureau of Narcotics").

59. House of Representatives. "Bureau of Narcotics," pp. 31–32.

60. *Washington Herald,* March 7, 1930.

61. Memorandum by Caldwell, March 12, 1930, RG 59 811.114N16–Porter Bill/24.

62. Ibid. *Congressional Record,* 71 Cong., 2 Sess., March 7, 1930, p. 5186; *New York Times,* March 9, 1930, I, p. 14.

63. Memorandum by Caldwell, March 12, 1930, RG 59 811.114N16–Porter Bill/24; Memorandum by Caldwell, June 3, 1930, RG 59 811.114N16–Porter Bill/40.5

64. Memorandum by Caldwell, March 26, 1930, RG 59 811.114N16–Porter Bill/26.

65. Caldwell to Cotton, April 1, 1930, RG 59 811.114N16–Porter Bill/29; Memorandum by Caldwell of a Conversation wtih Porter, April 4, 1930, RG 59 811.114N16–Porter Bill/31; Memorandum by Caldwell to Cotton, April 11, 1930, RG 59 811.114N16–Porter Bill/32.

66. Caldwell's Memorandum of a Conversation with Porter, April 22, 1930, RG 59 811.114N16–Porter Bill/37; Memorandum by Caldwell, June 6, 1930, RG 59 811.114N16–Porter Bill/40.5; Musto, *The American Disease,* p. 209.

67. *New York Times,* February 22, 1930, p. 25. In the early 1930s when Rep. Hamilton Fish tried to gain influence over drug policy similar to that which Porter had enjoyed, the State Department successfully resisted his efforts; Taylor, *American Diplomacy and the Narcotics Traffic,* p. 241.

68. *New York Times,* February 15, 1930, p. 4; and February 20, 1930, pp. 1, 3.

69. Ibid., February 20, 1930, pp. 1, 3; the quotation is on p. 1.

70. Ibid., March 1, 1930, p. 22; "Editorial Paragraphs," *The Nation,* March 12, 1930, p. 9; Andrew W. Mellon to Senator Reed Smoot, Chairman, Senate Finance Committee, December 4, 1930, National Archives, General Records of the Department of the Treasury, Record Group 56, Box 248, Folder: "Treasury Department: Narcotics Bureau, 1930–1932" (hereafter cited as RG 56, Box [number]).

71. Caldwell to Cotton, June 6, 1930, RG 59 811.114N16–Porter Bill/41; Memorandum by Caldwell to Cotton, June 7, 1930, RG 59 811.114N16–Porter Bill/43; Cotton to George Akerson, Secretary to the President, June 10, 1930, RG 59 811.114N16–Porter Bill/46; Cotton to Ogden L. Mills, Undersecretary of the Treasury, June 10, 1930, RG 59 811.114N16–Porter Bill/47; Akerson to Mills, June 20, 1930, RG 56, Box 248.

72. Memorandum by Caldwell of a Conversation with Harry J. Anslinger, June 17, 1930, RG 59 811.114N16–Porter Bill/50.

73. Mellon to Smoot, December 4, 1930, RG 56, Box 248.

74. Musto, *The American Disease*, p. 212. Musto's book reveals especially well the persistence of a strict enforcement policy under auspices of the Federal Bureau of Narcotics.

75. For a discussion of bureaucratic efficiency, see Peter M. Blau and Marshall W. Meyer, *Bureaucracy in Modern Society*, 2nd ed. (New York: Random House, 1971), p. 156; Eakins, "Liberal Policy Research," pp. 163–64; McConnell, *Private Power*, pp. 6–7, 27. The Hoover quotation is in Richard Hofstadter, *The American Political Tradition and the Men Who Made It* (New York: Alfred A. Knopf, 1948), p. 287. And see, United States. Department of the Treasury, Bureau of Narcotics, *Traffic in Opium and Other Dangerous Drugs for the Year Ended December 31, 1930* (Washington, D.C.: Government Printing Office, 1931), pp. 1–4, 12 (hereafter cited as Bureau of Narcotics, *Traffic in Opium* [*year*]).

76. *New York Times*, February 13, 1930, p. 15. Hoover's view of drug law enforcement cannot be determined with precision. His dismissal in 1929 of the flamboyant prohibitionist Assistant Attorney General Mabel Walker Willebrandt sugests that he may have favored an attitude similar to Porter's. That is, social issues of serious national concern had to be dealt with humanely and rationally, something Hoover attempted to do, for example, in the area of prison reform. Burner, *Herbert Hoover*, pp. 207, 210, 214, 217–19; Sanford Bates, *Prisons and Beyond* (New York: The Macmillan Company, 1936), pp. 14–18.

77. *New York Times*, January 13, 1931, p. 8. League of Nations, Advisory Committee on Traffic in Opium and Other Dangerous Drugs, *Minutes of the Fourteenth Session, held at Geneva from January 9th to February 7th, 1931* C.88.M.34.1931.XI. (Geneva, 1931), p. 21.

78. May, "The International Control of Narcotic Drugs," 333; *FRUS, 1931*, I, p. 656. The United States delegation was composed of Caldwell, Anslinger, Assistant Surgeon General Walter L. Treadway, and Sanborn Young, a member of the California state senate; Stimson to American Legation, Berne, March 17, 1931, RG 59 511.4A6/235.

79. *FRUS, 1931*, I, pp. 653–54; for more on Latin American reaction to the international antidrug campaign around 1930, see Walker, "The Politics of Drug Control," pp. 157–59.

80. League of Nations, *Records of the Conference for the Limitation of the Manufacture of Narcotic Drugs, Geneva, May 27th to July 13th, 1931*, "Volume I: Plenary Meetings, Text of the Debates," C.509.M.214.1931.XI. (Geneva, 1931), pp. 9–13, 39 (hereafter cited as League of Nations, *Conference for the Limitation of Manufacture*).

81. Ibid., pp. 19–20, 74–80; emphasis in original.

82. Taylor, *American Diplomacy and the Narcotics Traffic*, p. 247; *FRUS, 1931*, I, p. 657.

83. Taylor, *American Diplomacy and the Narcotics Traffic*, pp. 248–49; May, "The International Control of Narcotic Drugs," pp. 335–38.

84. *FRUS, 1931*, pp. 671–73; Taylor, *American Diplomacy and the Narcotics Traffic*, p. 255.

85. League of Nations, *Conference for the Limitation of Manufacture*, pp. 272, 369; Taylor, *American Diplomacy and the Narcotics Traffic*, pp. 259–60; *New York Times*, July 11, 1932, p. 4.

Chapter 4: Drug Control in the Americas, 1931–1936

1. "End of the Illicit Drug Traffic Now in Sight," *Literary Digest*, July 29, 1933, p. 19.

2. For the government's 1926 addiction figures, see Bureau of Narcotics, *Traffic in Opium, 1931* (Washington, D.C.: Government Printing Office, 1932), p. 8; for Porter's testimony, see House of Representatives, "Bureau of Narcotics," 15; for the government's 1932 addiction figures, see Mellon to Stimson, February 9, 1932, RG 59 500.C1197/510.5.

3. *St. Louis Post–Dispatch*, December 17, 1934; for the Bureau's response to the editorial, see Will S. Wood, Acting Commissioner of Narcotics, to Herbert E. Gaston, Assistant Secretary of the Treasury, January 16, 1935, RG 56, Box 191, "Treasury Department, Narcotics Bureau, 1933–1940."

4. For Mills's comments, see Mills to Stimson, February 9, 1932, RG 59 500.C1197/510.5; for Anslinger's assessment, see Harry J. Anslinger, "The Narcotic Problem," Delivered at the Attorney General's Conference on Crime, Washington, D.C., December 13, 1934, Bureau of Narcotics and Dangerous Drugs Library, Anslinger Papers: 1930–1940 (hereafter cited as Anslinger Papers, BNDD Library).

5. Dr. Walter L. Treadway, "La Narcomanía y las medidas para su prevención en los Estados Unidos," *Boletín OSP*, 11 (diciembre de 1932), pp. 1256–67.

6. Anslinger and Tompkins, *The Traffic in Narcotics*, pp. 156–59; Bonnie and Whitebread, *The Marihuana Conviction*, chap. 4 for the background of the uniform state narcotic law.

7. Anslinger and Tompkins, *The Traffic in Narcotics*, p. 160; Bonnie and Whitebread, *The Marihuana Conviction*, p. 90; Bureau of Narcotics, *Traffic in Opium, 1933* (Washington, D.C.: Government Printing Office, 1934), pp. 8, 61; idem, *Traffic in Opium, 1935* (Washington, D.C.: Government Printing Office, 1936), p. v; on support by the American Medical Association, see idem, *Traffic in Opium, 1931*, p. 10.

8. Memorandum of a Conversation with A. V. Dalrymple by Stuart J. Fuller, April 12, 1933, RG 59 102.196/33; more generally, see Barry Dean Karl, *Executive Reorganization and Reform in the New Deal: The Story of the Controversial First Steps toward Administrative Management, 1900–1939* (Cambridge: Harvard University Press, 1963).

9. Fuller to Undersecretary of State William Phillips, March 31, 1933, RG 59 102.196/31; emphasis in original. Anslinger welcomed the role of the Bureau as a model for other nations; see Harry J. Anslinger, "Peddling of Narcotic Drugs," *Journal of Criminal Law and Criminology*, XXIV (September–October 1933), pp. 636–55, especially pp. 637, 651.

10. Memorandum by Fuller to John T. Fowler, Department of Justice, April 4, 1933, RG 59 102.196/32; Memorandum of a Conversation with A. V. Dalrymple by Fuller, April 12, 1933, RG 59 102.196/33; Phillips to Louis Howe, April 12, 1933, RG 59 102.196/34b; Phillips to Director of the Budget Lewis W. Douglas, April 12, 1933, RG 59 511.4A6/983.

11. *New York Times*, April 20, 1933, p. 12; Memorandum for the Undersecretary of State from President Franklin D. Roosevelt, April 20, 1933, RG 102.196/35.

12. Dr. Juan Péon del Valle, "Algunos Aspectos de la Actual Lucha Contra La Toxicomanía en México," *Boletín OSP*, 12 (abril de 1933), pp. 347–55, especially pp. 347–50.

13. *Excélsior* (Mexico City), June 12, 1931; for the first United States response, see J. Reuben Clark to Stimson, June 12, 1931, RG 59 812.002/301.

14. Col. Gordon Johnson to Stimson, June 12, 1931, RG 59 812.114 Narcotics/176.

15. Clark to Stimson, June 18, 1931, RG 59 812.002/303; Clark to Stimson, June 22, 1931, RG 59 812.002/304; Clark to Stimson, August 11, 1931, RG 59 812.002/309.

16. *Diario Oficial*, Mexico, October 27, 1931.

17. For pertinent sections of the Mexican Sanitary Code, see ibid., August 30, 1934 and August 31, 1934.

18. *El Universal* (Mexico City), April 7, 1935; Stuart J. Fuller's *Report on the 17th Session of the Opium Advisory Committee of the League of Nations, Held at Geneva, from October 30–November 9, 1933*, January 9, 1934, RG 59 500.C1197/655; Marshall, "Opium and the Politics of Gangsterism," pp. 20–28.

19. Stanley V. Parker, Commander, United States Coast Guard, Chief, Division of Intelligence, to Anslinger, December 31, 1935, RG 59 812.114 Narcotics/501.

20. *FRUS, 1929*, 3 vols. (Washington, D.C.: Government Printing Office, 1943–44), I, p. 389 note 3; a similar agreement was reached with Cuba.

21. Blocker to Stimson, April 23, 1931, RG 59 812.114 Narcotics/163.

22. Blocker to Stimson, May 23, 1931, RG 59 812.114 Narcotics/166; Undersecretary of State William R. Castle to Mellon, June 13, 1931, RG 59 812.114 Narcotics/170; R. A. Darling to Wood, May 31, 1931, RG 59 812.114 Narcotics/173.

23. For information on continued border smuggling, see Clark to Stimson, June 18, 1931, RG 59 812.114 Narcotics/ 169; for the informal agreement of 1932, see Clark to Stimson, March 9, 1932, RG 59 711.129/217; Phillips to Clark, June 22, 1932, RG 59 ibid; and Fuller to Clark, June 16, 1932, RG 59 711.129/221.

24. League of Nations, Advisory Committee on Traffic in Opium and Other Dangerous Drugs, *Minutes of the Seventeenth Session Held at Geneva, October 30 to November 9, 1933* C.661.M.316.1933.XI. (Geneva, 1933), pp. 9–10 (hereafter cited as League of Nations, *Minutes of the Seventeenth Session*); Fuller's *Report on the Seventeenth Session of the Opium Advisory Committee*, January 9, 1934, RG 59 500.C1197/655.

25. William A. Smale, United States Consul Ensenada, to Secretary of State Cordell Hull, September 20, 1934, RG 59 811.114 Narcotics/300.

26. W. W. Robert, Jr., Acting Secretary of the Treasury, to Hull, October 12, 1934, RG 59 711.129/223 requesting Smale's presence at the Los Angeles meeting; Smale to Hull, October 30, 1934, RG 59 811.114 Mexico/303.

27. Smale to Hull, March 7, 1935, RG 59 811.114 Mexico/332.

28. Smale to Hull, October 30, 1934, RG 59 811.114 Mexico/303. At the same time, Mexico was minimizing the extent of its illicit drug traffic to the OAC; see League of Nations, Advisory Committee on Traffic in Opium and Other Dangerous Drugs, *Minutes of the Eighteenth Session Held at Geneva, May 18 to June 2, 1934* C.317.M.142.1934.XI. (Geneva, 1934), p. 19 (hereafter cited as League of Nations, *Minutes of the Eighteenth Session*).

29. Edward L. Reed to Smale, April 2, 1935, RG 59 811.114 Mexico/332.

30. Smale to Hull, March 3, 1936, RG 59 812.114 Narcotics/544; League of Nations, Advisory Committee on Traffic in Opium and Other Dangerous Drugs, *Minutes of the Twenty-First Session Held at Geneva, May 25 to June 5, 1936* C.290.M.176. 1936.XI. (Geneva, 1936), p. 32.

31. For the June 1931 questionnaire, see Department of State to American Diplomatic Officers and Certain American Consular Officials, June 10, 1931, RG 59 833.114 Narcotics/ 25; for Uruguay's reply, see Benjamin Muse to Stimson, April 2, 1932, RG 59 833.114 Narcotics/27.

32. Leslie Reed, Consul General, to Hull, June 6, 1933, RG 59 833.114 Narcotics/39; League of Nations, *Minutes of the Seventeenth Session*, pp. 5, 8.

33. *La Nación* (Buenos Aires), June 8, 1934; Anti-Opium Information Bureau to Fuller, July 5, 1934, RG 59 833.114 Narcotics/43.

34. Leon Dominian to Hull, September 18, 1934, RG 59 883.114 Narcotics/47; Prentiss B. Gilbert, United States Consul Geneva, to Hull, October 23, 1934, RG 59 833.114 Narcotics/48; Reed to the Department of State for the Division of Far Eastern Affairs, November 28, 1934, RG 59 833.114 Narcotics/52.

35. J. Butler Wright to Hull, October 8, 1933, RG 59 710.G1A/215; Wright to Hull, November 9, 1933, RG 59 710.G1A/278. In its proposal, Uruguay also recommended the creation of state drug monopolies should domestic laws so allow. The Final Act of the conference defined addicts as a class apart from "common delinquents." Division of International Law, Carnegie Endowment for International Peace, ed., *The International Conferences of American States: First Supplement, 1933–1940*, "Seventh International Conference of American States, Montevideo, December 3–26, 1933," (Washington, D.C.: Carnegie Endowment for International Peace, 1940), pp. 47–48.

36. League of Nations, *Minutes of the Eighteenth Session*, pp. 9, 34–37, 41–43.

37. República Oriental del Uruguay, Ministerio de Salud Pública, *Reglamentación del Movimiento de Los Estupefacientes Nocivos y Su Distribución* (Montevideo, 1934), pp. 3–4.

38. League of Nations, Advisory Committee on Traffic in Opium and Other Dangerous Drugs, *Measures Taken in Uruguay in the Campaign Against the Illicit Traffic* O. C. 1670 (Geneva, 1936); Julius Lay to Hull, February 4, 1937, RG 59 833.114 Narcotics/72. According to government claims, usage of opium had fallen 15 percent, morphine 40 percent, heroin 50 percent, and cocaine 27 percent. Lay had served previously in Honduras.

39. Lay to Hull, February 4, 1937, RG 59 833.114 Narcotics/72; Reed to Hull, September 21, 1937, RG 59 833.114 Narcotics/77.

40. Department of State to American Diplomatic Officers and Certain American Consular Officials, June 10, 1931, RG 59 835.114 Narcotics/8; Winthrop Greene, Geneva, to Stimson, December 4, 1931, RG 59 835.114 Narcotics/10.

41. Stanley Hawks, Secretary, United States Legation Berne, to Hull, November 23, 1935, RG 59 835.114 Narcotics/25; Hawks to Hull, December 5, 1935, RG 59 835.114 Narcotics/29.

42. Alexander Wilbourne Weddell, United States Ambassador Buenos Aires, to Hull, March 22, 1938, RG 59 835.114 Narcotics/54; Stephen B. Gibbons to Hull, April 29, 1938, RG 59 835.114 Narcotics/60; República Argentina, Ministerio del Interior, *Boletín Sanitario del Departmento Nacional Higiene*, año 1 (enero de 1937), p. 65.

43. League of Nations, *Minutes of the Eighteenth Session*, p. 83; Eric Einar Ekstrand, Report to Stuart J. Fuller, April 13, 1934, RG 59 815.114 Narcotics/111.

44. League of Nations, Advisory Committee on Traffic in Opium and Other Dangerous Drugs, *Minutes of the Nineteenth Session Held at Geneva, November 15 to 18, 1934* C.33.M.14.1935.XI. (Geneva, 1935), p. 21 (hereafter cited as League of Nations, *Minutes of the Nineteenth Session*); Lay to Hull, July 6, 1934, RG 59 815.114 Narcotics/157; MacLeod, *Spanish Central American*, pp. 280, 311, 373.

45. League of Nations, *Minutes of the Nineteenth Session*, p. 21.

46. Lawrence Higgins to Hull, July 27, 1933, RG 59 815.114 Narcotics/66; Lay to Hull, August 6, 1933, RG 59 815.114 Narcotics/77; Anslinger to Fuller (with a cable from Paris), March 26, 1934, RG 59 815.114 Narcotics/99.

47. Lay to Hull, May 1, 1934, RG 59 815.114 Narcotics/127; *FRUS, 1932*, 5 vols. (Washington, D.C.: Government Printing Office, 1947–48), V: *The American Republics*, p. 717.

48. For information on the growth of the banana industry and its domination of the Honduran economy from land ownership to railroad and rail construction, see generally Luis Mariñas Otero, *Honduras* (Madrid: Ediciones Cultura Hispanica, 1963), pp. 54–55, 65, 85, 88 (hereafter cited as Mariñas Otero, *Honduras*); more specifically, see Stacy May and Galo Plaza, *The United Fruit Company in Latin America* (Washington, D.C.: National Planning Association, 1958), pp. 10, 19–22 (hereafter cited as May and Plaza, *The United Fruit Company*); Thomas L. Karnes, *Tropical Enterprise: The Standard Fruit and Steamship Company in Latin America* (Baton Rouge: Louisiana State University Press, 1978), pp. 168–72, 180–88 (hereafter cited as Karnes, *Tropical Enterprise*). On the relationship between the banana companies and the quality of life in Honduras, see May and Plaza, *The United Fruit Company*, p. 154; Karnes, *Tropical Enterprise*, pp. 171–72, 180–82; and Mariñas Otero, *Honduras*, pp. 57, 62, 96. It should be pointed out that the Carías government did not permit labor to organize. The quotation by Willard L. Beaulac is in his book, *A Diplomat Looks at Aid to Latin America* (Carbondale and Edwardsville: Southern Illinois University Press, 1970), p. 70. Additional information on economic conditions in Honduras may be found in Gary W. Wynia, *Politics and Planners: Economic Development Policy in Central America* (Madison: University of Wisconsin Press, 1972), pp. 33–36; and Vincent Checchi and Associates, *Honduras: A Problem in Economic Development* (New York: The Twentieth Century Fund, 1959), pp. 1–2, 29, 33, 131–32.

49. Dana G. Munro, *The United States and the Caribbean Republics, 1921–1933* (Princeton: Princeton University Press, 1974), pp. 290–94; Ralph Lee Woodward, Jr., *Central*

America: A Nation Divided (New York: Oxford University Press, 1976), pp. 218–19; *FRUS, 1932,* V, pp. 709, 713–15, 720, 722; and William S. Stokes, *Honduras: An Area Study in Government* (Madison: University of Wisconsin Press, 1950), p. 56 (hereafter cited as Stokes, *Honduras*).

50. *FRUS, 1932,* V, pp. 717–28.

51. Ibid., p. 724. Carías, head of the conservative Nationalist Party, began his term in office with a policy of strict economy. He reduced the salaries of public employees, a move, as previously suggested, that was not likely to overcome official susceptibility to bribery. Stokes, *Honduras*, p. 56.

52. Lay to Fuller, August 9, 1933, RG 59 815.114 Narcotics/73; Higgins to Fuller, March 26, 1934, RG 59 815.114 Narcotics/100.

53. Lay to Hull, May 11, 1934, RG 59 815.114 Narcotics/131; *El Ciudadano* (Tegucigalpa), July 9, 1934.

54. See the representative discussions in Laurence Duggan, *The Americas: The Search for Hemisphere Security* (New York: Henry Holt and Company, 1949), pp. 61–65 (hereafter cited as Duggan, *The Americas*); Samuel Flagg Bemis, *The Latin-American Policy of the United States: An Historical Interpretation* (1943; reprint ed., New York: W. W. Norton & Company, 1967), pp. 258–59 (hereafter cited as Bemis, *Latin-American Policy*); Irwin F. Gellman, *Good Neighbor Diplomacy: United States Policies in Latin America, 1933–1945* (Baltimore: Johns Hopkins University Press, 1979), pp. 24–25, 27, 38–39 (hereafter cited as Gellman, *Good Neighbor Diplomacy*).

55. Josephus Daniels to Pierre Boal, Division of American Republics, September 27, 1938, in Library of Congress, Josephus Daniels Papers, Box 754, "Correspondence with Mexican and American Officials, 1933–1941." In an article in *Foreign Affairs* in 1928, Roosevelt previewed his future administration's policy; Franklin D. Roosevelt, "Our Foreign Policy: A Democratic View," *Foreign Affairs*, 6 (July 1928), pp. 573–86. For further discussion, see Welles, *The Time for Decision*, p. 192; Duggan, *The Americas*, pp. 59–61; Sumner Welles, *Seven Decisions That Shaped History* (New York: Harper & Brothers, 1950, 1951), pp. 103–4; Bemis, *The Latin-American Policy*, pp. 389–93; Bryce Wood, *The Making of the Good Neighbor Policy* (New York: Columbia University Press, 1961), pp. 159–60 (hereafter cited as Wood, *Good Neighbor Policy*); Gellman, *Good Neighbor Diplomacy*, pp. 50, 81. Gellman appears to minimize the crucial role of reciprocity.

56. *FRUS, 1933,* 5 vols. (Washington, D.C.: Government Printing Office, 1949–52), V: *The American Republics*, p. 393.

57. Lay to Hull, May 31, 1934, RG 59 815.114 Narcotics/139; Myron H. Schrand, United States Vice Consul Puerto Cortés, to Hull, June 7, 1934 RG 59 815.114 Narcotics/144; *New York American*, June 26, 1934.

58. Lay to Hull, July 13, 1934, RG 59 815.114 Narcotics/169; Lay to Hull, July 18, 1934, RG 815.114 Narcotics/174.

59. For the Honduran reaction to Fuller's remarks and the inquiry of the League of Nations, see the progovernment newspaper *El Cronista* (Tegucigalpa), July 23, 1934; Fuller's Memorandum to the Bureau of Narcotics, July 30, 1934, RG 59 815.114 Narcotics/187; Memorandum (unsigned) in the Division of Latin American Affairs, March 11, 1935, RG 59 815.114 Narcotics/292.

60. See chapter 7 *infra*.

61. Herbert O. Williams to the Department of State, March 11, 1933, RG 59 819.114 Narcotics/60; Antonio C. Gonzalez to the Department of State, February 6, 1934, RG 59 819.114 Narcotics/66; Bureau of Narcotics, *Traffic in Opium, 1934* (Washington, D.C.: Government Printing Office, 1935), p. 8.

62. Maxwell M. Hamilton to the United States Legation, Tegucigalpa, December 1, 1934, RG 59 815.114 Narcotics/265; Department of State to Raleigh A. Gibson, November 28, 1934, RG 59 815.114 Narcotics/264; Gibbons to H. Charles Spruks, November 17, 1934, RG 59 815.114 Narcotics/258; *El Cronista* (Tegucigalpa), September 1, 1934.

63. Gibson to Hull, December 5, 1934, RG 59 815.114 Narcotics/268; Anslinger to Fuller, January 10, 1935, RG 59 815.114 Narcotics/276; R. Austin Ady to the Department of State, July 25, 1935, RG 59 815.114 Narcotics/304.

64. Leo J. Keena to the Department of State, October 16, 1935, RG 59 815.114 Narcotics/309; Sumner Welles to the United States Legation, Tegucigalpa, October 16, 1935, RG 59 815.114 Narcotics/313; for the seizure of drugs in New Orleans, see Department of State to Ady, August 5, 1935, RG 59 815.114 Narcotics/305.

65. Division of Economic Research, Pan American Union, *The Foreign Trade of Latin America* (Washington, D.C: Pan American Union, 1952), pp. 25–28, 155; Richard F. Behrendt, *Inter-American Economic Relations: Problems and Prospects* (New York: The committee on International Economic Policy in cooperation with the Carnegie Endowment for International Peace, 1948), p. 4 (hereafter cited as Behrendt, *Inter-American Economic Relations*); *FRUS, 1934*, 5 vols. (Washington, D.C.: Government Printing Office, 1950–52), V: *The American Republics*, p. 372; Karnes, *Tropical Enterprise*, pp. 197–98.

66. *FRUS, 1934*, V, pp. 372–80; *FRUS, 1935*, 4 vols. (Washington, D.C.: Government Printing Office, 1952–53), IV: *The American Republics*, pp. 734–40; Behrendt, *Inter-American Economic Relations*, p. 77; Dick Steward, *Trade and Hemisphere: The Good Neighbor Policy and Reciprocal Trade* (Columbia: University of Missouri Press, 1975), pp. 212–14 (hereafter cited as Steward, *Trade and Hemisphere*); George Soule, David Efron, and Norman T. Ness, *Latin America in the Future World* (New York: Farrar & Rinehart, 1945), p. 358 for statistics on the low level of Honduran exports to nations in the hemisphere other than the United States.

67. Fred Morris Dearing to Stimson, March 21, 1932, RG 59 823.114 Narcotics/35.

68. William C. Burdett, United States Consul-General, Callao-Lima to Stimson, April 21, 1932, RG 59 823.114 Narcotics/41.

69. Ibid.; Pike, *The Modern History of Peru*, pp. 246–49.

70. Dearing to Hull, May 19, 1933, RG 59 823.114 Narcotics/70.

71. *El Comercio* (Lima), March 15, 1936; Louis G. Dreyfus, Jr., United States Counselor, Lima, to Hull, March 23, 1936, RG 59 823.114 Narcotics/107.

72. *La Crónica* (Lima), February 28, 1936; "Estupefacientes," *Boletín OSP*, 15 (enero de 1936), 64. See also a report on the Third Pan-American Conference of National Directors of Health in "Editoriales," *Boletín OSP*, 15 (junio de 1936), 592 for a good summation of the attitude of the Peruvian government on the relation between its domestic coca industry, the national economy, and international drug control.

73. Robert F. Fernald to Hull, April 12, 1933, RG 59 824.114 Narcotics/18 for the production figures; Dr. Nicanor T. Fernandez, *La Coca Boliviana* (La Paz: Sociedad de Proprietarios de Yungas, 1932), especially pp. 2–3.

74. *El Diario* (La Paz), October 1, 1933; "Estupefacientes," *Boletín OSP*, 13 (marzo de 1934), 234.

75. Taylor, *American Diplomacy and the Narcotics Traffic*, pp. 288–90; Department of State to Hugh R. Wilson, Berne, March 2, 1936, RG 59 511.4T1/36.

76. Hawks to Hull, March 24, 1936, RG 59 511.4T1/13 with the communication from Ekstrand; Department of State Press Release, May 1, 1936, RG 59 511.4T1/36.

77. Dreyfus to Hull, April 13, 1936, RG 59 511.4T1/20.

78. Ibid.; *El Comercio* (Lima), April 6, 1936 for more on the possibility of a national coca monopoly.

79. League of Nations, *Records of the Conference for the Suppression of the Illicit Traffic in Dangerous Drugs (Geneva, June 8 to 26, 1936)*, "Text of the Debates" C.341.M.216.1936.XI. (Geneva, 1936), pp. 7–11 (hereafter cited as League of Nations, *Conference for the Suppression of the Illicit Traffic*).

80. Ibid., pp. 14–15, 18–23.

81. Ibid., pp. 26, 29.

82. Gilbert to Hull (from Fuller and Anslinger), June 8, 1936, RG 59 511.4T1/41.

83. Phillips to Gilbert (for Fuller and Anslinger), June 9, 1936, RG 59 511.4T1/42.

84. Gilbert to Hull (from Fuller and Anslinger), received June 10, 1936, RG 59 511.4T1/44; League of Nations, *Conference for the Suppression of the Illicit Traffic*, pp. 39, 42, 47.

85. Gilbert to Hull (from Fuller and Anslinger), June 22, 1936, RG 59 511.4T1/48; Gilbert to Hull (from Fuller), June 26, 1936, RG 59 511.4T1/52; *New York Times*, June 27, 1936, p. 3.

86. League of Nations, *Conference for the Suppression of the Illicit Traffic*, pp. 174–76.

87. Anslinger and Tompkins, *The Traffic in Narcotics*, pp. 37–38.

Chapter 5: The United State Discovers an "Assassin of Youth"

1. Bonnie and Whitebread, *The Marihuana Conviction*, pp. 90–91.

2. David F. Musto, M.D., "The Marihuana Tax Act of 1937," *Archives of General Psychiatry*, XXVI (February 1972), p. 101 (hereafter cited as Musto, "The Marihuana Tax Act").

3. C. Mahlon Kline, "The Thirty-Seventh Annual Convention of the National Wholesale Druggists Association," *American Journal of Pharmacy*, 84 (January 1912), pp. 30–31.

4. "Our Home Hashheesh Crop," *Literary Digest*, April 3, 926, p. 64.

5. Lester Grinspoon, M.D., *Marihuana Reconsidered*, 2nd ed. (Cambridge: Harvard University Press, 1977), pp. 14–16 (hereafter cited as Grinspoon, *Marihuana Reconsidered*); Musto, "The Marihuana Tax Act," p. 103; Bonnie and Whitebread, *The Marihuana Conviction*, pp. 92–94; Harry J. Anslinger and Will Oursler, *The Murderers: The Story of the Narcotic Gangs* (New York: Farrar, Straus, and Cudahy, 1961), p. 6 (hereafter cited as Anslinger and Oursler, *The Murderers*).

6. Grinspoon, *Marihuana Reconsidered*, pp. 16, 174, 192–94; the quotation from the *New Orleans Medical and Surgical Journal* appears on p. 16.

7. Ibid., pp. 192–301; Eugene Stanley, "Marihuana as a Developer of Criminals," *American Journal of Police Science*, II (May–June 1931), pp. 254–56 (hereafter cited as Stanley, "Developer of Criminals").

8. Stanley, "Developer of Criminals," pp. 254–56.

9. Bureau of Narcotics, *Traffic in Opium, 1931*, p. 51.

10. Bureau of Narcotics, *Traffic in Opium, 1933*, p. 36.

11. Bureau of Narcotics, *Traffic in Opium, 1936* (Washington, D.C.: Government Printing Office, 1937), pp. iii–v; Harry J. Anslinger has written that at that time marijuana usage "spread across America like a roadside fever from state to state." Anslinger and Oursler, *The Murderers*, p. 6.

12. Bonnie and Whitebread, *The Marihuana Conviction*, p. 100.

13. "Medical News," *Journal of the American Medical Association*, March 17, 1934, p. 850 (hereafter cited as *JAMA*).

14. *New York Times*, September 16, 1934, IV, p. 6.

15. "Medical News," *JAMA*, August 8, 1936, p. 437.

16. Will S. Wood to Aaron W. Uris, June 5, 1935, as quoted in Bonnie and Whitebread, *The Marihuana Conviction*, p. 100.

17. Wolf, "Uncle Sam Fights a New Drug Menace," pp. 119–20.

18. *New York Times*, September 15, 1935, IV, p. 9; Musto, The Marihuana Tax Act," 103–4.

19. Musto, "The Marihuana Tax Act," pp. 104–5.

20. Bonnie and Whitebread, *The Marihuana Conviction*, pp. 118–24.

21. Joseph F. Siler, Colonel, M. C., U.S. Army, Chief Health Officer, et al., "Mariajuana Smoking in Panama," *Military Surgeon*, 73 (November 1933), pp. 269, 273–74.

22. Ibid., pp. 274–75.

23. Ibid., pp. 276, 279.

24. Bonnie and Whitebread, *The Marihuana Conviction*, pp. 127–36.

25. "Facts and Fancies about Marihuana," *Literary Digest*, October 14, 1936, pp. 7–8.

26. Walter Bromberg, M.D., "Marihuana Intoxication: A Clinical Study of Cannabis Sativa Intoxication," *American Journal of Psychiatry*, 91 (October 1934), pp. 304, 328.

27. Bonnie and Whitebread, *The Marihuana Conviction*, pp. 138–39.

28. Ibid., pp. 141–43.

29. Musto, "The Marihuana Tax Act," p. 106; as Musto points out: "The goal . . . was to have a prohibitive law to the fullest extent possible."

30. Ibid., p. 107.

31. *Washington Herald*, April 12, 1937.

32. United States Congress. House of Representatives, *Taxation of Marihuana, Hearings on HR 6385*, 75 Cong., 1 Sess., April 27–30 and May 4, 1937 (Washington, D.C.: Government Printing Office, 1937), pp. 18, 24.

33. Ibid., pp. 92, 103.

34. Ibid., p. 93.

35. United States Congress. House of Representatives, Report No. 792, *Marihuana Taxing Bill*, 75 Cong., 1 Sess., May 11, 1937 (Washington, D.C.: Government Printing Office, 1937), pp. 2–3. The House Ways and Means Committee believed that the bill's constitutionality would be upheld under the precedent set in *Veazie Bank v. Fenno*, 1869 (8 Wall. 533).

36. Bureau of Narcotics, *The Traffic in Opium, 1937* (Washington, D.C.: Government Printing Office, 1938), pp. 1–2, 53; Anslinger and Oursler, *The Murderers*, pp. 35, 38–39.

37. Bonnie and Whitebread, *The Marihuana Conviction*, chap. IX, especially p. 175.

38. Harry J. Anslinger, United States Commissioner of Narcotics, with Courtney Riley Cooper, "Marihuana: Assassin of Youth," *American Magazine*, July 1937, pp. 19, 150 (hereafter cited as Anslinger, "Assassin of Youth"); Howard Beckers, in *Outsiders*, p. 141, shows that the antimarijuana campaign produced at least seventeen articles from July 1937 to June 1939—ten of which either explicitly or with textual evidence acknowledged the assistance of the Federal Bureau of Narcotics.

39. Anslinger, "Assassin of Youth," pp. 18, 150.

40. Bureau of Narcotics, *The Traffic in Opium, 1937*, p. 57.

41. *Minneapolis Journal*, October 17, 1937. For a particularly sensational description of a marijuana user, see Anslinger and Tompkins, *The Traffic in Narcotics*, pp. 21–22. A fuller exposition of the alleged menace of marijuana can be found in the Papers of Harry J. Anslinger, Pennsylvania State University Library, University Park, Pa., Box 7: "Marijuana" folder.

42. Harry J. Anslinger, "Narcotic Enforcement," Anslinger Papers, BNDD Library.

43. "Marihuana Weed Grows Where Rope Factory Failed," *Science News Letter*, January 15, 1938, pp. 38–39.

44. Clair A. Brown, "Marihuana: The Mexican Dope Plant Is the Source of a Social Problem," *Nature Magazine*, May 1938, pp. 271–72; "Marihuana More Dangerous than Heroin or Cocaine," *Scientific American*, May 1938, p. 293; Wayne Gard, "Youth Gone Loco," *Christian Century*, June 29, 1938, pp. 812–13; "New Billion-Dollar Crop," *Popular Science Magazine*, February 1938, pp. 238–39, 145A–54A; on the repetition of articles influenced by the Bureau of Narcotics, see note 38 *supra*.

45. For a draft of the speech, see Harry J. Anslinger, "The Government's Fight on Marihuana," Address before the *New York Herald Tribune* Forum, October 25, 1938, Anslinger Papers, BNDD Library (hereafter cited as Anslinger, "The Government's Fight on Marihuana").

46. Robert P. Walton, *Marihuana: America's New Drug Problem* (Philadelphia: J. B. Lippincott Company, 1938), pp. 1, 19, 128–50.

47. Ibid., pp. 27–39, especially pp. 30–33, 39.

48. A. J. Hagen-Smit et al., "A Psychologically Active Principle from *Cannabis Sativa* (Marihuana)," *Science*, June 21, 1940, pp. 602–3.

49. Howard C. Curtis, M.D., "Psychosis Following the Use of Marihuana with Report of Cases," *Journal of the Kansas Medical Society*, 40 (December 1939), pp. 515–17, 526–28.

50. James M. Henninger, "exhibitionism," *Journal of Psychopathology*, 2 (January 1941), pp. 357–66, especially p. 360; Dr. N. S. Yawger, "Marihuana, el Nuevo Vicio," *Criminalia*. *México* (enero de 1939), pp. 269–72.

51. Harry J. Anslinger, "Marihuana . . . the Assassin of the Human Mind," *Law Enforcement*, 1 (October 1941), pp. 7–8, 10.

52. "United States Assumes Control of Cannabis," *JAMA*, September 11, 1937, pp. 31B–32B.

53. Lawrence Kolb, "Marihuana," *Federal Probation*, (July 1938), pp. 22–25.

54. Walter Bromberg, M.D., "Marihuana: A Psychiatric Study," *JAMA*, July 1, 1939, pp. 4–12. For a good overview of the suspected myths and realities of marijuana in 1940, see Maud A. Marshall, "Marihuana," *American Scholar*, 9 (Winter 1938–1939), pp. 95–101.

55. Roger Adams, "Marihuana," *Science*, August 9, 1940, pp. 115–19.

56. Bonnie and Whitebread, *The Marihuana Conviction*, pp. 187–89.

57. Samuel Allentuck, M.D., Ph.D., and Karl Bowman, M.D., "The Psychiatric Aspects of Marihuana Intoxication," *American Journal of Psychiatry*, 99 (September 1942), pp. 248–51 (hereafter cited as Allentuck and Bowman, "Psychiatric Aspects of Marihuana Intoxication").

58. Ibid., p. 251.

59. Harry J. Anslinger, "Correspondence," *JAMA*, January 16, 1943, p. 212–13.

60. James M. Phelan, Colonel, U.S. Amry, Ret., "Editorial: The Marihuana Bugaboo," *Military Surgeon*, 93 (July 1943), pp. 94–95.

61. Michael Schaller, "The Federal Prohibition of Marihuana," *Journal of Social History*, 4 (Fall 1970), p. 62.

62. New York City Mayor's Committee on Marihuana, George B. Wallace, M.D., Chairman, *The Marihuana Problem in the City of New York* (Lancaster, Pa.: Cattel Press, 1944), pp. ix–xi (hereafter cited as Mayor's Committee, *The Marihuana Problem*); Allentuck and Bowman, "Psychiatric Aspects of Marihuana Intoxication," p. 248.

63. Mayor's Committee, *The Marihuana Problem*, pp. 3–25.

64. Dr. J. D. Reichard, "Correspondence: The Marihuana Problem" *JAMA*, June 24, 1944, pp. 594–95.

65. "Marihuana Problems," *JAMA*, April 28, 1945, p. 1129. The Marcovitz and Myers study appeared as "The Marihuana Addict in the Army" in the December 1944 issue of *War Medicine*. See also, Anslinger and Oursler, *The Murderers*, pp. 39–42.

66. Karl M. Bowman, "Correspondence," *JAMA*, July 21, 1945, pp. 899–900.

67. Harry J. Anslinger, "Correspondence," *JAMA*, August 18, 1945, p. 1187. Through 1944 medical journals were printing antimarijuana articles that ignored the latest scientific research. John H. Foulger, M.D., "The Marihuana Problem," *Delaware State Medical Journal*, 16 (February 1944), pp. 24–28.

68. Harry J. Anslinger, "Criminal and Psychiatric Aspects Associated with Marihuana," *The Union Signal*, February 5, 1944, pp. 77–78.

69. Musto, "The Marihuana Tax Act," *passim*; and note 42 *supra* for more on Anslinger and marijuana. The 1939 Women's Christian Temperance Union convention asked that "publicity on marihuana be tempered to conform wtih the factual problem." See Bureau of Narcotics, *Traffic in Opium, 1939* (Washington, D.C.: Government Printing Office, 1940), p. 15.

70. Musto, *The American Disease*, p. 228.

71. Bonnie and Whitebread, *The Marihuana Conviction*, pp. 180–81.

72. King, *The Drug Hang-Up*, p. 63.

73. Ibid., pp. 63–64; World Narcotics Research Foundation, *Press Release* (September 24, 1939), RG 56, Box 191.

74. World Narcotics Research Foundation, *Press Release* (September 24, 1939), RG 56, Box 191.

75. Ibid. The 75 percent rate of recidivism was corroborated by the Public Health Service in 1942; see Musto, *The American Disease*, p. 98.

76. World Narcotics Research Foundation, *Press Release* (September 24, 1939), RG 56, Box 191; King, *The Drug Hang-Up*, p. 65.

77. Anslinger to Herbert Gaston, Assistant Secretary of the Treasury, October 5, 1939, RG 56, Box 191.

78. For an informative discussion of bureaucratic politics relevant to the pivotal role of the Federal Bureau of Narcotics, see Morton H. Halperin, with Priscilla Clapp and Arnold Cantor, *Bureaucratic Politics & Foreign Policy* (Washington, D.C.: The Brookings Institution, 1974), chap. 3, "Organizational Interests."

Chapter 6: Control Across the Border

1. See chapter 4, notes 22 and 23.

2. E. David Cronon, *Josephus Daniels in Mexico* (Madison: University of Wisconsin Press, 1960) gives the fullest treatment to the often tense relations between Washington and Mexico City in the late 1930s. See also, Josephus Daniels, *Shirt-Sleeve Diplomat* (Chapel Hill: University of North Carolina Press, 1947); Wood, *Good Neighbor Policy*, chaps. 8 and 9; David Green, *The Containment of Latin America: A History of the Myths and Realities of the Good Neighbor Policy* (Chicago: Quadrangle Books, 1971), passim; Steward, *Trade and Hemisphere*, pp. 198–207.

3. Josephus Daniels to Hull, November 6, 1936, RG 812.513/48; Carr to Daniels, December 5, 1936, RG 59 ibid.

4. Department of State to Daniels, March 5, 1934, RG 59 812.114 Narcotics/370.

5. For information from the *Weekly News Sheet*, see Department of State to Charles H. Derry, United States Consul Mazatlán, October 28, 1936, RG 59 812.114 Narcotics/584.

6. Daniels to Hull, November 27, 1936, RG 59 812.114 Narcotics/597.

7. Luis G. Franco to Daniels, January 30, 1937, RG 59 812.114 Narcotics/624.

8. Morgenthau to Hull, February 25, 1937, RG 59 812.114 Narcotics/639; for an earlier request, see Castle to Mellon, June 13, 1931, RG 59 812.114 Narcotics/170.

9. *El Universal* (Mexico City), February 25 and 27, 1937; *El Nacional* (Mexico City), February 23, 1937; Daniels to Hull, April 29, 1937, RG 59 812.114 Narcotics/691.

10. *El Universal* (Mexico City), April 25, 1937.

11. Political Report for April, submitted by United States Consul General James Stewart, Mexico City, May 14, 1937, RG 59 812.00/30449.

12. Department of State to Daniels, April 4, 1937, RG 59 812.114 Narcotics/671; *Excélsior* (Mexico City), May 21, 1937.

13. *Excélsior* (Mexico City), May 13, 1937.

14. Stewart to Hull, September 2, 1937, RG 59 812.114 Narcotics/733. The health official also remarked that control of border smuggling would not improve until Mexico's drug agents received better pay. Representative of the low pay and bribery syndrome existing in parts of the country was the announcement in December that federal officials had replaced state police at Ciudad Juárez because of the low level of antidrug activity; see Morgenthau to Hull, December 13, 1937, RG 59 812.114 Narcotics/749.

15. Hull, for Anslinger, to Daniels, July 10, 1937, RG 59 812.114 Narcotics/717; Daniels to Hull, July 10, 1937, RG 59 812.114 Narcotics/718.

16. League of Nations, *Conference for the Limitation of Manufacture*, p. 78.

17. League of Nations, *Minutes of the Nineteenth Session*, p. 29; *Excélsior* (Mexico City), May 21, 1937.

18. Gibbons to Hull, February 25, 1938, RG 59 812.114 Narcotics/760. From available evidence it is not possible to determine precisely why Siurob and Franco left their positions for others. Their new duties entailed comparable responsibilities; the quality of their antidrug work does not seem to have been in question. Moreover, United States diplomatic personnel maintained cordial relations with Siurob during his time away from the Public Health Department. The most reasonable explanation may be that the moves came as a result of bureaucratic changes accompanying the social and political reforms of the Cárdenas administation.

19. *El Universal* (Mexico City), February 27, 1937.

20. Stewart to Hull, April 7, 1938, RG 59 812.114 Narcotics/782.

21. Ibid.

22. Ibid.

23. Memorandum within the division of Far Eastern Affairs by Stuart J. Fuller, April 5, 1938, RG 59 812.114 Narcotics/766; Customs Agent Alvin F. Scharff to Deputy Commissioner of Customs Thomas A. Gorman, April 19, 1938, RG 59 812.14 Narcotics/786.

24. Stewart to Hull, April 7, 1938, RG 59 182.114 Narcotics/782; Thomas H. Lockett to Daniels, April 7, 1938, RG 59 812.114 Narcotics/804.

25. Musto, "The Marihuana Tax Act," p. 106.

26. Daniels to Hull, September 8, 1938, RG 59 812.114 Narcotics/845; one of the articles was later changed to make entrance mandatory.

27. R. Walton Moore to Daniels, October 7, 1938, RG 59 812.114 Narcotics/848.

28. Salazar Viniegra, "El Mito de la Marijuana," pp. 206–37.

29. *El Universal* (Mexico City), October 22 and 24, 1938; *Excélsior* (Mexico City), October 25, 1938; Anslinger, "The Government's Fight on Marihuana," Anslinger, Papers, BNDD Library.

30. Dr. Gregorio Oneto Barenque, "La Marijuana ante La Psiquiatría y el Código Penal," *Criminalia. México* (diciembre de 1938), pp. 238–56.

31. Fernando Rosales, director of the national drug addiction hospital, had conducted research on marijuana supporting the findings of Salazar Viniegra; see Stewart to Hull for the Division of Far Eastern Affairs, November 5, 1938, RG 59 812.114 Narcotics/868.

32. Salazar's statements are contained in Daniels to Hull, October 28, 1938, RG 59 812.114 Narcotics/855.

33. Anslinger, "The Government's Fight on Marihuana," Anslinger Papers, BNDD Library.

34. Leopoldo Salazar Viniegra, "El Sueño de Lexington," *Toxicomanías E Higiene Mental*, año 1 (enero-febrero de 1939), pp. 4–6.

35. League of Nations, Advisory Committee on Traffic in Opium and Other Dangerous Drugs, *Report to the Council on the Work of the Twenty-Fourth Session, Held at Geneva, May 15 to June 12, 1939* C.202.M.131.1939.XI. (Geneva, 1939), pp. 3–4, 20–21, 32, 47–48, 63.

36. Stewart to Hull, August 21, 1939, RG 59 812.114 Narcotics/914.

37. Ibid.

38. See *Excélsior* (Mexico City), March 13, 1939 for charges that Salazar had legalized widespread drug usage. Stewart alleges that Salazar had Communist connections. Stewart to Hull, April 18, 1939, RG 59 500.C1197/1314.

39. Daniels to Hull, September 22, 1939, RG 59 812.114 Narcotics/924; Hull to Daniels, October 3, 1939, RG 59 812.114 Narcotics/937; Hull to Morgenthau for the Customs Agency Service, October 3, 1939, RG 59 812.114 Narcotics/938.

40. José Siurob, "The Struggle Against Toxicomania," *Pacific Coast International*, November-December 1939, pp. 19–25; copy in Anslinger Papers, BNDD Library.

41. Ibid.

42. Hull to Morgenthau, December 7, 1939, RG 59 812.114 Narcotics/959; Dayle C. McDonough, United States Consul General Monterrey, to Hull, December 18, 1939, RG 59 812.114 Narcotics/963.

43. Siurob to Daniels, December 9, 1939, contained in Daniels to Hull, December 20, 1939, RG 59 812.114 Narcotics/964; Siurob to Anslinger, November 30, 1939, RG 59 812.114 Narcotics/978; Anslinger to Fuller, January 2, 1940, RG 59 812.114 Narcotics/978.

44. Department of State to Daniels, January 3, 1940, RG 59 812.114 Narcotics/987; Daniels to Hull, January 31, 1940, RG 59 812.114 Narcotics/1013.

45. Stewart to Hull, February 20, 1940, RG 59 812.114 Narcotics/1020; *Diario Official*, Mexico, February 17, 1940.

46. Anslinger to George A. Morlock, Division of Far Eastern Affairs, February 20, 1940, RG 59 812.114 Narcotics/1020. For the 1935 law that Anslinger invoked, see United States. Treasury Department, Bureau of Narcotics, *Regulation No. 2 Relating to the Importation, Exportation, and Transshipment of Opium or Coca Leaves or any Compound, Manufacture, Salt, Derivative, or Preparation Thereof* (under the Act of May 22, 1922, as amended by the . . . Act of August 5, 1935): "Narcotic Regulations Made by Commissioner of Narcotics with the Approval of the Secretary of the Treasury." (Washington, D. C.: Government Printing Office, 1938), p. 3 for the text of the pertinent section.

47. Memorandum by Fuller, January 23, 1940, RG 59 812.114 Narcotics/1022.

48. Ibid.; Treasury Department memorandum (unsigned), February 27, 1940, RG 59 812.114 Narcotics/1032.

49. Department of State to Daniels, February 28, 1940, RG 59 812.114 Narcotics/1034.

50. Stewart to Hull, March 1, 1940, RG 59 812.114 Narcotics/1042; for Mexico's protest of the narcotics embargo, see Luis Quintanella to Ellis O. Briggs, February 24, 1940, RG 59 812.114 Narcotics/1047.

51. Siurob's plan of conciliation is contained in Stewart to Hull, March 15, 1940, RG 59 812.114 Narcotics/1049.

52. Daniels to Hull, March 17, 1940, RG 59 812.114 Narcotics/1048; Daniels to Hull, March 21, 1940, RG 59 812.114 Narcotics/1053.

53. Copy of a telegram from Siurob to Dr. Thomas Parran, March 19, 1940, contained in Daniels to Hull, March 21, 1940, RG 59 812.114 Narcotics/1053. For Parran's reaction, see notation by Fuller, March 22, 1940, RG 59 ibid. The new regulations became the object of ridicule in Mexico despite Siurob's efforts; *Excélsior* (Mexico City), March 19, 1940.

54. Memorandum from Anslinger to Fuller, April 6, 1940, RG 59 812.114 Narcotics/1068; Memorandum by Herbert Bursley, April 9, 1940, RG 59 812.114 Narcotics/1075.

55. Memorandum by Herbert Bursley, April 9, 1940, RG 59 812.114 Narcotics/1075.

56. Department of State to Daniels, April 22, 1940, RG 59 812.114 Narcotics/1076; Stewart to the Department of State, May 8, 1940, RG 59 812.114 Narcotics/1079 for information about the suspension of the controversial regulations.

57. Report of a Conference held May 4, 1940, at Washington, D.C., for the Purpose of Discussing the Narcotic Regulations Recently Enacted in Mexico, RG 59 812.114 Narcotics/1083.

58. Conference Held on the Narcotic Regulations Recently Enacted in Mexico, on May 7, 1940, in the Office of Mr. Stuart J. Fuller, RG 59 ibid.

59. Memorandum from Herbert Gaston to Henry Morgenthau, May 8, 1940, RG 56, Box 191.

60. George P. Shaw, United States Consul Mexico City, to the Department of State, July 9, 1940, RG 59 812.114 Narcotics/1104.

61. Siurob to H.S. Creighton, June 17, 1940, RG 59 812.114 Narcotics/1115; Creighton to Siurob, June 28, 1940, RG 59 ibid.; emphasis added.

62. Creighton to the Commissioner of Customs, June 28, 1940, RG 59 ibid.

Chapter 7: A Window on the Future

1. "Estupefacientes," *Boletín OSP*, 15 (enero de 1936), pp. 61–66.

2. Carleton Beals, "The Drug Eaters of the High Andes," *Travel*, December 1937, pp. 29–31, 40.

3. *El Comercio* (Lima), December 17, 1937.

4. Ibid., December 20, 1938.

5. United States Consulate, Lima, to the Department of State, December 1, 1938, RG 59 823.114 Narcotics/152.

6. Homer Brett, United States Consul General Callao-Lima, to the Department of State, January 25, 1938, RG 59 823.114 Narcotics/141; Department of State to Morgenthau for the Bureau of Narcotics, February 17, 1938, RG 59 823.114 Narcotics/144.

7. *El Comercio* (Lima), December 3, 1939.

8. David M. Clark, United States Vice Consul Callao-Lima, to Hull, February 9, 1940, RG 59 823.114 Narcotics/189. Soon thereafter *El Comercio* published an executive decree prohibition opium poppy cultivation in Peru without explicit government approval; *El Comercio* (Lima), February 28, 1940. Carlos Monge Medrano became the first director of the National Institute of Andean Biology; see Hull to Morgenthau for the Bureau of Narcotics, September 25, 1940, RG 59 823.114 Narcotics/206.

9. Hull to R. Henry Norweb, United States Ambassador Lima, April 27, 1940, RG 59 823.114 Narcotics/195.

10. Norweb to Hull, April 30, 1940, RG 59 823.114 Narcotics/196.

11. Bureau of Narcotics, *Traffic in Opium, 1937*, pp. 16, 43–44; idem, *Traffic in Opium, 1938* (Washington, D.C.: Government Printing Office, 1939), p. 14; and see chapter 4, note 71.

12. United States. Department of State, *Report of the Delegation of the United States of America to the Inter-American Conference for the Maintenance of Peace, Buenos Aires, Argentina, December 1–23, 1936* (Washington, D.C.: Government Printing Office, 1937), p. 79; Alton Frye, *Nazi Germany and the Western Hemisphere, 1933–1941* (New Haven: Yale University Press, 1967), pp. 72–79, 109, 112–13 (hereafter cited as Frye, *Nazi Germany*); Pike, *The Andean Republics*, pp. 241–42; cf. Gellman, *Good Neighbor Diplomacy*, pp. 74–80, 83–85.

13. Frye, *Nazi Germany*, p. 109; Edwin Lieuwin, *Arms and Politics in Latin America*, rev. ed. (New York: Frederick A. Praeger, 1961), p. 62; Davies, *Indian Integration in Peru*, pp. 123–32.

14. "El Gob. [Gobierno] provincial de Jujuy reglamenta el expendio de la coca boliviana," *Boletín Comercial y Minero*. La Paz. (1 de julio de 1937), pp. 27–33.

15. *El Diario* (La Paz), "La industria y comercio de la coca en Bolivia," pp. 37, 39.

16. Orosco, "El alma de la humilde hoja," pp. 149–55.

17. H. Fossati, "Reflexiones sobre la organización del monopolio de la coca," *Boletín Comercial y Minero*. La Paz. (15 de noviembre de 1940), pp. 9–17.

18. League of Nations, Advisory Committee on Traffic in Opium and Other Dangerous Drugs. *Minutes of the Twenty-Third Session Held at Geneva from June 7 to 24, 1938* C.249.M.147.1938.XI. (Geneva, 1938), p. 11 (hereafter cited as League of Nations, *Minutes of the Twenty-Third Session*).

19. Department of State to the United States Consulate Geneva, October 31, 1939, RG 59 511.4A2A/918.

20. Herbert O. Williams, United States Consul Panama City, to the Department of State for the Division of Far Eastern Affairs, March 11, 1933, RG 59 819.114 Narcotics/60; Antonio C. Gonzales to the Department of State, February 6, 1934, RG 59 819.114 Narcotics/66.

21. For a report on heroin in Panama, see David Williamson, United States Embassy Berne, to the Department of State, July 2, 1934, RG 59 819.114 Narcotics/70; Williams to the Department of State, October 5, 1934, RG 59 819.00/1717.

22. Anslinger and Tompkins, *The Traffic in Narcotics*, p. 142; League of Nations, Advisory Committee on Traffic in Opium and Other Dangerous Drugs, *Minutes of the Twentieth Session Held at Geneva from May 20 to June 5, 1935* C.277.M.144.1935.XI. (Geneva, 1935), p. 52; idem, *Minutes of the Twenty- Third Session*, p. 43.

23. See chapter 4.

24. Gibbons to Hull, June 6, 1933, RG 59 815.114 Narcotics/61.

25. Lawrence Higgins to the Department of State, July 27, 1933, RG 59 815.114 Narcotics/65; for more on the Huber brothers, see Major A. R. Harris, Military Attaché, Costa Rica, to the Division of Latin American Affairs, July 19, 1934, RG 59 816.114 Narcotics/27.

26. Higgins to the Department of State, July 27, 1933, RG 59 815.114 Narcotics/65; Warren C. Stewart to Hull, August 9, 1933, RG 59 815.114 Narcotics/72.

27. Stewart to Hull, August 1, 1934, RG 59 815.114 Narcotics/209.

28. Lay to Hull, March 7, 1934, RG 59 815.114 Narcotics/92; Hull to Lay, March 8, 1934, RG 59 815.114 Narcotics/93.

29. Ekstrand to Fuller, April 13, 1934, RG 59 815.114 Narcotics/111; Lay to Hull, May 1, 1934, RG 59 815.114 Narcotics/127.

30. R. Austin Ady, United States Vice Consul Tegucigalpa, to the Department of State, July 25, 1935, RG 59 815.114 Narcotics/304. Maloney, it should be noted, helped put down the anti-Carías revolt following the election of 1932; and TACA ferried munition from El Salvador to the forces supporting the Carías government; see *FRUS, 1932*, V, pp. 722–23, 727.

31. Department of State to the United States Legation Tegucigalpa, October 15, 1935, RG 59 815.114 Narcotics/308; Sidney E. O'Donoghue, United States Legation Guatemala City, to the Department of State, October 18, 1935, RG 59 815.114 Narcotics/311.

32. Keena to Hull, October 25, 1935, RG 59 815.114 Narcotics/317; O'Donoghue to Hull, October 29, 1935, RG 59 815.114 Narcotics/320; Keena to Hull, October 29, 1935, RG 59 815.114 Narcotics/321; Fletcher Warren, United States Consul Managua, to Hull, November 13, 1935, RG 59 815.114 Narcotics/331; Sumner Welles to the United States Legation Tegucigalpa, November 19, 1935, RG 59 815.114 Narcotics/337. For more on Kennett's travels after mid-November, see Keena to Hull, November 20, 1935, RG 59 815.114 Narcotics/343; Matthew E. Hanna, United States Minister Guatemala City, to Hull, November 29, 1935, RG 59, 815.114 Narcotics/344; Hanna to Hull, December 5, 1935, RG 59 815.114 Narcotics/349.

33. United States Legation to the Department of State, October 23, 1935, RG 59 815.114 Narcotics/ 323; Keena to Hull, October 31, 1935, RG 59 815.114 Narcotics/325 enclosing a summary of an article appearing in *La Epoca* (Tegucigalpa), October 30, 1935 giving the government's view of the traffic in the illicit, imported drugs.

34. Bureau of Narcotics, *Traffic in Opium, 1935*, pp. 24–26.

35. Keena to Hull, November 29, 1935, RG 59 815.114 Narcotics/350; William A. M. Burden, *The Struggle for Airways in Latin America* (New York: Council on Foreign Relations, 1943), pp. 20, 31 (hereafter cited as Burden, *The Struggle for Airways*).

36. Keena to Hull, December 26, 1935, RG 59 815.114 Narcotics/370; Keena to Hull for the Bureau of Narcotics, January 17, 1936, RG 59 815.114 Narcotics/378.

37. Fuller to the United States Legation Guatemala City, February 14, 1936, RG 59 815.114 Narcotics/389.

38. Keena to the Department of State, March 10, 1936, RG 59 815.114 Narcotics/394; Keena to the Department of State, November 10, 1936, RG 59 815.114 Narcotics/416; Bureau of Customs report to Fuller, November 24, 1936, RG 59 815.114 Narcotics/418;

Stokes, *Honduras*, pp. 57, 225, 296–97; *FRUS, 1936*, 5 vols. (Washington, D.C.: Government Printing Office, 1953–54), V: *The American Republics*, pp. 682, 685–87.

39. Bureau of Customs memorandum to the Department of State, January 13, 1937, RG 59 815.114 Narcotics/421; H. S. Creighton to the Investigative Unit of the Commissioner of Customs, January 16, 1937, RG 59 815.114 Narcotics/426; Culver E. Gidden, United States Vice Consul Belize, to the Department of State, February 2, 1937, RG 59 815.114 Narcotics/428. There existed limits, however, to the American solicitude for the Carías government. As reports of incipient revolution persisted into 1937, the Department of State tried without success to elicit a pledge from Carías that American nationals, serving as instructors at the *Escuela Militar de Aviación*, would not participate in air raids against suspected insurrectionists. *FRUS, 1937*, 5 vols. (Washington, D.C.: Government Printing Office, 1954), V: *The American Republics*, pp. 597–601.

40. C. H. Calhoun, Chief of the Division of Civil Affairs, Panama, to Anslinger, January 20, 1937, RG 59 815.114 Narcotics/427.

41. Keena to Hull, March 5, 1937, RG 59 815.114 Narcotics/436; Memorandum to the Department of State from Thomas J. Gorman, April 1, 1937, RG 59 815.114 Narcotics/445.

42. Keena to Hull, April 12, 1937, RG 59 815.114 Narcotics/449; Rae V. Vader to the Department of State, July 12, 1937, RG 59 815.114 Narcotics/458.

43. John D. Erwin, United States Minister Tegucigalpa, to the Division of Far Eastern Affairs, April 1, 1938, RG 59 815.114 Narcotics/477; Far Eastern Affairs to Erwin, April 26, 1938, RG 59 815.114 Narcotics/479. TACA's primary competition in Central America came from Pan American Airways; Burden, *The Struggle for Airways*, passim.

44. *FRUS, 1937*, V, p. 601.

45. Memorandum of a Conversation Held June 24, 1938 between Lowell Yerex, Harold White, John W. Bulkley, and George A. Morlock, RG 59 815.114 Narcotics/487.

46. General Memorandum from the Department of State to the United States Legations in Central America, July 25, 1938, RG 59 815.114 Narcotics/488–492.

47. Behrendt, *Inter-American Economic Relations*, pp. 8–9; Frye, *Nazi Germany*, pp. 109, 120; D. M. Phelps, ed., *Economic Relations with Latin America*, Michigan Business Papers, No. 6 (Ann Arbor: University of Michigan, School of Business Administration, Bureau of Business Research, 1940), p. 26; *FRUS, 1936*, V, p. 684.

48. Erwin to Hull, March 6, 1939, RG 59 815.114 Narcotics/502.

49. *New York Times*, March 14, 1939, p. 9. In 1941, Guatemala revoked TACA's concession under pressure from Pan American Airways; Burden, *The Struggle for Airways*, p. 146.

50. Department of State to the Treasury Department with a report on Eugene LeBaron, April 5, 1939, RG 59 815.114 Narcotics/505; Fred K. Salter, Tegucigalpa, to the Division of Far Eastern Affairs, September 1, 1939, RG 59 815.114 Narcotics/509.

51. Fuller's Memorandum of talk with Eugene LeBaron, December 18, 1939, RG 59 815.114 Narcotics/516. With Kennett finally out of the way, TACA was able to expand its operations into Panama and the Canal Zone in late 1941; Burden, *The Struggle for Airways*, pp. 146, 148.

52. LeBaron to Fuller, July 27, 1940, RG 59 815.114 Narcotics/520; Meredith Nicholson, United States Minister Managua, to Hull, September 23, 1940, RG 59 815.114 Narcotics/525; Erwin to Hull, October 25, 1940, RG 59 815.114 Narcotics/530; Nicholson to Hull, December 7, 1940, RG 59 815.114 Narcotics/538 all containing reports on Kennett's travels immediately after his dismissal from TACA. For more on the profitability of TACA's routes in Central America, see Burden, *The Struggle for Airways*, pp. 32, 99, 113, 127.

53. In 1945, for reasons that cannot be determined, the government of Honduras published a pamphlet defending the drug control policies of the Carías administration. The pamphlet, prepared anonymously by the Facultad de Farmacia of Honduras, blamed the influx of drugs in the early 1930s on the administration of Vicente Mejía Colindres, mentioned Dr. Ricardo Alduvín without noting his resignation under questionable circum-

stances, praised Dr. Francisco Sánchez without mentioning his murder, and was silent on the relationship between drugs and both José María Guillen Velez and TACA. See Facultad de Farmacia de la República de Honduras, *En Defensa del Gobierno de Honduras: nuestro pais no es como se pretende, un pais traficante en estupefacientes* (Tegucigalpa: Talleres Tipograficos Nacionales, 1945).

54. Fuller to R. Walton Moore, September 4, 1937, RG 59 500.C1197/1115; Memorandum by Joseph F. McGurk, Tokyo, June 20, 1938, RG 59 500.C1197/1225.

55. Koki Hirota, Minister for Foreign Affairs, to Joseph C. Grew, November 4, 1937, RG 59 894.114 Narcotics/312; Memorandum by McGurk, June 20, 1938, RG 59 500.C1197/1225; Grew to Hull, December 20, 1938, RG 59 500.C1197/1282.

56. Fuller to Moore, September 4, 1937, RG 59 500.C1197/1115; Memorandum on the Narcotics Situation in Japanese Controlled Areas in China (unsigned), January 14, 1939, RG 59 893.114 Narcotics/2458; Marshall, "Opium and the Politics of Gangsterism," passim.

57. Martin G. Scott, Treasury Attaché, Kobe, Japan, to the Commissioner of Customs, May 11, 1937, RG 59 894.114 Narcotics/271; Hull to Grew, April 11, 1938, RG 59 894.114 Narcotics/329.

58. Stanley K. Hornbeck to Governor W. Cameron Forbes, Thomasville, Georgia, February 12, 1940, RG 59 894.114 Narcotics/374.

59. However deficient Honduran drug control policies may have been, United States officials no doubt were pleased with the way the Carías government lined up behind the United States in resisting Axis influence in the Americas. By the end of 1940, Honduras was actively participating in the planning of hemispheric defense. See *FRUS, 1940*, 5 vols. (Washington, D.C.: Government Printing Office, 1955–61), V: *The American Republics*, pp. 130–33. It is worth noting also that TACA's image improved steadily during the Second World War. Officials in Washington may have considered Americanizing TACA to protect it in its competition with Pan American. As one official put it at the end of May 1940: "If Germany comes out on top we can't afford to have TACA bereft of all protection from a strong and friendly government." Financial protection for the Yerex airline finally arrived in November 1943 when Trans Continental and Western Air (TWA) purchased a controlling interest. Expansion of cargo operations throughout the Caribbean soon followed. Two years later Yerex announced his retirement as president and general manager of TACA. At the age of fifty, he was a wealthy man no longer burdened, thanks to the war, by allegations of drug smuggling. Memorandum by Gerald A. Drew, May 31, 1940 RG 59 813.796 TACA 8 for the quotation; and see Walker, "The Politics of Drug Control," pp. 307–11 for the wartime improvement of TACA's fortunes.

Chapter 8: World War II and After — Patterns of Drug Control

1. For information on the activities of Argentina at the 1942 Rio de Janeiro Conference, see *FRUS, 1942*, 6 vols. (Washington, D.C.: Government Printing Office, 1960–63), V: *The American Republics*, p. 11. Cordell Hull, *The Memoirs of Cordell Hull*, 2 vols. (New York: The Macmillan Company, 1948), II, p. 1144; David H. Popper, "The Rio de Janeiro Conference of 1942," *Foreign Policy Reports*, April 15, 1942, p. 30.

2. Department of State to Norman Armour, United States Ambassador Buenos Aires, February 9, 1942, RG 59 835.114 Narcotics/76.

3. Armour to Hull, May 5, 1942. RG 59 835.114 Narcotics/78. For information on the planting of opiates, see Morlock to the chargé d'affaires a. i., July 20, 1942, RG 59 835.114 Narcotics/83; Thomas Hughes, Commercial Attaché, to Hull, August 12, 1942, RG 59 835.114 Narcotics/86.

4. Merwin L. Bohan, Commercial Attaché, to Hull, November 3, 1942, RG 59 835.114 Narcotics/94.

5. Bohan to Hull, May 21, 1943, RG 59 835.114 Narcotics/101. For the Anslinger letter to Hoffman-LaRoche, Inc., see Anslinger to N. F. Peterson, February 23, 1943, RG 59 835.114 Narcotics/103.

6. Armour to Hull, October 28, 1943, RG 59 835.114 Narcotics/105. For information on narcotic production in Chile, see Claude G. Bowers, United States Ambassador Santiago, to Hull (for Anslinger), November 3, 1943, RG 59 835.114 Narcotics/106.

7. Armour to Hull, December 8, 1943, RG 59 835.114 Narcotics/109.

8. Harold M. Rundall to Hull, December 8, 1943, RG 59 835.114 Narcotics/108.

9. Armour to Hull, December 17, 1943, RG 59 835.114 Narcotics/111; Armour to Hull, December 23, 1943, RG 59 835.114 Narcotics/113.

10. Hull to Armour, December 30, 1943, RG 59 835.114 Narcotics/114; Armour to Hull, December 31, 1943, RG 59 835.114 Narcotics/116; Armour to the Department of State, September 22, 1944, RG 59 835.114 Narcotics/9-2244.

11. Carlos Gutiérrez-Noriega and Victor Wolfgang von Hagen, "The Strange Case of the Coca Leaf," *Scientific Monthly*, February 1950, p. 82 (hereafter cited as Gutiérrez-Noriega and von Hagen, "The Strange Case of the Coca Leaf").

12. Lillian Whittenhall Hughes, "The Curse of Coca," *Inter-American*, V (September 1946), pp. 21–22; Davies, *Indian Integration in Peru*, pp. 130–39.

13. C. A. Ricketts, "El Cocaísmo en el Perú," *América Indígena*, XII (octubre de 1952), p. 310.

14. Ibid., pp. 311–12.

15. League of Nations, Advisory Committee on Traffic in Opium and Other Dangerous Drugs, *Minutes of the Twenty-Fifth Session Held at Geneva from May 17 to 30, 1940*, Annex II: "Progress Report by the Secretary," C.162.M.147.1940.XI. (Geneva, 1940), pp. 52–53.

16. Gutiérrez-Noriega and von Hagen, "The Strange Case of the Coca Leaf,"p. 82.

17. Joseph F. McGurk, United States Counselor Lima, to the Department of State, April 25, 1941, RG 59 823.114 Narcotics/220. The Department of State sent McGurk's report on cocaine to the Bureau of Narcotics in May; see Gaston to Hull for Morlock, May 16, 1941, RG 59 823.114 Narcotics/222.

18. McGurk to Hull, June 10, 1941, RG 59 823.114 Narcotics/223. For Great Britain's position on the Peruvian cocaine, see Howard Trueblood to Lynn R. Edminster, June 5, 1941, RG 59 823.114 Narcotics/224.

19. Anslinger to Morlock, November 25, 1941, RG 59 823.114 Narcotics/234; Hull to Norweb, November 28, 1941, RG 59 823.114 Narcotics/235. For data on the extensive cocaine supply in Peru, see Julian Greenup, Commercial Attaché, to Hull, December 4, 1941, RG 59 823.114 Narcotics/237.

20. McGurk to Hull, June 17, 1941, RG 59 823.114 Narcotics/226.

21. Jefferson Patterson to Hull, August 9, 1941, R 59 823.114 Narcotics/228.

22. Greenup to Hull, December 6, 1941, RG 59 823.114 Narcotics/240; Department of State files do not reveal whether the transaction with Japan was carried out, but it is unlikely given Peru's position at the 1942 Rio conference.

23. Hull to Norweb, March 30, 1942, RG 59 823.114 Narcotics/246.

24. Unsigned Memorandum in the Division of American Republics, April 11, 1942, RG 59 823.114 Narcotics/254.

25. Gaston to the Division of Far Eastern Affairs, March 27, 1942, RG 59 823.114 Narcotics/243; Morlock's notation is handwritten.

26. Adolf A. Berle, for Hull, to Norweb, April 16, 1942, RG 59 823.114 Narcotics/252; Greenup to Hull, May 22, 1942, RG 59 823.114 Narcotics/259.

27. Greenup to Hull, May 22, 1942, RG 59 823.114 Narcotics/259; Gaston to Morlock, June 5, 1942, RG 59 823.114 Narcotics/261.

28. Greenup to Hull, June 16, 1942, RG 59 823.114 Narcotics/266; Anslinger to Morlock, July 20, 1942, RG 59 823.114 Narcotics/278.

29. Greenup to Hull, February 2, 1943, RG 59 823.114 Narcotics/288.

30. Ibid.

31. Memorandum by Morlock, February 20, 1943, RG 59 823.114 Narcotics/290.

32. Berle to Norweb, March 2, 1943, RG 59 823.114 Narcotics/291.

33. Greenup to Hull, April 19, 1943, RG 59 823.114 Narcotics/299.

34. Hull to Norweb, April 7, 1943, RG 59 823.114 Narcotics/295; Greenup to Hull, June 22, 1943, RG 823.114 Narcotics/304; Anslinger to Dr. César Gordillo Zuleta, June 24, 1943, RG 59 823.114 Narcotics/309.

35. Greenup to Hull, November 3, 1943, RG 59 823.114 Narcotics/315; Gaston to the Division of Far Eastern Affairs, December 2, 1943, RG 59 823.114 Narcotics/316.

36. Greenup to Hull, December 3, 1943, RG 59 823.114 Narcotics/318; Greenup to Hull, May 19, 1944, RG 59 823.114 Narcotics/324.

37. Gaston to Morlock, June 17, 1944, RG 59 823.114 Narcotics/327; Greenup to the Department of State, March 26, 1945, RG 59 823.114 Narcotics/3-2645; El Comercio (Lima), March 23, 1945.

38. Morlock to Fuller, December 11, 1940, RG 59 812.114 Narcotics/1131.

39. Excélsior (Mexico City), December 7, 1940.

40. Ibid., December 8, 1940.

41. Morris N. Hughes, Mexico City, to Hull, December 18, 1940, RG 59 812.114 Narcotics/1135.

42. Department of State to the United States Embassy Mexico City, December 11, 1940, RG 59 812.114 Narcotics/1132.

43. Excélsior (Mexico City), December 18, 1940.

44. United States Embassy to the Department of State, January 10, 1941, RG 59 812.114 Narcotics/ 1150.

45. El Universal (Mexico City), December 28, 1940.

46. Memorandum of a telephone conversation between Fuller and Gorman, January 27, 1941, RG 59 812.114 Narcotics/1151; Dallas News, January 20, 1941.

47. Shaw to Hull, February 12, 1941, RG 59 812.114 Narcotics/1158 containing a memorandum of a conversation, February 4, 1941, between Victor Fernández Manero and H. S. Creighton.

48. Ibid. for a conversation on February 12, 1941.

49. Ibid., Ailshie remarked of Creighton: "He is not as tactful as he might be."

50. Shaw to Hull, February 19, 1941, RG 59 812.114 Narcotics/1160.

51. Shaw to Hull, February 12, 1941, RG 59 812.114 Narcotics/1158 containing Bursley's notation.

52. Daniels to the Department of State, February 10, 1941, RG 59 812.114 Narcotics/ 1157.

53. Morlock to George H. Winters, September 18, 1941, RG 59 812.114 Narcotics/1175; Department of State to the chargé d'affaires a. i., October 16, 1941, RG 59 812.114 Narcotics/1178.

54. Memorandum by Morlock, October 13, 1941, RG 59 812.114 Narcotics/1204.

55. Blocker to Hull, January 9, 1942, RG 59 812.114 Narcotics/1209.

56. Blocker to Hull, March 2, 1942, RG 59 812.114 Narcotics/1223.

57. Rufus H. Lane, United States Consul Mazatlán, to Hull, May 26, 1942, RG 59 812.114 Narcotics/1243; Bureau of Narcotics, Traffic in Opium, 1942 (Washington, D.C.: Government Printing Office, 1943), pp. 13, 16.

58. Creighton to the Customs Agency Service Division of Investigations, January 31, 1942, RG 59 812.114 Narcotics/1246.

59. El Universal (Mexico City), January 30, 1942; Salvador Peña to the Customs Agency Service, April 9, 1942, RG 59 812.114 Narcotics/1247.

60. Peña to the Customs Agency Service, April 30, 1942, RG 59 812.114 Narcotics/1328.

61. Secretary of the Treasury to Morlock, June 11, 1942, RG 59 812.114 Narcotics/1331 containing Creighton's memorandum of June 4, 1942.

62. Lane to Hull, April 24, 1942, RG 59 812.114 Narcotics/1234; Raleigh A. Gibson to Hull, June 8, 1942, RG 59 812.114 Narcotics/1244 containing Creighton's memorandum of May 6, 1942.

63. Blocker to Hull, October 29, 1942, RG 59 812.114 Narcotics/1341; Memorandum by Morlock, October 27, 1942, RG 59 812.114 Narcotics/1343.

64. Blocker to Hull, December 29, 1942, RG 59 812.114 Narcotics/1346.

65. Memorandum by Morlock, April 9, 1943, RG 59 812.114 Narcotics/1351.

66. Department of State to George S. Messersmith, United States Ambassador Mexico City, May 11, 1943, RG 59 812.114 Narcotics/1356.

67. Memorandum by Morlock of a conversation between Bulkley, Creighton, and Morlock, June 11, 1943, RG 59 812.114 Narcotics/1367.

68. Bursley to Hull, August 7, 1943, RG 59 812.114 Narcotics/1356; Messersmith to Hull, August 2, 1943, RG 59 812.114 Narcotics/1363.

69. Memorandum, November 15, 1943, in Paul J. Revely to Hull, February 22, 1944, RG 59 812.114 Narcotics/1372.

70. Bureau of Narcotics, *Traffic in Opium, 1943* (Washington, D.C.: Government Printing Office, 1944), p. 19; Sidney J. Kennedy to the Department of State, March 16, 1944, RG 59 812.114 Narcotics/1374.

71. Memorandum by Kennedy, April 17, 1944, RG 59 812.114 Narcotics/1376.

72. E. W. Eaton, United States Vice Consul, to the Department of State, June 27, 1944, RG 59 812.114 Narcotics/6-2744.

73. League of Nations, Advisory Committee on Traffic in Opium and Other Dangerous Drugs, *Minutes of the Twenty-Fourth Session Held at Geneva from May 15 to June 12, 1939* C.209.M.136.1939.XI. (Geneva, 1939), pp. 9–10, 86–87.

74. United Nations. Economic and Social Council, Commission on Narcotic Drugs, *Illicit Traffic in Narcotic Drugs*, "I : Review of World Traffic from 1 January 1940 to 30 June 1946," "II: World Trends During the War, 1939–1945," E/CN.7/68 (Lake Success, N.Y., 1947), pp. 3, 6–7, 9–14, 17, 19–23 (hereafter cited as United Nations, *Illicit Traffic in Narcotic Drugs*).

75. Ibid., pp. 24–30, 34–35, 46–49.

76. Anslinger and Tompkins, *The Traffic in Narcotics*, p. 137.

77. United Nations, *Illicit Traffic in Narcotic Drugs*, p. 45.

78. Anslinger and Tompkins, *The Traffic in Narcotics*, p. 165; see p. 257 for the Public Health Service estimate of addiction. The low figure of 20,000 is in Lindesmith, *The Addict and the Law*, p. 105.

79. Anslinger and Tompkins, *The Traffic in Narcotics*,, p. 284.

80. Lindesmith, *The Addict and the Law*, pp. 105–9.

81. Anslinger and Tompkins, *The Traffic in Narcotics*, p. 168.

82. Harry J. Anslinger, "Letter on Drug Addiction," *JAMA*, September 23, 1950, p. 333.

83. *New York Herald Tribune*, March 7, 1948.

84. Anslinger and Tompkins, *The Traffic in Narcotics*, chap. 9, "Narcotics, Crime, and Publicity." The commissioner failed to mention his own article, "Marihuana: Assassin of Youth."

85. Ibid., p. 168.

86. United States Congress. House of Representatives, *Hearings Before a Subcommittee of the Committee on Ways and Means on HR 3490*, "A Bill to Amend the Penalty Provisions Applicable to Persons Convicted of Violating Certain Narcotic Laws, and for Other Purposes," and *HR 348*, "A Bill to Provide for the Coverage of Barbiturates Under the Federal Narcotic Laws," 82 Cong., 1 Sess., April 7, 14, and 17, 1951 (Washington, D.C.: Government Printing Office, 1951), p. 206.

87. United States Congress. Senate, *Hearings Before a Subcommittee of the Committee on Finance on HR 6906*, "An Act to Impose an Occupational Excise Tax upon Certain Dealers in Marihuana, to Impose a Transfer Tax upon Certain Dealers in Marihuana, and to Safeguard the Revenue Therefrom by Registry and Recording," 75 Cong., 1 Sess., July 12, 1937 (Washington, D.C.: Government Printing Office, 1937), pp. 14–15.

88. Walker, "The Politics of Drug Control," pp. 352–56; Bonnie and Whitebread, *The Marihuana Conviction*, chap. 10.

89. Anslinger and Tompkins, *The Traffic in Narcotics*, p. 168.

90. Ibid., pp. 225-26.

91. Milton "Mezz" Mezzrow and Bernard Wolf, *Really the Blues* (New York: Random House, 1946); Anslinger and Tompkins, *The Traffic in Narcotics*, p. 166.

92. Harry J. Anslinger, "The Physician and the Federal Narcotic Law," *American Journal of Psychiatry*, 102 (March 1946), pp. 609–18; the quotation is on p. 615.

93. Anslinger and Tompkins, *The Traffic in Narcotics*, pp. 294–95.

94. Bonnie and Whitebread, *The Marihuana Conviction*, p. 204.

95. Dr. Harry Berger and Dr. Andrew A. Eggston, "Should We Legalize Narcotics?" *Coronet*, June 1955, pp. 30–35; the quotation is on p. 34.

96. Alfred R. Lindesmith, "Dope: Congress Encourages the Traffic," *The Nation*, March 16, 1957, pp. 228-31.

97. Dr. Pablo Osvaldo Wolff, *Aspectos Sociales de Las Narcomanías* (Publicado en la *Revista de la Asociación Medica Argentina*, Toma LV, 15–30 de enero de 1941). This twenty-four page pamphlet is contained in Armour to Hull, April 23, 1941, RG 59 835.114 Narcotics/72.

98. Dr. Pablo Osvaldo Wolff, "Narcomanías y Criminalidad," *Revista de Psiquiatría y Criminología*. Buenos Aires, año VI (septiembre–octubre de 1941), pp. 433-54, especially pp. 433-34, 445-49.

99. Dr. Pablo Osvaldo Wolff, *Marihuana in Latin America: The Threat It Constitutes* (Washington, D.C.: Linacre Press, 1949).

100. Gutiérrez-Noriega y Zapata Ortiz, *Estudios Sobre La Coca*, pp. 28–30; cf. Edward M. Brecher and the editors of *Consumer Reports, Licit and Illicit Drugs* (Boston: Little, Brown and Company, 1972), chap. 34.

101. Gutiérrez-Noriega y Zapata Ortiz, *Estudios Sobre La Coca*, pp. 31–33, 71–73; the quotation is on p. 73, emphasis in original.

102. Ibid., pp. 49–56, 74–77, 113; Davies, *Indian Integration in Peru*, pp. 155–62.

103. Mrs. Helen H. Moorehead, "International Narcotics Control, 1939–1946," *Foreign Policy Reports*, July 1, 1946, pp. 94–103 (hereafter cited as Moorehead, "International Narcotics Control").

104. *The Reminiscences of Herbert L. May*, p. 92.

105. Moorehead, "International Narcotics Control," pp. 101–2; Mrs. Helen H. Moorehead, "Control of the Narcotic Drugs," *Foreign Policy Reports*, September 30, 1946, pp. 10–13.

106. Moorehead, "International Narcotics Control," pp. 102–3. After the war there was no doubt that the United States under Anslinger's leadership became the dominant force in the world antidrug movement.

107. May, "The International Control of Narcotic Drugs," pp. 346–47, 352–55; "New Protocol on Narcotic Drugs Signed," *United Nations Bulletin*, December 31, 1946, p. 37.

108. "New Protocol on Narcotic Drugs Signed," *United Nations Bulletin*, December 31, 1946, p. 37; "Old and New Narcotic Perils," *United Nations Bulletin*, September 16, 1947, pp. 363–64; "The Coca Leaf Habit," *United Nations Bulletin*, October 21, 1947, p. 525. The increased interest in the coca leaf appeared at approximately the same time as *Estudios Sobre La Coca*. See also, Bureau of Narcotics, *Traffic in Opium, 1948* (Washington, D. C.: Government Printing Office, 1949), p. 15. Department of State files confirm the findings drawn from the public record; see Greenup to the Department of State, March 26, 1945,

RG 59 823.114 Narcotics/3-2645; Treasury Department memorandum to Morlock, January 13, 1947, RG 59 823.114 Narcotics/1-1347.

109. *St. Louis Post-Dispatch*, March 26, 1948; Salvador Peña to the Commissioner of Customs, October 10, 1946, RG 59 812.114 Narcotics/11-846 for information on clandestine opium production in Mexico, and also for data on Dr. José Quevado Bazan, the Mexican representative to the United Nations Commission on Narcotic Drugs.

110. Commissioner Anslinger's statement of protest is contained in an unsigned memorandum to the American mission, Mexico City, August 9, 1947, RG 59 812.114 Narcotics/8-947. For the optimistic report about the eradication campaign, see Paul H. Nitze to Walter Thurston, United States Ambassador Mexico City, April 22, 1947, RG 59 812.114 Narcotics/3-1747. In fact, the 1947 crop was "the largest ever produced in Mexico." See Willard L. Thorp to Raymond H. Geist, Chargé d'Affaires a. i., May 19, 1947, RG 59 812.114 Narcotics/4-3047. The D. G. DeLagrave memorandum is contained in Geist to the Secretary of State, May 12, 1947, RG 59 812.114 Narcotics/5-1247. For more on the situation in Mexico in the immediate postwar years, see Bureau of Narcotics, *Traffic in Opium, 1945* (Washington, D.C.: Government Printing Office, 1946), pp. 19–20; idem, *Traffic in Opium, 1946* (Washington, D.C.: Government Printing Office, 1947), p. 17; idem, *Traffic in Opium, 1947* (Washington, D.C.: Government Printing Office, 1948), pp. 2, 15–16.

111. For the move toward cooperation, see *Diario Oficial*, Mexico, November 14, 1947; Geist to the Department of State, November 24, 1947, RG 59 812.114 Narcotics/11-2447; Morlock's note on the change in United States policy is contained in RG 59 812.114 Narcotics/1-1948. Antidrug cooperation may have been in the offing, but problems continued—including a substantial increase in the smuggling of marijuana; see Bureau of Narcotics, *Traffic in Opium, 1948*, pp. 12, 16–17.

112. Anslinger placed much of the blame for the continuing influx of illicit drugs on underworld leader Charles "Lucky" Luciano. In a dictated memoir, Luciano claimed that the commissioner's actions constituted a personal vendetta. Luciano averred that he considered drug operations too risky a business to indulge in, unlike some of his compatriots and competitors. In any event, organized illicit drug activity was a rapidly increasing phenomenon after the Second World War. See Bureau of Narcotics, *Traffic in Opium, 1944* (Washington, D.C.: Government Printing Office, 1945), pp. 21–25; Martin A. Gosch and Richard Hammer, *The Last Testament of Lucky Luciano* (Boston: Little, Brown and Company, 1974, 1975), pp. 293, 314-15, 323-26; Anslinger and Oursler, *The Murderers*, chap. 7.

Chapter 9: "The Horror and Damnation of Poor Little Human Flies"

1. Walter Duranty, "Opium Smoking," *Atlantic Monthly*, February 1943, pp. 106–7 (hereafter cited as Duranty, "Opium Smoking").

2. On Brown's career, see Margaret Ripley Wolfe, *Lucius Polk Brown and Progressive Food and Drug Control: Tennessee and New York City, 1908–1920* (Lawrence: The Regents Press of Kansas, 1978), pp. 64–72.

3. Bruun, Pan, and Rexed, *The Gentleman's Club*, p. 41.

4. Musto, *The American Disease*, pp. 184, 189, 204–6.

5. Ibid., p. 212. For informative comments on the operation of bureaucracies, although in a different context, see Howard S. Becker and Irving Louis Horowitz, "Radical Politics and Sociological Research: Observations on Methodology and Ideology," *American Journal of Sociology*, 78 (July 1972), pp. 54–55.

6. Padden, *Hummingbird and the Hawk*, p. 95.

7. Harold E. Driver, *Indians of North America*, 2nd rev. ed. (Chicago: University of Chicago Press, 1969), maps 12 and 13.

8. John Hemming, *The Conquest of the Incas* (New York: Harcourt Brace Jovanovich, 1970), pp. 52, 367–68.

9. Terry and Pellens, *The Opium Problem*, p. 630.

10. One analyst finds the postwar antidrug campaign beginning as early as 1947. See Richard B. Craig, " *La Campaña Permanente:* Mexico's Anti-drug Campaign," unpublished manuscript, 1977; copy in author's possession (hereafter cited as Craig, "*La Campaña Permanente*").

11. Duranty, "Opium Smoking," p. 109.

Epilogue: The Limits of Flexibility

1. For the information upon which this assessment is based, see Memorandum by George A. Morlock, May 2, 1949, RG 59 823.114/5-249; Memorandum by Garland H. Williams for Harry Anslinger, May 17, 1949, RG 59 823.114 Narcotics/5-1749; Bureau of Narcotics, *Traffic in Opium*, [*1948–1959*] (Washington, D.C.: Government Printing Office, 1949–60), passim; "The White Goddess," *Time*, April 11, 1949, p. 44; Timothy Green, *The Smugglers: An Investigation into the World of the Contemporary Smuggler* (New York: Walker and Company, 1969), pp. 75, 79 (hereafter cited as Green, *The Smugglers*).

2. "Plans for Extending the Global Control of Narcotic Drugs," *United Nations Bulletin*, February 1, 1951, pp. 126–28; "Action on Coca Leaf Problem," *United Nations Bulletin*, May 15, 1952, p. 410.

3. The Peruvian Indian Institute began operating in 1946. Carlos Monge Medrano, "La Necesidad de Estudiar el Problema de la Masticación de las Hojas de Coca," *América Indígena*, XIII (enero de 1953), pp. 47–53; C. A. Ricketts, "La Masticación de las Hojas de Coca en el Perú," *América Indígena*, XIV (abril de 1954), pp. 113–26. Timothy Green claimed that by the mid-1960s the annual legitimate demand for cocaine was approximately 500 tons, while the estimated annual production ranged from 13,000 to 35,000 tons; Green, *The Smugglers*, p. 77.

4. Bruun, Pan, and Rexed, *The Gentleman's Club*, pp. 16–18. An effort to expand the kinds of drugs covered by international agreements, as attempted at Geneva in 1971 with the Convention on Psychotropic Substances, has not yet proven successful; ratifications are few.

5. Bonnie and Whitebread, *The Marihuana Conviction*, p. 242; James Q. Wilson, *The Investigators: Managing FBI and Narcotics Agents* (New York: Basic Books, 1978), pp. 4, 6–7, 86–87, 188.

6. United States Congress. Senate, *Hearing on S. 509, S. 694, S. 1944, S.J. Res. 78 and S. Con. Res. 8*, "International Traffic in Narcotics," 92 Cong., 1 Sess., July 1, 1971 (Washington, D.C.: Government Printing Office, 1971), pp. 25-30, 71–74; United States Congress. House of Representatives, *Report of a Special Study Mission*, "The World Heroin Problem," 92 Cong., 1 Sess., May 27, 1971 (Washington, D.C.: Government Printing Office, 1971), pp. 3, 5, 7. The heroin epidemic was most visibly associated with veterans of the war in Indochina. The Nixon administration established a rehabilitation program which by August 1972 was termed a "national hoax." If a veteran received a less than honorable discharge, he was ineligible for the rehabilitation program conducted by the Veterans Administration. A review of discharge might take as long as two years. The dilemma, of course, was that in many cases the unfavorable classification bore a direct relationship to drug dependence. *Los Angeles Times*, August 14, 1972.

7. Catherine Lamour and Michel R. Lamberti, *The International Connection: Opium from Growers to Pushers*, trans. Peter and Betty Ross (New York: Pantheon Books, 1974), p. 50 (hereafter cited as Lamour and Lamberti, *The International Connection*); Richard C. Schroeder, *The Politics of Drugs: Marijuana to Mainlining* (Washington, D.C.: Congressional Quarterly, 1975), p. 119, 121, 127; Craig, "*La Campaña Permanente*," pp. 5–6; Lyle

C. Brown, "The Politics of United States–Mexican Relations: Problems of the 1970s in Historical Perspective," in *Contemporary Mexico: Papers of the IV Congress of Mexican History*, ed. James W. Wilkie, Michael C. Meyer, and Edna Monzón de Wilkie (Berkeley and Los Angeles: University of California Press, 1976), pp. 482–83 (hereafter cited as Brown, "United States–Mexican Relations"); David Harris, "The Dark and Violent World of the Mexican Connection," *New York Times Magazine*, December 18, 1977, passim (hereafter cited as Harris, "The Mexican Connection"); Richard B. Craig, "Operation Intercept: The International Politics of Pressure," Paper: Organization of American Historians Convention, Atlanta, April 1977. Substantial grants of assistance were also made to Mexico in 1961 and 1965, but had no discernible effect on opium or marijuana cultivation; see Bruun, Pan, and Rexed, *The Gentleman's Club*, p. 214.

8. United States Congress. House of Representatives, *Report by Hon. Lou Frey, Jr.*, "The Drug Problem in the Caribbean and Central America," 94 Cong., 1 Sess., December 1975 (Washington, D.C.: Government Printing Office, 1975), p. 1 (hereafter cited as House of Representatives, "The Drug Problem in the Caribbean and Central America"); idem, *Report of a Study Mission to Mexico, Costa Rica, Panama, and Colombia, January 6–18, 1976*, "The Shifting Patterns of Narcotics Trafficking: Latin America," 94 Cong., 2 Sess. (Washington, D.C.: Government Printing Office, 1976), pp. 3, 8, 11 (hereafter cited as House of Representatives, "The Shifting Patterns of Narcotics Trafficking"); idem, *Hearings before the Select Committee on Narcotics Abuse and Control*, "Oversight Hearings on Narcotics Abuse and Current Federal and International Narcotics Control Effort," 94 Cong., 2 Sess., September 21–23 and 27–30, 1976 (Washington, D.C.: Government Printing Office, 1977), p. 3 (hereafter cited as House of Representatives, "Oversight Hearings on Narcotics Abuse").

9. House of Representatives, "Oversight Hearings on Narcotics Abuse," pp. 47–48; *New York Times*, August 3, 1977, p. 1; United States Congress. House of Representatives, *Hearings before the Committee on International Relations*, "International Security Assistance and Arms Export Control Act of 1976," 94 Cong., 2 Sess., March 23–24, 29–31, and April 5, 1976 (Washington, D.C.: Government Printing Office, 1976), pp. 166–69 (hereafter cited as House of Representatives, "International Security Assistance . . . 1976"); *Sacramento Bee*, September 22, 1976 and December 27, 1976.

10. *New York Times*, August 3, 1977, p. 1; Wilson McKinney, *Fred Carrasco: The Heroin Merchant* (Austin: Heidelberg Publishers, 1975), passim; Johnson, *Mexican Democracy*, pp. 187–94; Harris, "The Mexican Connection."

11. Carmen García Liñán to the author, March 20, 1979, with information on the operation of the Centros de Integración Juvenil; United States Congress. Senate, *Hearings before the Subcommittee to Investigate Juvenile Delinquency of the Committee on the Judiciary*, "The Mexican Connection," 95 Cong., 2 Sess., February 10 and April 19, 1978 (Washington, D.C.: Government Printing Office, 1978), pp. 7, 13, and 51–54 wherein it is estimated that perhaps only 6 percent of the heroin traffic was being interdicted. See also United States Congress. House of Representatives, *Hearings before the Subcommittee on Asian and Pacific Affairs of the Committee on Foreign Relations*, "Foreign Assistance Legislation for Fiscal Year 1979 (Part 6): Economic and Security Assistance in Asia and the Pacific," 95 Cong., 2 Sess., March 7, 9, 14, 16, 21–22, 1978 (Washington, D.C.: Government Printing Office, 1978), pp. 202, 261 (hereafter cited as House of Representatives, "Foreign Assistance Legislation for Fiscal Year 1979").

12. Johnson, *Mexican Democracy*, pp. 190, 192–93, 194 note 56; Jack Anderson's column, *Sacramento Bee*, July 25, 1979; House of Representatives, "Foreign Assistance Legislation for Fiscal Year 1979," pp. 220–21, 234, 236, 294, 309; United States Congress. Senate, *Hearings before the Subcommittee on International Operations of the Committee on Foreign Relations*, "International Narcotics Control Programs—Mexico," 95 Cong., 2 Sess., May 9, 1978 (Washington, D.C.: Government Printing Office, 1978), pp. 5–6.

13. United States Congress. House of Representatives, *A Report of the Select Committee on Narcotics Abuse and Control*, "The Use of Paraquat-Contaminated Marihuana on the U.S. Market," 96 Cong., 2 Sess. (Washington, D.C.: Government Printing Office, 1980), pp. 1, 3, 12–17, and 65–67 containing the quotations from the Percy Amendment; interview with Daniel Stein, staff member, House Select Committee on Narcotics Abuse and Control, August 7, 1980 (hereafter cited as Stein interview).

14. Interview with Ralph Saucedo, Assistant Chief, South American Operations, Drug Enforcement Administration, July 31, 1980 (hereafter cited as Saucedo interview).

15. The quotation is from Brown, "United States–Mexican Relations," p. 485. As long as the need exists, even the poorest Mexicans will play a role in the illicit drug trade. For a look at the roles these Indians, mestizos, and others ("mules" in the parlance of the trade) play, see Jacklyn Becker et al., "The Dope Trail," *Contemporary Drug Problems*, 1 (Summer 1972), pp. 413–52; Harris, "The Mexican Connection."

16. Lamour and Lamberti, *The International Connection*, pp. 51–54, 57.

17. Bureau of Narcotics, *Traffic in Opium, 1957*, p. 22. Reports for the next two years suggested that Colombia continued as a supplier of cocaine.

18. Lester Grinspoon and James B. Bakalar, *Cocaine: A Drug and Its Social Evolution* (New York: Basic Books, 1976), pp. 49–50, 52 (hereafter cited as Grinspoon and Bakalar, *Cocaine*); House of Representatives, "The Drug Problem in the Caribbean and Central America," pp. 2–3; idem, "The Shifting Patterns of Narcotics Trafficking," p. 15; *New York Times*, April 22, 1975, p. 1.

19. United States Congress. House of Representatives, *Report of the Select Committee on Narcotics Abuse and Control*, "South American Study Mission: August 9–23, 1977," 95 Cong., 1 Sess. (Washington, D.C.: Government Printing Office, 1977), pp. 2–3 (hereafter cited as House of Representatives, "South American Study Mission"); House of Representatives, "The Shifting Patterns of Narcotics Trafficking," p. 23.

20. House of Representatives, "International Security Assistance . . . 1976," pp. 13, 156; idem, "Oversight Hearings on Narcotics Abuse," pp. 375, 387, 395–407.

21. United States Congress. House of Representatives, *A Report of the Select Committee on Narcotics Abuse and Control*," "Factfinding Mission to Colombia and Puerto Rico," 96 Cong., 1 Sess., [April 13–21, 1979] (Washington, D.C.: Government Printing Office, 1979), pp. 1, 3, 6, 8–9 (hereafter cited as House of Representatives, "Factfinding Mission"); idem, *Hearings before the Select Committee on Narcotics Abuse and Control*, "Cocaine and Marihuana Trafficking in Southeastern United States," 95 Cong., 2 Sess., June 9 and 10, 1978 (Washington, D.C.: Government Printing Office, 1978), p. 16; as described on pp. 2 and 11 of the hearings, there is an annual outflow of perhaps $7 billion from Florida, Georgia, South Carolina, and Puerto Rico into the drug trade. In south Florida, drug trafficking means the exchange of more money than the tourist trade. The proposal in Colombia for the legalization of marijuana has raised fears that "Colombia will not eradicate"; Stein interview.

22. House of Representatives, "Factfinding Mission," 4 note 1; United States Congress. House of Representatives, *Hearings and Markup before the Subcommittee on Inter-American Affairs of the Committee on Foreign Affairs*, "Foreign Assistance Legislation for Fiscal Years 1980–81 (Part 5): Economic and Military Assistance for Latin America," 96 Cong., 1 Sess., February 13, 14, 20, 21; March 7 and 8, 1979 (Washington, D.C.: Government Printing Office, 1979), pp. 14, 22 (hereafter cited as House of Representatives, "Foreign Assistance Legislation for Fiscal Years 1980–81"); House of Representatives, "Foreign Assistance Legislation for Fiscal Year 1979," p. 191; Saucedo interview.

23. Green, *The Smugglers*, p. 78; House of Representatives, "South American Study Mission," p. 14; Julio Cotler, "State and Regime: Comparative Notes on the Southern Cone and the 'Enclave' Societies," in *The New Authoritarianism in Latin America*, ed. David Collier (Princeton: Princeton University Press, 1979), p. 277 (hereafter cited as Cotler, "State and Regime").

24. *New York Times*, April 21, 1975, p. 1.

25. Green, *The Smugglers*, pp. 78–79; Grinspoon and Bakalar, *Cocaine*, pp. 49–50, 52–55; House of Representatives, "The Shifting Patterns of Narcotics Trafficking," p. 19; idem, "South American Study Mission," pp. 3, 19; idem, "Foreign Assistance Legislation for Fiscal Year 1979," p. 278.

26. House of Representatives, "Oversight Hearings on Narcotics Abuse," pp. 297, 374–75, 415–16, and 435 for the statement of Commissioner Acree; idem, "International Security Assistance . . . 1976," pp. 13, 156.

27. House of Representatives, "Foreign Assistance Legislation for Fiscal Year 1979," pp. 203–5. The United Nations official is quoted in Green, *The Smugglers*, p.78.

28. House of Representatives, "South American Study Mission," pp. 7, 15, 20–23, 27. An additional problem was that growers were producing two distinct types of coca: one for coqueros—the traditional chewers, and the other—of greater acidity—for the illicit international trade; interview with Donald E. Mudd, Chief, Americas Division, Bureau of International Narcotics Matters, Department of State, July 31, 1980 (hereafter cited as Mudd interview).

29. House of Representatives, "South American Study Mission," p. 17; idem, "Foreign Assistance Legislation for Fiscal Years 1980–81," pp. 22–23; Mudd interview.

30. House of Representatives, "South American Study Mission," p. 16; Allan R. Holmberg, "The Role of Power in Changing Values and Institutions of Vicos," in *Peasants, Power, and Applied Social Change: Vicos as a Model*, ed. Henry F. Dobyns, Paul L. Doughty, Harold D. Lasswell (Beverly Hills: Sage Publications, 1964, 1971), pp. 36, 45; Pierre L. van den Berghe and George P. Primov, *Inequality in the Peruvian Andes: Class and Ethnicity in Cuzco* (Columbia: University of Missouri Press, 1977), pp. 5, 7–22, 92–93, 117–22, 137, 253; Mudd interview.

31. Alejandro Costa is quoted in the *San Francisco Sunday Examiner and Chronicle*, August 22, 1976.

32. Cotler, "State and Regime," pp. 278–80; Stephen Kinzer, "The World's Biggest Deadbeat," *The New Republic*, April 21, 1979, pp. 14, 16–18, with the quotation on p. 17; Abraham F. Lowenthal, "Dateline Peru: A Sagging Revolution," *Foreign Policy*, no. 38 (Spring 1980), pp. 182–90.

33. *New York Times*, July 18, 1980, p. A3; and July 19, 1980, p. 3.

34. Larry Rohter, "A Brutal 'Cocaine Coup,'" *Newsweek*, August 11, 1980, pp. 39–40 (hereafter cited as Rohter, "A Brutal 'Cocaine Coup'"). *New York Times*, July 19, 1980, p. 3; July 26, 1980, p. 1; and August 14, 1980, p. A13.

35. Rohter, "A Brutal 'Cocaine Coup,'" pp. 39–40; *Washington Post*, July 31, 1980; *New York Times*, August 14, 1980, pp. A1, A12. And see *Miami Herald*, May 26 and 28, 1981.

36. Interview with Patrick L. Carpentier, Chief Counsel, House Select Committee on Narcotics Abuse and Control, August 5, 1980.

37. *New York Times*, July 29, 1980, p. A3; see also Jane B. Baird, "The Source," *Miami Herald: Tropic*, May 23, 1980, pp. 12–14, 16–20, 36–38.

38. Saucedo interview.

39. Ibid.

40. *New York Times*, January 11, 1980, pp. 1, 6.

Bibliography

Unpublished Documents

Anslinger, Harry J. Papers. Bureau of Narcotics and Dangerous Drugs Library. Washington, D.C.

—. Papers. Pennsylvania State University Library. University Park, Pa.

Daniels, Josephus. Papers. Manuscript Division, Library of Congress. Washington, D.C.

Johnson, Nelson Trusler. Papers. Manuscript Division, Library of Congress. Washington, D.C.

The Reminiscences of Herbert L. May. Oral History Research Office, Butler Library, Columbia University. New York, N.Y.

United States. Department of State, General Records of the Department of State. Record Group 59. National Archives, Washington, D.C.

—. Department of the Treasury, General Records of the Department of the Treasury. Record Group 56. National Archives, Washington, D.C.

Published Documents

Argentina:
República Argentina. Ministerio del Interior, *Boletín Sanitario del Departmento Nacional de Higiene,* 1 (enero de 1937).

Carnegie Endowment for International Peace:
Division of International Law, Carnegie Endowment for International Peace, ed. *The International Conferences of American States: First Supplement, 1933–1940.* "Seventh International Conference of American States: Montevideo, December 3–26, 1933." Washington, D.C.: Carnegie Endowment for International Peace, 1940.

Honduras:
Facultad de Farmacia de la República de Honduras. *En Defensa del Gobierno de Honduras: nuestro pais no es como se pretende, un pais traficante en estupefacientes.* Tegucigalpa: Talleres Tipograficos Nacionales, 1945.

League of Nations:
League of Nations. *Records of the Second Opium Conference, November 17th, 1924 to February 19th* C.760.M.260.1924.XI. Geneva, 1925.

255

—. *Records of the Conference for the Limitation of the Manufacture of Narcotic Drugs, Geneva, May 27th to July 13th, 1931,* "Volume I: Plenary Meetings, Text of the Debates" C.509.M.214.1931.XI. Geneva, 1931.

—. *Records of the Conference for the Suppression of the Illicit Traffic in Dangerous Drugs (Geneva, June 8 to 26, 1936),* "Text of the Debates" C.341.M.216.1936.XI. Geneva, 1936.

—. *Traffic in Opium and Other Dangerous Drugs, Report of the Fifth Committee to the Assembly* A.86.1929.XI. Geneva, 1929.

—. Advisory Committee on Traffic in Opium and Other Dangerous Drugs. *Measures Taken in Uruguay in the Campaign against the Illicit Traffic.* O. C. 1670. Geneva, 1936.

—. Report of the Advisory Committee on Traffic in Opium and Other Dangerous Drugs. *Minutes of the [First to the Twenty-Fifth] Sessions, Held at Geneva from [1921–1940].* Geneva, 1921–40.

—. Report of the Advisory Committee on Traffic in Opium. *Report on the Work of the Committee During Its Second Session, Held at Geneva from April 19th–29th, 1922* C.223(1).1922.XI. Geneva, 1922.

—. Advisory Committee on Traffic in Opium and Other Dangerous Drugs. *Report to the Council on the Work of the Fifth Session (May 24th to June 7th, 1923)* A.13.1923.XI. Geneva, 1923.

—. —. *Report to the Council on the Work of the Sixth Session, August 4th–14th, 1924* A.32.1924.XI. Geneva, 1924.

—. —. *Report to the Council on the Work of the Seventh Session, August 24th–31st, 1925* A.28.1925.XI. Geneva, 1925.

—. —. *Report to the Council on the Work of the Ninth Session of the Committee, Held at Geneva, from January 17th to February 3rd, 1927* C.29.M.19.1927.XI. Geneva, 1927.

—. —. *Report to the Council on the Work of the Tenth Session, Geneva, September 28th to October 8th, 1927* C.521.M.179.1927.XI. Geneva, 1927.

—. —. *Report to the Council on the Work of the Thirteenth Session, Held at Geneva from January 20th to February 14th, 1930* C.138.M.51.1930.XI. Geneva, 1930.

—. —. *Report to the Council on the Work of the Twenty-Fourth Session Held at Geneva from May 15th to June 12th, 1939* C.202.M.131.1939.XI. Geneva, 1939.

Mexico:

Almada, Francisco R. *La Revolución en el Estado de Chihuahua.* 2 vols. Chihuahua: Biblioteca del Instituto Nacional de Estudios Historicos de la Revolución Mexicana, 1964.

Diario Oficial, Mexico. 1923, 1931, 1934, 1940, 1947.

Pan American Union:

Division of Economic Research, Pan American Union. *The Foreign Trade of Latin America.* Washington, D.C.: Pan American Union, 1952.

Peru:

Basadre, Jorge. *Historia de la República del Perú.* 5th ed., rev. and enl. 10 vols. Lima: Ediciones "Historia," 1961–64.

United Nations:

United Nations. Economic and Social Council, Commission on Narcotic Drugs, *Illicit Traffic in Narcotic Drugs,* "I: Review of World Traffic from 1 January 1940 to 30 June 1946" and "II: World Trends During the War, 1939–1945" E/CN.7/68. Lake Success, N.Y., 1947.

United States:

United States. Department of State, *Papers Relating to the Foreign Relations of the United States, 1916.* Washington, D.C.: Government Printing Office, 1925.

—. —, *Papers Relating to the Foreign Relations of the United States, 1923.* 2 vols. Washington, D.C.: Government Printing Office, 1938. Vol. I (1938).

—. —, *Papers Relating to the Foreign Relations of the United States, 1927.* 3 vols. Washington, D.C.: Government Printing Office, 1942. Vol. III (1942).

—. —, *Papers Relating to the Foreign Relations of the United States, 1928.* 3 vols. Washington, D.C.: Government Printing Office, 1942–43. Vol. I(1942).

—. —, *Papers Relating to the Foreign Relations of the United States, 1929.* 3 vols. Washington, D.C.: Government Printing Office, 1943–44. Vol. I (1943).

—. —, *Foreign Relations of the United States, 1931.* 3 vols. Washington, D.C.: Government Printing Office, 1946. Vol. I (1946).

—. —, *Foreign Relations of the United States, 1932.* 5 vols. Washington, D.C.: Government Printing Office, 1947–48. Vol. V: *The American Republics* (1948).

—. —, *Foreign Relations of the United States, 1933.* 5 vols. Washington, D.C.: Government Printing Office, 1949–52. Vol. V: *The American Republics* (1952).

—. —, *Foreign Relations of the United States, 1934.* 5 vols. Washington, D.C.: Government Printing Office, 1950–52. Vol. V: *The American Republics* (1952).

—. —, *Foreign Relations of the United States, 1935.* 4 vols. Washington, D.C. Government Printing Office, 1952–53. Vol. IV: *The American Republics* (1953).

—. —, *Foreign Relations of the United States, 1936.* 5 vols. Washington, D.C.: Government Printing Office, 1953–54. Vol. V: *The American Republics* (1954).

—. —, *Foreign Relations of the United States, 1937.* 5 vols. Washington, D.C.: Government Printing Office, 1954. Vol. V: *The American Republics* (1954).

—. —, *Foreign Relations of the United States, 1940.* 5 vols. Washington, D.C.: Government Printing Office, 1955–61. Vol. V: *The American Republics* (1961).

—. —, *Foreign Relations of the United States, 1942.* 6 vols. Washington, D.C.: Government Printing Office, 1960–1963. Vol. V: *The American Republics* (1963).

—. —, *Report of the Delegation of the United States of America to the Inter-American Conference for the Maintenance of Peace, Buenos Aires, Argentina, December 1–23, 1936.* Washington, D.C.: Government Printing Office, 1937.

—. Department of the Treasury, *Annual Report of the Commissioner of Internal Revenue for the Fiscal Year Ended June 30, 1919.* Washington, D.C.: Government Printing Office, 1919.

—. —, *Annual Report to the Commissioner of Internal Revenue for the Fiscal Year Ended June 30, 1920.* Washington, D.C.: Government Printing Office, 1920.

—. —, *Traffic in Narcotic Drugs: Report of the Special Committee of Investigation Appointed March 25, 1918 by the Secretary of the Treasury.* June 1919. Washington, D.C.: Government Printing Office, 1919.

—. —, Bureau of Narcotics, *Regulation No. 2 Relating to the Importation, Exportation, and Transshipment of Opium or Coca Leaves or any Compound, Manufacture, Salt, Derivative, or Preparation Thereof* (under the Act of May 22, 1922, as amended by the . . . Act of August 5, 1935): "Narcotics Regulations Made by the Commissioner of Narcotics with the Approval of the Secretary of the Treasury." Washington, D.C.: Government Printing Office, 1938.

—. —, *Traffic in Opium and Other Dangerous Drugs for the Year Ended December 31, [1930–1959].* Washington, D.C.: Government Printing Office, 1931–1960.

—. Federal Narcotics Control Board, *The Traffic in Opium and Other Dangerous Drugs for the Year Ended June 30, 1927.* Washington, D.C.: Government Printing Office, 1927.

—. —, *The Traffic in Opium and Other Dangerous Drugs for the Year Ended December 31, 1929.* Washington, D.C.: Government Printing Office, 1930.

United States Congress. House of Representatives, Committee on Ways and Means, Report No. 852. *Importation and Exportation of Narcotic Drugs,* 67 Cong., 2 Sess., March 27, 1922. Washington, D.C.: Government Printing Office, 1922.

—. —, Document No. 380. *The Traffic in Habit-Forming Drugs: Hearings before the Committee on Foreign Affairs,* 68 Cong., 1 Sess., on H.J. Res. 195, "Authorizing an Appropriation for the Participation of the United States in Two International Conferences for the Control of the Traffic in Habit-Forming Narcotic Drugs," February 21, 1924. Washington, D.C.: Government Printing Office, 1924.

—. —, *Hearings before the Committee on Ways and Means, House of Representatives,* 71 Cong., 2 Sess., on H.R. 10,561, "A Bill to Create in the Treasury Department a Bureau of Narcotics and for Other Purposes," March 7 and 8, 1930. Washington, D.C.: Government Printing Office, 1930.

—. —, Report No. 792. *Marihuana Taxing Bill,* 75 Cong., 1 Sess., May 11, 1937. Washington, D.C.: Government Printing Office, 1937.

—. —, *Taxation of Marijuana, Hearings on H.R. 6,385,* 75 Cong., 1 Sess., April 27-30 and May 4, 1937, Washington, D.C.: Government Printing Office, 1937.

—. —, *Hearings before a Subcommittee of the Committee on Ways and Means on H.R. 3,490,* "A Bill to Amend the Penalty Provisions Applicable to Persons Convicted of Violating Certain Narcotic Laws, and for Other Purposes," and *H.R. 348,* "A Bill to Provide for the Coverage of Barbiturates under the Federal Narcotic Laws." 82 Cong., 1 Sess., April 7, 14, and 17, 1951. Washington, D.C.: Government Printing Office, 1951.

—. —, *Report of a Special Study Mission,* "The World Heroin Problem." 92 Cong., 1 Sess., May 27, 1971. Washington, D.C.: Government Printing Office, 1971.

—. —, *Report by Hon. Lou Frey, Jr.,* "The Drug Problem in the Caribbean and Central America." 93 Cong., 1 Sess., December 1975. Washington, D.C.: Government Printing Office, 1975.

—. —, *Report of a Study Mission to Mexico, Costa Rica, Panama, and Colombia, January 6–18, 1976,* "The Shifting Patterns of Narcotics Trafficking: Latin America." 94 Cong., 2 Sess. Washington, D.C.: Government Printing Office, 1976.

—. —, *Hearings before the Committee on International Relations,* "International Security Assistance and Arms Export Control Act of 1976." 94 Cong., 2 Sess., March 23–24, 29–31, and April 5, 1976. Washington, D.C.: Government Printing Office, 1976.

—. —, *Hearings before the Select Committee on Narcotics Abuse and Control,* "Oversight Hearings on Narcotics Abuse and Current Federal and International Narcotics Control Effort." 94 Cong., 2 Sess., September 21–23, 27–30, 1976. Washington, D.C.: Government Printing Office, 1977.

—. —, *A Report of the Select Committee on Narcotics Abuse and Control,* "South American Study Mission: August 9–23, 1977." 95 Cong., 1 Sess. Washington, D.C.: Government Printing Office, 1977.

—. —, *Hearings before the Subcommittee on Asian and Pacific Affairs of the Committee on International Relations,* "Foreign Assistance Legislation for Fiscal Year 1979 (Part 6): Economic and Security Assistance in Asia and the Pacific." 95 Cong., 2 Sess., March 7, 9, 14, 16, 21–22, 1978. Washington, D.C.: Government Printing Office, 1978.

—. —, *Hearings before the Select Committee on Narcotics Abuse and Control,* "Cocaine and Marihuana Trafficking in Southeastern United States." 95 Cong., 2 Sess., June 9–10, 1978. Washington, D.C.: Government Printing Office, 1978.

—. —, *Hearings before the Subcommittee on Inter-American Affairs of the Committee on Foreign Affairs,* "Foreign Assistance Legislation for Fiscal years 1980–81 (Part 5): Economic and Military Assistance for Latin America." 96 Cong., 1 Sess., February 13–14, 20–21, and March 7–8, 1979, Washington, D.C.: Government Printing Office, 1979.

—. —, *A Report of the Select Committee on Narcotics Abuse and Control,* "Factfinding Mission to Colombia and Puerto Rico." 96 Cong., 1 Sess., [April 13–21, 1979]. Washington, D.C.: Government Printing Office, 1979.

—. —, *A Report of the Select Committee on Narcotics Abuse and Control,* "The Use of Paraquat-Contaminated Marihuana on the U.S. Market." 96 Cong., 2 Sess. Washington, D.C.: Government Printing Office, 1980.

—. Senate, *Hearings before a Subcommittee of the Committee on Finance on H.R. 6,906,* "An Act to Impose an Occupational Excise Tax upon Certain Dealers in Marihuana, to Impose a Transfer Tax on Certain Dealings in Marihuana, and to Safeguard the Revenue

Therefrom by Registry and Recording," 75 Cong., 1 Sess., July 12, 1937. Washington, D.C.: Government Printing Office, 1937.

—. —, *Hearings on S. 509, S. 694, S. 1188, S. 1944, S.J. Res. 78, and S. Con. Res. 8,* "International Traffic in Narcotics." 92 Cong., 1 Sess., July 1, 1971. Washington, D.C.: Government Printing Office, 1971.

—. —, *Hearings before the Subcommittee to Investigate Juvenile Delinquency of the Committee on the Judiciary,* "The Mexican Connection." 95 Cong., 2 Sess., February 10 and April 19, 1978. Washington, D.C.: Government Printing Office, 1978.

—. —, *Hearings before the Subcommittee on International Operations of the Committee on Foreign Relations,* "International Narcotics Control Programs–Mexico." 95 Cong., 2 Sess., May 9, 1978. Washington, D.C.: Government Printing Office, 1978.

—. Statutes at Large, "An Act To provide for the registration of, with collectors of internal revenue, and to impose a special tax upon all persons who produce, import, manufacture, compound, deal in, dispense, sell, distribute, or give away opium or coca leaves, their salts, derivatives, or preparations, and for other purposes." Vol. 38, 63 Cong., 3 Sess., December 17, 1914 (Part I, pp. 785–90). Washington, D.C.: Government Printing Office, 1915.

—. —, "An Act to Amend the Act entitled 'An Act to prohibit the importation and use of opium for other than medicinal purposes,' approved February 9, 1909, as amended." Vol. 42, 67 Cong., 2 Sess., May 26, 1922 (Part I, pp. 596–98). Washington, D.C.: Government Printing Office, 1923.

United States Treaty Series, No. 732. *Convention between the United States and Mexico to Prevent Smuggling and for Certain Other Objects.* Washington, D.C.: Government Printing Office, 1926.

—, No. 739. *Convention between the United States and Cuba to Prevent Smuggling.* Washington, D.C.: Government Printing Office, 1926.

Uruguay:

República Oriental del Uruguay. Ministerio de Salud Pública, *Reglamentación del Movimiento de los Estupefacientes Nocivos y su Distribución.* Montevideo, 1934.

Memoirs

Beaulac, Willard L. *A Diplomat Looks at Aid to Latin America.* Carbondale and Edwardsville: Southern Illinois University Press, 1970.

Daniels, Josephus. *Shirt-Sleeve Diplomat.* Chapel Hill: University of North Carolina Press, 1947.

Hull, Cordell. *The Memoirs of Cordell Hull,* 2 vols. New York: The Macmillan Company, 1948.

Maldonado, Braulio. *Baja California: Comentarios Politicos.* 2nd ed. México, D.F.: Costa-Amic, 1960.

Newspapers

Argentina:

La Nación (Buenos Aires). 1934.

Bolivia:

El Diario (La Paz). 1933.

Honduras:

El Ciudadano (Tegucigalpa). 1934.

El Cronista (Tegucigalpa). 1934.

Mexico:
El Nacional (Mexico City). 1937.
El Universal (Mexico City). 1929–30, 1935, 1937–40, 1942.
Excélsior (Mexico City). 1923, 1931, 1937–40.
Peru:
El Comercio (Lima). 1932, 1936–40, 1945.
La Cronica (Lima). 1936.
United States:
Boston Globe. 1923.
Christian Science Monitor. 1922.
Dallas News. 1941.
Los Angeles Times. 1972.
Miami Herald. 1980–81.
Minneapolis Journal. 1937.
New York American. 1934.
New York Herald Tribune. 1938, 1948.
New York Times. 1923, 1925, 1928, 1930–36, 1939–45, 1975, 1977, 1980.
Sacramento Bee. 1976, 1979.
San Francisco Sunday Examiner & Chronicle. 1976.
St. Louis Post-Dispatch. 1934, 1948.
Wall Street Journal. 1978.
Washington Herald. 1930, 1937.
Washington Post. 1980.

Interviews and Personal Communications

Interview with Patrick L. Carpentier, Chief Counsel, House Select Committee on Narcotics Abuse and Control. Washington, D.C., August 5, 1980.

Letter from Carmen García Liñán, Centros de Integración Juvenile, to the author, March 20, 1979.

Interview with Donald E. Mudd, Chief, Americas Division, Bureau of International Narcotics Matters, Department of State. Washington, D.C., July 31, 1980.

Interview with Ralph Saucedo, Assistant Chief, South American Operations, Drug Enforcement Administration. Washington, D.C., July 31, 1980.

Interview with Daniel Stein, staff member, House Select Committee on Narcotics Abuse and Control. Washington, D.C., August 7, 1980.

Books

Almond, Gabriel A., and Verba, Sidney. *The Civic Culture: Political Attitudes and Democracy in Five Nations.* Princeton: Princeton University Press, 1963.

Andrews, Kenneth R. *The Spanish Caribbean: Trade and Plunder, 1530–1630.* New Haven: Yale University Press, 1978.

Anslinger, Harry J., and Oursler, Will. *The Murderers: The Story of the Narcotic Gangs.* New York: Farrar, Straus and Cudahy, 1961.

—, and Tompkins, William F. *The Traffic in Narcotics.* New York: Funk and Wagnalls, 1953.

Barnes, William, and Morgan, John Heath. *The Foreign Service of the United States: Origins, Development, and Functions.* Washington, D.C.: Government Printing Office, 1961.

Bates, Sanford. *Prisons and Beyond.* New York: The Macmillan Company, 1936.

Bazant, Jan. *A Concise History of Mexico from Hidalgo to Cárdenas, 1805–1940.*
   Cambridge: At the University Press, 1977.
Becker, Howard S. *Outsiders: Studies in the Sociology of Deviance.* New York: The Free
   Press of Glencoe, 1963.
Behrendt, Richard F. *Inter-American Economic Relations: Problems and Prospects.* New
   York: The Committee on International Economic Policy in cooperation with the Carnegie
   Endowment for International Peace, 1948.
Bemis, Samuel Flagg. *The Latin-American Policy of the United States: An Historical
   Interpretation.* 1943. Reprint. New York: W. W. Norton & Company, 1967.
Best, Gary Dean. *The Politics of American Individualism: Herbert Hoover in Transition,
   1918–1921.* Westport: Greenwood Press, 1975.
Blau, Peter M., and Meyer, Marshall W. *Bureaucracy in Modern Society.* 2nd ed. New
   York: Random House, 1971.
Bonnie, Richard J., and Whitebread II, Charles H. *The Marihuana Conviction: A History
   of Marihuana Prohibition in the United States.* Charlottesville: University Press of
   Virginia, 1974.
Borah, Woodrow. *Early Colonial Trade and Navigation between Mexico and Peru.* Berkeley
   and Los Angeles: University of California Press, 1954.
Braddy, Haldeen. *Cock of the Walk: The Legend of Pancho Villa.* Port Washington, N.Y.:
   Kennikat Press, [1955], 1970.
Brandenburg, Frank R. *The Making of Modern Mexico.* Englewood Cliffs: Prentice-Hall,
   1964.
Brandes, Joseph. *Herbert Hoover and Economic Diplomacy: Department of Commerce
   Policy, 1921–1928.* Pittsburgh: University of Pittsburgh Press, 1962.
Brecher, Edward M., and the Editors of *Consumer Reports. Licit and Illicit Drugs.* Boston:
   Little, Brown and Company, 1972.
Bruun, Kettil; Pan, Lynn; and Rexed, Ingemar. *The Gentleman's Club: International
   Control of Drugs and Alcohol.* Chicago: University of Chicago Press, 1975.
Buenker, John D. *Urban Liberalism and Progressive Reform.* New York: Charles Scribner's
   Sons, 1973.
Burden, William A. M. *The Struggle for Airways in Latin America.* New York: Council on
   Foreign Relations, 1943.
Burner, David. *Herbert Hoover: A Public Life.* New York: Alfred A. Knopf, 1979.
Burrow, James G. *AMA: Voice of American Medicine.* Baltimore: Johns Hopkins Press,
   1963.
Carey, James C. *Peru and the United States, 1900–1962.* Notre Dame: University of Notre
   Dame Press, 1964.
Centro de Investigaciones Agrarias [Reyes Osorio, Sergio, et al.]. *Estructura Agraria y
   Desarrollo Agrícola en México: Estudio Sobre Las Relaciones entro La Tenencia y Uso de
   la Tierra y El Desarrollo Agrícola de México.* México, D.F.: Fondo de Cultura
   Económica, 1974.
Chambers, Clarke A. *Seedtime of Reform: American Social Service and Social Action,
   1918–1933.* Minneapolis: University of Minnesota Press, 1963.
Checchi, Vincent, and Associates. *Honduras: A Problem in Economic Development.* New
   York: The Twentieth Century Fund, 1959.
Chevalier, François. *Land and Society in Colonial Mexico: The Great Hacienda.* Translated
   by Alvin Eustis. Berkeley and Los Angeles: University of California Press, 1963.
Clark, Norman H. *Deliver Us from Evil: An Interpretation of American Prohibition.* New
   York: W. W. Norton & Company, 1976.
Cornelius, Wayne A. *Politics and the Migrant Poor in Mexico City.* Stanford: Stanford
   University Press, 1975.
Cronon, E. David. *Josephus Daniels in Mexico.* Madison: University of Wisconsin Press,
   1960.

Cumberland, Charles C. *Mexico: The Struggle for Modernity.* New York: Oxford University Press, 1968.

Davies, Jr., Thomas M. *Indian Integration in Peru: A Half Century of Experience, 1900–1948.* Lincoln: University of Nebraska Press, 1974.

Davis, Allen F. *Spearheads for Reform: The Social Settlements and the Progressive Movement, 1890–1914.* New York: Oxford University Press, 1967.

Dobyns, Henry E., and Doughty, Paul L. *Peru: A Cultural History,* New York: Oxford University Press, 1976.

Driver, Harold E. *Indians of North America.* 2nd rev. ed. Chicago: University of Chicago Press, 1969.

Duggan, Laurence. *The Americas: Search for Hemisphere Security.* New York: Henry Holt and Company, 1949.

Duster, Troy. *The Legislation of Morality: Law, Drugs, and Moral Judgment.* New York: The Free Press, 1970.

Eckstein, Susan. *The Poverty of Revolution: The State and the Urban Poor in Mexico.* Princeton: Princeton University Press, 1977.

Ellis, L. Ethan. *Frank B. Kellogg and American Foreign Relations, 1925–1929.* New Brunswick: Rutgers University Press, 1961.

—. *Republican Foreign Policy, 1921–1933.* New Brunswick: Rutgers University Press, 1968.

Fagen, Richard R., and Tuohy, William S. *Politics and Privilege in a Mexican City.* Stanford: Stanford University Press, 1972.

Fernandez, Dr. Nicanor T. *La Coca Boliviana.* La Paz: Sociedad de Proprietarios de Yungas, 1932.

Fernandez, Raul A. *The United States–Mexican Border: A Politico-Economic Profile.* Notre Dame: University of Notre Dame Press, 1977.

Fine, Sidney. *Laissez-Faire and the General Welfare State, 1865–1901: A Study in Conflict in American Thought.* Ann Arbor: University of Michigan Press, 1966.

Fleming, Denna Frank. *The United States and World Organization, 1920–1933.* 1938. Reprint. New York: AMS Press, 1966.

Frye, Alton. *Nazi Germany and the Western Hemisphere, 1933–1941.* New Haven: Yale University Press, 1967.

Furman, Bess, in consultation with Williams, M.D., Ralph C. *A Profile of the United States Public Health Service, 1798–1948.* Washington, D.C.: Government Printing Office, 1973.

Gardiner, C. Harvey. *The Japanese and Peru, 1873–1973.* Albuquerque: University of New Mexico Press, 1975.

Geertz, Clifford. *The Interpretation of Cultures.* New York: Basic Books, 1973.

Gellman, Irwin F. *Good Neighbor Diplomacy: United States Policies in Latin America, 1933–1945.* Baltimore: Johns Hopkins University Press, 1979.

Gilderhus, Mark T. *Diplomacy and Revolution: U.S.–Mexican Relations under Wilson and Carranza.* Tucson: University of Arizona Press, 1977.

González Casanova, Pablo. *Democracy in Mexico.* Translated by Danielle Sati. 2nd ed. New York: Oxford University Press, 1970.

Gosch, Martin A., and Hammer, Richard. *The Last Testament of Lucky Luciano.* Boston: Little, Brown and Company, 1974, 1975.

Graham, Jr., Otis L. *The Great Campaigns: Reform and War in America, 1900–1928.* Englewood Cliffs: Prentice-Hall, 1971.

Green, David. *The Containment of Latin America: A History of the Myths and Realities of the Good Neighbor Policy.* Chicago: Quadrangle Books, 1971.

Green, Timothy. *The Smugglers: An Investigation into the World of the Contemporary Smuggler.* New York: Walker and Company, 1969.

Greib, Kenneth J. *The Latin American Policy of Warren G. Harding.* Fort Worth: Texas Christian University Press, 1976.

Grindle, Merilee Serrill. *Bureaucrats, Politicians, and Peasants in Mexico.* Berkeley and Los Angeles: University of California Press, 1977.

Grinspoon, M.D., Lester. *Marihuana Reconsidered.* 2nd ed. Cambridge: Harvard University Press, 1977.

—, and Bakalar, James B. *Cocaine: A Drug and Its Social Evolution.* New York: Basic Books, 1976.

Guerra, F[rancisco], y Olivera, H. *Las Plantas Fantásticas de México.* México, D.F.: Imprenta del Diario Español, 1954.

Gutiérrez-Noriega, Carlos, y Zapata Ortiz, Vicente. *Estudios Sobre La Coca y La Cocaina en el Perú.* Lima: Ministerio de Educación Pública, 1947.

Gutman, Herbert G. *Work, Culture, and Society in Industrializing America: Essays in American Working Class and Social History.* New York: Alfred A. Knopf, 1976.

Haber, Samuel. *Efficiency and Uplift: Scientific Management in the Progressive Era, 1890–1920.* Chicago: University of Chicago Press, 1964.

Halperin, Maurice H., with Clapp, Priscilla, and Kanter, Arnold. *Bureaucratic Politics & Foreign Policy.* Washington, D.C.: The Brookings Institution, 1974.

Hansen, Roger D. *The Politics of Mexican Development.* Baltimore: Johns Hopkins Press, 1971.

Hays, Samuel P. *Conservation and the Gospel of Efficiency: The Progressive Conservation Movement, 1890–1920.* Cambridge: Harvard University Press, 1959.

Hemming, John. *The Conquest of the Incas.* New York: Harcourt Brace Jovanovich, 1970.

Himmelberg, Robert F. *The Origins of the National Recovery Administration: Business, Government, and the Trade Association Issue, 1921–1933.* New York: Fordham University Press, 1976.

Hofstadter, Richard. *The American Political Tradition and the Men Who Made It.* New York: Alfred A. Knopf, 1948.

Hogan, Michael J. *Informal Entente: The Private Structure of Cooperation in Anglo-American Economic Diplomacy, 1918–1928.* Columbia: University of Missouri Press, 1977.

Hughes, Emmet John. *The Living Presidency: The Resources and Dilemmas of the American Presidential Office.* New York: Coward, McCann & Geohegan, 1973,

Ilchman, Warren Frederick. *Professional Diplomacy in the United States, 1779–1939: A Study in Administrative History.* Chicago: University of Chicago Press, 1961.

Johnson, Kenneth F. *Mexican Democracy: A Critical View.* Rev. ed. New York: Praeger Publishers, 1978.

Karl, Barry Dean. *Executive Reorganization and Reform in the New Deal: The Story of the Controversial First Steps toward Administrative Management, 1900–1939.* Cambridge: Harvard University Press, 1963.

Karnes, Thomas L. *Tropical Enterprise: The Standard Fruit and Steamship Company in Latin America.* Baton Rouge: Louisiana State University Press, 1978.

King, Rufus. *The Drug Hang-Up: America's Fifty Year Folly.* New York: W. W. Norton & Company, 1972.

Lamour, Catherine, and Lamberti, Michel R. *The International Connection: Opium from Growers to Pushers.* Translated by Peter and Betty Ross. New York: Pantheon Books, 1974.

Lasch, Christopher. *The New Radicalism in America, 1889-1963: The Intellectual as a Social Type.* New York: Alfred A. Knopf, 1965.

—. *The World of Nations: Reflections on American History, Politics, and Culture.* New York: Alfred A. Knopf, 1973.

Leffler, Melvyn P. *The Elusive Quest: America's Pursuit of European Stability and French Security, 1919–1933.* Chapel Hill: University of North Carolina Press, 1979.

Leon-Portilla, Miguel, ed. *The Broken Spears: The Aztec Account of the Conquest of Mexico.* Boston: Beacon Press, 1962.

Lieuwin, Edwin. *Arms and Politics in Latin America.* Rev. ed. New York: Frederick A. Praeger, 1961.

Lindesmith, Alfred R. *The Addict and the Law.* Bloomington: Indiana University Press, 1965.

Lockhart, James. *Spanish Peru, 1532–1560: A Colonial Society.* Madison: University of Wisconsin Press, 1968.

Lowi, Theodore J. *The End of Liberalism: Ideology, Policy, and the Crisis of Public Authority.* New York: W. W. Norton & Company, 1969.

Lubove, Roy. *The Professional Altruist: The Emergence of Social Work as a Career, 1880–1930.* Cambridge: Harvard University Press, 1965.

—. *The Struggle for Social Security, 1900–1935.* Cambridge: Harvard University Press, 1968.

McConnell, Grant. *Private Power and American Democracy.* New York: Alfred A. Knopf, 1966.

McCoy, Alfred W., with Read, Cathleen B., and Adams II, Leonard P. *The Politics of Heroin in Southeast Asia.* New York: Harper & Row, 1972.

McCoy, Donald R. *Calvin Coolidge: The Quiet President.* New York: The Macmillan Company, 1967.

McKinney, Wilson. *Fred Carrasco: The Heroin Merchant.* Austin: Heidelberg Publishers, 1975.

MacLeod, Murdo J. *Spanish Central America: A Socioeonomic History, 1520–1720.* Berkeley and Los Angeles: University of California Press, 1973.

Maier, Charles S. *Recasting Bourgeois Europe: Stabilization in France, Germany, and Italy in the Decade after World War I.* Princeton: Princeton University Press, 1975.

Mariñas Otero, Luis. *Honduras.* Madrid: Ediciones Cultura Hispanica, 1963.

Martinez, Oscar J. *Border Boom Town: Ciudad Juárez since 1848.* Austin: University of Texas Press, 1978.

May, Stacy, and Plaza, Galo. *The United Fruit Company in Latin America.* Washington, D.C.: National Planning Association, 1958.

Métraux, Alfred. *The History of the Incas.* Translated by George Ordish. New York: Schocken Books, 1970.

Mezzrow, Milton "Mezz", and Wolfe, Bernard. *Really the Blues.* New York: Random House, 1946.

Miller, Stuart Creighton. *The Unwelcome Immigrant: The American Image of the Chinese, 1785–1882.* Berkeley and Los Angeles: University of California Press, 1969.

Morgan, H. Wayne, ed. *Yesterday's Addicts: American Society and Drug Abuse, 1865–1920.* Norman: University of Oklahoma Press, 1974.

Mörner, Magnus. *Race Mixture in the History of Latin America.* Boston: Little, Brown and Company, 1967.

Mortimer, M.D., W. Golden. *History of Coca: "The Divine Plant" of the Incas.* Edited by Michael Horowitz. San Francisco: And/Or Press, 1974.

Munro, Dana G. *The United States and the Caribbean Republics, 1921–1933.* Princeton: Princeton University Press, 1974.

Murray, Robert K. *The Politics of Normalcy: Governmental Theory and Practice in the Harding-Coolidge Era.* New York: W. W. Norton & Company, 1973.

Musto, M.D., David F. *The American Disease: Origins of Narcotic Control.* New Haven: Yale University Press, 1973.

New York City Mayor's Committee on Marihuana, Wallace, M.D., George B., Chairman. *The Marihuana Problem in the City of New York.* Lancaster, Pa.: Cattell Press, 1944.

Osborne, Harold. *Indians of the Andes: Aymaras and Quechuas.* Cambridge: Harvard University Press, 1952.

Padden, R. C. *The Hummingbird and the Hawk: Conquest and Sovereignty in the Valley of Mexico, 1503–1541.* Columbus: Ohio State University Press, 1967.

Phelps, D. M., ed. *Economic Relations with Latin America.* Michigan Business Papers, No. 6. Ann Arbor: University of Michigan, School of Business Administration, Bureau of Business Research, 1940.

Picón-Salas, Mariano. *A Cultural History of Spanish America: From Conquest to Independence.* Translated by Irving A. Leonard. Berkeley and Los Angeles: University of California Press, 1971.

Pike, Frederick B. *The Modern History of Peru.* New York: Frederick A. Praeger, 1967.

—. *The United States and the Andean Republics: Peru, Bolivia, and Ecuador.* Cambridge: Harvard University Press, 1977.

Powell, Philip Wayne. *Soldiers, Indians, and Silver: North America's First Frontier War.* Rev. ed. Tempe: Arizona State University Press, 1975.

Price, John A. *Tijuana: Urbanization in a Border Culture.* Notre Dame: University of Notre Dame Press, 1973.

Reed, John. *Insurgent Mexico.* 1914. Reprint. New York: International Publishers, 1969.

Reynolds, Clark W. *The Mexican Economy: Twentieth-Century Structure and Growth.* New Haven: Yale University Press, 1970.

Rothman, David J. *The Discovery of the Asylum: Social Order and Disorder in the New Republic.* Boston: Little, Brown and Company, 1971.

Sandmeyer, Elmer Clarence. *The Anti-Chinese Movement in California.* Urbana: University of Illinois Press, 1973.

Saxton, Alexander. *The Indispensable Enemy: Labor and the Anti-Chinese Movement in California.* Berkeley and Los Angeles: University of California Press, 1971.

Schmeckebier, Lawrence F. *The Bureau of Prohibition: Its History, Activities and Organization.* Washington, D.C.: The Brookings Institution, 1929.

—. *The Customs Service: Its History, Activities and Organization.* Baltimore: Johns Hopkins Press, 1924.

—, and Eble, Francis X. A. *The Bureau of Internal Revenue: Its History, Activities and Organization.* Baltimore: Johns Hopkins Press, 1923.

Schroeder, Richard C. *The Politics of Drugs: Marijuana to Mainlining.* Washington, D.C.: Congressional Quarterly, 1975.

Sheridan, James E. *China in Disintegration: The Republican Era in Chinese History, 1912–1949.* New York: The Free Press, 1975.

Simpson, Eyler N. *The Ejido: Mexico's Way Out.* Chapel Hill: University of North Carolina Press, 1937.

Smith, Peter H. *Labyrinths of Power: Political Recruitment in Twentieth-Century Mexico.* Princeton: Princeton University Press, 1979.

Soule, George; Efron, David; and Ness, Norman T. *Latin America in the Future World.* New York: Farrar & Rinehart, 1945.

Soustelle, Jacques. *Daily Life of the Aztecs on the Eve of the Spanish Conquest.* Translated by Patrick O'Brian. New York: The Macmillan Company, 1962.

Spicer, Edward H. *Cycles of Conquest: The Impact of Spain, Mexico, and the United States on the Indians of the Southwest, 1533–1960.* Tucson: University of Arizona Press, 1962.

Stavenhagen, Rodolfo. *Les classes sociales dans les sociétés agraires.* Paris: Editions Anthropos, 1969.

Stevens, Rosemary. *American Medicine and the Public Interest.* New Haven: Yale University Press, 1971.

Steward, Dick. *Trade and Hemisphere: The Good Neighbor Policy and Reciprocal Trade.* Columbia: University of Missouri Press, 1975.

Stokes, William S. *Honduras: An Area Study in Government.* Madison: University of Wisconsin Press, 1950.

Stuart, Graham H. *American Diplomatic and Consular Practice.* 2nd ed. New York: Appleton-Century Crofts, 1962.

—. *The Department of State: A History of Its Organization, Procedure, and Personnel.* New York: The Macmillan Company, 1949.

Tannenbaum, Frank. *The Mexican Agrarian Revolution.* Washington, D.C.: The Brookings Institution, 1929.

Taylor, Arnold H. *American Diplomacy and the Narcotics Traffic, 1900–1939: A Study in International Humanitarian Reform.* Durham: Duke University Press, 1969.

Terry, M.D., Charles E., and Pellens, Mildred. *The Opium Problem.* New York: The Bureau of Social Hygiene, 1928.

Trani, Eugene P., and Wilson, David L. *The Presidency of Warren G. Harding.* Lawrence: The Regents Press of Kansas, 1977.

Tulchin, Joseph. *The Aftermath of War: World War I and U.S. Policy Toward Latin America.* New York: New York University Press, 1971.

Turner, Frederick C. *The Dynamic of Mexican Nationalism.* Chapel Hill: University of North Carolina Press, 1968.

van den Berghe, Pierre L., and Primov, George P. *Inequality in the Peruvian Andes: Class and Ethnicity in Cuzco.* Columbia: University of Missouri Press, 1977.

Villa, Eduardo W. *Compendio de Historia del Estado de Sonora.* México, D.F.: Editorial "Patria Nueva," 1937.

von Hagen, Victor Wolfgang, ed. *The Incas of Pedro de Cieza de León.* Translated by Harriet de Onis. Norman: University of Oklahoma Press, 1959.

Walton, Robert P. *Marihuana: America's New Drug Problem.* Philadelphia: J. B. Lippincott Company, 1938.

Weil, Martin. *A Pretty Good Club: The Founding Fathers of the U.S. Foreign Service.* New York: W. W. Norton & Company, 1978.

Welles, Sumner. *Seven Decisions That Shaped History.* New York: Harper & Brothers, 1950, 1951.

—. *The Time for Decision.* New York: Harper & Brothers, 1944.

Werking, Richard Hume, *The Master Architects: Building the United States Foreign Service, 1890–1913.* Lexington: University Press of Kentucky, 1977.

Whetten, Nathan L. *Rural Mexico.* Chicago: University of Chicago Press, 1948.

Wiebe, Robert H. *The Search for Order, 1877–1920.* New York: Hill and Wang, 1967.

Wilkie, James W. *The Mexican Revolution: Federal Expenditure and Social Change since 1910.* 2nd rev. ed. Berkeley and Los Angeles: University of California Press, 1970.

Wilson, James Q. *The Investigators: Managing FBI and Narcotics Agents.* New York: Basic Books, 1978.

Wilson, Joan Hoff. *American Business and Foreign Policy, 1920–1933.* Lexington: University Press of Kentucky, 1971.

—. *Herbert Hoover: Forgotten Progressive.* Boston: Little, Brown and Company, 1975.

—. *Ideology and Economics: U.S. Relations with the Soviet Union, 1918–1933.* Columbia: University of Missouri Press, 1974.

Wolf, Eric. *Sons of the Shaking Earth: The People of Mexico and Guatemala—Their Land, History, and Culture.* Chicago: University of Chicago Press, 1959.

—. and Hansen, Edward C. *The Human Condition in Latin America.* New York: Oxford University Press, 1972.

Wolfe, Margaret Ripley. *Lucius Polk Brown and Progressive Food and Drug Control: Tennessee and New York City, 1908–1920.* Lawrence: The Regents Press of Kansas, 1978.

Wolff, M.D., Pablo Osvaldo. *Aspectos Sociales de las Narcomanías.* Buenos Aires: Revista de la Asociación Medica Argentina, 1941.

—. *Marihuana in Latin America: The Threat It Constitutes.* Washington, D.C.: Linacre Press, 1949.

Womack, Jr., John. *Zapata and the Mexican Revolution.* New York: Random House, 1968.

Wood, Bryce. *The Making of the Good Neighbor Policy.* New York: Columbia University Press, 1961.

Woodward, Jr., Ralph Lee. *Central America: A Nation Divided.* New York: Oxford University Press, 1976.

Wynia, Gary W. *Politics and Planners: Economic Development Policy in Central America.* Madison: University of Wisconsin Press, 1972.

Young, James Harvey. *The Toadstool Millionaires: A Social History of Patent Medicines in America before Federal Regulation.* Princeton: Princeton University Press, 1961.

Articles

"Action on Coca Leaf Problem." *United Nations Bulletin,* May 15, 1952, p. 410.

Adams, Roger. "Marihuana." *Science,* August 9, 1940, pp. 115–19.

Allentuck, M.D., Ph.D., Samuel, and Bowman, M.D., Karl. "The Psychiatric Aspects of Marihuana Intoxication." *American Journal of Psychiatry,* 99 (September 1942), pp. 248–51.

Anslinger, Harry J. "Correspondence." *Journal of the American Medical Association,* January 16, 1943, pp. 212–13.

—. "Correspondence." *Journal of the American Medical Association,* August 18, 1945, p. 1187.

—. "Criminal and Psychiatric Aspects Associated with Marihuana." *The Union Signal,* February 5, 1944, pp. 77–78.

—. "Letter on Drug Addiction." *Journal of the American Medical Association,* September 23, 1950, p. 333.

—. "Marihuana . . . the Assassin of the Human Mind." *Law Enforcement,* 1 (October 1941), pp. 7–8, 10.

—. "Peddling of Narcotic Drugs." *Journal of Criminal Law and Criminology,* XXIV (September–October 1933), pp. 636–55.

—. "The Physician and the Federal Narcotic Law." *American Journal of Psychiatry,* 102 (March 1946), pp. 609–18.

—, with Cooper, Courtney Riley. "Marihuana: Assassin of Youth." *American Magazine,* July 1937, pp. 18–19, 150–53.

Arnold, Peri Ethan. "Herbert Hoover and the Continuity of American Public Policy." *Public Policy,* XX (Fall 1972), pp. 525–44.

Baird, Jane B. "The Source." *Miami Herald: Tropic,* May 23, 1980, p. 12.

Bauer, Arnold J. "Rural Workers in Spanish America: Problems of Peonage and Oppression." *Hispanic American Historical Review,* 59 (February 1979), pp. 34–63.

Beals, Carleton. "The Drug Eaters of the High Andes." *Travel,* December 1937, pp. 29–31, 40.

Becker, Howard S., and Horowitz, Irving Louis. "Radical Politics and Sociological Research: Observations on Methodology and Ideology." *American Journal of Sociology,* 78 (July 1972), pp. 48–66.

Becker, Jacklyn, et al. "The Dope Trail." *Contemporary Drug Problems,* 1 (Summer 1972), pp. 413–52.

Bejarano, Jorge. "El Cocaísmo en Colombia." *América Indígena,* V (enero de 1945), pp. 11–20.

Berger, Dr. Harry, and Eggston, Dr. Andrew A. "Should We Legalize Narcotics?" *Coronet,* June 1955, pp. 30–35.

Blake, S. F. "The 'Divine Plant of the Incas.'" *Agriculture in the Americas,* III (June 1943), pp. 114–16.

Borah, Woodrow. "Discontinuity and Continuity in Mexican History." *Pacific Historical Review,* 48 (February 1979), pp. 1–25.

Bowman, Karl M. "Correspondence." *Journal of the American Medical Association*, July 21, 1945, pp. 899–900.

Bromberg, M.D., Walter. "Marihuana: A Psychiatric Study." *Journal of the American Medical Association*, July 1, 1939, pp. 4–12.

—. "Marihuana Intoxication: A Clinical Study of Cannabis Sativa Intoxication." *American Journal of Psychiatry*, 91 (October 1934), pp. 303–30.

Bromberg, M. C. (5), U.S.N.R., Commander Walter, and Rodgers, M. C., U.S.N., Lieutenant Terry C. "Marihuana and Aggressive Crime." *American Journal of Psychiatry*, 102 (May 1946), pp. 825–27.

Brown, Clair A. "Marihuana: the Mexican Dope Plant Is the Source of a Social Problem." *Nature Magazine*, May 1938, pp. 271–72.

Brown, Lyle C. "The Politics of United States–Mexican Relations: Problems of the 1970s in Historical Perspective." In *Contemporary Mexico: Papers of the IV Congress of Mexican History*, edited by James W. Wilkie, Michael C. Meyer, and Edna Monzón de Wilkie, pp. 471–93. Berkeley and Los Angeles: University of California Press, 1976.

César Perez, Julio. "El Problema Social de la Coca en Bolivia." *Protección Social. La Paz*, agosto de 1942, pp. 31–32.

Charen, B.A., M.A., Sol, and Perelman, B.H., B.M., Lic. M., Luis. "Personality Status of Marihuana Addicts." *American Journal of Psychiatry*, 102 (March 1946), pp. 674–82.

Class, F. E. "The Sacred Coca Plant." *Pan-American Magazine*, December 1922, pp. 297–303.

"The Coca Leaf Habit." *United Nations Bulletin*, October 21, 1947, p. 525.

"Coca Leaves and Cocaine." *Pan-American Magazine*, May–June 1922, pp. 2–3.

"The Colombian Connection." *Time*, January 29, 1979, pp. 22–26, 28–29.

El Consejo Nacional de Higiene. "La Higiene en el Uruguay." *Boletín de la Oficina Sanitaria Panamericana*, 7 (junio de 1928), pp. 672–83.

Cotler, Julio. "State and Regime: Comparative Notes on the Southern Cone and the 'Enclave' Societies." In *The New Authoritarianism in Latin America*, edited by David Collier, pp. 255–82. Princeton: Princeton University Press, 1979.

The Council on Health and Public Instruction. "Report of the Committee on Narcotic Drugs of the Council on Health and Public Instruction." *Journal of the American Medical Association*, June 11, 1921, pp. 1669–71.

Curtis, M.D., Howard C. "Psychosis Following the Use of Marihuana with Report of Cases." *Journal of the Kansas Medical Society*, 40 (December 1939), pp. 515–17, 526–28.

Dell'Occhio, Elsa. "La coca, el cocaísmo y los problemas de la hora presente." *Runa: Archivo Para Las Ciencias Del Hombre*, II (1949), pp. 191–97.

"Drug Curse is Pall on Roof of World." *Popular Mechanics*, February 1924, pp. 248–49.

Duque Gómez, Luis. "Notas Sobre el Cocaísmo en Colombia." *Boletín de Arqueologia*, I (septiembre–octubre de 1945), pp. 445–51.

Duranty, Walter. "Opium Smoking." *Atlantic Monthly*, February 1943, pp. 106–13.

Eakins, David W. "The Origins of Corporate Liberal Policy Research, 1916–1922: The Political-Economic Expert and the Decline of Public Debate." In *Building the Organizational Society: Essays on Associational Activities in Modern America*, edited by Jerry Israel, pp. 163–79, 288–91. New York: The Free Press, 1972.

"Editoriales." (Tercera Conferencia Panamericana de Directores Nacionales de Sanidad). *Boletín de la Oficina Sanitaria Panamericana*, 15 (junio 1936), pp. 581–97.

"Editorial Paragraphs." *The Nation*, March 12, 1930, p. 284.

El Diario (La Paz). "La Industria y Comercio de la Coca en Bolivia." *Boletín Comercial y Minero*. La Paz (15 de junio de 1938), pp. 37, 39.

"End of the Illicit Drug Traffic Now In Sight." *Literary Digest*, July 29, 1933, p. 19.

"Estupefacientes." *Boletín de la Oficina Sanitaria Panamericana*, 13 (marzo de 1934), pp. 232–38.

—. *Boletín de la Oficina Sanitaria Panamericana*, 15 (enero de 1936), pp. 61–66.

"Facts and Fancies about Marihuana." *Literary Digest*, October 24, 1936, pp. 7–8.

Fossati, H. "Reflexiones sobre la organización del monopolio de la coca." *Boletín Comercial y Minero*. La Paz (15 de noviembre de 1940), pp. 9–17.

Foulger, M.D., John H. "The Marihuana Problem." *Delaware State Medical Journal*, 16 (February 1944), pp. 24–28.

Fredrickson, George M., and Lasch, Christopher. "Resistance to Slavery." *Civil War History*, 13 (December 1967), pp. 315–29.

Freedman, Major Harry L., M.C. (Director, Mental Hygiene Division, Armed Service Forces Training Center, Camp Planche, La.), and Rockmore, S/Sgt. Myron J. (Chief Psychiatric Social Worker, Mental Hygiene Division, Camp Planche, La.). "Marihuana: A Factor in Personality Evaluation and Army Maladjustment." Part I, *Journal of Clinical Psychopathology*, 7 (April 1946), pp. 756–82.

—. "Marihuana: A Factor in Personality Evaluation and Army Maladjustment." Part II, *Journal of Clinical Psychopathology*, 8 (October 1946), pp. 221–36.

Gabriel Garcés, Victor. "El Indio Ecuatoriano y La Coca." *América Indígena*, V (octubre de 1945), pp. 287–93.

Galambos, Louis. "The Emerging Organizational Synthesis in Modern American History." *Business History Review*, 44 (Autumn 1970), pp. 279–90.

Gard, Wayne. "Youth Gone Loco." *Christian Century*, June 29, 1938, pp. 812–13.

"El Gob. [Gobierno] provincial de Jujuy reglamenta el expendio de la coca Boliviana." *Boletín Comercial y Minero*. La Paz (1 de julio de 1937), pp. 27–33.

Gutiérrez-Noriega, Carlos. "El Hábito de la Coca en el Perú." *América Indígena*, IX (abril de 1949), pp. 143–54.

—. "El Hábito de la Coca en Sud América." *América Indígena*, XII (abril de 1952), pp. 111–20.

—, and von Hagen, Victor Wolfgang. "The Strange Case of the Coca Leaf." *Scientific Monthly*, February 1950, pp. 81–89.

Hagen-Smit, A. J., et al. "A Physiologically Active Principle from *Cannabis Sativa* (Marihuana)." *Science*, June 21, 1940, pp. 602–3.

Harbaugh, William H. "The Republican Party, 1893–1932." In *History of U.S. Political Parties*, edited by Arthur M. Schlesinger, Jr., pp. 2069–2125, vol. 3: *1910–1945: From Square Deal to New Deal*. New York: Chelsea House in association with R. R. Bowker, 1973.

Harris, David. "The Dark and Violent World of the Mexican Connection." *New York Times Magazine*, December 18, 1977, p. 15.

Hawley, Ellis W. "Herbert Hoover and American Corporatism, 1929–1933." In *The Hoover Presidency: A Reappraisal*, edited by Martin L. Fausold and George T. Mazuzan, pp. 101–19, 207–15. Albany: State University of New York Press, 1974.

—. "Herbert Hoover, the Commerce Secretariat, and the Vision of an 'Associative State,' 1921–1928." *Journal of American History*, 61 (June 1974), pp. 116–40.

Heinrichs, Jr., Waldo H. "Bureaucracy and Professionalism in the Development of American Career Diplomacy." In *Twentieth-Century American Foreign Policy*, edited by John Braeman, Robert H. Bremner, and David Brody, pp. 119–206. Columbus: Ohio State University Press, 1971.

Henninger, James M. "exhibitionism." *Journal of Psychopathology*, 2 (January 1941), pp. 357–66.

Hernández, Salomé. "Innocence or Guilt? Mexico's Arrest of the Yaquis, 1899–1909." *Journal of the West*, 14 (October 1975), pp. 15–26.

Hiaasen, Carl, and Messerschmidt, Al. "Cocaine Killers." *Rolling Stone*, September 20, 1979, pp. 82–85.

Higbee, E. C. "America's Drug Plants." *Agriculture in the Americas*, II (May 1942), pp. 91–93.

Higginson, Eduardo. "Memoria del Consulado General del Perú en Nueva York correspondiente al año 1912." *Anales de la Dirreción de Fomento:* no. 6 (junio de 1913), pp. 39–95.

Holmberg, Allan R. "The Role of Power in Changing Values and Institutions of Vicos." In *Peasants, Power and Applied Social Change: Vicos as a Model,* edited by Henry F. Dobyns, Paul L. Doughty, Harold D. Lasswell, pp. 33–63. Beverly Hills: Sage Publications, 1964, 1971.

Hughes, Lilian Whittenhall. "The Curse of Coca." *Inter-American,* V (September 1946), pp. 18–22, 42.

Israel, Jerry. "A Diplomatic Machine: Scientific Management in the Department of State, 1906–1924." In *Building the Organizational Society: Essays on Associational Activity in Modern America,* edited by Jerry Israel, pp. 183–96, 291–95. New York: The Free Press, 1972.

Jardines Carrion, Dr. H. "La Marihuana en América." *Revista Farmaceutica de Cuba,* 29 (junio de 1951), pp. 34–44.

Jones, Robert F. "Powerboat Racing Has Gone to Pot." *Sports Illustrated,* April 9, 1979, pp. 28–30, 33.

Kane, Francis Fisher. "Coca-chewing." *The Survey,* June 15, 1927, p. 347.

Katz, Friedrich. "Pancho Villa and the Attack on Columbus, New Mexico." *American Historical Review,* 83 (February 1978), pp. 101–30.

Katz, Michael B. "Origins of the Institutional State." *Marxist Perspectives,* 1 (Winter 1978), pp. 6–22.

Kinzer, Stephen. "The World's Biggest Deadbeat." *The New Republic,* April 21, 1979, pp. 14, 16–18.

Kirschner, Don S. "The Ambiguous Legacy: Social Justice and Social Control in the Progressive Era." *Historical Reflections,* 2 (Summer 1975), pp. 69–88.

Kline, C. Mahlon. "The Thirty-Seventh Annual Convention of the National Wholesale Druggists Association." *American Journal of Pharmacy,* 84 (January 1912), pp. 24–33.

Kolb, Lawrence. "Marihuana." *Federal Probation,* II (July 1938), pp. 22–25.

—, and DuMez, A. G. "The Prevalence and Trend of Drug Addiction in the United States and the Factors Influencing It." *Public Health Reports,* May 23, 1924, pp. 1179–1204.

LaBarre, Weston. "The Aymara Indians of Lake Titicaca Plateau, Bolivia." *American Anthropologist,* 50 (January 1948), pp. 1–250.

La Motte, Ellen. "'Limiting' Drug Manufacture." *The Nation,* April 13, 1932, pp. 418–19.

Larrabure y Correa, Carlos. "Ensayos culturales de la coca en las colonias europeas." *Boletín de la Dirrecion de Fomento,* año IX (noviembre de 1911), pp. 9–11.

Leffler, Melvyn P. "Political Isolationism, Economic Expansionism, or Diplomatic Realism: American Policy Toward Western Europe, 1921–1933." *Perspectives in American History,* VIII (1974), pp. 413–61.

Léon, Luis A. "Historia y Extinción del Cocaísmo en el Ecuador." *América Indígena,* XII (enero de 1952), pp. 7–32.

Lindesmith, Alfred R. "Dope: Congress Encourages the Traffic." *The Nation,* March 16, 1957, pp. 228–31.

Lorente, Sebastían, y Caravedo, Baltazar. "Bases Fundamentales para la Organización de la Defensa Social contra la Toxicomanía." *Boletín de la Oficina Sanitaria Panamericana,* 7 (enero de 1928), pp. 192–97.

Lowenthal, Abraham F. "Dateline Peru: A Sagging Revolution." *Foreign Policy,* no. 38 (Spring 1980), pp. 182–90.

McCormack, George Randall. "Marihuana." *Hygeia,* October 1937, pp. 898–99.

"Marihuana More Dangerous than Heroin or Cocaine." *Scientific American,* May 1938, p. 293.

"Marihuana Problems." *Journal of the American Medical Association,* April 28, 1945, p. 1129.

"Marihuana Weed Grows Where Rope Factory Failed." *Science News Letter*, January 15, 1938, pp. 38–39.

Marroquin, José. "Cocaísmo entre los indigenos peruanos." *Boletín Identificación y Policia Tecnica, Lima* (julio–agosto de 1945), pp. 67–76.

Marshall, Johnathan. "Opium and the Politics of Gangsterism in Nationalist China, 1927–1945," *Bulletin of Concerned Asian Scholars*, 8 (July–September 1976), pp. 19–48.

Marshall, Maud A. "Marihuana." *American Scholar*, 8 (Winter 1938–1939), pp. 95–101.

Martin, Richard T. "The Role of Coca in the History, Religion, and Medicine of South American Indians." In *The Coca Leaf and Cocaine Papers*, edited by George Andrews and David Solomon, pp. 20–37. New York: Harcourt Brace Jovanovich, 1975.

May, Herbert L. "The International Control of Narcotic Drugs." *International Conciliation*, no. 441 (May 1948), pp. 301–73.

—. "Narcotic Drug Control." *International Conciliation*, no. 485 (November 1952), pp. 489–536.

"Medical News." *Journal of the American Medical Association*, March 17, 1934, p. 850.

—. *Journal of the American Medical Association*, August 8, 1936, p. 437.

Mintz, Sidney W. "Foreword." In *Afro-American Anthropology: Contemporary Perspectives*, edited by Norman E. Whitten and John F. Szwed, pp. 1–16. New York: The Free Press, 1970.

—. "History and Anthropology: A Brief Reprise." In *Race and Slavery in the Western Hemisphere: Quantitative Studies*, edited by Stanley L. Engerman and Eugene D. Genovese, pp. 477–94. Princeton: Princeton University Press, 1975.

Monge Medrano, Carlos, "La Necesidad de Estudiar el Problema de la Masticación de las Hojas de Coca." *América Indígena*, XIV (abril de 1954), pp. 113–26.

Monsiváis, Carlos. "The Culture of the Frontier: The Mexican Side." In *Views Across the Border: The United States and Mexico*, edited by Stanley R. Ross, pp. 50–67. Albuquerque: University of New Mexico Press, in cooperation with the Weatherhead Foundation, 1978.

Moorehead, Mrs. Helen H. "Control of Narcotic Drugs." *Foreign Policy Reports*, September 30, 1946, pp. 10–13.

—. "International Narcotics Control, 1939–1945." *Foreign Policy Reports*, July 1, 1946, pp. 94–103.

Musto, M.D., David F. "The Marihuana Tax Act of 1937." *Archives of General Psychiatry*, XXVI (February 1972), pp. 101–08.

"New Billion-Dollar Crop." *Popular Mechanics Magazine*, February 1938, pp. 238–39, 144A–45A.

"New Protocol on Narcotic Drugs Signed." *United Nations Bulletin*, September 16, 1947, p. 37.

"Notas y Revistas." *Boletín de la Oficina Sanitaria Panamericana*, 10 (marzo de 1931), pp. 373–74.

"Nueva Legislación." *Boletín de la Oficina Sanitaria Panamericana*, 8 (diciembre de 1929), p. 1422.

—. *Boletín de la Oficina Sanitaria Panamericana*, 9 (marzo de 1930), p. 347.

"Old and New Narcotic Perils." *United Nations Bulletin*, September 16, 1947, pp. 363–64.

Oneto Barenque, Dr. Gregorio. "La Marijuana ante La Psiquiatría y el Código Penal." *Criminalia*. *México* (diciembre de 1938), pp. 238–56.

Orosco, Dr. German. "El alma de la humilde hoja del indio dominó el refinamiento del blanco." *Revista Geographica Americana*, XVI (septiembre de 1941), pp. 149–55.

"Our Home Hasheesh Crop." *Literary Digest*, April 3, 1926, pp. 64–65.

Peón del Valle, Dr. Juan. "Algunos Aspectos de la Actual Lucha Contra La Toxicomanía en México." *Boletín de la Oficina Sanitaria Panamericana*, 12 (abril de 1933), pp. 347–55.

Perez de Barradas, José. "Antiguedad del uso de la coca en Colombia." *Academia Colombiana de Ciencias Exactas, Fisicas y Naturales, Revista.* Bogotá, III (enero-abril de 1940), pp. 323–26.

Phelan, James M., Colonel, U.S. Army Ret. "Editorial: The Marihuana Bugaboo." *Military Surgeon*, 93 (July 1943), pp. 94–95.

"Plans for Extending Global Control of Narcotic Drugs." *United Nations Bulletin*, February 1, 1951, pp. 126–28.

Popper, David H. "The Rio de Janeiro Conference of 1942." *Foreign Policy Reports*, April 15, 1942, pp. 25–35.

Reichard, Dr. J. D. "Correspondence: The Marihuana Problem." *Journal of the American Medical Association*, June 24, 1944, pp. 594–95.

Ricketts, C. A. "El Cocaísmo en el Perú." *América Indígena*, XII (octubre de 1952), pp. 309–22.

—. "La Masticación de las Hojas de Coca en el Perú." *América Indígena*, XIV (abril de 1954), pp. 113–26.

Rohter, Larry. "A Brutal 'Cocaine Coup.'" *Newsweek*, August 11, 1980, pp. 39–40.

Roosevelt, Franklin D. "Our Foreign Policy: A Democratic View." *Foreign Affairs*, 6 (July 1928), pp. 573–86.

Ross, Stanley R. "Commentaries: Introduction." In *Views Across the Border: The United States and Mexico*, edited by Stanley R. Ross, pp. 361–82. Albuquerque: University of New Mexico Press, in cooperation with the Weatherhead Foundation, 1978.

Salazar Viniegra, Dr. Leopoldo. "El Mito de la Marijuana." *Criminalia. México* (diciembre de 1938), pp. 206–37.

—. "El Sueño de Lexington." *Toxicomanías E Higiene Mental*, 1 (enero-febrero de 1939), pp. 4–6.

Schaller, Michael. "The Federal Prohibition of Marihuana." *Journal of Social History*, 4 (Fall 1970), pp. 71–74.

Schwarz, Jordan A. "Hoover and Congress: Politics, Personality, and Perspective in the Presidency." In *The Hoover Presidency: A Reappraisal*, edited by Martin L. Fausold and George T. Mazuzan, pp. 87–100, 204–7. Albany: State University of New York Press, 1974.

Siler, Joseph F., Colonel, M.C., U.S. Army, Chief Health Officer, et al. "Marijuana Smoking in Panama." *Military Surgeon*, 73 (November 1933), pp. 269–80.

Siurob, José. "The Struggle Against Toxicomania." *Pacific Coast International*, November–December 1939, pp. 19–25.

Spicer, Edward H. "Yaqui." In *Perspectives in American Indian Culture Change*, edited by Edward H. Spicer, pp. 7–93. Chicago: University of Chicago Press, 1961.

Stanley, Eugene. "Marihuana as a Developer of Criminals." *American Journal of Police Science*, II (May–June 1931), pp. 252–61.

Stavenhagen, Rodolfo. "Social Aspects of Agrarian Structure in Mexico." In *Agrarian Problems and Peasant Movements*, edited by Rodolfo Stavenhagen, pp. 225–70. New York: Anchor Books, 1970.

Treadway, Dr. Walter L. "La Narcomanía y las medidas para su prevención en los Estados Unidos." *Boletín de la Oficina Sanitaria Panamericana*, 11 (diciembre de 1932), pp. 1256–67.

"United States Assumes Control of Cannabis." *Journal of the American Medical Association*, September 11, 1937, pp. 31B–32B.

"The White Goddess." *Time*, April 11, 1949, p. 44.

Williams, William Appleman. "The Legend of Isolationism in the 1920's." *Science and Society*, XVIII (Winter 1954), pp. 1–20.

Wolf, William. "Uncle Sam Fights a New Drug Menace . . . Marihuana." *Popular Science*, May 1936, pp. 119–20.

Wolff, Dr. Pablo Osvaldo. "Narcomanías y Criminalidad." *Revista de Psiquiatría y Criminología*. Buenos Aires, VI (septiembre–octubre de 1941), pp. 433–54.

Womack, Jr., John. "The Mexican Economy During the Revolution, 1910–1920: Historiography and Analysis." *Marxist Perspectives*, 1 (Winter 1978), pp. 80–123.

Wright, Elizabeth Washburn. "American at the Geneva Opium Conference," *The Outlook*, July 11, 1923, pp. 360–61.

Yawger, N. S. "Marihuana, el Nuevo Vicio." *Criminalia. México* (enero de 1939), pp. 269–72.

Unpublished Manuscripts and Dissertations

Costigliola, Frank Charles. "The Politics of Financial Stabilization: American Reconstruction Policy in Europe: 1924–30." Ph.D. dissertation, Cornell University, 1973.

Craig, Richard B. *La campaña permanente:* "Mexico's Anti-drug Campaign." Photoduplication. Kent, Ohio: Kent State University, 1977.

—. "Operation Intercept: The International Politics of Pressure." Photoduplication. Paper: Organization of American Historians Convention, Atlanta, April 1977.

Jaffe, Arnold. "Addiction Reform in the Progressive Age: Scientific and Social Response to Drug Dependence in the United States, 1870–1930." Ph.D. dissertation, University of Kentucky, 1977.

McNeely, John Hamilton. "The Politics and Development of the Mexican Land Program." Ph.D. dissertation, The University of Texas, 1958.

Van Meter, Robert H. "The United States and European Recovery, 1918–1923: A Study of Public Policy and Private Finance." Ph.D. dissertation, The University of Wisconsin, 1971.

Walker III, William O. "The Politics of Drug Control: The United States and Latin America, 1900–1945." Ph.D. dissertation, University of California, Santa Barbara, 1974.

Index

Acree, Vernon D., 197–98
A Cultural History of Spanish America, 2–3
Acuna, Gorgonio, 208
Adams, Roger, 112
Advisory Committee on Traffic in Opium and Other Dangerous Drugs. *See* Opium Advisory Committee
Afghanistan, 201–2
Ailshie, William K., 164
Alcázar, Heberto, 126, 162–63
alcohol, 184; alternatives to, 12; and Andeans, 45, 156; in Ecuador, 11; in Mexico, 124, 185; in Peru, 136; liquor smuggling, 82; United States use of, 13, 15, 101, 105
Alduvín, Ricardo, 87–88, 90
Allende government, 197
Allentuck, Samuel, 113–14
Almazán, Leonidas Andreu, 122, 126, 127
AMA. *See* American Medical Association
America Indígena, 190
American Bar Association, Committee on Narcotics and Alcohol, 173

American Chamber of Commerce, 155
American Journal of Clinical Medicine, 17–18
American Journal of Psychiatry, 113
American Magazine, 108
American Medical Association, (AMA), Bureau of Legal Medicine, 111; Committee on Habit-Forming Drugs, 19; on domestic drug controls, 16; on health insurance, 26–27, 106; on heroin, 13; on marijuana, 106, 113–15; opposition to drug controls, 30, 31, 66; support for drug controls, 77
American Psychiatric Association, 105
analfabetismo, 175
Andean Common Market, 200
Anslinger, Harry J., at Geneva, 71, 95–96, 126; career of, 64, 68–69, 183, 191; cocaine sale by, 157; policy of, 78, 81–82, 90, 99, 107, 125, 147, 149–50, 185, 188, and Argentina, 154, 174, and Mexico, 121, 128–33, 162–63, 178, and Peru, 159–60,

on addiction, 76, 170–73, on
   drug traffic, 102, 170, 250 n.
   112, on marijuana, 103–16, 124,
   on Porter bill, 66
Anti-Opium Information Bureau,
   84
Arce Gómez, Luis, 200–201
Argentina, 169, 174, 200; at
   Geneva, 70–72; drug control
   effort by, 85–86, 139, 153–56,
   177, 197
Armour, Norman, 154–55
Aruak Indians, 9
Asia, obstacles to drug control in,
   150–51
Assassins of Persia legend, 101,
   104, 106, 111
associational activity, 24–27
Attorney General's Conference on
   Crime, (1934), 76
Ávila Camacho, Manuel, 162–64,
   166–67
Axis powers, 89, 148, 153–55, 157
Aymara Indians, 41, 56

Bailey, Charles A., 126
Baja California, 22, 35–36, 59,
   82–83, 164
banana industry, 87–88, 91
Barnes, Roy, 155
Bassols, Francisco, 162
Baz, Gustavo, 168
Bazant, Jan, 5
Beam Test, 112
Beaulac, Willard L., 87
Behavior Clinic of the Criminal
   Court, 110
Belaúnde Terry, Fernando, 197,
   201
Benavides, Oscar R., 139
Bensinger, Peter B., 201
Bermúdez, Antonio, 91, 143,
   165–66
Blocker, William P., 60, 81,
   164–65
Blue, Rupert, 30, 32–34
BNDD, (Bureau of Narcotics and
   Dangerous Drugs), 191–92
Board of Economic Welfare, 160
Bohr, Frank, 58–59
*Boletín de la Oficina Sanitaria
   Panamericana*, 136

Bolivia, 73, 169, 177; and Geneva,
   48, 50, 60, 70, 72, 94; and The
   Hague, 21; drug control effort
   by, 22, 45, 47, 56, 93, 139–40,
   149–50, 197–201
Bonnie, Richard J., 99, 104, 108,
   173
Bourne, Peter G., 193
Bowers, Claude G., 154
Bowman, Karl, 113–15
Brazil, 200; and the United States,
   89; at Geneva, 60, 70, 94, 96;
   drug traffic through, 84–85, 157
Brent, Charles H., 15, 34, 51, 181
Bromberg Walter, 104–6, 112–13
Brown, Lucius Polk, 17, 182
Brown, Preston, 104
Bruun, Kettil, 184
bubonic plague, 30
Bulkley, John W., 130, 147–48, 167
Burdett, William C., 92
Bureau of Indian Affairs, Peru, 43
Bureau of Internal Revenue, 18–19,
   182
Bureau of Narcotics. *See* Federal
   Bureau of Narcotics
Bureau of Narcotics and Dangerous
   Drugs, (BNDD), 191–92
Bureau of Prisons, 106
Bureau of Public Health, Peru, 43,
   92
Bureau of the Budget, 78
Bursley, Herbert, 130, 164, 167

caciques, 3, 4, 6
Caldwell, John Kenneth, 53–54,
   61–68, 70–72
Califano, Joseph A., 194
California Institute of Technology,
   110
Calles, Plutarco Elías, 49, 58, 60,
   79–80
campesino, 39–40
Canada, 103, 126, 169
Canal Zone, 90, 103–4, 140
cannabis. *See* marijuana
Cantú, Esteban, 35–36
Caravedo, Baltazar, 56
Cárdenas, Lázaro, 38, 80–81, 119,
   162–63
Carías Andino, Tiburcio, 87–91;
   and drug traffic through

Honduras, 141, 145–48 passim
Caribbean zone, 7–9, 195
Carillo Puerto, Felipe, 37
Carr, Paul, 82
Carr, Wilbur J., 28
Carranza, Venustiano, 22, 35–36, 40–41
Carter, Jimmy, 191, 193
Carvallo, Constantino J., 159
cédulas, 7–9
Central America, air freight in, 148; drug control in. *See by country, and* drug traffic through, 1, 75, 86; rescates in, 7–9; United States role in, 140–49 passim
Centros de Integración Juvenil, 193
Chamberlain, Joseph, 54
chasqui, 9
Chevalier, François, 4
Chiapas, 167
Chihuahua, 35. *See also* Ciudad Juárez
child care, 27
Children's Bureau, 106
Chile, 45, 154, 177, 200; and Geneva, 35, 60, 70, 72, 94
China, 81, 176. *See also* Mexico, Chinese in
Chopra, R. N., 115
Christian Science Monitor, 44
Christianity and Andean Indians, 57
Ciudad Juárez, 36–37, 59, 81, 132, 164–65
Civilian Conservation Corps, 109
Clark, J. Reuben, 54
Coast Guard, 140, 151
coca, (*Erythroxylon coca*), 1, 9–11; at The Hague, 21; in Argentina, 139; in Bolivia, 50, 93, 198–99; in Peru, 3–6, 41, 56, 92, 94, 186, 198–99. *See also* cocaine; coca leaf chewing; coca leaves; el coqueo
Coca, Ariel, 200
Coca-Cola Company, 66
cocaine, 16, 21, 50, 59, 110, 169, 190; from Bolivia, 56, 84, 135, 140, 189, 195, 199–200; from Chile, 189, 195, 197; from Colombia, 189, 195; from

Ecuador, 189, 195, 197; from Europe, 75–76; from Peru, 43–45, 56, 94, 135, 137–38, 140, 154, 156–58, 189, 195, 199; United States' use of, 67, 77, 102, 106. *See also* coca
cocaístas, 10
coca leaf chewing, 57, 177, 190; Andean historical role of, 1, 9–11, 185–86, 198; in Bolivia, 139, 189; in Peru, 92, 136–37, 175, 213–14 n. 30. *See also* coca
coca leaves, 156, 175, 198; Commission on, 190; League control of, 47, 50, 72, 95; used in Bolivia, 22, 45, 48, 187, 195, 201; used in Peru, 22, 43, 45, 48–49, 92–93, 161, 187, 195, 199, 201; used in the United States, 30, 66–67, 158. *See also* cocaine
coca paste, 195, 197. *See also* cocaine
codeine, 13, 160
Coffee, John M., 115–16
Cohen, Harry, 64–65
Colombia, 156, 177, 200; drug control effort by, 57, 73, 195–96, 201
Colonia. *See* Free Zone of Colonia
Columbia University, 54
Columbus, New Mexico, 40–41
Commission of Inquiry on the Coca Leaf, 190
Commission on Narcotic Drugs, 177–78, 187, 190
communicable diseases, 15
communidades, 139
Compañía Nacional de Aviación, 143
Conference for the Limitation of the Manufacture of Narcotic Drugs, (1931), 70–72
Conference for the Suppression of the Illicit Traffic in Narcotic Drugs, (1936), 93–95
Congress of Pan-American Health Directors, Fourth, (1940), 130
Coolidge administration, 25–26, 55
coqueros, 6, 9, 20, 156, 175. *See also* el coqueo
Costa, Alejandro, 199

Costa Rica, 148; at Geneva, 70, 72;
    drug traffic through, 90, 195
Cottrell, Jesse, 45, 48
Cozumel, 145
Creighton, H. S., 122–23, 127, 129,
    132–33, 145; and Mexico,
    162–67 passim
Criminalia, 124
criminality, 18, 174
Cuba, and Geneva, 35, 46, 70, 72,
    94, 96; expatriate Cubans, 197
Cuellar García, Zaragoza, 164
culture, 2
Cumming, Hugh S., 32–33, 104
Curiel, Juan Francisco, 206
Customs Agency Service, 30, 147,
    151, 165, 191
Customs Border Patrol Office, 82
Customs Bureau Division of
    Investigations and Patrol, 130
Cuzco, 92

Daladier, Edouard, 49
Dalrymple, A. V., 78
Damm, Henry, 58
Daniels, Josephus, 89, 166; and
    Mexico, 119–23, 127–30,
    132–33
d'Arcy, Captain, 144, 146
Davies, Thomas M., Jr., 176
debt peonage, 3, 8. *See also* mita
de Castro, Alfredo, 84–85
Declaration of Lima, 138
Declaration of Panama, 138
de la Garza Brito, Ángel, 121
DeLagrave, D. G., 178
Denmark, 50
Department of Agriculture, Bureau
    of Plant Industry, 100
Department of Health, Education
    and Welfare, Bureau of Drug
    Abuse Policy, 191, 194
Department of Public Health,
    Labor, and Social Welfare, 137
Department of State, 28, 47; and
    Argentina, 154, 156; and Asia,
    150; and Bolivia, 198, 200; and
    Colombia, 196; and domestic
    drug policy, 67–69, 77–78; and
    drug traffic control, 86, 89,
    through Honduras, 143–46,
    148–49; and League of Nations,

32; and Mexico, 81–82, 123,
    128–29, 163; and Peru, 137,
    157–58, 160, 198; at Geneva,
    47–48, 72, 94–96; Division of
    American Republics, 130, 158;
    Division of Far Eastern Affairs,
    147; entreaty on opium, 176; on
    cocaine, 189; on the Percy
    Amendment, 194
diacetylmorphine, 13. *See also*
    heroin
Diario Oficial, 132
Division of Foreign Control, 69
Division of Mental Hygiene, 105
Dominican Republic, 70
Doran, James M., 64
Doughton, Robert L., 107
Douglas, Lewis W., 78
Drogas Botanicas, 154
drug addiction, curative solutions
    to, 19; Mexican definition of,
    125, 127, treatment for, 80–81,
    123, 128, 131–32; United States'
    definition of, 31, 182–84,
    statistics on, 13, 17, 20, 29, 64,
    76, 115, 173, 191, 216 n. 55,
    treatment for, 16–19, 30–31,
    69–70, 77, 116, 171–72,
    182–85; Uruguay treatment for,
    85; war effect on, 170
drug control, and progressivism,
    14–17, 19, 30, 182; Asian
    obstacles to, 150–51; histories
    on, 23–24; impact on indigenous
    cultures of, 9–12; Latin
    American support for, 20–22, 35,
    45–47, 93. *See also by country;*
    origin of licit, 1, 15; since 1948,
    189–203; summary on, 181–88;
    United States' legislative process
    for, 16. *See also* United States,
    domestic drug control in, foreign
    drug control effort by; war effect
    on, 169, 173–74, 187
drug dealers, licensing of, 64–65
drug education, 84, 171, 192
Drug Enforcement Administration,
    (DEA), 191–92, 194–95, 197–98,
    201
drug law enforcement, budget for,
    of United States, 69, 192, 195, of
    Uruguay, 84; evidence of

violation, 96
drug production and manufacture, 33, 62–63, 70
drug source limitations, 16, 33, 47, 49, 61, 65, 71, 95, 151, 161, 177, 183, 192, 202–3
Drug Supervisory Body, 177
drug use, as social problem, 60; overview of Latin American, 2–6, 9–12; overview of United States', 12–20; significance of, 1. *See also* drug addiction
dry zone, 41, 49, 59
Du Mez, A. G., 17–19
Durango, 168–69, 205–9
Duranty, Walter, 181, 188
Dye, John W., 36–37, 60

Eastern Medical Society of New York, 64–66
Ecuador, 177, 189, 195, 197, 200; at Geneva, 94, 96
ejido, 38
Ekstrand, Eric Einar, 94–95
El Comercio, 57, 136
el coqueo, 9–11, 50, 56, 139, 156, 175, 186, 190, 199, 213–14 n. 30
El Cronista, 90
el oncenio, 41–43. *See also* Leguía, Augusto B.
El Paso, 59
El Salvador, 88, 142, 144, 148–49
El Universal, 120, 124
encomenderos, 6
encomienda system, 3, 4, 8
Ensenada, 82
Escuela Militar de Aviación, 146
estancieros, 6
Estudios Sobre La Coca y La Cocaina en el Perú, 175
Excelsior, 37, 79, 121–22, 124, 162–63, 207

Falco, Mathea, 196–97
FBI Law Enforcement Bulletin, 109
Federal Bureau of Narcotics, and cocaine, 177, 189; and Colombia, 194; and Honduras, 91, 145, 147; and marijuana, 99–115 passim, 124; and Mexico, 81, 121, 157, 165; and

Peru, 159–60; domestic activity of, 67–69, 76–78, 90, 115, 184; establishment and further delineation of, 63, 72, 77–78, 178–79, 183–84, 191; foreign activity of, 96, 170, 173, 184
Federal Narcotics Control Board, 30, 63–64, 66, 69
Federal Narcotics Farm, 116, 125
Federal Narcotics Service, Mexico, 122
Fernández Manero, Victor, 163–64, 166–67
First World War, 26, 30, 41, 48
Ford, Gerald R., 193
Foreign Affairs Committee, 34, 53
Foreign Policy Association, 34, 54
Foreign Service. *See* United States Foreign Service
France, 33, 49, 62, 86, 176
Franco-Japanese proposal, 71
Franco, Luis G., 120–22
Free Zone of Colonia, 84
"French Connection," 192
Frye, Alton, 148
Fuller, Stuart J., 78; and Geneva, 85, 95–96; and Mexico, 126, 128–29, 130–31, 133; on drug traffic, 83, 89, 141, 148–50
Fund for Drug Abuse Control, 192, 202

Gamiz, Ramon, 207
Garner, John Nance, 66
García Meza Tejada, Luis, 199–201
Gaston, Herbert, 132, 158
Geertz, Clifford, 2
Geneva Convention, Fifth Committee of the Assembly, 34–35
Geneva Opium Conference, First, (1924–25), 46–47
Geneva Opium Conference, Second, (1924–25), 47–51, 151, 183
Geneva Opium Convention, (1925), 50, 53, 60, 83, 85, 228 n. 42
Geneva Opium Convention, (1931), 70–73, 78, 84, 88, 124, 126, 128–29, 186, 232 n. 35
George, Walter, 158–59
Germany, 33, 86, 91, 158; and

Geneva, 71–72; and The Hague, 21; in South America, 138, 157
Gibbons, Stephen B., 86
Goethe, C. M., 102
Golden Triangle, 191, 202
Gómez Carrasco, Fred, 193
Gomilla, Frank R., 110
González, Octavio, 195
Good Neighbor Policy, 83, 88–89, 119, 133, 138, 145
Gordillo Zuleta, César, 160
Great Britain, 33, 81, 91, 157–58, 176, 194; at Geneva, 48, 72, 95; at The Hague, 16, 21
Greenup, Julian, 159–61
Grieb, Kenneth J., 28
Grinspoon, Lester, 101
Guatemala, 143, 148; and Geneva, 35, 70, 72; and The Hague, 22
Gueiler Tejada, Lydia, 199–200
Guevara Oropesa, Manuel, 124
Guillen Velez, José María, 86–87, 89–90, 141, 143, 145
Gutiérrez-Noriega, Carlos, 175
Gutman, Herbert G., 2

hacienda, 4–5, 199
Hague Opium Conference, First, (1911–12), 20–21
Hague Opium Conference, Second, (1913), 21
Hague Opium Conference, Third, (1914), 21–22
Hague Opium Convention, (1912), 16, 21, 31–33, 55, 60, 62, 186; and Mexico, 48–49; and Peru, 43–44; United States' support for, 45
Hague, The, 16, 21, 51, 69, 182, 186
Haiti, 35
Hamburg, Germany, 69
Harding, Warren G., 25–29, 31–32, 45–46, 55
Harrison Narcotic Act, (1914), 12, 15–18, 64, 76–77, 103, 173, 182; and *Behrman* ruling, 29; and Public Health Service, 30–31; violators of, 20, 184
hashish, 101, 115. *See also* marijuana
Havana, 55, 60

health insurance, 26–27, 30, 106
herbicides. *See* paraquat
heroin, (diacetylmorphine), 251 n. 6; from Mexico, 58, 169, 177, 191–93, 201–2; from the Mideast, 201; from Southeast Asia, 191; from Turkey, 191; origin of, 13
Higgins, Lawrence, 141–42
Hobson, Richmond P., 75
Hoffman-La Roche, Incorporated, 154–55
Honduras, and Geneva, 94, 96; and The Hague, 22; drug control effort by, 86–88, 90–92, 141–51, 187, 244–45 n. 53, 245 n. 59. *See also* Guillen Velez, José María
Hong Kong, 170
Hoover, Herbert, 24–31 passim, 63, 67–69, 219 n. 18, 230 n. 76
Hornbeck, Stanley K., 151
House Foreign Affairs Committee. *See* Foreign Affairs Committee
House Subcommittee on Inter-American Affairs, 197
House Ways and Means Committee, 106
Huber, Edwin E., 141–42
Huber-Honduras Company, La Ceiba branch, 141, 143
Huerta, Victoriano, 40
Hughes, Charles Evans, 28, 31–32, 34, 48, 219 n. 18
Hughes, Thomas L., 154
Hull, Cordell, 91
human sacrifice, 3

ICI, Ltd., 194
import-export certificate system, 35, 50, 83–84
India, 115, 178
Indian hemp, 16, 50, 111, 121. *See also* marijuana
indigenismo, 43
Ingersoll, John, 191
Institute of Hygiene, Mexico City, 130
Inter-American Conference, Sixth, (1928). *See* Pan-American Conference, Sixth, (1928)
Inter-American Conference for the

Maintenance of Peace and War, (1936), 138
Inter-American Consultative Group on Coca Leaf Problems, 197
interest-group pluralism, 25
international drug cartel, 63
International Labor Organization, 169
International Opium Conference. *See* Hague Opium Conference
International Security Assistance Act, (1961), 194
International Security Assistance Act, (1979), 194
Iran, 55, 176, 178, 201–2
Italy, 157

Jackson, William K., 148
Japan, 33, 91, 164, 169, 176; at Geneva, 72
Japanese, and Peru, 44, 158; in China, 150–51; in Colonia, 84
Johnson, Gordon, 80
Johnson, Nelson T., 54–55, 61, 64
Journal of the American Medical Association, 113
Journal of the Kansas Medical Society, 110
Judd Resolution, (1944), 176–77
Judd, Walter, 176
Justice Department. *See* United States Justice Department

Kellogg, Frank, 60
Kennedy, Sidney, 168
Kennett, Raymond J., 141–50
King, Rufus G., 173
Kinzer, Stephen, 199
Kissinger, Henry A., 197
Kolb, Lawrence, 17, 19, 31, 111–13, 130

La Ceiba, 144. *See also* Huber-Honduras Company
la conscripción vial, 43
La Crónica, 93
La Guaira, 69
La Guardia, Fiorello, 114
La Guardia Report, 113–14, 171–72, 174
Lasch, Christopher, 15
latifundistas, 40

Latin America, and German threat, 138–39; support for drug control by, 20–22, 35–47, 150, 174–76, 185–87. *See also by country, and* United States
Lay, Julius, 85, 87–91, 142
League of Nations, 23, 68, 139, 156, 173, 176; Advisory Committee on Traffic in Opium and Other Dangerous Drugs. *See* Opium Advisory Committee; and Honduras, 86, 89, 94, 142; antileague activity, 45, 55–56; mission to Latin America, 169; Opium Traffic and Social Question Section, 94; report on Mexico, 81, 162; United States' opposition to, 28, 31–35, 45; United States' relations with, 24, 47, 49, 53–55, 60–61, 73
League of Nations Assembly, Fifth Committee, 34–35
League of Nations Assembly, Tenth, (1929), 62
LeBaron, Eugene, 148–49
Leguía, Augusto B., 41–44, 56–57, 92, 156–57
Lend-Lease program, 157
León, Albert P., 162
Lima, conferences at, 138, 197; study by School of Medicine, 175
Linder v. United States, (1925), 29
Lindesmith, Alfred R., 173
Literary Digest, 75
Loaiza, Rudolfo, 165, 167, 207
Lockett, Thomas H., 123
Lockhart, James, 4
London, 63, 177
London Conference for the Suppression of Liquor, (1926), 69
López Portillo, José, 193–94
Lorente, Sebastían, 56
Los Angeles, 82
Lowi, Theodore, 19
Lowman, Seymour, 64
Lufthansa Airline, 157

macehualtin, 3
MacLeod, Murdo, 8
malaria, 138
Maloney, Guy R., 142, 144, 146
Manchuria, 81, 150

Marcovitz, Eli, 114
marijuana, (*Cannabis sativa*), 6,
    11–12, 172; from Colombia,
    189, 195; from Mexico, 58, 83,
    164, 166, 169, 189, 191–92;
    paraquat on, 194; rulings on, 16,
    94–96; trilateral pact on, 103;
    United States' attitude toward,
    102, 105, 108–11, 124, 128,
    195; United States' studies on,
    101–6, 140; United States'
    scientific opinion on, 111–15,
    171–72; United States' use of,
    11, 12, 77, 170; war effect on,
    170
*Marijuana: America's New Drug
    Problem*, 109–10
*Marijuana in Latin America: The
    Threat It Constitutes*, 174
Marijuana Tax Act, (1937), 99,
    107, 116, 121, 124, 171;
    hearings for, 105–6, 123
Marseilles, 170
Martínez de Alva, 70
Matamoros-Brownsville, 59
Matienzo de Peralta, Juan, 157
May, Herbert L., 54–55, 62, 176
mayorazgos, 8
Mazatlán, 120–21, 165–66
McGurk, Joseph, 157
Mejía Colindres, Vicente, 87–88
Mellon, Andrew W., 29, 66, 76
Messersmith, George S., 166–68
Mexicali, 58–59
Mexican Association of Neurology
    and Psychiatry, 124
Mexican Health Code, 121
Mexican Revolution, 37–41, 161
Mexican War, 36
Mexico, agrarian reform in, 38–40,
    223 n. 62; and Geneva, 45,
    70–72, 94, 96; and The Hague,
    21; Chinese in, 167, 227 n. 28;
    drug control effort by, 22, 37,
    48–49, 59–60, 73, 80–83, 186,
    192–95, 201, obstacles to,
    35–41, with the United States,
    133, 149, 176, under Salazar,
    122–26, under Siurob, 119–22,
    127–32; social order in, 3–6, 41;
    United States' anti-Mexican
    sentiment, 102; wartime drug

control effort, 161–64, 167–68.
    See also Durango
Meyer Brothers Drug Company, 90
Mezzrow, Milton "Mezz", 172
Military Surgeon, 113
Ministry of Development, Peru, 43
Ministry of Foreign Affairs, Mexico,
    120, 122
Ministry of Public Health, Labor,
    and Social Welfare, 157, 159
Minneapolis *Journal*, 109
Mintz, Sidney W., 2
Missouri Peace Officers Association,
    111
mita, 5. *See also* debt peonage
Monge Medrano, Carlos, 190
montaña, 10
Montevideo, 95
Montezuma the Elder, 185
Montezuma II, 3
Moore, R. Walton, 123
Moorehead, Helen Howell, 34, 54,
    62
Mora, José, 84
Morlock, George A., 147–48,
    158–60, 164, 166–67
morphine, 13; and The Hague, 16;
    from Mexico, 58, 169, 177; from
    United States to Peru, 90,
    159–60; Honduras imports of,
    86–87, 89–90, 143; United
    States' use of, 12
Moshar-ol-Molk, 50–51
Murray, Robert K., 25
Musto, David F., 16, 24, 115, 185
Myers, Henry J., 114

Narcotic Division of Treasury
    Department. *See* Treasury
    Department, Narcotics Division
    of Prohibition Unit
Narcotic Drug Import and Export
    Act, (1922), 30, 128
Nassau, 69
National Association of Financial
    Institutions, 196
National Auxiliary Committee, 120
National Coca Monopoly, 197, 199
National Conference of
    Commissioners on Uniform State
    Laws, 77
National Council of Public Health,

Uruguay, 57, 84
National Defense Headquarters, 157
National Drug Trade Conference, 16
National Institute of Andean Biology, 137, 139
National Institute of Health, 105
national narcotic monopolies, 125, 128, 131, 137, 140, 161, 197
Nazi Germany, 138, 148
Netherlands, 32, 176; at Geneva, 72; at The Hague, 21, 31
Neville, Edwin L., 32, 34, 47, 53
New Deal, 26, 116
New Orleans, 100, 144
New Orleans Medical and Surgical Journal, 100-1
New York Academy of Medicine, 113-14
New York City, 102, 114
New York *Herald Tribune*, 171; Forum, 109
New York Stock Exchange, 146
New York Times, 49, 102, 148
Nicaragua, 142-44, 148; at Geneva, 60, 72, 94
Nixon, Richard M., 191
Nogales, Mexico, 58
nonintervention. *See* Good Neighbor Policy
Norweb, R. Henry, 137, 159
Nutley, New Jersey, 155
Nutt, Levi G., 20, 29, 30, 68

Obregón, Alvaro, 37, 45
octli, 3. *See also* pulque
Office Internationale d'Hygiene Publique, 33
Office of Control of Medicine and Pharmacopoeia, 162
Office of Drug Abuse, 191, 193
Office of Price Management, 157
Oliphant, Herman, 103
Onesimo Calderon, Miguel, 206
Operation Cooperation, 192
Operation Intercept, 82, 192, 202
opiates, 110, 172; from Argentina, 154; from Europe, 75-76; from Mexico, 166; United States on, 34, 77, 102; war effect on, 170. *See also* heroin; morphine; opium
opium (*Papaver somniferum*), 6, 13, 15-16, 181; and The Hague, 21, 33, 35, 47; as medicinal, 12; from Argentina, 154-55; from China, 55, 150; from Europe, 96; from India, 178; from Iran, 55, 178, 202; from Mexico, 58, 165-67, 169, 177-78; from Persia, 50-51, 81; from Peru, 159-60; from the Mideast, 177; from Turkey, 178, 192, 202; United States' use of, 30, 64, 160. *See also* opiates; opium poppies
Opium Advisory Committee (OAC), 28, 61, 93-96, 177, 183, 186, 190; and Bolivia, 50, 56; and Latin America, 35, 46; and Mexico, 45, 121, 125-26; and Peru, 45; and Uruguay, 84; and the United States, 28-29, 32-35, 53-54, 62-63, 70, 72, 78, 83, 141; of 1931, 70-71
Opium Advisory Committee, First Session, (1921), 32
Opium Advisory Committee, Second Session, (1922), 32
Opium Advisory Committee, Fourth Session, 33
Opium Advisory Committee, Fifth Session, 33-35
Opium Advisory Committee, Eleventh Session, (1928), 53
opium poppies, in Mexico, 83, 123, 153, 163-64, 193, 205-9; in Peru, 159-60; in the United States, 96, 170; League control of, 33, 72, 95; United Nations' control of, 177. *See also* opium
opium smoking, 1, 59, 137, 150, 176
Ordonez Díaz, P. H., 87
Organization of American States, Permanent Council, 200
Oroso, German, 139

Pacific Coast International Association of Law Enforcement Officials, 127, 131
Padden, R. C., 185
Pakistan, 201-202
Pan, Lynn, 184
Panama, 35, 90, 104; at Geneva,

70, 72, 94, 96; drug traffic through, 140, 145–46, 149–50
Pan-American Airways, 148
Pan-American Conference, Sixth, (1928), 55
Pan-American Conference, Seventh, (1933), 84
Pan-American Conference, Eighth, (1938), 138
Pan-American Health Conference, (1942), 153, 159
Pan-American Sanitary Bureau, 93–94
Pan-American Sanitary Conference, Fifth, (1923), 45
Pan-American Sanitary Conference, Eighth, (1927), 56
Paraguay, 195, 200; at Geneva, 70, 72
paraquat, 194, 196
Paris Peace Conference, 16
Parran, Thomas, 130
patent medicine, 12
Patronato de la Raza Indígena, 43
Paz Soldán, Carlos Enrique, 94
Pearl Harbor, 158
Pellens, Mildred, 13, 17, 20, 186
Peña, Salvador, 165–66, 168, 206
Pennsylvania State College, 68
Penrose, Boies, 27
peones, 40
Percy Amendment, 194
Percy, Charles, 194
Perdonio Benítez, José, 162–63
Perez, Fernando, 71
Permanent Central Opium Board, 50, 54–55, 72, 128, 140, 176
Peru, 45, 169, 189, 195, 200; and Geneva, 48–50, 70, 94, 96; and The Hague, 21; drug control effort by, 22, 35, 41–45, 47, 56–57, 73, 92–93, 136–39, 149–50, 175–77, 197–98, 201; social order in, 3–4, 5–6, 9; wartime drug control effort by, 156–61. *See also* Lima
Peruvian Indian Institute, 190
Peterson, N. F., 154
peyote, in Mexico, 1, 6, 185
Philip II, 7, 9, 10
Philippines, 15
Phillips, William, 78

Picón-Salas, Mariano, 2–3
Pike, Fredrick B., 138
Pinto-Escalier, Arturo, 50
pipiltin, 3
poppy, 94. *See also* opium poppies
Porfiriato, 39
Porter bill, 66–67
Porter Narcotic Act, 67
Porter, Stephen G., 34, 49, 53–55, 61, 62–67 passim, 69–70, 76, 184
Portugal, 95
Potosí, 4
Prado y Ugarteche, Manuel, 139
Preliminary Report on Indian Hemp and Peyote, 104
Productos Roche, S. A., 154–56
Progressive Era, 14–16, 19; and progressivism, 17, 30, 182
prohibition, 13, 36–37
Prohibition Bureau, 63–64, 68
Public Health Department, Mexico, 80, 120–24, 126, 130–31, 162–63, 206–7, 209
Public Health Service, (PHS), 17, 19, 32, 65, 76, 104, 127, 130, 170, 183; and Congressional hearings, 115; and the Harrison Act, 18, 30–31; on marijuana, 104–6
Puerto Cortés, 144
Puerto Rico, 158
pulque, 1, 6. *See also* alcohol
Pure Food and Drug Act, (1906), 12, 100

Quechua Indians, 41

Reagan, Ronald, 200
reconstruction, European, 28
repartimiento, 8
rescates, 7–9, 20. *See also* smuggling
Rexed, Ingemar, 184
Ricketts, C. A., 190
Rio de Janeiro, 159
Rio Grande, 170
Riva Palacio, Carlos, 79–80
Rockefeller Foundation, in Mexico, 126
Rogers Act, (1924), 28. *See also* United States Foreign Service

Roosevelt, Franklin D., 26, 77, 88–89, 119, 133, 138
Roper, Daniel C., 19–20, 29, 30
Rothstein, Arnold, 68
Rubio Ortiz, Pascual, 79–80
Rush, Benjamin, 12
Russia, 176. *See also* Soviet Union

St. *Louis Post-Dispatch*, 76, 177–78
Salamanca, Daniel, 93
Salazar, Viniegra, Leopoldo, 122–27, 131, 133
Sánchez Anaya, Pascual, 163
Sánchez, Francisco, 90–91, 142–43
Sandino, Augusto, 142
Saucedo, Ralph, 194, 196
Scharff, Alvin F., 119, 163
Second World War, 78, 151, 153, 159, 187, 195
Section of Narcotics Control, Argentina, 86
Select Committee on Narcotics Abuse and Control, House of Representatives, 193, 195–96, 198
Shanghai Opium Commission, (1909), 15, 51, 182
Sheppard-Towner Act, (1921), 26–27
Siles Zuazo, Hernán, 200
Sinaloa, 123, 164–67, 194
Single Convention on Narcotic Drugs, (1961), 190, 197
Sirovich, William I., 66
Siurob, José, 120–23, 126–33, 162, 167
Slobotsky, Isidore, 142, 144, 146–47
Smale, William, 82–83
Smith, Peter H., 39
smuggling, 47, 177, 193, 197–98; as cultural phenomenon, 7–9, 151; control of, 94, 140–41; from Brazil, 84; from Peru, 159; in Argentina, 85; into the United States, 29, 30–31, 93, 177, 189, from Asia, 150–51, from Mexico, 37, 59–60, 81–82, 119, 128–29, 162–66, 170, 191–93, from Turkey, 192; through Central America, 90, 140. *See also* Central America; Honduras;

rescates; through Colonia, 84; through Colombia, 75, 90; war effect on, 169–70, 178
social alienation, active and passive, 6
Social Security Act, (1935), 106
Sociedad Anónima Fausto Piaggio, 159
Sociedad Nacional Agraria, 94, 137
Sonora, 123, 164, 166, 178
Soto Burciaga, Romulo, 206–7
Soviet Union, 71, 157, 202. *See also* Russia
Spanish conquest, 3–12 passim
Standard Fruit and Steamship Company, 87
Stanley, Eugene, 101
Star Furniture Company, 142, 144–45
State Department, United States, 68. *See also* Department of State
states' rights, 27
Sterling, Frederick A., 43–44
Stewart, James, 124, 126, 129
Stewart, Warren, 142
Stimson, Henry L., 62–64, 70
Stockberger, W. W., 100
Stroessner, Alfredo, 195
Supreme Court, United States, 18–19, 21, 103, 107, 182
Switzerland, 72, 81, 86
Symes, J. Foster, 108–9
syphilis, 156

TACA, (Transportes Aereos Centro-Americanos), 142–50, passim
Tacna-Arica boundary dispute, 45
Taft, William Howard, 15
Taylor, Arnold H., 24
Taylor, J. T., 110
Tegucigalpa, 143
Tello, Manuel, 83, 121, 125–26
Terry, Charles E., 13, 17, 20, 182, 186
Texas, 81–82
The Traffic in Narcotics, 171
tourism, 36–37
traficantes, 192
Transportes Aereos Centro-Americanos, (TACA), 142–50, passim
Travel magazine, 136

Treadway, Walter L., 76–77, 105
Treasury Department, 18, 30, 32, 53, 66, 68, 82, 112, 115, 130, 158, 165; agents in Mexico, 81, 119–20, 164, 166–67, 194; and Kennett, 141, 147; and marijuana hearings, 105; and the Porter bill, 67; Narcotic Division of the Prohibition Unit, 19, 20, 29–30, 63, 77–78, 182; Special Committee, (1919), 17–19
True, Rodney, 100
Trujillo Bravo, Enrique, 94
Tuck, Pinkney, 53
Turbay Ayala, Julio César, 196, 201
Turkey, 176, 178, 191–92, 202

Uniform State Narcotic Act, (1932), 77, 99, 101
United Fruit Company, 87, 148
United Nations, 170, 176–77, 198; Commission on Narcotic Drugs, 177–78, 187, 190; Preparatory Commission, 177
United States, and Geneva, 28, 31–35, 47–49, 51, 54–55, 61–63, 70–73, 85, 94; and Latin America, 45–46, 202; and Mexico, 36–37; and Peru, 42, 44; and The Hague, 22; anti-League sentiment of, 55–56; domestic drug control, 29–31, as reform, 1, 14–16, 19, 181–82, marijuana studies for, 103–4, 114–16. *See also* Anslinger, Harry J.; reassessments of, 63–69, 77–79, 182–84, 187–88, 191; foreign drug control effort by, 20–23, 45, 70, 135–40, assistance for, 197–201, wartime effort for, with Mexico, 161, 164–66, with Peru, 158–60, with Honduras. *See* Honduras, drug control effort by; with Mexico, 119–33, 178, 191–95. *See also* smuggling, into the United States from Mexico; interventionism, 60–61, 133. *See also* Good Neighbor Policy; isolationism, 28, 51, 54; public policy making in, 24–29; social order in, 20, 76–77; summary of antidrug involvement by, 181–88
United States Congress, 25, 30, 63, 72, 105, 158–59, 170, 176
United States Customs Service, 30. *See also* Customs Agency Service
United States Department of State. *See* Department of State
United States Foreign Service, professionalism, 28
United States grand jury on law enforcement, 67–68
United States Justice Department, 18, 78, 191
United States v. Behrman, (1922), 18, 29
United States v. Doremus, (1919), 18
United States v. Jin Fuey Moy, (1915), 18
University of Illinois, 112
University of Mississippi Medical School, 109
Uruguay, 169, 200; and Geneva, 60, 70, 72, 94–96; drug control effort by, 57–58, 73, 83–85, 140, 149, 186–87, 232 n. 35; Special Commission for the Defense Against Toxicomania and Controls of the Narcotics Traffic, 84

Vaeder, Rae, 146
Valladares Pineda, Casimiro, 206–8
Valverde, Vincente, 10
vecinos, 8
Velasco Alvarado, Juan, 197
Venezuela, 200; and Geneva, 35, 70, 72, 94, 96; and The Hague, 22
Villa, Pancho, 40–41, 102
Voegtlin, Carl, 105
Volstead Act, (1919), 19

Walton, Robert P., 109–10
Ward, Frank S., 95
Washington College of Law, 68
Washington Herald, 66
Washington Post, 200
Watson, J. W., 14
Wayne County Medical Society, 102

Webb et al v. United States, (1919), 18

Weekly News Sheet, 120

welfare legislation, 27

Weissman, Marvin, 200

White, Harold A., 146–47

White House Conference on Unemployment, (1921), 25

White House Office of Drug Abuse Policy. *See* Office of Drug Abuse

Whitebread II, Charles H., 99, 104, 108, 172

Wholesale Druggists Association, 100

Williams, Abraham, 142

Williams, Vicente, 142

Wilson, Hugh, 28

Wilson, Woodrow, 16, 27, 41, 138

withdrawal distress, 110

Wolff, Lester L., 193

Wolff, Pablo Osvaldo, 174, 176

Wollner, Herbert, 112

Womack, John, Jr., 40

Womens' Christian Temperance Union, (WCTU), 41, 102

Woodward, William C., 106

Works Progress Administration, 102

World Health Organization, 190–91

World Narcotic Defense Association, 75

World Narcotics Research Foundation, 116

Wright, Elizabeth Washburn, 31–33, 51, 55, 61, 181

Wright, Hamilton, 32, 51, 100, 181; at Shanghai, 15–16; at The Hague, 16, 21

Yaqui Indians, 5, 6, 40, 212–13 n. 16

Yerex, Lowell, 142–44, 146–48

Yugoslavia, 176

Yuma, 41, 59

Yungas, 93

Zacatecas, 4

Zahle, Herluf, 49–50

Zapata Ortiz, Vicente, 175

Zapatistas, 40

Zona Libre, 36

Zozaya, José, 130–32